D1394360

The Marketing Series is one of the most comprehensive collections of books in marketing and sales available from the UK today.

Published by Butterworth-Heinemann on behalf of The Chartered Institute of Marketing, the series is divided into three distinct groups: *Student* (fulfilling the needs of those taking the Institute's certificate and diploma qualifications); *Professional Development* (for those on formal or self-study vocational training programmes); and *Practitioner* (presented in a more informal, motivating and highly practical manner for the busy marketer).

Formed in 1911, The Chartered Institute of Marketing is now the largest professional marketing management body in Europe with over 60,000 members located worldwide. Its primary objectives are focused on the development of awareness and understanding of marketing throughout UK industry and commerce and in the raising of standards of professionalism in the education, training and practice of this key business discipline.

Books in the series

Royal Mail Guide to Direct Mail for Small Businesses
Brian Thomas

The CIM Handbook of Selling and Sales Strategy
David Jobber

The CIM Handbook of Export Marketing
Chris Noonan

The Creative Marketer
Simon Majaro

The Customer Service Planner
Martin Christopher

The Effective Advertiser
Tom Brannan

Integrated Marketing Communications
Ian Linton and Kevin Morley

The Marketing Audit
Malcolm H. B. McDonald

The Marketing Planner
Malcolm H. B. McDonald

Marketing Strategy
Paul Fifield

Cybermarketing
Pauline Bickerton, Matthew Bickerton and Upkar Pardesi

(Forthcoming: *The CIM Handbook of Strategic Marketing* by Colin Egan and Michael Thomas; *The CIM Handbook of Service Marketing* by Colin Egan)

Sales Management

Chris J. Noonan

Butterworth-Heinemann
Linacre House, Jordan Hill, Oxford OX2 8DP
225 Wildwood Avenue, Woburn MA 01801-2041
A division of Reed Educational and Professional Publishing Ltd

A member of the Reed Elsevier plc group

OXFORD   AUCKLAND   BOSTON
JOHANNESBURG   MELBOURNE   NEW DELHI

First published 1998
Transferred to digital printing 2001

British Library Cataloguing in Publication Data
A catalogue record for this book is available from the British Library

ISBN 0 7506 3361 1

Printed in Great Britain by Antony Rowe Ltd, Eastbourne

www.bh.com

Contents _____

Preface

Sales management is an integral part of marketing management. The sales team are the implementers of marketing strategy and tactics at the customer interface. Modern sales management is not about leading a team of foot-in-the-door salespersons. It is a complex and disciplined mix of: marketing skills, professional selling and negotiation skills, people management skills (including selection, motivation, communicating and training), sales strategy and tactical planning skills, data management and performance monitoring skills (involving a high level of numeracy and experience in using computers to advantage in sales and customer management). The material coverage of this text addresses many of these topics in a practical way that sales managers can use in self-development, or adapt to team development needs.

This text is targeted at the professional sales manager, who wants to make the most of the market opportunities, and develop the productivity of his or her sales team. Companies are facing increasing competition, with threats to many traditional markets and customer bases, as supply and purchase points in many market segments become more concentrated. To tackle the threats and capitalize on opportunities the modern sales manager needs a far broader range of selling and managerial skills and experience than in past decades. The aim of this text is to provide some skill-developing inputs that will enable the proactive sales manager to build on this material in managing the sales team and sales environment more profitably and productively.

The contents of this text should be of interest to:

- senior sales and marketing directors charged with responsibilities for overall development of markets, planning and strategy, and who may find this a useful reference text
- field sales managers who may find that much of this text has practical application by adapting the principles as relating to team management into their own environment
- salespersons and students of marketing and sales management, who will find that the text provides a comprehensive coverage of practical sales management principles that will provide a firmer base for their entry into sales line management.

The reader with international responsibilities, or with a broader interest in marketing aspects of management, can usefully supplement reading of this work with reference to my companion volume *The CIM Handbook of Export Marketing* (Butterworth-Heinemann 1996, ISBN 0 7506 2573 2).

Throughout this text use of the masculine gender can be taken as including the feminine gender, without intention to discriminate or imply anything other than that marketers of both sexes are equal in all respects in selling and sales management.

Chris J. Noonan
E-mail: Noonan@cjn.co.uk

Part One

Functions and Organization of the Sales Force

1

Roles and functions in the sales force ____

The sales organization, commonly referred to as the sales force, plays a key role in the growth, development, profitability and impact on customers (whether trade or direct customers) of most companies. It may represent only one department, or division, within a company organization, and often be relatively small in numbers in relation to total employees, especially in manufacturing industries, but it is a critical resource that must be nurtured, developed and motivated to fulfil its potential within the company organization and the external market place.

Key sales and marketing functional activities

The functional activities undertaken by the sales and marketing departments can normally be allocated into one of the three categories of **management**, **administration** or **planning**, as illustrated in Figure 1.1, and expanded in Table 1.2.

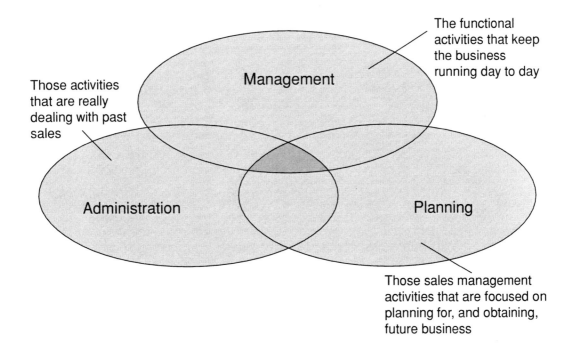

Those activities that are really dealing with past sales

Management

The functional activities that keep the business running day to day

Administration

Planning

Those sales management activities that are focused on planning for, and obtaining, future business

Figure 1.1 The main categories of sales and marketing activity

Table 1.2 *Main functional responsibilities in sales and marketing departments*

Functional responsibilities	
Sales	**Marketing**
Management	
<ul><li>Achieving sales volume requirements</li><li>Achieving distribution objectives</li><li>Product display/merchandising</li><li>Call (outlet) coverage</li><li>Sales force recruitment</li><li>Sales force training</li><li>Provision of feedback to sales force<ul><li>bulletins</li><li>conferences</li><li>personal contact</li></ul></li><li>Trade terms<ul><li>financial terms of trade</li><li>warranties and sale conditions</li><li>order size and delivery</li></ul></li><li>Performance measurement<ul><li>sales volumes/values</li><li>call coverage</li><li>distribution</li><li>display achievements</li></ul></li></ul>	<ul><li>Brand management (including profitability)</li><li>Market research</li><li>Product performance and market share analysis</li><li>Brand publicity including public relations, sponsorship, etc.</li><li>Advertising and promotion</li></ul>
Administration	
<ul><li>Credit control</li><li>Collection of payments</li><li>Customer service and care</li><li>Order processing</li><li>Maintaining records on sales force activity and customer activity</li></ul>	<ul><li>Packaging supplies (ordering and stock control if not an allocated responsibility of purchasing or production functions)</li><li>Production scheduling (if not an allocated responsibility of another department)</li><li>Regulatory compliance of product and packaging in domestic (and export) markets</li></ul>
Planning	
<ul><li>Sales forecasting</li><li>Pricing policies and profit planning</li><li>Sales promotions and competitions</li><li>Sales force rewards and incentives</li><li>Management training</li></ul>	<ul><li>Sales & marketing forecasts</li><li>Pricing policies & profit planning</li><li>New product development</li><li>New product test marketing</li><li>Product design (physical attributes, size, shape, packaging)</li></ul>

Sales functional activities

Table 1.1 can be expanded with the following additional commentary on the main sales management functional activities.

Achieving sales volume	Once a forecast or target is set or agreed, the sales manager becomes responsible for its achievement. Achievement of sales forecasts is usually critical to achievement of the company's financial plans (profitability, ability to meet operating expenses, etc.).
Distribution	Product distribution targets may be set independently of sales volume targets, but higher sales volume is commonly a function of increasing distribution as well as generating more product offtake or usage through existing users or outlets.
Product display and merchandising	These are traditional sales force functions in consumer product companies, and also with some industrial products distributed through trade stockists. Where offtake is a factor of display, the salesperson should have display guide-lines and objectives, possibly for regular shelf space in the trade outlet (retail outlets, cash and carry stores) and for off-shelf promotional or feature displays.
	The merchandising function may be performed by the sales force, or by a separate team (possibly of part-timers) charged with that responsibility. Many consumer goods companies contract the merchandising to specialist companies that provide merchandising services to a range of suppliers.
Call coverage	This is the actual process of making physical calls on customers. Where a company has a stable customer base, calling might be scheduled at some regular frequency relating to actual or potential sales (see later sections on journey planning), or to the amount of stock a customer can (or will) carry.
Sales recruitment and training	The identification of suitable persons for a selling position, and their subsequent training, must be a fundamental responsibility of sales managers. Clear job specifications and job holder profiles should be developed, based upon qualities and skills known to be relevant to performance in the company's trading environment.
	Once suitable persons are identified and recruited, there are three levels of training that the sales manager needs to incorporate into his or her management activities:

- initial induction training, likely to include industry and product knowledge, as well as basic selling skills
- ongoing field sales training
- supporting training provided at sales meetings and conferences.

Provision of feedback	It is essential to communicate achievements, objectives, plans, programmes, and policies, in order to provide support and motivation. Sales managers typically hold (area or national) sales meetings at regular frequencies to provide a feedback forum and to give sales team members a chance to interrelate, and these can be supplemented by sales bulletins or newsletters.
Trade terms	Marketing and finance departments will usually have an input to a company's trade terms. The sales manager should be the expert on the custom and practice within his or her markets, knowing industry

	norms, and constantly reviewing competitive pricing, trade terms, and promotions.
Performance measurement	Statistical sales performance measures must relate sales achievements to targets, plans, and budgets, and form part of a programme of rapid feedback to salespersons. Performance statistics need to be broken down to give measures for each territory and customer, and, wherever practical, should be benchmarked against comparable external data, e.g. for the industry or product category. Comparative figures for performance against plans often cover:

- **sales volumes** by product and customer
- **sales values** by product and customer
- **profitability** by product and customer (not measured often enough!)
- **call coverage** achieved versus the scheduled or optimum coverage as related to sales
- **product distribution** achieved by product and sales territory, or by target market sector
- **display** achievements by product, territory, etc., where this is a relevant measure for consumer products.

Credit control	This functional responsibility is often shared with a section of the finance department. In the final analysis, however, it must be accepted as a sales management responsibility to collect overdue payments, as the sales force are involved in selecting customers and advising on their suitability for credit.
Collection of payments	In most developed markets payment for goods despatched is made by cheque, or direct bank-to-bank transfers. Late payers are usually reminded by a letter serving as a *polite reminder*, followed subsequently if payment is not made by more terse *chasers*. In some markets salespersons traditionally collect payment while calling on customers, but this is not ideal as it distracts from the salesperson focusing on selling, and may bring a negative atmosphere into what should be a positive environment.
Customer service and care	This function has grown in importance over recent years, as suppliers work not just to meet customer expectations from products and service, but to exceed them. This may include a very broad range of activities, from providing product leaflets and information, to answering queries about where orders are in a supply pipeline, to provision of after sales service and technical support.
Order processing	This activity also might fit within a sales organization, within customer service, or possibly a separate distribution department. Wherever it is placed as an activity, its function impacts on the selling activities, as salespersons and their customers clearly have particular concerns about the speed and accuracy of processing orders, and the management of order processing from all stages through collection (by a sales call or telephone call) to delivery and payment.
Maintaining activity records	The sales force needs to have information on its customers and its own activities. Most companies have a customer record system, such as a customer card where the salesperson records all customer details and sales history, call dates, etc. Salespersons should have information that shows when calls are scheduled or have been made, and the results, as well as recording sales objectives for each customer.

Sales forecasting While this is a function that often overlaps with marketing, sales managers do have a key contribution to make to the forecasting and planning process, notably in relation to sales volume and value estimates, in establishing distribution and display objectives, and in setting budgets for a sales organization that can achieve its objectives.

Pricing policies The marketing and sales departments will both be closely involved in developing and implementing market pricing policies, to ensure correct positioning versus competitors' products while also satisfying company profit objectives.

Sales promotions and competitions While a marketing department might initiate much tactical promotional activity, in support of strategic objectives (e.g. aimed at increasing distribution, display, and user/consumer trial), some promotional activity aimed at improving performance against the same key result areas might be under the control of the sales manager alone, such as sales force incentives and competitions.

Sales force rewards and incentives The sales manager (often with advice from a human resources department) will have responsibility to ensure that rewards and incentives promote a high level of morale, motivating achievement of goals and objectives, encouraging excellence, and developing loyalty amongst the good performers. While this could be seen as a management function, I prefer to assign it to planning, as reward packages have a great bearing on future success.

Sales management training While many sales managers recognize the need for training their sales teams, they often neglect their own development. Management training, to meet the future needs of the business and demands of sales management jobs, is a key activity. A well-trained team of sales managers will contribute to their own further self-development, to company performance, and to the morale and training of salespersons.

Typical job functions in a sales organization ▬▬▬

The sales manager or sales director ▬▬

This is the person who is head of the sales organization, by whatever title. Frequently he will either sit on the company board or executive committee, or, at least, report directly to it. In some companies the sales manager comes within a combined sales and marketing department, possibly reporting to a marketing director or commercial director. Here we are less concerned with titles than with job functions. The main functions of the position would include:

- forecasting potential sales volumes and prices
- identifying, setting, and achieving sales objectives, targets, budgets and profit plans

- assigning sales force priorities in line with objectives and plans
- developing programmes for field implementation of the company's marketing plan (including developing supporting sales promotional activity within budgetary limits and in conjunction with the marketers)
- designing and developing a sales organization and structure to achieve company plans and objectives, and suited to the company, industry and markets (and which might include selection of agents, distributors, etc.)
- developing motivational reward and incentive packages
- converting overall plans and objectives into specific standards of performance, sales targets, and programmes for subordinate functions and managers, including regional/area managers and

key account executives, ensuring that each is allocated a fair share in relation to historical performance or potential
- developing systems of monitoring sales performance at all levels of the organization and for all trade sectors, including systems for benchmarking company performance versus competitors' performance and trade/customer expectations
- developing a head office sales support organization that may include:
  - operational planning and forecasting;
  - sales recruitment and sales training;
  - sales performance monitoring and performance feedback reporting;
  - sales promotions department (planning promotions, in liaison with the marketers, and providing all sales aids including product literature, display aids, samples, etc.);
  - customer service departments;
  - order processing departments;
  - tele-sales departments;
  - product distribution (if this responsibility is under the sales function);
  - production scheduling (if this responsibility is under the sales function)
- selecting and training all subordinate managers and salespersons
- setting terms of trade, including basic prices (in conjunction with marketing), scale discounts and allowances, promotional allowances, etc.
- communicating with the sales force and with customers as necessary (including agents and distributors as appropriate) on matters concerned with plans, programmes, policies, and performance feedback
- assisting with the test marketing of new products
- building good internal relationships and liaising with all other departments concerned with forecasting and planning, marketing, production, finance, distribution, etc.

The field sales manager

The **field sales manager** is the person with specific responsibility for the field implementation of the marketing programme. Larger companies have a network of field sales managers, often entitled area managers or district managers, leading smaller teams usually of from six to ten salespersons. The field sales manager:

- accepts responsibility for achieving assigned objectives, targets, forecasts, budgets, etc., with and through the team
- liaises with salespersons and superiors in setting sales performance targets, objectives, standards of performance, etc. by territory
- plans and monitors call coverage to optimize effective frequency of calling in relation to potential
- implements field programmes supporting company marketing plans
- maximizes the sales effort by providing training, counselling and feedback
- exercises control and maintains team discipline
- interprets and filters company policies
- communicates effectively with salespersons through regular sales meetings and bulletins
- selects, trains, manages, motivates and controls his or her sales team
- advises superiors on market intelligence, competitive products, promotions, terms of trade
- liaises between head office departments and field personnel
- ensures each of his or her sales team achieves high job satisfaction through:
  - job content
  - team spirit and membership
  - management
  - monetary and non-monetary rewards
  - recognition of achievements
  - quality of products sold
  - the company as a good employer.

The effective field sales manager will work to accomplish his or her goals and maximize sales team performance by:

- ensuring he or she is well briefed on company policies, objectives and activities
- putting subordinates first in his or her priorities.

The key account manager

Management of the company's business and relations with major customers will normally be the responsibility of a **key account manager** who:

- liaises with Sales Director and marketing departments in setting customer targets/forecasts, which would be broken down by product and branch or use location (depending on whether the supplier is offering industrial inputs or products for resale through trade distribution channels)
- liaises with buyers to agree annual sales volume forecasts, and to negotiate any ongoing supply contracts
- advises on setting terms of trade for each key account, and then manages the business to these trade terms
- conducts negotiations on products (standard products or special production runs such as customized industrial products or private label retail products), quantities, prices, promotions, special offers, etc.
- implements the company's sales and marketing programme at the key account level
- negotiates special distribution requirements
- monitors key account profit performance and achieves satisfactory profit contributions from accounts
- recommends key account special promotional activity to senior managers
- reports market intelligence concerning the key account's own strategies and performance, and that of competitors with the account

- follows up at individual locations of multi-branch customers to ensure programme implementation, ensuring that all branch locations receive adequate direct coverage (either personally or through other members of the sales team)
- develops relationships with other key account personnel influential in the buying process (e.g. users, specifiers, budget controllers, other authorizers, etc.) – this networking within major accounts is normally critical to successful business development
- liaises internally with all departments and colleagues involved in supplying or servicing the key account
- monitors performance of the key account in terms of sales volumes, turnover, profitability, usage/distribution, and any other relevant criteria, comparing performance with plans agreed with the account head office buying team, giving breakdowns for branches/subsidiaries, providing feedback and promoting corrective action to counter any deviations from plans.

The territory manager (or salesperson)

The person who most frequently provides the direct interface with the mass of customers is the territory salesperson, who

- agrees with his or her field sales manager the individual customer and territory objectives, targets and programmes, breaking down the larger territory target by product and customer, for each measured time period or journey cycle
- agrees additional business development objectives for the territory or for individual customers to encourage growth beyond the normal levels expected
- develops a professional rapport and business relationship with all buyers and influential contacts
- develops his or her professional selling skills, not just relying on relationship selling
- maintains planned call coverage

- develops a programme of prospecting/pioneer calling to identify new worthwhile customers on the assigned territory
- identifies new product and new prospect opportunities
- maintains full and accurate customer call records
- avoids out-of-stock situations, checking stock in all outlets, and sells in product to satisfy demand and offtake
- achieves maximum levels of sales and distribution in current and potential outlets
- achieves optimum levels of product display for retailed products in all appropriate outlets
- motivates and trains customer staff to promote company brands against competition, giving them guidance in any necessary technical knowledge, and helping them understand and communicate the product features and benefits
- provides market intelligence feedback on competitive activity.

The merchandiser

This role is primarily a function in consumer product companies, where goods are offered for resale through a network of retailers or trade distributors, and where there is considerable competition for display space and display impact on consumers who face a mass of similar competing products. Typically the merchandiser, whether directly employed by the supplier or engaged through a contract merchandising company, will work to:

- locate products and display material at key selling spots within any product category (where the merchandiser can arrange this locally)
- maximize display of company products in assigned retail outlets
- tidy any displays, ensuring damaged product is not left on display
- ensure products in retail outlets are correctly priced according to the retail outlet's pricing structure (and can advise a store on competitor pricing where an individual branch manager has any authority to vary prices)
- rotate products according to any sell by code
- support products on promotion through construction of feature displays and placement of promotional point of sale (POS) material
- motivate retail outlets to re-order company products as necessary to maintain stock levels avoiding out-of-stock situations
- report on competitive activity.

Product promoters

When a supplier is running certain types of promotional activity with trade dealers or retail customers it is sometimes appropriate for them to place product promoters at the customer's locations to communicate product features and benefits directly to customers. These promoters can fulfil a useful role, if suitable persons are selected and trained, by:

- promoting consumer trial through:
  - sampling/demonstrating products
  - direct customer contact
  - supporting promotional activity at the point of sale
- motivating display retention through presence and activity
- providing a direct interface between the distribution company and the customer, reporting on attitudes, reactions, etc.
- cementing relationships between the distribution company and on or off trade retailer.

Here we have only reviewed some of the typical field selling job functions within a selling organization. These will be supported by a range of specialist functions or departments to ensure that they can perform optimally, possibly including order processing, telesales, customer service, sales training, sales planning, sales promotions, with additional clerical support. There is no definitively correct sales organization, as it must be designed to reflect the needs of the company, the trade channels, the products, and final users/consumers. This will be looked at further in Chapter 2.

Sales management qualities ▬▬▬

While the later chapter on sales personnel selection will look in more detail at qualities of persons suited to selling, at this early stage it is perhaps worth a comment on some basic personal qualities appropriate to sales managers. He should be:

- a good organizer and administrator, able to plan, implement and monitor sales activity

- a good communicator, with colleagues, subordinates, customers and trade contacts at all levels
- decisive, thereby inspiring colleagues and subordinates with a sense of leadership, direction and confidence
- fair, objective and impartial in allocating objectives and dealing with business and personnel issues
- a team leader, with that intangible leadership quality that inspires others to follow and take direction, with initiative to identify and take advantage of opportunities, and not given to panic in times of adversity but cool-headed in working towards corrective action.

A sales manager's personal audit

As a short self-analysis exercise take a moment to assign a rating against each of the questions listed below. This is not all-comprehensive, but will serve to alert you to your strengths and development areas, and act as a prompt in planning self-development.

Factors you are weaker on should score lower, and factors you consider your strengths should score high. How would your subordinate salespersons rate you on each of these factors? You can then either sit with your own line manager and discuss the ratings versus the importance of each of the factors in the job, or use your notes to assess personal training needs objectively.

Do You	SCORE 1, 2, 3, 4, 5, 6	NOTES
● Provide leadership?		
● Motivate your team?		
● Set goals and objectives?		
● Develop sales strategies and tactics?		
● Prepare forecasts, plans or set targets?		
● Develop promotional programmes?		
● Recruit the right people?		
● Provide training to meet job and individual needs?		
● Communicate effectively?		
● Measure performance?		
● Provide feedback?		
● Exercise control and discipline?		
● Counsel effectively?		
● Recognize or anticipate problems?		
● Exercise initiative?		
● Take decisions promptly?		
● Exercise good judgement?		
● Develop corrective action programmes?		
● Manage resources cost effectively?		
● Delegate effectively?		
● Develop organizational structures to suit the company business and trading environment?		
● Develop or cooperate with sales support functions?		
● Develop control systems and procedures?		
● Have all the necessary skills for your job?		
● Recognize the need for motivating reward programmes?		

2

Sales structures and organization

Considerations in organizing the sales force

The sales organization, as illustrated in Figure 2.1, should be designed to take account of certain key factors, such as:

- marketing strategy
  - marketing goals and market share objectives;
  - market segmentation and product positioning issues;
  - arget market sectors;
  - marketing communications reaching the target market (prospective customers influenced by advertising and promotion must have a means to try and buy the product)
- sales strategy
  - identifying and servicing trade customers or product users;
  - market coverage objectives;
  - sales volume/value objectives (to meet marketing objectives)
- distribution channels
  - needs of each level of the distribution chain;
  - market distribution infrastructure
- product needs.

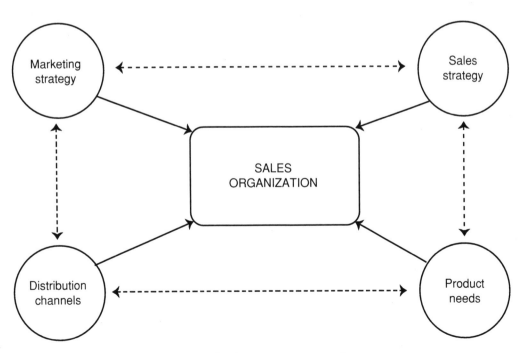

Figure 2.1 *Key factors impacting on sales force organization design*

...al factors

...normally
...l spread of
...will grow
...dded, and
...nands the
...ositions. In
...n of trade
...et sectors

Geographically

Sales and management responsibilities could be divided by geographical area (possibly based on population locations or customer locations), so that certain functions are provided within a defined area. Typically sales territories are assigned on a geographical basis, and with some organizations a network of regional distribution centres is strategically located to service customers. In a larger sales organization sales support services might also be split geographically, e.g. with a network of regional sales trainers, or customer service staff with a specific regional responsibility.

Horizontally

Functions are mutually exclusive as a departmental sub-activity, e.g. sales training, customer service, sales planning,

Vertically

Within a department, as workload grows beyond the capacity of existing personnel, functional responsibilities are delegated downwards, with new tiers of management and non-management functional positions appearing. Each new level should have clearly defined responsibilities, objectives and standards of performance.

Trade channel structures

In some organizations that sell products in several market sectors a different sales team is developed to handle sales activity in separate trade channel market sectors with greater specialization, e.g. in the wines and spirits trade it is common to have separate sales teams servicing the ON trade (hotels, restaurants, food service and institutional customers) and OFF trade (supermarkets, liquor stores). Pharmaceutical companies commonly develop separate sales teams to sell into pharmacies and hospitals, and to brief doctors. Suppliers of components might have one sales team servicing other manufacturers who would use the components as original equipment in another finished product, and a separate team servicing the (larger) network of replacement parts dealers.

Management span of control

Consideration will also have to be given to the **span of control** limits of each manager to manage, motivate, train and control salespersons, which is dependent on:

- the nature of work being performed (skilled or unskilled)
- the knowledge or experience of the persons involved in managing or being managed
- the physical proximity of jobs
- the similarity of content of the jobs being managed
- the time available and required for training, planning, communicating and supervising.

There is a general view that any single manager is limited in the number of persons he or she can supervise directly, and in the number of different functions he or she can manage effectively. Typically a manager might supervise four to six functions (sub-departments). In managing a sales team experience shows that first line field sales managers (area or district managers) can only supervise effectively between six and ten salespersons, providing all the inputs to management, control, training, performance monitoring, planning, communicating, etc. While some companies'

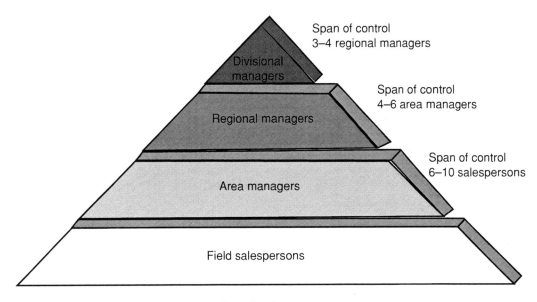

Figure 2.2 *Adding management tiers as the sales force grows in size*

will try to run with much larger teams, the normal result is a fire-fighting approach to field sales management, with a negligible focus on training, and very little time being spent with any individual. A good rule of thumb for a field sales manager would be to spend at least half a day to a day with each salesperson in his or her team each two weeks.

From this commentary we see that the size of a sales force will vary with the number of management tiers, and effective span of control at each level. Figure 2.2 and Table 2.1 illustrate how an organization might grow as levels are added. In these examples I have assumed that the span on control reduces the higher the position, as the higher the level of management the more time must be given to activities such as planning, rather than field salesperson management. Very large sales

Table 2.1 *Relationship between sales force size and span of control*

	Span of control of first line manager (area manager) = 6			Span of control of first line manager (area manager) = 8			Span of control of first line manger (area manager) = 10		
Required number of field salespersons to cover customer base	Hierarchical management organization required			Hierarchical management organization required			Hierarchical management organization required		
	AM	RM	DM	AM	RM	DM	AM	RM	DM
50	8	1 or 2		6			5		
100	17	3		13	2 or 3		10	2	
200	33	5	1	25	4	1	20	3	1
300	50	8	2	38	6 or 7	2	30	5	1 or 2
400	66	11	3	50	8	2	40	7	2

Notes to table

AM = Area manager   RM = Regional manager   DM = Divisional manager

It is assumed for the calculation that the regional manager can manage six area managers, and the divisional manager can manage four regional managers.

forces are more commonly found in developed markets for consumer products and some service industries (such as insurance) rather than in industrial products, as the former normally have a much greater potential customer base to contact and service than do industrial product suppliers.

Other organizational considerations

There are some other considerations in planning the organization structure, including those listed below.

- **Workloads of individuals** The number of positions at any level depends on the workload capacity of individuals within each functional activity in the sales force.
- **Functional activities** It is necessary to identify the functions requiring separate management input, control and development to improve the quality and quantity of output.
- **Communications within the sales organization** Effective communications are essential to provide feedback, motivation, planning, recognition, and achievement of common objectives through coordinated activities.
- **Flexibility** The sales organization should be flexible enough to adapt to changing market conditions. Barriers to flexibility should be avoided or removed.
- **Role clarification** Avoid internal conflict and non-functioning by ensuring each person in the sales team is very clear on his/her role, and avoid duplication of functional responsibilities, assign clear

responsibilities, and promote good formal and informal communications.

In a field selling organization management control and motivation are more likely to be effective in an environment of 'one person, one boss'. One salesperson is normally responsible for all sales through an account or, at least, of a clearly defined product category. Various forms of functional or matrix management structures that might work in the office environment often result in confusion and under-performance if introduced to a field selling organization. Any factor that can introduce confusion into the field management equation may need to be addressed. For example, companies that introduce the role of field sales trainer, to supplement the work of the area field sales managers, usually find that those trainers rapidly become aware of the need not to usurp the authority of the line managers and be seen as an 'alternative manager'.

Some typical evolving organization structures

Developing a basic structure

Readers in medium to larger companies may have quite substantial selling organizations, and perhaps forget how the sales organization developed from its embryonic beginnings, when there were probably few customers and products, and very few personnel managed by a single sales manager, illustrated in outline in Figure 2.3.

Figure 2.3 A basic sales organization structure

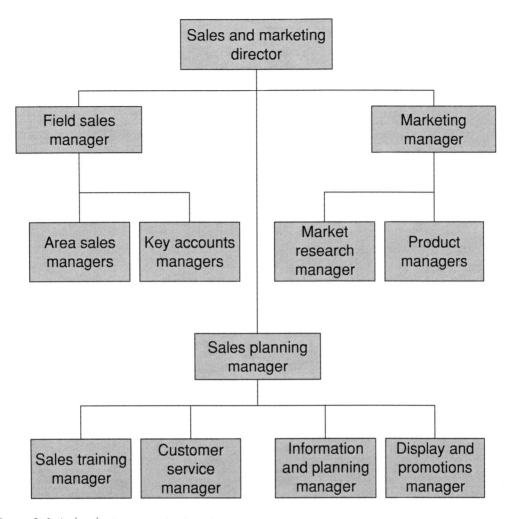

Figure 2.4 *A developing organization structure*

As the sales volume increases, or the product range or product complexity grows, a larger, more sophisticated organization will be required to handle workloads or provide additional support functions, possibly along the lines illustrated in Figure 2.4. A number of the job functions do not have line management responsibility over field selling operations, but provide essential support. A formal job evaluation process will need to be developed at this point to fairly assess the relative values in terms of contribution to sales division goals and objectives, and seniority of each position. In this illustration, the functions reporting to the sales planning manager would be quite different, but would all work in close proximity to him or her and each other, therefore being a manageable mix of functions.

A further stage of development typically occurs as sales grow to new levels, and it is felt necessary to split sales and marketing functions. Workloads might also be increasing, product ranges further expanding, market infrastructures changing, and target segments becoming more defined, with growing product service needs. The structure adopted will vary according to the nature of the market, i.e. whether consumer goods, industrial goods, or consumer services or business-to-business services are being provided.

Any particular organization structure should have scope for **flexibility** to take account of and develop with environmental changes. For example, the buying needs and practices of retail or industrial customers might change (buying may be consolidated at fewer buying points within large customer organizations), product distribution patterns might change (e.g. the advent of a growing direct marketing and home shopping culture).

The final organization should reflect skills of individuals and accountabilities of managers. For example, in Figure 2.5, the position of sales training manager could, logically, report to the national sales manager (in that the outcomes of the job impact directly on his or her responsibilities and key performance indicators); but he or she may have neither the skills, time, nor be well located to manage the function on a day-to-day basis. Figure 2.5 illustrates examples of geographical, horizontal and vertical specialization.

A geographically organized sales force

As has been mentioned, a common way to organize a sales force is with some geographical split of responsibilities, breaking the country into similar sized areas and territories, where the size comparison might consist of population bases, number of outlets or customers, or the relative turnover values or potential. Figure 2.6 illustrates a typical basic geographical structure.

Trade sector specialization _____

In many fast moving consumer goods and industrial product companies more than one sales force emerges over time to serve different trade sectors with the same product range (albeit the products may be presented and packed slightly differently to better suit each trade sector). The various trade sectors may have very different service needs, or requirements for promotional support, and require different inputs of selling time to develop business optimally. Figures 2.7 and 2.8 illustrate some example structures.

An example of the same products requiring more than one sales force to serve different trade sectors is the wines and spirits trade. The retail (off-trade) sector will require a more aggressive selling style in a very competitive retail environment, product merchandising, in-store promotional displays and consumer promotions encouraging a take-home trial, with selling activity taking place during normal daytime hours. But the on-trade (bars, clubs, etc.) will require a different selling style (less aggressive, perhaps, with emphasis on relationship development with owners/managers), probably a sales team that calls on customers when they are open for trade (which in many markets will not be until late in the day or the evenings), different formats of promotional support during peak evening opening hours, not with major feature displays, but perhaps with sponsored events and theme nights. Other examples follow.

- Food companies frequently have products sold through more than one type of outlet (e.g. supermarkets and smaller independent general stores or confectionery/tobacco/news stores).
- Pharmaceutical companies and other suppliers of over-the-counter remedies are frequently supplying to pharmacies, sundry non-pharmacy outlets (such as drug stores), and to hospitals and medical centres, while also needing to have a specialist team for briefing the medical professions (who will not be ordering personally for resale).
- An industrial manufacturer of paints typically would develop a separate selling structure to service the very different end use markets, likely to include industrial manufacturers of equipment that requires painting (e.g. by dipping or spraying), the professional decorating trade, as well as the home do-it-yourself market.
- A manufacturer of electrical components, such as switches, connectors, plugs, sockets, etc., might have quite a variety of potential trade sectors to supply (see Figure 2.8), and all might require different service formats, and product variations.

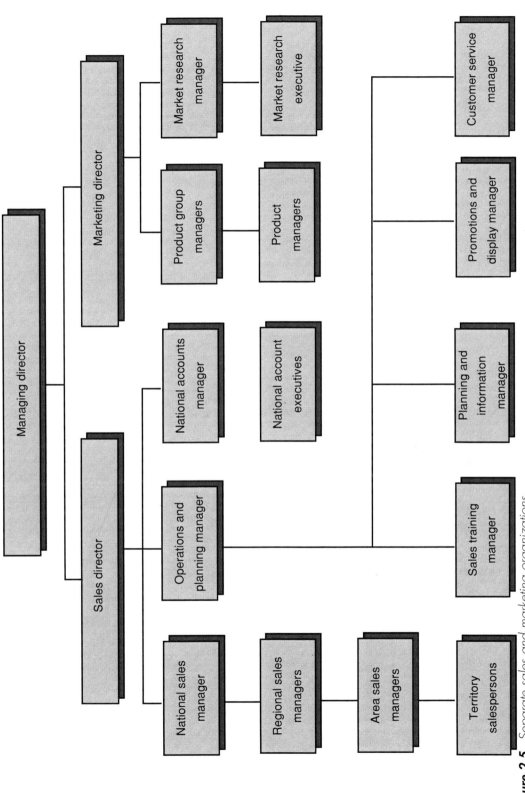

Figure 2.5 Separate sales and marketing organizations

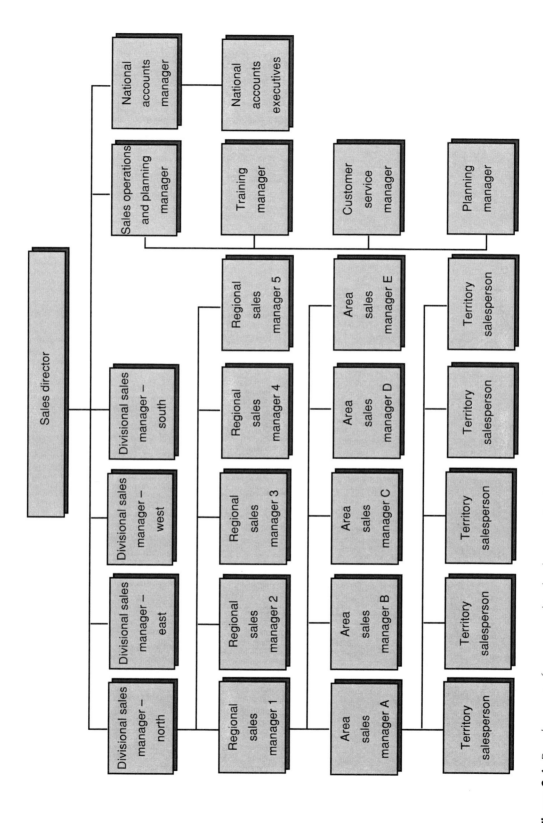

Figure 2.6 Development of a geographical sales organization structure

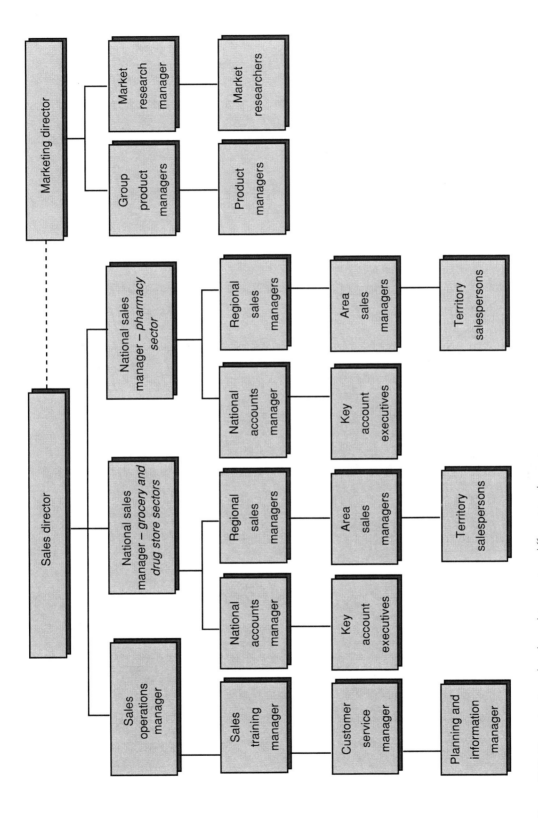

Figure 2.7 Organization developed to service different trade sectors

In the example shown in Figure 2.8, retailers, such as the multiple do-it-yourself chains, might prefer single unit bubble packs. Building and electrical contractors would want to purchase bulk quantities with price a key selection factor. Manufacturers of other forms of electrical products would want component inputs, for designing into their own products, where the component supplier might have to custom design a product of special size or shape to meet the customer's needs. In addition the component manufacturer is likely to want to promote to persons who specify components (such as architects of public sector bodies concerned with public housing). All this can make for a sales force structure with several separate sales teams who are each specialized in a market sector, possibly with special training or experience. Also, in this example I have deliberately used the title *sales operations manager* rather than sales office manager, to highlight that the job is much more than an administrative function, with considerable input to planning, customer service strategy development, and development of sales promotion support.

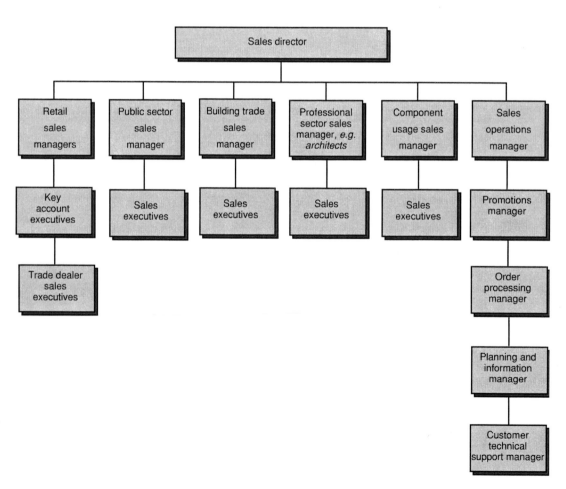

Figure 2.8 Sales organization for a manufacturer of electrical components

Product specialization

Many companies offer more than one product range, and these might be offered to a common customer base, or to different target market users/consumers. In such situations there may also be a need for different sales teams to specialize in the different product groups, even where they might overlap, calling on some of the same customers. In some instances the different sales teams might call on the same corporate customers, but deal with quite a different group of buyers or specifiers. Figures 2.9 and 2.10 give some illustrations.

● Insurance companies typically offer products to meet very different personal needs, such as household insurance, life assurance, and pension and investment plans. Some of these categories are frequently promoted by professional advisers (who typically receive a commission for recommendations), such as lawyers and accountants, and these advisers will need product briefings from specialist salespersons.

● A company selling industrial machinery and consumable materials for use with the machinery, such as print binding machinery and the binding materials, or shoe making machinery and shoe components, may also decide to split the sales force into product teams. The machinery may be purchased by one type of buyer supported by specialist specifiers, such as engineers, and the consumables might be purchased by another buyer supported by finished product designers and production managers. Each buying team will have very different objectives and criteria for judging products they are responsible for. The machinery buyers may have concerns for capital cost, operating

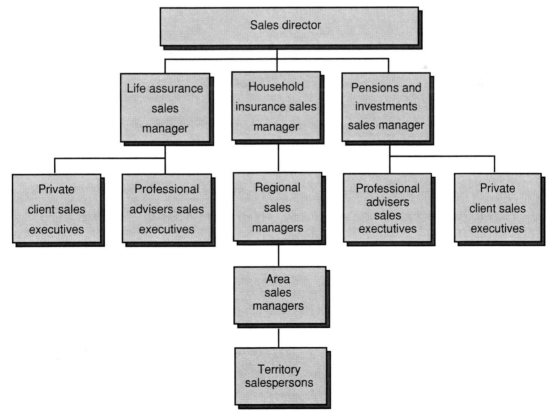

Figure 2.9 *Sales organization for an insurance company*

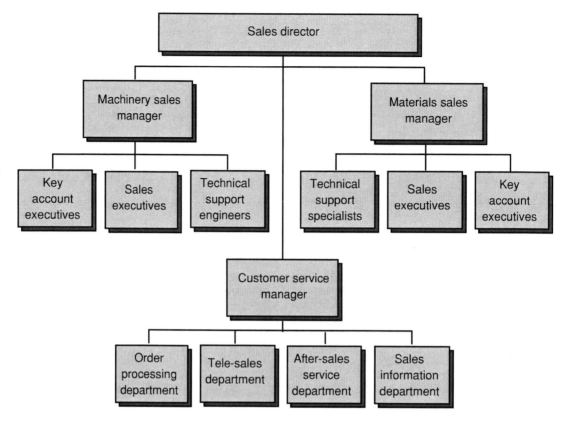

Figure 2.10 *Sales organization for a supplier of machines and related consumables*

costs, spare part and service availability and support, and the sales team may need a level of engineering expertise. The consumable products buying team may be concerned for durability of the consumable inputs in finished products, design and aesthetic factors, ease of use by production operatives, minimum down-time through consumables jamming in machinery, etc. If the products are very technical, it is likely that the sales teams may need to be supported by technical experts who can survey needs or work with engineers in specifying product modifications, as well as supervising tests and trials and providing installation support. A customer service function may need a particular focus on after-sales technical support.

Key account management

Some of the examples illustrated show a key accounts selling structure, sometimes also referred to as national accounts management. Some comment on the development and role of such a sub-organization is warranted here.

In many markets there is a growing concentration of buying points, in part through mergers and acquisitions, and in part through organic expansion. In retailing concentration is found in food, furniture, electrical goods, toys, pharmaceuticals, clothing, service products such as travel and cleaning, and so on. Smaller independent retailers have often banded into voluntary buying groups in an attempt to remain competitive and to buy on better terms from suppliers. Similar trends are found in manufacturing for many product categories, where mergers provide benefits from synergy of operations. Buying then often becomes centralized, rather than each branch or subsidiary organizing its own supply purchasing.

As purchasing becomes more concentrated many suppliers become concerned for their margins (as buyers demand larger discounts, performance rebates, promotional and display allowances in retailing, and so on), and for security of their supply contracts. But there can also be benefits from purchasing concentration and proactive key account management, such as:

- an improved ability to forecast sales as more and better information becomes available
- better production planning and plant utilization
- improved control over supplies of inputs and inventories
- more flexibility and control in developing specific sales promotions to support ongoing marketing programmes
- opportunities to negotiate larger and longer-term supply contracts
- new opportunities to supplement standard products with products customized to customer needs (e.g. private label products for retailers, or customized design of industrial products)
- concentration of key selling functions to few highly skilled key account business development executives, trained to negotiate with professional buyers
- a possible reduction in the size of a field sales force, with resultant cost savings, and an opportunity to focus more management time and effort on developing business with the major accounts (nationally and internationally).

Key account management thrives on mutual respect and recognition of professionalism, in all aspects of business relations and negotiating. Neither party benefits from ignoring problems, either in relationships or technically with products or service, and both have a strong interest in satisfactory resolution of problems standing in the way of mutually profitable business development. The account manager must, above all, be an efficient and effective communicator, both with the customers and internally within the selling organization, with a strong ability to influence senior managers. It is critical to select suitable persons to fulfil the job functions, as not all salespersons will have the personal and technical skills and qualities to work as equals with buyers, authorizers, specifiers and any other persons inputting to the buying process within major account organizations.

The size of a national accounts organization will depend on the number of major accounts warranting treatment as key accounts. Many companies find that a few customers contribute most sales turnover and profit, and analysis normally confirms the broad *Pareto* findings that 80 per cent of sales comes from 20 per cent of turnover (i.e. the 80/20 rule, or *Pareto* rule). Typically, when trying to assess the number of key account executives needed, look at:

- how many customers provide at least 50 per cent of turnover, or individually represent more than one per cent of sales (then this list can be refined to include the largest and those with most potential as key accounts)
- the number of subsidiaries or branch locations that need servicing for each account (as these should all be the responsibility of a single account manager)
- the amount of time needed for planning and performance monitoring
- the expected frequency of account contact (at head office and branches).

A simple tabulation of customer sales normally highlights the potential candidates for key account treatment (see Table 2.2). If there are different product groups or market sectors, the key account structure may have specialists in product groups or trade sectors, as illustrated in Figure 2.11.

Table 2.2 *Tabulating data to identify the key accounts*

Alton Plastic Mouldings		Top 50 customers (domestic market)					
Sales rank	Customer name	Cum % sales	Cumulative sales	Sales value	Gross margin	Cumulative gross margin	Cum % margin
1	Highbury Computers Ltd	6	835,827	835 827	591 397	591 397	10
2	Alsop Electronics	10	1 369 403	533 576	126 979	718 376	13
3	Standard Toys	14	1 898 884	529 481	226 387	944 763	16
4	Fairburn & Wilson	18	2 397 283	498 399	213 468	1 158 231	20
5	Alpha Instruments	21	2 715 545	318 262	73 495	1 231 726	21
6	Xenon Packaging Supplies	23	3 031 307	315 762	112 209	1 343 935	23
7	Wirex Components	25	3 337 375	306 068	88 331	1 432 266	25
8	Multiparts	27	3 613 210	275 834	115 618	1 547 884	27
9	Acme Superstores	29	3 886 421	273 211	58 509	1 606 393	28
10	Delsey Sales Promotions	31	4 123 897	237 476	95 077	1 701 470	30
11	Hyper Hyper Stores	33	4 351 292	227 395	68 971	1 770 441	31
12	Solex	34	4 563 589	212 297	60 085	1 830 526	32
13	Generation Games Ltd	36	4 755 552	191 962	72 244	1 902 770	33
14	Urquart Dept. Stores	37	4 936 053	180 502	28 454	1 931 224	34
15	DDC Electronics	39	5 103 482	167 429	52 638	1 983 862	35
16	Plastiploy	40	5 269 057	165 574	83 692	2 067 554	36
17	Computer Components Plc	41	5 418 114	149 057	148 310	2 215 864	39
18	Renshaw	42	5 563 042	144 928	50 618	2 266 482	40
19	Whyte & Wilson	43	5 707 801	144 759	38 407	2 304 889	40
20	Astari Computers	44	5 847 844	140 043	57 726	2 362 615	41
21	Maxi-Markets	45	5 986 287	138 443	70 485	2 433 100	42
22	Depal Packaging Supplies	46	6 119 113	132 826	70 535	2 503 635	44
23	Holstein Factors	47	6 251 021	131 908	65 959	2 569 594	45
24	Universal Exports Ltd	48	6 382 529	131508	51 230	2 620 824	46
25	Senstronic	49	6 507 890	125 361	60 640	2 681 464	47
26	Guardall Security	50	6 631 805	123 915	42 656	2 724 120	48
27	Betta Housewares	51	6 754 083	122 278	50 974	2 775 094	48
28	LoCost Stores	52	6 876 224	122 141	46 904	2 821 998	49
29	Universal Car Parts	53	6 976 553	100 330	32 532	2 854 530	50
30	Bendi Toys	53	7 072 785	96 232	31 440	2 885 970	50
31	Wastall Partners	54	7 168 443	95 658	25 367	2 911 337	51
32	Midland Auto Spares	55	7 262 237	93 795	37 250	2 948 587	51
33	HomeGuard Security	56	7 355 458	93 220	60 929	3 009 516	53
34	Lylle & McKay	56	7 447 026	91 568	40 282	3 049 798	53
35	Partytime Games	57	7 537 986	90 960	31 970	3 081 768	54
36	Welstart Components	58	7 625 394	87 408	28 598	3 110 366	54
37	Rustall Plastics	58	7 711 163	85 769	41 221	3 151 587	55
38	Sonheim	59	7 796 767	85 605	74 493	3 226 080	56
39	Kut Kost Markets	60	7 881 037	84 270	66 143	3 292 223	57
40	Tennison Storage Ltd	60	7 963 944	82 907	62 362	3 354 585	59
41	Nordic Office Supplies	61	8 046 055	82 111	29 325	3 383 910	59
42	Wyman Stationers	61	8 126 835	80 781	39 250	3 423 160	60
43	Caruthers Dept. Store	62	8 207 360	80 524	37 533	3 460 693	60
44	Flex-tone Fitness Equipment	63	8 284 787	77 427	14 962	3 475 655	61
45	Beauchamp Lighting	63	8 356 784	71 997	33 245	3 508 900	61
46	Morrison Mallory Ltd	64	8 425 696	68 913	21 769	3 530 669	62
47	Modern Bathrooms	64	8 493 407	67 711	27 618	3 558 287	62

Table 2.2 *Tabulating data to identify the key accounts (continued)*

Alton Plastic Mouldings		Top 50 customers (domestic market)					
Sales rank	Customer name	Cum % sales	Cumulative sales	Sales value	Gross margin	Cumulative gross margin	Cum % margin
48	Huntingdon Spares	65	8 556 003	6 2596	22 283	3 580 570	62
49	Raschid Electronics	65	8 617 985	6 1981	34 984	3 615 554	63
50	Southern Garden Centres	66	8 679 655	6 1670	26 943	3 642 497	64
Top 50 totals				8 679 655	3 642 496		
UK totals 1996							
(845 active customers)				13 231 111	5 732 214		
Top 50 as %age of UK customers				66%	64%		
AVERAGES PER CUSTOMER				15 658	6784		

The example customer mix shown in Table 2.2 shows that 50 customers of a total active base of 845 (six per cent of customers) accounted for two-thirds of sales and profits with our model company! And from amongst the top 50 there are probably at least a dozen that should warrant special development as key accounts, since each contributes between one and six per cent of sales. Even from the brief customer names we can see a mix of some industrial and some retail clients, as the plastic moulding company supplies moulded parts for industry as well as a range of retail plastic house wares.

It is interesting to note in this example that, while the top 50 represent a similar proportion of both sales and profits, the ranking for sales and gross margin would not be exactly the same, and there are significant differences between the gross margin yields from the various customers. Key account management is not just about generating and managing

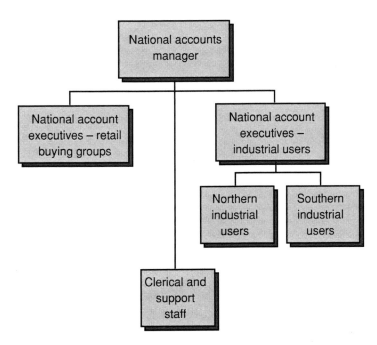

Figure 2.11 *An example key account sales structure*

turnover, but managing the total business partnership of supplier and customer, with a focus on the profitability of trading.

The key account organization structure, as a sub-department of the sales division, can incorporate, as appropriate, elements of horizontal, vertical and geographical specialization, with an example illustrated in Figure 2.11.

Export department organization

All of the basic principles of developing a sales and marketing organization outlined in this chapter can be applied when structuring an export organization. In some companies export sales operations fall under the control of a sales or marketing director, while in larger organizations export will often be a separate function with its own director heading the organization. Readers who have a particular interest in export marketing and management are referred to the author's companion book *The CIM Handbook of Export Marketing* (Butterworth-Heinemann), which includes a number of developing organization examples. Figures 2.12 and 2.13 illustrate typically how the basic principles expounded here might look for a company with a larger export sales and marketing organization. In Figure 2.12 the technical services manager is shown with a dotted line linking to the

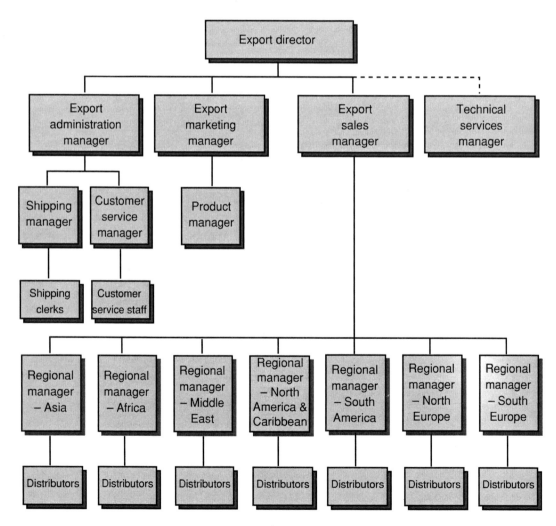

Figure 2.12 *A typical export department organized geographically*

export director, just to indicate that this position only functionally supports export operations rather than being a direct line report (probably reporting in to the research and development or engineering director, depending on the nature of the products).

Matrix organizations

Some companies have found that the traditional pyramidical organizational hierarchy has not always been effective or easy to manage as a company grows in size, and the product ranges and market sectors served diversify. Internal politics and communication blockages or barriers can result in delays in implementation of strategies and tactics through all the departments that contribute to achievement of an effective plan. Marketing and sales managers cannot manage their own departments in isolation from other specialist functions or production and distribution departments.

The result in some companies has been for a form of **matrix** management to develop, to supervise projects and sometimes product development and management (with Figure 2.14 providing an illustration). In this scenario the team can control planning, decision taking, evaluation and resource allocation, as well as performance monitoring against plans and objectives.

Typically, within the matrix, team leadership would be from a department with key inputs to contribute, such as marketing or possibly sales. Hierarchical reporting relationships would still exist, in that each team member has line superiors who would expect reports. As any reader who has experience of this type of matrix team has probably

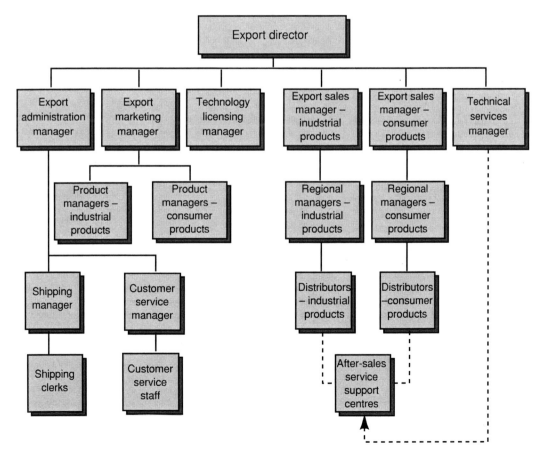

Figure 2.13 *An export organization developed to serve market sectors*

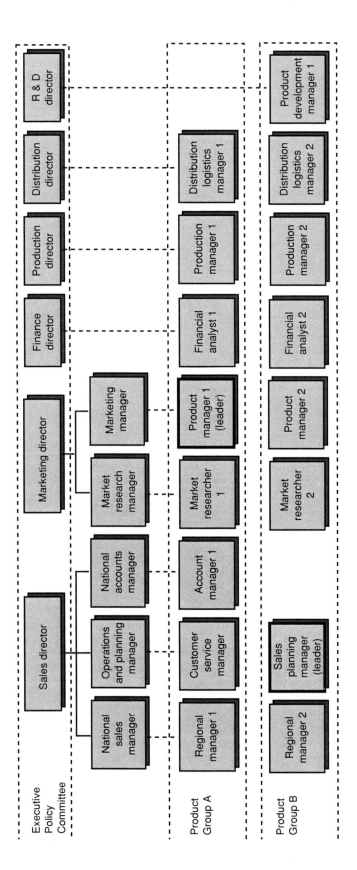

Figure 2.14 *A form of team matrix management*

Notes:
Within each department and division there is a hierarchical structure (the management pyramid), although membership of any particular matrix group need not depend on seniority but upon a manager's functional contribution to that group. If it is felt that particular functions need to be represented on several projects or product groups, then one functional representative might sit on several groups. Each matrix group has a clear team leader.

discovered, the teams can only function effectively where each person has clearly defined roles and contributions, so that disfunctionality and confusion do not hamper progress while managers argue over what they view as incursions into their sphere of operations. While, on the one hand, to internal managers it seems essential to avoid conflict and confusion, what can frequently be overlooked in the melee of internal politics is the confusion customers experience when they do not know who, in a company, can effectively manage their business and relationship.

Customers who find they are being contacted by several persons (from the same or different departments), whether on separate or overlapping issues, will first become confused but soon learn to play the supplier's weaknesses in managing communications to their advantage. So whether a traditional pyramidical structure or some form of matrix organizational structure is preferred, lines of communication, both internally and externally, must be clearly drawn, and the roles and responsibilities of individuals clarified.

Checklist 2.1
Effective organizational structures

Action points

Is your sales organization designed to:

- prepare sales forecasts, plans, budgets, sales and marketing programmes?
- increase and/or maximize distribution?
- merchandise and display product optimally?
- provide timely and efficient distribution to all outlets?
- provide field management to sales persons or outlets?
- identify and develop new stockists/consumer locations?
- recruit and develop the most suitable sales personnel?
- provide comprehensive initial and ongoing training to staff?
- measure performance?
- provide performance feedback?
- communicate effectively between all levels and to all staff?
- control customer credit/cash management?
- provide support services to the sales staff and trade outlets?
- provide comprehensive customer service?
- process orders promptly and efficiently?
- provide support and service to key accounts and customers?
- provide customer after-sales service?
- respond to changing market needs for products?
- reflect customer needs in terms of distribution, product trends, etc.?
- have in-built flexibility to meet changing markets and environments?

Are the following effective and realistic for all sales team operatives?

- reporting relationships?
- spans of control?
- workloads?
- number/mix/range of functional activities?
- internal and external communications?
- organizational format?
- reporting procedures, administrative systems and controls?

If the answer to any of these is a 'no' or qualified 'yes', there may be scope for organizational modifications or improvements that might increase the productivity and effectiveness of the organization.

Part Two

Developing a Motivating Sales Environment

3

Motivational management in the sales force

What is motivation?

Motivation is generally seen as the process of getting people to work towards achievement of an objective. Management may often take a rather limited view, or perhaps selfish approach, to motivation, seeing it only as getting subordinate employees to work towards achievement of a company goal or objective, possibly achieving the current sales targets. Traditional motivational theory (e.g. Maslow's theory, subsequently developed and modified by others – see later) postulates that individuals are motivated only when they see an opportunity to fulfil some personal need, within a hierarchy of needs that may change over time as some of them are satisfied. In fact, we can then see needs as being positively satisfied, in that something is added (perhaps a new automobile, or holiday), or negatively satisfied in that some source of dissatisfaction is lessened or removed (such as accomplishing a task that stops the pressures from the manager, allowing the achiever a quieter life, for a while). If we define motivation as follows, then we see that achievement of a goal or objective that

> **Motivation**
> This is the process of getting people to act willingly towards achieving greater satisfaction of their personal needs through the achievement of company goals and objectives.

the company values should be accompanied by some reciprocation that the individual values (which might be as simple as praise in a sales bulletin, a bonus, or positive feedback through promotion).

Why salespersons need motivation

Many sales managers apparently expect their sales teams to be self-motivated, rather like a perpetual motion machine or self-winding watch. Some readers may recognize this symptom as common amongst those sales managers who spend little time working in the field with their team. Many even comment that when recruiting they seek to identify self-motivated individuals. Perhaps what they are failing to recognize is that the apparently 'self-motivated' individual is actually highly motivated towards achieving his or her clearly defined goals and objectives at that point in time (including landing the job on offer at the interview), and once certain objectives are achieved, that person needs new horizons to aim at, and new motivations to drive achievement towards those horizons.

Salespersons need constant motivation to maintain performance and productivity to satisfactory levels, and to present challenges that encourage them to raise their performance and productivity to greater than satisfactory levels by offering ways that address the personal needs of each. The sales manager who, when asked how he treats his sales

Figure 3.1 *A simple motivational model*

team, comments that he treats them all the same is missing the point. They are not all the same, any more than two children in a family have the same behavioural and motivational pattern. Individual difference in motivation must be identified, recognized and addressed if team performance is to be improved. It would be fairer to talk of treating all members of the sales team equally, that is by addressing equally each person's balance of needs.

Motivational factors

To maintain and improve performance and productivity becomes a full-time job for many supervisors and managers within their teams. This is particularly likely to be the case where managers fail to understand and apply some basic principles of motivation. While this is the subject of many specialized texts, from the practical perspective there are several interesting approaches that readily translate into a sales environment. They have all been tested over the years, each having some validity in various circumstances. However, most of the attempts to verify motivation theo-ries are based on tests in western cultures, and even within these there are found to be varia-tions in cultural response to efforts to motivate improved performance and productivity.

Hierarchy of needs theory

This approach to understanding motivation (initially propagated by Maslow, see Figure 3.2) recognized five main types of needs:

- **physiological** needs, addressing the basic survival requirements of the individual (e.g. food, health, security)
- **safety** needs, addressing the need for physical and emotional security
- **social** needs, such as the need to belong and to be accepted within social groups, to give and receive affection
- need for **esteem**, both internal esteem (self-respect, achievement) and external esteem (status, recognition, public attention)
- **self-actualization** needs, those higher-level needs relating to self-achievement and self-fulfilment.

Primary physiological and safety needs in the main are more easily met in developed

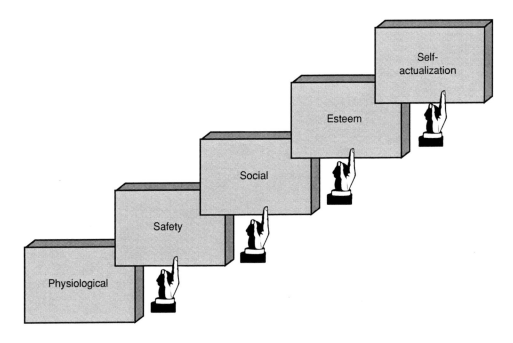

Figure 3.2 *The traditional model of a hierarchy of needs*

nations, as an employer is providing a job, income and range of benefits that address these needs, usually satisfying basic comfort and survival needs through:

- security of employment
- basic salary meeting financial commitments
- earnings protection during periods of sickness
- pensions to provide for post-retirement income
- sickness and life assurance cover
- safe working environments.

Goal setting theory

This approach to management and motivation has gained many supporters amongst practising managers. It postulates that setting and agreeing specific and difficult goals will lead to higher performance. Goals tell people what effort they can expect to have to expend to achieve it, and, if broken down, what actions they need to take. Gaining acceptance of, and commitment to, a goal presupposes the individual sees it as realistic and achiev-

able. Self-set goals typically have more impact on individual behaviour, particularly where the goals are made public within a team.

While on the one hand easier goals are more likely to find acceptance with many employees, once a harder goal is accepted effort towards achieving it normally increases until it is achieved, lowered or abandoned. While it is also recognized that feedback on progress towards a goal is important, it is also recognized that self-generated feedback is a more powerful motivator than external feedback.

Goal setting also assumes that:

- individuals can influence outcomes
- individuals have the independence to pursue options
- challenging goals will be accepted
- performance is seen as important in the work and cultural environment.

Managers who travel internationally will realize that this goal setting approach to motivation is less effective in some cultures, particularly where:

- employees are adverse to taking risks
- employees have little independence, and possibly have little involvement in active management and decision-making processes
- personal performance is not such a driving force in motivation.

Equity theory

This theory will, again, be recognized by managers who are familiar with situations the theory depicts. It recognizes that individuals in a work environment will be concerned not just with the absolute levels of rewards from a job, but also with their rewards relative to those received by others in appropriate reference groups, such as colleagues doing similar jobs. It assumes then that they are likely to seek to eliminate what they judge to be inequities. It is this desire to remove inequities that provides scope for motivation towards increased productivity and performance.

Individual employees have four main reference options (illustrated in the table following) in making equity comparisons.

Internal self	Experiences of an employee in different positions in the current company organization
External self	Experiences of an employee in or with different positions in other (former employer) company organizations
Internal others	Comparisons by an employee with other individuals or groups within the current company organization
External others	Comparisons by an employee with other individuals or groups outside the current company organization

Employees do make frequent comparisons with colleagues, friends and neighbours, and form views about their relative income and value. How they judge themselves in relation to other reference groups or individuals is considered within equity theory to affect their motivation and behaviour. When making comparisons individuals do tend to consider the variables of sex (most men favour comparisons with other males, most women favour comparisons with other women), length of service with an employer, seniority within the organization, and education or training that will give a measure of comparative suitability or professionalism in the job.

Where any individual employee judges that he or she is in an inequitable relationship to others in reference groups, then possible courses of action include:

- reducing effort and input to the job, thereby balancing their perception of their relative equity (rewards) with their inputs
- increasing effort and input, trying to raise their equity to a higher level commensurate with that of reference groups or individuals
- justifying the inequity with particular reference groups by looking for other reference groups where there would not be such an imbalance (i.e. instead of making comparisons with colleagues in, say, the private sector, making comparisons with persons employed in public service)
- distorting perceptions of themselves and their contributions, self-justifying positions (such as developing a view that they are indispensable in a role, or that they work harder than others)
- distorting perceptions of others they have drawn relative reward comparisons with, such as by claiming they have no interest in the job functions or responsibilities of some of those who they consider inequitably rewarded in relation to themselves
- quitting the job and going to look for another that appears to offer a better equity relationship with reference groups.

McClelland's achievement – power – affiliation theory _____

This theory postulates three key needs of:

- **achievement**: the individual's striving to perform to a high level, excelling in relation to standards and colleagues
- **power**: the desire for power and control over other persons, influencing their activities and behaviour, the desire to make an impact
- **affiliation**: the desire to build close and harmonious relationships.

Within the scope of this theory it has been recognized that in a business organization environment high achievers tend to be people who have stronger needs for achievement and power, and who prefer to tackle tasks or projects where they have a reasonable chance of success, but which are also not too simple to accomplish. They like responsibility, good feedback, and a moderate (preferably measurable) level of risk. Typically they would like successful outcomes to be the result of their inputs rather than as a result of uncontrollable external factors.

High achievement does not necessarily equate to a good management style, as high achievers are often more self-centred in pursuing achievement. The good manager tends to be stronger in the power drive area, with less concern to develop close affiliations.

Expectancy theory _____

Another motivational theory that has gained credibility is Vroom's **expectancy theory**. This proposes that the strength of an employee's inclination to act in certain (predictable) ways will depend on his or her expectation that the act will be followed by a predictable result (outcome or reward) and the attractiveness of that to the individual. The desired outcome or reward might be to benefit from a good performance appraisal,

move up the promotion ladder, receive a pay increase or bonus. It is implicit that the rewards will satisfy an employee's personal goals. Figure 3.3 illustrates how expectancy theory is seen to work. Readers may note that this is a development of the most basic motivational model illustrated earlier in Figure 3.1. Managers must understand the goals of individual employees, and show how improved performance resulting from individual effort leads to company rewards, leading on to satisfaction of personal goals.

The expectancy theory offers some insights into why some employees might appear not to be motivated to increase productivity or improve performance. They may be asking themselves a number of questions, such as:

- 'Is the reward worth the effort?'
- 'Will the performance improvements justify the effort?'
- 'Will the effort and performance improvements give me extra recognition through appraisals?'
- 'If my appraisal rating improves, will it lead to promotion or new responsibilities I value?'
- 'Will all my extra effort and performance improvements increase my job security?'

As this section illustrates, there is quite a range of traditional and more contemporary theories concerning motivation. They all have merit, and the practising manager probably adopts a number of them. In a sales context the sales manager concerned to improve performance must ensure that:

- there are no obstacles that can prevent the salesperson increasing effort or improving performance (while the sales manager cannot control external limiting factors, he should ensure internal factors are addressed; e.g. if there are production or supply limitations these will work against improving sales through extra effort)
- appropriate resources are made available to assist the salesperson.

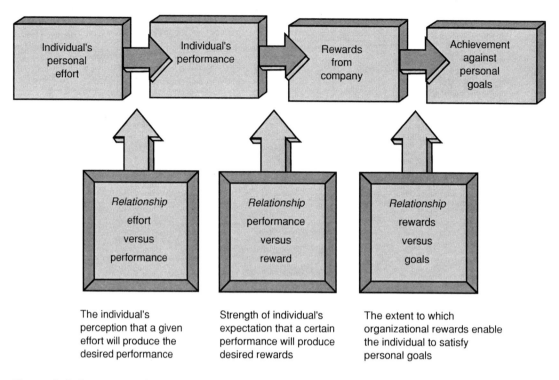

The individual's perception that a given effort will produce the desired performance

Strength of individual's expectation that a certain performance will produce desired rewards

The extent to which organizational rewards enable the individual to satisfy personal goals

Figure 3.3 *Expectancy theory*

Practical motivation

From the practical perspective the starting point in looking at motivation of a sales team might be considered as looking at issues of job dissatisfaction and satisfaction. This, as the reader will recall, is basically looking at the **motivation-hygiene** theory as it applies to the sales environment. Ideally factors that cause demotivation should be neutralized or otherwise tackled if they are seen to detract from efforts to input positive motivation. Then we can move forward with a framework for practical positive motivation.

Job satisfaction

Every job will include a number of interesting (motivating) and uninteresting (demotivating) factors, and each individual performing job functions is likely to have different views on which factors fall into each category. To maximize individual and team productivity, and continuously improve per-

formance, managers must develop job content and provide an environment seen by each salesperson as motivating and rewarding in terms of each of their collection of personal drives and needs. As a starting point to positive motivation we must analyse the job functions, activities and working environments, and establish the typical motivating and demotivating factors.

Demotivators

Demotivating factors should be eliminated or neutralized before motivation can begin. Figure 3.4 highlights a range of typical demotivators, which can most frequently can be categorized under the headings of:

- job uncertainties
- job imbalances
- inadequate management
- inadequate working environment
- poor compensation
- poor prospects.

Causes of demotivation

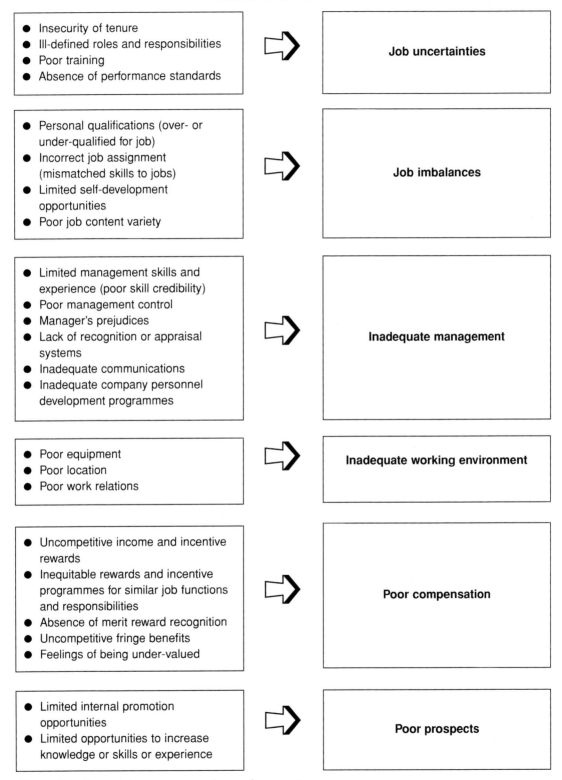

Figure 3.4 *Typical demotivators in the working environment*

The sales manager should constantly be aware of any signs that there are problems in the motivational aspects of his sales team. Frequent signs of demotivation include:

- increased absence
- higher incidence of sickness
- complaints about demotivating factors
- deteriorating performance
- requests for transfers
- active job hunting
- increased staff turnover
- non-compliance with administrative procedures
- increased cynicism (at meetings).

In addition there are a host of attitudinal indications through changed or modified behaviour the manager might spot.

It is a useful management exercise (sometimes monitored by a human resource department) to record and plot demotivational indicators that can be quantifiably measured (such as absence, sickness, staff turnover). These might be graphed, and variations from levels considered normal can be highlighted for further investigation of

root causes as a precursor to corrective action.

Motivators

Now that we have identified a range of potential demotivators, some of which can be labelled as hygiene factors, a basic practical approach to motivation of the salesperson is to focus on providing:

- an understanding of what is expected of him or her
- confidence that he or she has the skills to do the job
- training
- feedback on company and personal performance
- security in the job
- pride in the company and job
- a good working environment
- fair reward.

We will build on these in the next section.

A framework for practical motivation

Before the sales manager can start to motivate a salesperson to achieve anything, the salesperson must know what is expected of him or her. The table following highlights some things the sales manager can address in developing a motivational selling environment. Then the sales manager can work at motivation by recognizing the major motivational drives within each salesperson (see Table 3.1), and working to help the salesperson increase the satisfaction of his or her main motivational drives.

Tackling demotivation
- If morale and motivation are weakening, search out the root causes.
- Find the cause before treating the symptoms.
- Be brutal in self-analysis and recognition of your own role in demotivation – work with other members of your management team to resolve problems

Promoting a motivational environment

Clarify the job
- Clarify the job content and responsibilities of the jobs in your team, preparing and issuing job descriptions.

Recruit only qualified personnel
- Develop a job holder profile modelled on successful performers, and recruit against objective criteria of skills, personal characteristics and experience.

Provide thorough initial and ongoing skills training
- Avoid inadequate performance, frustration, or demotivation through inadequate skills.
- Provide induction training and company orientation.
- Provide job-specific training on an initial and ongoing basis.

Establish goals and objectives
- Agree goals and objectives with each team member.
- Clarify the relationship between individuals' goals, objectives and standards, and company objectives.

Set standards of performance
- Identify key performance indicators from the job description and set standards of performance against which the salesperson can personally measure performance.

Set specific targets or quotas as motivational tools and performance measures
- Establish periodic quantified **sales targets** that are seen as realistic and achievable by the salespersons involved.
- Provide the **sales tools** (information, sales leads, sales aids and literature, etc.) that facilitate achieving the targets.
- Work to **time span**s, with relevant feedback and related rewards, that are long enough to allow achievement, but short enough to generate momentum behind pursuing the target. For example, in retail selling, where sales activity is immediate after a customer enters the premises, targets might be established on a daily and weekly basis; selling to trade customers or business-to-business customers may take longer to develop contacts and progress to a sale, so targets might be established for monthly and quarterly intervals.
- Provide constant **performance feedbac**k against the sales targets throughout the period to which the target applies (e.g. daily, weekly, monthly updates).

Provide a motivational rewards and benefits package
- Ensure that the basic **rewards package** is competitive and reflective of skills required and effort demanded to achieve the desired results.
- Ensure **sales incentives** (commissions, bonuses, etc.) reflect opportunity to achieve sales in relation to effort and skill expended. There is a high risk that if high 'on target earnings' quoted in recruitment advertisements prove to be elusive to those persons making a concerted effort to generate sales, then the incentive package

loses credibility, and is demotivational not motivational (usually with a high sales team turnover).

- Ensure that the basic rewards package is competitive, reflecting skills required and effort demanded to achieve the desired results.
- Ensure sales incentives (commissions, bonuses, etc.) reflect opportunity to achieve sales in relation to effort and skill expended.

Demonstrate efficient and effective management

- Recruit and train managers who have the qualifications, skills and experience to provide leadership, training and motivation.

Establish sales controls geared to the key performance indiscators of sales performance

- Ensure that controls (continuous and warning controls) are in place to measure and monitor sales activity and performance.

Communicate information

- Ensure that the salesperson has all technical information to perform the job.
- Ensure all company policies, goals and objectives are communicated to each salesperson and that they understand how their personal goals and objectives interrelate.

Develop communications and contact forums

- Provide periodic information **newsletters** or **sales bulletins**.
- Maintain frequent **telephone contact** with all sales team members.
- Organize and run periodic **sales meetings** (such as monthly area sales meetings, supported by an annual national sales conference) that provide:
  - information;
  - a forum for exchanging experiences and ideas;
  - skill development training;
  - an opportunity for salespersons to network internally with colleagues;
  - motivation through collective membership of a successful sales team.
- Develop a pattern of regular **personal field contact** by ensuring that field sales managers work with all salespersons frequently (typically at least every two weeks), and that more senior sales managers accompany salespersons with noticeable frequency.

Provide regular performance feedback

- Develop a system of regular feedback on aspects of **quantitative performance**, such as sales targets and quotas, with team comparisons and league tables showing measurement against several criteria (so that there is less likelihood that one person always dominates performance leagues).

	• Measurements might cover sales volumes, sales values (turnover), territory profitability, new accounts opened, special promotions organized, new product listings obtained, and so on.
Provide feedback and appraisal	• Develop skill audits and identify and communicate training needs. • Develop a pattern of providing **informal personal feedback** on skill performance, achievements, and training and development needs. This might be pro- vided as an input when accompanying salespersons on customer visits, or on occasions that they visit the office. • Develop formal **performance feedback appraisals** at peri- odic intervals, typically at six- or twelve-month intervals. • Appraisals should be constructive and seen as relevant to the activities and responsibilities of each individual in the sales team, and not be seen as a *'moan and groan'* session of criticisms of personal weaknesses. • Appraisals should have a clear focus on performance against standards and objectives with structured pro- posals for self-development with supportive training from line managers.
Encourage staff development	• Recognize the individual needs of salespersons, and provide opportunities to grow with the job. • Develop training to advance existing skills and to add new skills that stretch salespersons.
Promote the use of advanced technology systems and procedures where appropriate	• Association with a company that is seen in the market place as modern, progressive and innovative is a source of motivation. Make use of technology to increase job satisfaction, reduce administrative burdens, free up time for selling, etc.
Involve salespersons in the planning process	• Encourage participation in sales planning and the decision-making processes, gaining commitment to goal.
Delegate responsibilities whenever possible	• Encourage development through increased and varied responsibility, including through delegation of tasks, func- tions and projects.
Recognize the individual salesperson's personal motivational needs and drives	• Clarify to each salesperson how achieving their personal job goals and objectives, and the higher-level department/area/company objectives, will increase their personal satisfaction of needs.
Manage and motivate through needs satisfaction	• No two people are the same, and each salesperson has a different mix of needs priorities. The mix of needs priorities will change over time, as some become more sat- isfied. Identify the salesperson's priority attached to satisfy- ing each major need.

Table 3.1 *Using a motivational needs audit to recognize individual differences*

Motivational needs audit	Salesperson	
	Rating 1 to 6	Notes
Prepare an audit of the needs of each team member from time to time (the priority attached to needs changes over time). Assign scores or rankings to key individual motivations. **Acceptance** The need for acceptance by family, friends, peer groups, etc. **Affection** The need for close relationships within home, social and work environments **Respect** The need to receive or to show respect in home, social or work environments **Harmony** Preference for order and harmony in work or social environments, rather than conflict and disharmony **Dependence** The need for support and supervision **Consolidation** A level of satisfaction with present role and status rather than seeking change **Change** A need to diversify skills or work responsibilities and to find new challenges **Activity** A need for physical and/or intellectual activity beyond minimum job inputs **Knowledge** A desire to pursue new knowledge and experiences **Achievement** A need for tangible achievements in terms of results, status, benefits, recognition, knowledge, etc. **Recognition** Preference for public recognition (within peer groups) rather than obscurity. **Responsibility** The need to have or seek responsibility rather than avoid it **Status** The need for a feeling of self-worth or recognition of status **Power** The need for power through position or knowledge **Acquisition** The need for additional material things beyond survival needs, and these need not be functional		
Summary	Date	

The manager's motivational role _____

The sales manager is key in the motivational process. He identifies the motivational drives within his team, and offers ways to increase satisfaction of personal needs. The sales manager has a range of tools he or she can use to motivate the sales team, including those listed below.

- **Counselling** Use counselling to direct motivation to key performance indicators. Frank, honest counselling builds trust and a relationship of respect between a sales manager and the team.
- **Recognition** Provide a forum for recognition for specific efforts and outstanding results.
- **Praise** Give sincere and timely praise as a form of personal recognition for a job well done.
- **Involvement/participation** Involve the salespersons in activities beyond day-to-day routine. The more a person is involved in a wider range of functions, particularly those that hold an interest, the greater the commitment to achievement of goals and objectives.
- **Delegation** Give authority to take specific decisions or positive action, increasing motivation within those salespersons who have stronger needs for responsibility, power, personal growth, achievement, and so on.
- **Training** Provide training in all the requisite skills for the job, and recognize and respond to the additional training needs of high fliers.
- **Promotion and self-development** Create an environment where progress is possible and promotion is recognized as on merit. Encourage personal development through reading, study and networking with colleagues who have other skills and experiences to share.
- **Team building** Develop teamwork aimed at achieving common goals and objectives.

The manager's leadership role _____

The sales team will look to their sales manager for **leadership** in addition to motivation. Leadership means providing direction (particularly by example), and guiding actions and opinions. The authority that accompanies leadership may derive from several sources:

- **election** by peers to hold a position of authority in a group
- **appointment** by higher-placed persons who believe they are in a position to exercise judgement about skills, experience and personal qualities, and to appoint a person to a leadership role
- **knowledge**, where an individual has a degree of specialist knowledge on a subject that is critical to group performance, and can command the attention and respect of team subordinates
- **structure**, where an organization is structured such that it is clear which jobs are more senior to others, and which subordinate positions report to each higher management tier
- **personal authority**, where an individual has personal characteristics and attributes that command attention and respect within peer groups (for example, exhibiting high levels of energy, enthusiasm, leadership, influence, intelligence, integrity, determination, and so on).

A manager's claim to leadership is commonly based on a mix of these factors. Recognition as a leader commonly comes when team members realize the manager can and does help them achieve their own goals and objectives. As a leader the sales manager must:

- achieve the group's goals and objectives
- maintain a team committed and motivated to achieving the group objectives
- satisfy the personal needs of individual team members through achieving the

group's goals and objective

- lead in a fashion that motivates staff through their personal commitment
- be seen by staff as decisive, rational and consistent
- be objective and impartial
- accept full responsibility for the actions, activities and performance results of team members
- lead by example and exhibit the highest standards of personal integrity, reliability, dependability, loyalty, etc.
- be seen as a constant source of motivation and stimulation while exhibiting high levels of personal energy, enthusiasm, commitment and work effort.

The good manager

- He sees, knows, and notes everything going on in his department.
- He controls many of the activities through his formal system of continuous controls and warning indicators.
- He overlooks many of the non-critical happenings.
- He corrects through counselling and training, focusing on a few of the points that particularly influence key performance indicators.

Motivation through involvement in decision making

The management style adopted may be influenced by the manager's views of the ability of team members to understand issues and make constructive comment. Some managers believe that they alone have the skills and experience to make decisions. This somewhat cynical view is unlikely to be very motivational. If you, as sales manager, want your sales team to take ownership for decisions and their implementation then it is important to involve them whenever appropriate in the decision-making processes. Discussion amongst team members who have experience and relevant input to make on subjects usually produces better decisions, and active involvement helps produce a more cooperative environment and a team committed to implementing the decisions they participated in making.

In deciding whom to involve in the decision-making process, consider:

- Whose problem is it?
- Have I the authority to decide and act?
- Is there time to consult and communicate with other interested persons?
- Are there alternative courses of action?
- Who else has information, knowledge or experience that can contribute to an evaluation of alternatives?
- Who else is being committed to involvement, participation, action or decisions?
- Who might benefit or suffer from any course of action?
- Who might benefit from the experience of involvement in management decision-making processes?

In arriving at decisions within the sales team it is often useful to check that each of the stages in Figure 3.5 is covered.

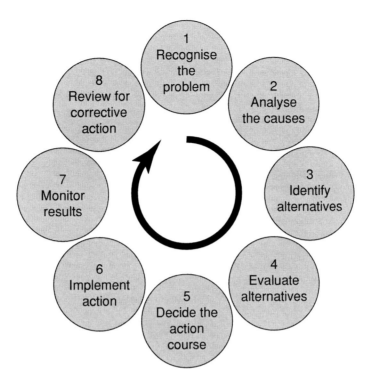

Figure 3.5 *The decision-making process*

Action points

Check if potential or actual DEMOTIVATORS have been identified and removed or neutralized, including:

Job uncertainties
- insecurity of tenure
- ill-defined roles and responsibilities
- poor training
- absence of performance standards

Job imbalances
- personal qualifications (over- or under-qualified)
- incorrect job assignment (mismatching skills to jobs)
- limited self-development opportunities
- poor job content variety

Inadequate management
- limited management skills and experience
- poor management control
- managers' prejudices
- lack of recognition or appraisal systems
- inadequate communications
- inadequate company personnel development programmes

Inadequate working environment
- poor equipment
- poor location
- poor relations

Poor compensation
- uncompetitive income and incentive awards
- inequitable incentive programmes
- absence of merit award recognition
- uncompetitive fringe benefits
- feelings of being under-valued

Poor prospects
- limited internal promotional opportunities
- limited opportunities to increase knowledge or skills or experience

Checklist 3.2
Practical motivation

Action points

Have you conducted a motivational audit covering the following factors?
- Have job descriptions clearly identified the job functions, duties, responsibilities, and relationships?
- Have goals and objectives been established?
- Have standards of performance been set and agreed?
- Has a needs audit analysis been prepared for each team member?
    Does each salesperson see how personal needs and goals can be met by achieving company goals and objectives?
    Do sales managers manage and motivate through needs satisfaction?
- Are sales managers appropriately skilled and experienced to provide leadership, training and motivation?
- Is the motivational environment right in respect of:
    correct selection of suitable job holders?
    training programmes (induction and ongoing development)?
    self-development opportunities?
    company development?
    specific , realistic and achievable targets?
    fair reward and incentive programmes?
    control systems and procedures geared to key performance indicators of performance?
    formal and informal communications?
    performance feedback systems?
    formal appraisal systems?
    career development?
    use of technology?

In addition to the foregoing, do you, the sales manager, make use of the opportunities for:
- counselling/feedback?
- expressing recognition?
- giving praise?
- involvement/participation in planning and decision making?
- delegation?
- training?
- promotion?
- team building?

4

Sales management by objectives _____

Establishing a hierarchy of objectives ▬▬▬▬▬

Objectives should be set and agreed at the company and department level. The objectives for all the departments should be mutually compatible between departments, and all focused towards promoting the achievement of company objectives.

Once company objectives are established, then each department should produce a plan with its own objectives. These department objectives should clearly contribute to the achievement of company objectives. Within each department its objectives should be further broken down to lower-level objectives, also demonstrably contributing to department and company objectives, for each sub-department and job function. That way each person is set goals and objectives within their sphere of responsibility that contribute to overall achievement of company objectives.

Within the sales division objectives (see Figure 4.1) should be set for:

- each product
- each customer
- each territory or salesperson
- each sales call

A hierarchy of objectives for retail products _____

Retail customers typically receive sales calls from territory salespersons, or, in the instances of major retailers, from key account managers (possibly supported by territory salespersons making calls on branches of a multiple retailer). Objectives (see Figure 4.2) should be developed for each relevant functional activity within the account, and at each level of your organization servicing the account, e.g. at the account head office, branch, and sales territory level.

- **Agree objectives for each sales and marketing functional activity within the key account, and at each branch, e.g.:**
  Market share by brand
  Overall account volumes by brand by specific time period
  Performance rebates – rebates related to volume objectives/achievements
  Marketing and promotional programmes specific to account or supporting main stream activity
  Cooperative advertising (i.e. where supplier and customer contribute)
  Price positioning and policies
  Display standards by brand and category
  Distribution procedures, i.e. branch ordering or central deliveries
  Product knowledge training for the customer's staff
- **Set objectives at each level and for each function within your company sales organization servicing the key account, e.g.:**
  Branch distribution and ordering
  Display locations and space allocation by brand
  Volume targets by brand
  Demonstration programmes

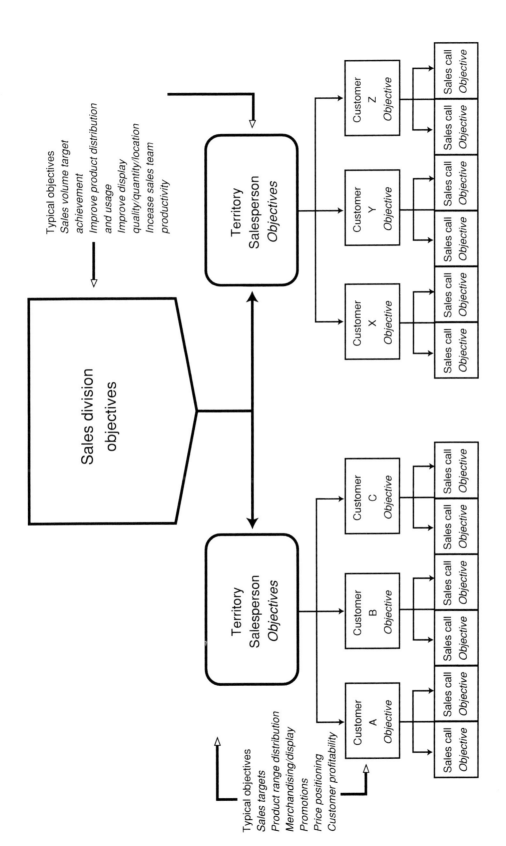

Figure 4.1 A typical hierarchy of sales division objectives

Promotional activity – localized branch programmes or supporting mainstream brand marketing strategies
Stock and order controls
Outlet coverage.

A hierarchy of objectives for industrial products

As Figure 4.3 illustrates, individuals or departments within the industrial customer or business-to-business client organization will often have a quite different focus of objectives, depending on whether their functional activity is as a commercial buyer, product user or product specifier (or other form of influencer in the buying process). The salesperson servicing the customer must recognize and address these internal customer objectives in sourcing product as well as attempting to achieve his or her own company's objectives with the customer. The salesperson should develop objectives for each customer department that can use a product, and for each functional department or manager involved in the buying process, either in placing orders or in approving the product for use.

- **Develop objectives within the account's organization, e.g.:**
  Purchase and usage volumes
  Product trial and testing by all parties or departments that influence purchase decisions
  Formal reports (feedback to the account manager) on any trials and tests (technical tests, productivity tests, performance tests, etc.)
  Product knowledge or technical training (if necessary)
  New opportunities to expand usage (such as in other locations or departments that could benefit from use of the product)
  Opportunities to customize products to the account's specific environment or needs (binding the account to the supplier in a supply chain partnership).
- **Develop objectives within your own company organization, involving all departments concerned with developing products for, or servicing, the customer. The objectives should be specific to that department's functional activity, e.g.:**
  Product design or formulation/ specification to meet client needs

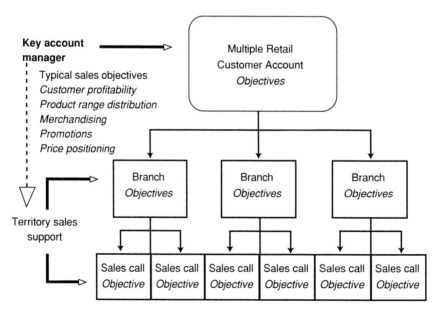

Figure 4.2 An outline objectives hierarchy for a multiple retailer

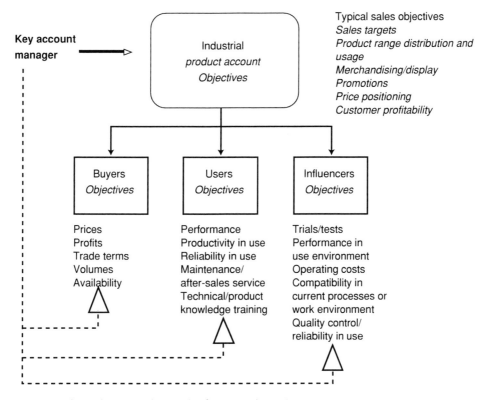

Figure 4.3 *An outline objectives hierarchy for an industrial customer*

Production quantities and time frames
Product demonstration, trial and testing
and quality control
Distribution (availability and timeliness to
meet client needs)
Product after-sales servicing (product
installation, technical training,
maintenance)
Customer service (order processing,
liaison, service levels)
Sales contact and support (sales volumes,
terms of trade, prices and profit, building
relationships and contacts within the
account organization).

Managing to sales objectives ▬

The objectives set must be agreed with each
individual charged with achieving them, and
must be accepted by him or her as:

● their personal responsibility

● achievable within the scope of their skills
(possibly with additional training).

> **Increase individual satisfaction through
> achievement of personal job-related
> objectives that make a tangible contri-
> bution to developing each customer
> account.**

The basic principles of establishing objectives

Most managers are aware that, when setting
and agreeing objectives, they should follow
the principle that objectives should be **specific**, **measurable**, **achievable**, **realistic** and
timed (SMART). This is outlined in Table 4.1.

This commonly accepted approach to
establishing objectives to motivate higher
performance and personal achievement is

just as applicable in sales team management as in other aspects of a business. However, I would extend it to consider the importance of ensuring that all objectives must fit together in a compatible fashion, and, above all, be agreed and communicated.

A framework for managing to sales objectives

1. **Agree objectives for each sales and marketing functional activity within the company sales and marketing team**

   - Market share by brand.
   - Overall volumes by brand by specific time period.
   - Product positioning, trial and loyalty building through media campaigns.
   - Marketing and promotional programmes supporting mainstream activity (including brands publicity activity).
   - Achieving price positioning and policies.
   - Display objectives standards by brand and by outlet.
   - Distribution targets by brand and by outlet.
   - Sales skill and product knowledge training.

2. **Set objectives at each level and for each function within the selling organization servicing customers, e.g. for key account managers and territory salespersons, e.g.:**

   - Branch/outlet distribution and ordering (percentage increase over base period).
   - Display locations and space allocation by brand (shelf layouts and product positioning, etc.).
   - Volume targets by brand and by outlet.
   - Demonstration programmes.
   - Promotional activity – localized branch programmes or supporting mainstream brand marketing strategies.
   - Stock and order controls.
   - Outlet coverage.

3. **Agree standards of performance for each job function, setting the basic standards expected to be achieved with priority to key result areas**

   - Distribution achievements versus a base period (measured from salesperson recording on called-on outlets or from Nielsen data).
   - Average sales value/volumes.
   - Sales value/volume levels.
   - Product brand listings.
   - Display (facings per brand).
   - Daily call rate.
   - Percentage conversion of calls to orders.
   - Percentage effective coverage of territory accounts each journey cycle, etc.
   - New customer prospecting.

4. **Assign business development projects**

   - Assign each individual involved with customer sales activity some **special projects** he/she can undertake to benefit the company/area/department and personal development, e.g.: for retail products, undertaking a project to measure the proportion of category display space allocated to the various major brands, and relating that to sales volumes; or display site relocations, promotions, etc. With industrial products a project might study the training needs of potential users at customer locations, with a view to improving product use training.

5. **Personal development** • Encourage personal development through study, taking additional responsibility, enhancing sales skills, etc. For example, study on part-time courses covering management and marketing will raise their skills and value, and also reading professional journals or books dealing with the product will raise expertise.

6. **Management training** • Train your subordinates to understand and support your job, to accept responsibility for delegated functions, and to be more effective territory managers.

7. **Promote team building** • Include all staff involved in servicing accounts in regular planning and feedback meetings.

Table 4.1 Establishing objectives

Objectives must be: S-M-A-R-T	
Specific	**Set detailed numbers**
	e.g. 10% increase on last year's turnover £15000 increase in sales turnover monthly 2 new accounts per territory per week, etc.
Measurable	**Measure by quantitative not qualitative criteria**
	e.g. Number of customers covered is measurable; service quality is subjective except through reduced incidence of complaints or customer waiting time.
Achievable	**Can be achieved within the time frame**
	e.g. To aim to double turnover in the time period without changing any other factors might be unachievable: to double turnover through increased sales activity, coverage, extra staff and better training might be achievable.
Realistic	**Reasonable for the salesperson's territory or customers**
	e.g. Based upon historical performance or sound assessments of potential.
Timed	**To be achieved within a prescribed time period**
	e.g. Increase sales by 15% versus same quarter last year. Increase the average order value by 2 cases within 3 months.

Some information inputs for setting sales objectives

Historical customer performance data	● Review supplier's previous years' sales performance with customers. ● Consider customers' expenditure on the product category.
Assessment of sales area and customer potential	● Allow for sales area factors (e.g. boundary changes or reallocation of sales responsibilities). ● Allow for changing market conditions, customer or consumer locations, local economic conditions, or other relevant demographic factors. ● Use knowledge of customer activity and policies. ● Consider customers' growth and shares in their market sectors. ● Consider customers' future policies in respect of the product category. ● Consider market trends (growth or decline) in the product categories.
Recognition of competitor activity	● Locations, ranges, prices, promotions, quality, supply limitations, innovations, etc. ● Consider any special relationships of competitors with customers.
Knowledge of market conditions	● Competitors' prices and activity. ● Consumer spending (or budgets for industrial or business-to-business customers). ● Consider trends in the product categories. ● Consider impact of economic factors (inflation, income trends, employment levels, credit availability, industrial output trends, etc.).
Knowledge of company production capabilities and stock availability	● Supplier sales activity may be limited by capacity or stock availability.
Company's new marketing initiatives	● Consider new product developments coming on stream during the plan period and their impact on other products in the supplier's portfolio. ● Consider supplier advertising and promotion activity and budgets, etc.
ACTION	● Set and agree sales objectives by product, customer, and salesperson. ● Develop strategies and tactics to achieve objectives. ● Periodically evaluate performance against objectives, and provide feedback. ● Re-plan or modify strategies/tactics as necessary.

Typical focus of sales objectives ▪

Most **sales objectives** fall into the classifications of:

- **higher sales volume**
- **improved profitability from sales activity**
- **cost control and/or cost reduction within the sales organization.**

Table 4.2 illustrates strategic or tactical actions (right column) that the sales team can address to produce improvement against the key focus of objectives (left column).

The sales manager should develop an objective planning form, where each salesperson records his or her objectives against those areas of sales activity that are key to improving sales performance for the company. There is no single format for an objective planning form, but Table 4.3 illustrates an example. Table 4.4 illustrates some opportunities for salespersons to impact on key result areas.

Table 4.2 *Strategic and tactical factors addressing key sales objectives*

Sales objectives with customer accounts	
Focus of sales objectives	**Some strategic/tactical areas**
Increase sales volume	● Improve company inventory control ● Increase company production capability ● Improve company production planning ● Improve distribution efficiency ● Expand marketing resources ● Expand product range available for sale ● Expand number of market outlets in customer base – Locate and qualify more potential customers ● Expand outlet coverage – Increase call frequency ● Increase focus on key account development ● Expand market sales promotional activity ● Improve trade service levels ● Expand sales force resources ● Expand number of wholesale distributors ● Improve wholesaler/retailer training ● Increase minimum order requirements ● Improve customer stock and order controls ● Expand product range stocked or used by customers ● Improve merchandising support and attention to space management issues (for retail products) ● Increase promotional support for trade stockists or direct users (where promotions influence volume) ● Adjust trade and retail pricing to boost volume ● Improve after-sales service offered by trade stockists ● Improve trade channel product knowledge through training staff of customers ● Improve technical support for customer product trials and ongoing product usage

Table 4.2 *Strategic and tactical factors addressing key sales objectives (continued)*

Sales objectives with customer accounts
Focus of sales objectives   **Some strategic/tactical areas**

Increase profits
- Increase sales (see above)
  - number of wholesale distributors
  - number of outlets
  - new listings for existing products
  - listing for new products
- Increase product prices
- Vary product portfolio mix in relation to price and product profitability
- Develop new higher valued added products, provding opportunities to increase margins
- Improve cash flow through tighter management to trade terms
- Control company costs, e.g. through:
  - reduced sales organization costs (see below)
  - reduced input costs
  - improved productivity
  - improved supply chain management
  - improved quality of inputs
  - reduced input usage in finished products
  - reduced materials and resource wastage
  - improved expenditure controls
  - improved distribution efficiency
  - limiting number of delivery points
  - increasing delivery drop size
  - improved human resource productivity
  - reduced inventories of raw materials and finished products

Reduce sales force costs
- Increase sales team productivity
  - increase call rate
  - increase time available for selling (i.e. reduce administration or improve use of technology)
- Reduce sundry selling expenses
- Reduce size of sales organization
  - discontinue calls on small or unprofitable customers
  - increase salesperson/territory workloads
  - develop alternative means of communicating with customers
- Develop sales through third parties (wholesalers or sub-distributors)
- Develop a tele-sales operation
- Reduce sales promotion and marketing communication budgets

Table 4.3 *An example of a sales objective form*

Union Packaging Machinery Company Customer objective plan		

Customer detail:		Contacts	Position
Name:	Acme Foods Products Plc.	John Williams	Commercial Director (Buyer)
Address:	Unit 12	Gilbert Johnson	Technical Director
	Highbridge Industrial	Roy Yelland	Production Director
	Estate	Edward Lester	Finance Director
	Copthorne Road	Robert Atherton	Managing Director
	Duddington XX1 2YY		
Telephone:	01234 – 987654		
Fax:	01234 – 987653		
Business:	pre-packed fresh foods		

Current machine portfolio		Opportunity/objective

Suppliers	Models/year	Location	
Union	1020DX 1982	Highbridge plant	Offer: UPM Maxiflow
Union	102DX 1985	Netherton	Offer: UPM Compact 1100SX
Astral	Starpack 80 1983	Highbridge plant	
Astral	Starpack 80 1986	Netherton plant	
Astral	Starpack 100 1990	Highbridge plant	
Mishimoto	Maxipack 1995	Netherton plant	

Current material sources Product	Last year usage	Opportunity/objective Product	Target
Union Traypack 20/30 140gsm	1 150 000 m	Traypack 20/30 140 gsm	750 000 m
Traypack 15/25 140gsm	950 000 m	Traypack 15/25 140 gsm	600 000 m
Traytop 20 lid film 140gsm	1 200 000 m	Traytop 20 lid film 140 gsm	750 000 m
Traytop 15 lid film 140gsm	1 010 000 m	Traytop 15 lid film 140 gsm	600 000 m
		Varifilm tray 20/30 140 gsm	500 000 m
Astral Astrafilm 15/15 9 gauge trays	1 450 000 m	Varifilm tray 15/25 120 gsm	490 000 m
Astrafilm 15-9 gauge lidding	1 400 000 m	Varifilm tray15/15 120 gsm	1 000 000 m
		Varifilm lid 20/30 120 gsm	500 000 m
Eurofilm Formpack 20/20 100 gauge	1 750 000 m	Varifilm lid 15/25 100 gsm	490 000 m
Formpack 20 100 gauge	1 760 000 m	Varifilm lid 15/15 80 gsm	1 000 000m

Other objectives
1. Build closer relations between Union engineering designers and technical staff and Acme Technical and Production teams.
2. Build a better supply chain relationship on consumable film supplies, to improve Union planning and Acme stock holding.

Comments
1. Both Union machines in use and the earlier Astral model are nearing the ends of their economic lives. Proposals to be developed to promote our new variable speed models for production trials, with package to encourage new investment now, before competitors develop presentations and gain advantage.
2. Taking account of knowledge of different uses and throughputs, recommend optimum flexibility with 3 models.
3. If machine sales are achieved, then consumption of Traypack & Traytop film varieties will reduce, depending on timing of sales, expected here to be about mid year. Acme will switch to the new Variflow film, with its advantages of greater rigidity, clarity, and resistance to punctures. There is also an assumption for next year of 20% steal from competitive packaging film as Acme makes greater use of the new higher performance machines.

Table 4.4 *Some opportunities for salespersons to impact on key result areas*

Setting objectives in key result areas	
Key result area and focus of objectives	**Main area of impact**
Call coverage	
● Finding new productive outlets (trade stockists or users)	● Sales volumes
● Improve sales journey planning, relating frequency to potential	● Costs and productivity
● Reduce call frequencies without volume loss	● Costs and productivity
● Increase coverage of worthwhile outlets	● Sales volumes/profit
Distribution	
● Reduce out of stocks in trade outlets or with end users	● Sales volumes and profit
● Increase usage at new usage points within existing customer base	● Sales volumes and profit
● Obtain additional product listings in existing outlets	● Sales volumes and profit
● Identify new target customers meeting product profile criteria	● Sales volumes and profit
● Obtain new distribution in worthwhile outlets	● Sales volumes and profit
● New products sold through existing and new outlets	● Sales volumes and profit
● Discontinue coverage and supplies to unprofitable outlets	● Costs
Display (products sold through distributive trade channels)	
● Promote good space management principles in the product category	● Sales volumes and profit
● Improved key site display positioning	● Sales volumes and profit
● Increase product facings and display quality on display fixtures	● Sales volumes
● Shift display emphasis from lower to higher margin products	● Profits
● Improved use of point of sale material	● Sales volumes
● Improve impact of product merchandising	● Sales volumes
● Negotiate promotional displays	● Sales volumes
Sales volumes	
● Set specific targets for each account and time period	● Sales volumes and profit
● Increase average order sizes	● Sales volumes and profits
● Increase re-order frequency by encouraging increased usage	● Sales volumes and profits
● Promotional sales and product features (e.g. displays)	● Sales volumes
Efficiency	
● Improve management of key resource of TIME	● Costs and productivity
● Improve expense controls	● Profit
● Improve journey planning*	● Costs and productivity
● Reduce call frequencies without volume loss*	● Costs and productivity
● Improve customer record database	● Sales productivity
● Improve post-call administration and order processing efficiency (*also noted under call coverage above)	● Costs and productivity
Self-development	
● Improved selling and marketing skills	● Sales volumes
● Improved customer care skills	● Sales volumes
● Increased product knowledge	● Sales volumes
● Greater depth of understanding of customers' businesses	● Sales volumes/profits
● Greater understanding of customers' markets	● Sales volumes/profit

Action points

- When planning agree objectives for each functional activity within the sales and marketing team, e.g.:
  - Market share by brand
  - Overall volumes by brand by specific time period
  - Product positioning, trial and loyalty building through media campaigns
  - Marketing and promotional programmes specific to accounts or supporting mainstream activity
  - Brand price positioning and policies
  - Display objectives and standards by brand
  - Distribution targets by brand and by outlet
  - Sales skill and product knowledge training
- Agree supporting standards and objectives with other company departments such as:
  - Marketing department
  - Sales operations and support department
  - Distribution departments
  - Customer service departments
- Set standards and objectives at each level and for each function within the company's field selling organization servicing the customers, e.g.:
  - Outlet distribution and ordering
  - Display locations and square footage by brand
  - Volume targets by brand
  - Demonstration programmes
  - Promotional activity – localized branch programmes or supporting mainstream brand strategies
  - Stock and order controls
  - Outlet coverage
- Assign salespersons individual projects.
- Encourage personal development through study, giving additional responsibility, skill training, etc.
- Provide continuous training to develop skills and competencies, and to promote an environment that facilitates delegation.
- Promote team building through regular planning and feedback meetings.

Checklist 4.1 continued	**Action points**

● Divide the year into shorter sales cycles. Set specific objectives supported by sales activity plans, e.g.:
  – Marketing communications
  – Sales promotions
  – Sales targets
  – Distribution
  – Display	

5

Motivating through rewards and incentives

Developing motivational rewards ■

Traditionally in most markets salespersons have a significant portion of earnings from bonus incentive schemes. It is important that a sales incentive scheme is designed to motivate increases in sales effort and productivity, and not just to be earned automatically.

Sales managers should recognize that:

- financial rewards and incentives satisfy only some of the salesperson's personal needs
- marginal increases in productivity motivated through financial rewards may cost more than motivational alternatives (such as product knowledge and skill training, praise, recognition, promotion, feedback counselling and appraisals, and good internal communications).

Incentives should not be looked at in isolation, but as part of the overall rewards and benefits compensation package used to recruit, retain and motivate the sales team, and also be considered in relation to the other non-monetary rewards from the job and working environment.

The sales compensation programme should provide:

- security of income sufficient to meet everyday lifestyle needs
- flexibility to motivate through merit and incentive schemes

- a responsiveness to changes in the job and product market place.

In each market environment the local sales manager should look at a total rewards scheme in relation to the factors in Table 5.1, i.e.:

- team and individual performance standards and objectives
- individual expectations
- relative values of tangible and intangible rewards.

The main options and their suitability ■

The selection of options you use of salary, commissions, bonuses or competitions will depend on local practices and culture. In some cultures people entering the sales profession expect little security and basic income, being prepared to work largely on performance-related rewards, an approach commonly found in some of the developing markets such as in Asia. In other cultures, as seen in some of the developed markets of the west, people have high fixed outgoings in the way of living expenses, and may prefer a higher basic salary with a lower level of performance-related rewards. Basic salaries may tend to act more as a maintenance than a motivational factor. The rewards scheme developed for any market should meet the

Table 5.1 Developing motivational rewards – some factors to consider

Factors to consider in developing rewards		
Team and individual performance standards and objectives	Individual expectations	Relative values of tangible and intangible rewards

• Relative emphasis on team and individual performance
• Ability of the individual to influence the outcome of sales presentations
• Degree of integration of individuals into a team with common goals
	• Industry norms
	• Territory or account potential
	• Job functions and tasks
	• Personal aspirations
		• Cash now versus cash later – personal valuations of present job or through promotion
		• Intangible personal rewards on offer:
		  – recognition
		  – status
		  – praise
		  – achievement
		• Opportunities for changing job functions and responsibilities, e.g. promotion

employees' needs and expectations, but must also meet the company's needs (such as achieving sales volumes at set prices and margins, and to recruit, train and retain effective salespersons) and its financial means.

The main forms of alternative rewards are shown in Figure 5.1. This highlights that the salesperson will see the immediate benefit of some forms of reward, but that other forms of reward do not provide an immediate visible benefit, only being valued when they come into effect to meet needs and situations.

The sales manager also must consider his or her particular motivational objectives, i.e. are incentive rewards being used to direct attention to either longer- or short-term strategic or tactical matters?

Basic salary or wages

Salary is a fixed reward for work done, and it may be the only reward or linked with other incentive schemes. It should:

• be competitive with that for similar positions in similar companies
• fit with company job-grading schemes that

reflect the differing duties and levels of responsibility of positions within the company
• relate to the skills, experience and responsibilities required of the position.

Many companies prefer to keep individuals' incomes confidential, perhaps with the concern that publicizing information will produce a distraction as individuals concern themselves over their relative level of rewards. Other companies take quite the opposite approach, believing that publicizing income information provides motivation to lower earners to strive harder for the bigger rewards. An in-between approach is to publish job grade scales, but not to indicate where any salesperson is within the scale band.

Commissions

Commissions generally take the format of a straight percentage commission on sales values or profits, usually over the longer term. If commissions are the sole form of remuneration, the company needs to ensure that sales-

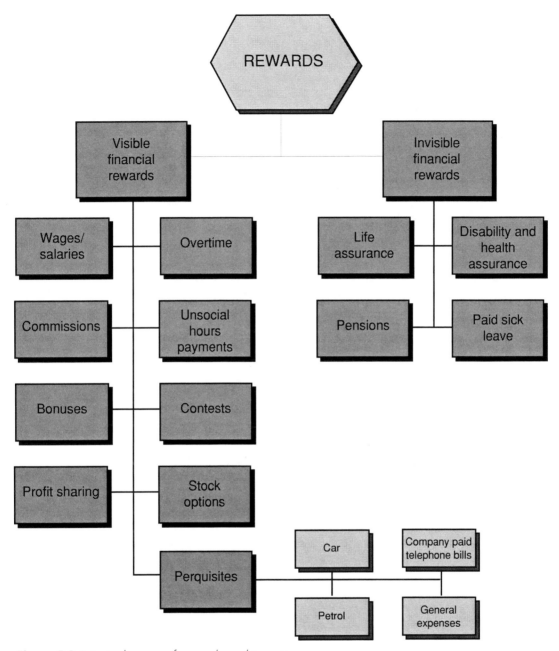

Figure 5.1 *A typical range of rewards and incentives*

persons can expect earnings to provide a reasonable standard of living for self and family, otherwise they will not stay long in the job. Many companies that reward largely or entirely by commission take the approach that since they have no investment it does not matter who is recruited into sales positions, and hence recruits are often unsuited to sell-

ing, lacking skills, training and suitable personalities.

The advantage of commissions to the company is that selling costs relate directly to sales values, and they are often favoured for companies selling into new markets. There may be disadvantages where all products do not produce the same gross margins, because if the products most easy to sell offer lower margins, salespersons may be boosting their earnings while eroding company profits. One way to tackle that problem is to reward with differential commissions related to product profitability. Commission schemes may encourage salespersons to focus on established customers where the products are consumables, rather than devoting adequate time to pioneer calling for new customers. Commission schemes are difficult to structure and manage for products in cyclical market sectors, or where several persons and not just one individual are involved in developing a sale to a successful conclusion. Attention must also be given to product returns to avoid salespersons loading trade stockists to boost their commission earnings to suit their own immediate needs. Where commission has been paid for goods subsequently returned, the system might allow for this to be recovered from the salesperson.

Bonuses

Bonuses are normally a lump sum payment made when specific achievements occur, i.e. a certain level of distribution or profit is achieved, or an agreed number of units is sold, or a pre-set number of promotions are sold in. Bonuses might be instead of, or in addition to, other rewards such as commission and other incentives, and can be readily geared to team efforts. Bonuses are not usually a regular reward, unlike salary and commission, but just paid periodically in recognition of special achievements. Where bonuses are used to reward team effort it is common to create a team bonus pool, and then allocate bonuses by some formula relating to seniority or perhaps as a percentage of basic income. Bonuses, like commissions, should relate to a key performance indicator of activity where the individual can clearly affect an outcome, such as profitability of customers or a sales territory.

Contests

Contests normally offer non-cash prizes (but cash may be offered) for very specific and measurable achievements for effort and results against short-term priorities and objectives, i.e. for the salesperson who organizes the biggest supermarket display, or for the salesperson who organizes the most on-trade promotions supporting a product, or the person opening the most new accounts over a defined time period. A contest where there can be only one winner could actually be counter-productive, as those salespersons who fall behind early in the contest may simply 'tune out' and effectively become non-contestants. A well-structured competition will ensure that all salespersons have an equal chance to win a prize, which may put pressure on a sales manager to develop a territory handicapping system where all sales territories are not equal in performance and potential.

When structuring contests it may be worth considering the following points.

- Prizes rather than cash may be more motivating, and not produce an irregular cash earnings pattern.
- Prizes of family interest often prove particularly motivational.
- Offer a range of prizes so that all eligible participants feel motivated to achieve the required performance results.
- Ongoing award schemes, where points are accumulated by all participants, leading to the acquisition of any of a range of merchandise when redeemed, can be a good motivator.
- Contests should not always be geared to the same goals and objectives, but varied frequently to avoid staleness.
- Contests should home in on particular functional activities of the selling job that impact on key performance indicators, e.g. achieving displays or promotional activities, or gaining new distribution locations.
- Structure the competition to minimize abuse (more common where certain parameters are less objectively measurable): any penalty for identified abuse should be sufficient to discourage it.

- Competitions geared to a single objective often distract from other important goals and objectives or functional activities, and the structuring of a competition may need to consider applying penalties for under-performing against other criteria (e.g., minimum performance standards must be met against basic standards of performance before additional activity counts towards the competition).

Stock options and profit sharing

Incentive schemes that offer annual profit sharing bonuses or periodic stock options are becoming more popular, and not just for management staff in companies. These tend to develop a recognition that the employees are important stakeholders in the prosperity of the company, and can also encourage greater loyalty.

Job perquisites

Managers are commonly seen as the main beneficiaries of job 'perks', but salespersons can also benefit from quite a range of perks that add value to the job. There are the tangible benefits of company cars and insurance, mobile telephones, laptop computers, petrol allowances (since often liberal petrol expenses cover some or all of private driving costs), and so on, and intangible benefits of freedom from close supervision, working from a home base (for many salespersons). Perks can be used as part of a motivational system, where, for example, there is an increase in perks or their value in relation to performance, e.g. a larger car as salespersons are promoted, or where certain levels of longer-term achievement are maintained.

Some companies have exclusive 'clubs' (e.g. a 'President's Club') open only to high performers, which encourages competition to gain entry, and then to maintain the minimum qualification standard to avoid loss of face from removal of membership status.

Additional holiday entitlement can also be used as a motivational reward.

Sales managers should consider carefully before conferring benefits where loss of those benefits later could be very demotivating.

Incentive scheme principles ▄▄▄

The structuring of a motivational rewards package might use any or all of the formats discussed here, and a seemingly endless range of variations on these themes. If too many incentive programmes are running at any one time it might be confusing for salespersons to clarify their own priorities, and there may be some conflict between schemes aimed at short-term versus longer-term goals. Therefore, when more than one incentive scheme is operating at the same time it should be planned that they all address compatible objectives. For example, a commission scheme that gave varying commission relating to the profitability of customer accounts, with a minimum level of profit required for eligibility for the commission, would work against an incentive scheme relating to opening new customer accounts, which would take some time to reach minimum profit levels. Giving time to developing new accounts might put at risk the maintenance of minimum profits with established profit (and commission) earners. In this sort of situation the scheme could waive profit-level requirements for new accounts, say for the first year.

When devising a motivational incentive scheme adopt the following basic principles:

- Ensure the scheme's relevancy and compatibility with established company portfolio goals, objectives and priorities.
- Base rewards on specific measurable and quantifiable criteria.
- Required achievements should be realistic and achievable by the sales team within any set time spans.
- The timing of incentives relating to company products and sales activities should match in with the timing and priorities of mainstream marketing activity.

- Base incentive awards on efforts and activities controlled or influenced by the salesperson or manager.
- The scheme should be fair and equitable to all team members, offering rewards related to individual productivity and performance.
- Schemes should not penalize individuals if circumstances outside their control (e.g. strikes) affect results unless all are so penalized.
- The scale and level of rewards should relate to the specific potential of the territory or accounts under the salesperson's direct control.
- Earnings of incentives are usually better spread evenly over a longer period, rather than all or nothing on a few orders.
- Earnings from incentive schemes, and the targets and objectives to which they relate, should be assessed at regular intervals to facilitate personal planning and budgeting, and to maintain motivational momentum.
- Reward, like criticism, should follow quickly the activity to which it relates.
- Avoid 'all or nothing' sales reward schemes, as restrictive schemes where few can win are demotivators to the rest of the sales team.
- Keep the incentive scheme
  simple,
  easy to administer,
  with minimum requirement of time and special training,
  and ensure it dovetails with existing systems, procedures, priorities and programmes.

The following checklist helps in the choice of which scheme or what combination of rewards to use.

The introduction of motivational reward and incentive schemes is no substitute for thorough training and development by line managers, as under-trained salespersons will not achieve within their true potential and will become demotivated. Also, programmes should be designed so that they will not impose control burdens on the sales managers.

Checklist 5.1
Reward systems as motivational tools

What	When	Advantages	Disadvantages
Salary A fixed form of reward unrelated to group or individual performance.	• Sales projects take a long time to produce orders. • It is not practical to identify the real contribution of any one person, and sales activity and results are a team effort. • Sales force tasks and objectives are not related to direct product sales, e.g. merchandising. • Individual salesperson's activity has little direct impact on sales levels, e.g. repeat purchase products.	• Administratively simple. • Equitable rewards system. • Promotes and satisfies security-driven motivations. • Predictable incomes and sales force budgets. • Rewards can be linked to longer-term objectives. • Rewards reflect longer-term merit and loyalty.	• Does not relate territory sales costs to sales volumes. • Favours security-motivated rather than achievement-motivated salespersons. • No flexibility to direct longer- or shorter-term effort to objectives through the use of incentives. • The sales force costs are relatively fixed whereas performance may exceed or fall short of targets set when budgets are prepared.
Commission A variable reward related normally either to sales turnover or profit	• Products are not cyclical in sales pattern. • For newer products or companies with limited resources. • Pre-trained experienced salespersons are recruited. • Attention is to be devoted only to new or repeat sales orders and not to non-selling activities.	• Directly links sales costs to sales values or profitability, as a percentage figure. • Differential; commission levels can direct effort to certain products or markets. • Motivates materially oriented salespersons.	• Limits recruitment to salespersons not highly security motivated. • Higher sales force turnover of less productive salespersons, possibly with higher ongoing training costs. • Insecurity of individual earn-ings. • Unsuitable where it is not feasible to identify individual sales contribution. • Requires adjustment for product returns and other credit allowances.

What	When	Advantages	Disadvantages
Bonuses Normally fixed pre-set payments linked to achievement of specific objectives or performance standards.	● It is difficult to separate each individual's contribution to an objective or result but where an incentive is considered an essential motivator. ● For achievement of longer-term objectives. ● Results depend on the effort of a team of salespersons.	● Good motivator to longer-term goals and objectives. ● Useful team incentive programme. ● Encourages the development of a system to recognize individual contributions to team efforts to achieve objectives and results (e.g. sales and profits).	● Not ideal for short-term objectives or corrective action. ● Less easy to budget. ● More complex administratively to measure and control in relation to performance and results. ● Subjectivity may enter the final valuation process e.g. external disruptive factors that impacted on performance.
Contests Competitions between salespersons where some but not all may benefit.	● To direct attention to short-term objectives or limited goals, or to motivate activity and attention towards corrective action.	● A good short-term motivator to limited goals and objectives. ● Frequently more motivationally beneficial where goods rather than cash form the basis of reward. ● Acts as an ongoing motivator where a points or other ongoing accrual system for recognizing effort and achievement is developed so that all participants receive benefit.	● May distract from longer-term objectives and activity. ● If there is one or few winners this acts as a demotivator to all other participants. ● Generally very complex to administer. ● Often more open to abuse than other incentive schemes. ● Can distract management unless it can be centrally controlled or managed by external specialists.

6

Providing appraisals and feedback for motivation, training and discipline ————

The role of appraisals ━━━━━

The process of appraisal is the comparison of individual performance against agreed standards and objectives.

- Sub-standard performance should result in corrective action programmes.
- Above-standard performance may result in merit rewards, promotion or more advanced training and development.

The appraisal system formalizes the process of the sales manager sitting with individual team members to review performance and to recognize the needs of each team member and his or her ability to satisfy those needs through the job. It is important that performance appraisals are conducted regularly, and form part of the normal sales management practices in motivating and providing feedback to the members of the sales team. Each one of us likes to know how we are doing in our job and whether we meet our line managers' expectations, how we compare with our colleagues, and what prospects we might have in the company (including advice on our personal development needs to fit us for new and bigger jobs).

Sales force appraisals should normally be conducted each half-year. This is long enough for a salesperson to implement changes in performance and behaviour from the previous performance appraisal, but not too wide a gap where the appraisal system

loses its impact and role in the ongoing provision of feedback and performance improvement. The formal appraisals should be supplemented with very regular informal feedback, so that whatever is to be communicated in the formal appraisal feedback does not come as a surprise, but more as a summary.

If periodic formal appraisals are conducted then sales managers should recognize that there will be changes in the market environment during the appraisal period. Changes may occur in:

- the competitive environment
- the company's own policies and strategies or organization
- sales territory workloads, boundaries of customer responsibilities
- the regulatory environment for the product categories.

Many of these changes may be outside the control of any individual salesperson, yet impact on his performance against his goals and standards. The appraiser must make objective judgements taking account of the impact of any extrinsic changes on salesperson performance and achievements.

What to measure and appraise ▬

There are three main areas that should form part of the salesperson's appraisal: **job per-**

formance and achievement, **personal skills and competencies** that affect performance, and **subjective factors** which impact on performance. Each of these can be broken down to a number of specific criteria or factors that can be measured.

Standards of performance

Standards of performance are those aspects of job performance where there is a level of achievement that is set as the standard. It is not a target of what the sales manager hopes to achieve, but a measure based upon historical or average levels of performance achievement. The standard of performance is the level at which a sales person would be considered a satisfactory achiever on any criteria. A salesperson who consistently failed to meet standards that were demonstrably being met by other salespersons in the team would need special counselling and training to raise performance, and could be subject to disciplinary action where that person continually failed to raise performance to meet minimum standards.

Typically standards can be set in all or most of the following aspects of performance:

- Call rate (daily average or number made in a pre-agreed time period)
- Call coverage (making customer visits to a plan ensuring all are visited at pre-set intervals)
- Pioneer calling (finding new prospective customers)
- Conversion ratio of orders to calls
- Distribution achievements (number of customers stocking or using the products)
- Display (for retail products, the quality of display and allocation of space)
- Market share
- Territory/area and customer profitability
- Sales value/volume targets
- Distributor sales performance (where products are sold through trade distributors)
- Complaints.

Skills and competencies

A range of skills and competencies are needed by a professional salesperson, with additional skills needed by a sales manager. Typical skills needed by the salesperson include the following:

- Professional selling and negotiating skills
- Product knowledge
- Verbal communication skills
- Numerical skills
- Administrative skills
- Organizational skills
- Planning
- Interpersonal (relationship building, people management) and motivational/persuasive skills – the ability to influence people

In each of these areas we can form some objective measure of what is satisfactory, good or unsatisfactory. The sales manager should make notes on the performance of each of his sales team's abilities in each of these areas, and any others he feels particularly relevant to selling in the local environment. When conducting the periodic appraisal it is important to be able to give specific examples of what is good or unacceptable.

Subjective factors

Subjective factors are those areas that are not directly concerned with actual achievement or performance, but where the factors do impact in some tangible way on a salesperson's achievements or ability to perform to a satisfactory level. Because any assessment involving subjective factors has no firm base in measurement, the appraisal comments on subjective factors should carry much less weight in an overall appraisal than the objective measurements of performance and achievement. Typically appraisals will cover commentary on subjective factors including the following.

Personal characteristics

Comparisons might be made with strengths and weaknesses of characteristics identified in a job holder profile, particularly drawing attention to how they impact on performance, e.g.:

Enthusiasm	Appearance	Maturity
Integrity	Persistence	Initiative
Reliability	Resilience	Loyalty
Sincerity	Intelligence	Commitment
Empathy	Adaptability	Sense of
Self-confidence	Self-motivation	loyalty

Attitudes

The salesperson's attitude to the job, the company, his customers and colleagues all have a bearing on resultant performance, and negative attitudes warrant comment just as positive attitudes justify praise.

Development and training needs

The appraisal should address the development needs of each salesperson to ensure that they have the skills to meet the demands and requirements of the current job, and they should be given the opportunity to develop within their potential to meet both future needs of this job and to take on new jobs and responsibilities.

Potential

The manager should assess the potential for promotion or assignment to new responsibilities within the sales force or elsewhere within the company. Salespersons often want to know where they stand in respect of career development within the company, and the sales manager has a duty to communicate on this subject while not demotivating those persons who may offer less development potential than others in the team.

Sources of appraisal information ■

There are always a number of sources of information on the performance of individual sales managers and salespersons and their areas of responsibility, i.e. territories. The sales manager should keep a file of data that provides measures of performance. Some of the typical sources of appraisal information available include:

- Previous appraisal forms
- Training assessment reports
- Field check reports relevant to the territory or customer accounts
- Agreed objectives and standards of performance
- Company published sales statistics or measurements kept by the line manager
- Relevant correspondence or bulletins noting appraisee performance
- Notes on any special activities or contributions, or special achievements
- Notes on any (good or bad) critical occurrences
- Skill assessment reports
- Feedback from customers.

Guidelines for managers operating an appraisal system ▬▬▬

The following summarizes the main guidelines the sales manager should follow when working within a formal appraisal framework.

- The appraiser should communicate clearly (in writing) to the salesperson at the beginning of each appraisal period specific objectives and performance standards for the appraisal period.
- Objective measurements should be provided on a regular basis to enable the appraiser and appraisee constantly to review performance and to implement corrective action as appropriate.

- When an appraisal is due the appraiser should not review performance alone but in cooperation with another involved party (line superior), objectively appraising on measurable criteria, commenting on relevant subjective factors.
- Where objective and subjective factors are involved in an appraisal, a weighting should be applied giving predominance to objective factors.
- The appraisee should participate in his or her own appraisal, and contribute his or her own comments to achievement against standards and objectives, on strengths and weaknesses and training needs, and on external factors that have impacted on performance.

The most difficult part of an appraisal is not compiling the assessment but communicating the feedback to the appraisee. The intention of counselling is to improve or modify performance, so it should:

- let the appraisee see, understand and agree his or her actual performance in relation to agreed standards
- ensure that the appraisee learns his or her manager's views of his or her role and performance
- advise the appraisee what prospects he or she might have, and how to realize those prospects through further development
- confirm and consolidate with the appraisee the ongoing mini-appraisals communicated at counselling and training sessions
- increase the motivation of the appraisee to improve his or her productivity and performance through agreed objectives and development programmes.

The appraisee should be notified well in advance of the time, place and date, and the counselling should:

- be conducted in a reasonably relaxed and informal atmosphere, away from the normal work environment (and not in the salesperson's car)
- be unbroken by interruptions and distractions
- have plenty of time specifically allocated to the appraisal so that the salesperson does not feel rushed
- be a two-way exchange of views.

When the appraisal is finished the appraiser should write up notes immediately, and have the appraisee sign as acknowledgement of the appraisal after adding his or her own summary comments.

Developing an appraisal scheme ■

The starting point in an appraisal system is to design a basic appraisal form that will measure the performance and other key factors affecting performance, and provide a reference document when giving feedback. There are a few basic guidelines that might help a sales manager design a form (see Table 6.1), if none already exists within a company.

- Keep the form simple in structure and format with clear instructions on completion.
- The form should identify key aspects of performance, personality and potential.
- Criteria listed should be relevant to the particular job being appraised and be capable of objective measurement.
- The design should encourage consistency in rating between different raters who are familiar with the job and appraisee.
- The form should encourage consistency in rating between subsequent appraisals.
- Rating scales should be used against key criteria, e.g. possibly numerical or verbal (good, satisfactory, etc.), with whichever is preferred having clearly defined meanings to all parties.

Table 6.1 An example appraisal form

Appraisee:			Date of appraisal:	
JOB PERFORMANCE				
Key performance indicators Call rate Call coverage Conversion ratio Pioneer calling Distribution Display Sales targets Market share Territory profitability Complaints	**Standards of performance**	**Actual achievement**	**Rating**	**Comments**
Overall rating	1 2 3 4 5 6 7 8 9		**Comment**	
Skills and competencies Selling skills Administration Organization Communications Planning Decision making Time management Interpersonal	**Rating**		**Comment**	
Overall rating	1 2 3 4 5 6 7 8 9		**Comment**	
Job performance summary	1 2 3 4 5 6 7 8 9		**Comment**	

Table 6.1 An example appraisal form (continued)

SUBJECTIVE FACTORS		
Strengths		**Development area**
Personal characteristics and attitudes Initiative Integrity Decisiveness Adaptability Flexibility Judgement Tenacity Enthusiasm Reliability Energy Motivation Right mental attitude	**Rating**	**Comment**
Overall rating on subjective factors	1 2 3 4 5 6 7 8 9	**Overall comment on subjective factors**
Potential		
Training and development		
Overall appraisal rating 1 2 3 4 5 6 7 8 9 **Overall appraisal comment**		**Appraisee's summary comment**
Signed: 1st line manager 2nd line manager		**Signed appraisee:** **Date**
Notes to appraisers: Ratings should be given on the 1–9 scale (1 being less than satisfactory, 9 being most satisfactory). Job performance factors should carry more weight than subjective factors.		

Giving feedback for motivation, appraisal, training and discipline ■

Giving effective feedback is a skill to be developed by sales managers, as feedback given incorrectly can be very demotivating to the salesperson. The model shown in the Figure 6.1 provides a basic framework for giving feedback, and is applicable in appraisal, discipline or training situations.

Feedback can be either **informal** or **formal,** and the choice will depend on the nature of the topic to be discussed. A regular periodic appraisal would normally be better conducted as formal feedback, but a comment on a personal matter such as appearance would normally be better presented as informal feedback. Figure 6.2 outlines a model that helps decide whether formal or informal feedback is more appropriate to a situation.

Formal feedback guidelines

We can develop a basic framework for giving feedback under three headings:

- Setting the scene for the feedback session
- Making a plan for change with the salesperson
- Controlling the environment in which you give the feedback.

Setting the scene

- Prepare for the feedback session.
- Advise the salesperson in advance of the time, date and place and subject.
- Establish your rapport with the salesperson.
- State any issue clearly, concisely and in comprehensible terms to the salesperson.
- Let the salesperson see, understand and agree his/her actual performance in relation to agreed standards.
- Check that the salesperson agrees that the issue/problem or need for change exists.
- Seek to develop a mutual understanding of why the issue/problem is arising.

- Develop a two-way exchange of communications, views, comments, opinions.
- Ensure the salesperson learns your views of his role and performance (check by asking the salesperson to summarize).

Planning for change

- Obtain agreement that changes would be beneficial to the salesperson (use questioning techniques).
- Seek a commitment to work for a change in performance through modified behaviour (plans/activities) or skills application.
- Confirm and consolidate with the salesperson the ongoing feedback communicated at other sessions, training or meeting forums.
- Develop a programme (with time spans) to promote change, develop skills or modify behaviour.
- Demonstrate your commitment to assist the salesperson achieve the desired results.
- Increase the salesperson's personal motivation to improve productivity and performance through agreed objectives and development programmes.
- Where appropriate confirm the discussions and action plans in writing.
- Monitor progress, provide regular feedback in relation to the agreed programme and changes.
- Develop further corrective action programmes (or training) as necessary.

Feedback environment

- Avoid interruptions and distractions.
- Allow plenty of time so that neither you nor the salesperson feels pressured.
- Providing informal feedback should be conducted in a relaxed informal environment, possibly away from the normal work environment, but should not be projected in a flippant or sarcastic fashion.

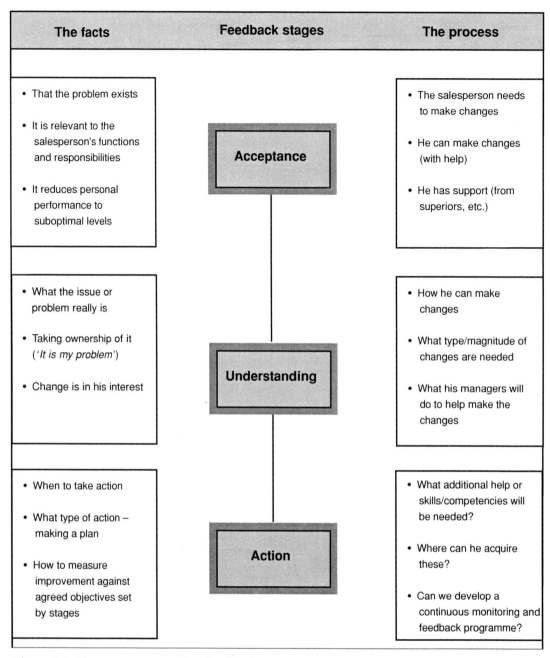

Figure 6.1 *The stages in providing feedback*

Getting a commitment to change

The purpose of appraisal, disciplinary or training feedback is to promote a change, either in performance or attitudes that affect performance. A model that helps in this process is shown in Table 6.2, which breaks

the process down to the process of getting change, i.e. **how**; the steps we need to go through, i.e. the **stages**; and the results we want to achieve, i.e. the **outcome**. Working to this model will assist in arriving at satisfactory and lasting outcomes to feedback sessions.

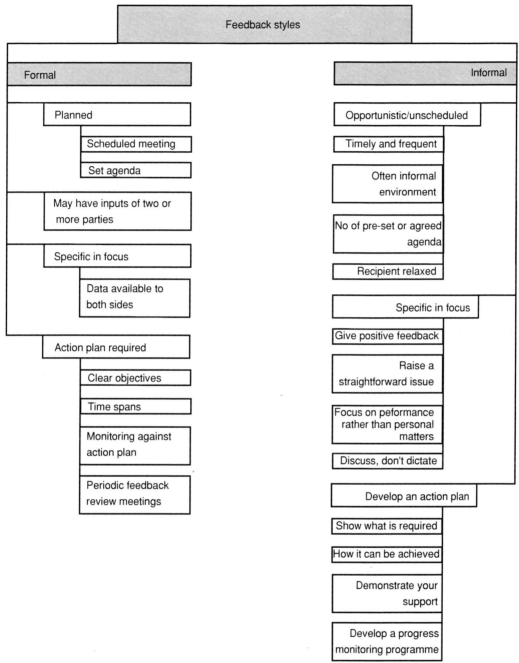

Figure 6.2 *The main feedback styles used by managers*

The salesperson should leave an appraisal or feedback meeting with a clear understanding of:

- what he or she has achieved
- his or her strengths and development areas
- his or her potential
- what is expected of him or her now (including his or her objectives for the next appraisal period)
- and the help you, his or her manager, will provide to help the appraisee progress his or her skills and effectiveness.

Table 6.2 Using feedback to create change in behaviour and performance

Objective: commitment to change		
How	**Stages**	**Outcome**

<ul><li>Establish rapport</li><li>Establish equality</li><li>Controlling content and structure of meeting</li><li>Involvement in two-way discussion</li><li>Presenting the benefits of change to the salesperson</li><li>Closing on an agreement/ commitment</li><li>Using the tools of the communications process, e.g.:
  – questioning techniques
  – listening
  – benefit selling
  – negotiating principles
  – body language</li></ul>
	<ul><li>Present the data</li><li>State the issues</li><li>Agree interpretations</li><li>Develop a common understanding of the causes/consequences of the situation or issues</li><li>Sell benefits of change/action to salesperson</li><li>Obtain interim agreements</li><li>Summarize regularly</li><li>Identify the options to address the situations/issues</li><li>Evaluate alternatives</li></ul>	<ul><li>Develop an agreed action plan and objectives</li><li>Ensure the action plan can be implemented by the salesperson within his resources and skill limitations</li><li>Set review time spans and benchmarks</li><li>Develop progress monitoring and reporting criteria</li><li>Agree the salespersons' support needs from sales manager</li><li>Write up the programme</li></ul>

An appraisal meeting should be motivational while giving honest feedback. The sales manager will find the appraisal progresses more smoothly if he or she:

- makes good use of questions to help take the heat and emotions from feedback situations, to involve the salesperson, to help gain recognition and acceptance of the need for change, and to lead towards performance and/or attitude improvement
- listens and actively responds to the salesperson's inputs and comments, as these will provide insight to the salesperson's attitudes and understanding of the issues being discussed in the feedback appraisal
- is sensitive to body language, controlling his own so as not to convey negative or judgemental feelings, and observing the salesperson's body language to be alert for positive or negative non-verbal feedback.

**Checklist 6.1
Feedback**

Action points

Feedback stages: check that you take your feedback session through the following stages.

Acceptance
- That the problem exists
- It is relevant to the salesperson's functional responsibilities
- It reduces performance to sub-optimal levels
- The salesperson needs to make changes
- The salesperson can make changes (with help)
- The salesperson has his or her superior's support

Understanding
- The nature of the problem (causes/consequences)
- The salesperson takes ownership that it is his or her problem
- Change is in the salesperson's interest
- What type/magnitude of change is required
- How appropriate change can be made
- What help/support is available

Action
- What action is to be taken
- When will it start
- What additional skills/training are needed
- Where can the skills be obtained
- How can progress be monitored
  - Agreeing interim objectives/reviews
- Continuous monitoring and feedback

Style of feedback: what style is best suited to the issue and individual?

Formal
- Planned
- Prepared inputs by both parties
- Specific in focus
- Agreed action plans resulting:
  - Objectives
  - Time framed
  - Performance monitored
  - Periodic reviews

Checklist 6.1 continued	Action points
Informal	

Informal

- Opportunistic
  - Unscheduled
  - Frequent
  - No pre-agreed agenda or detailed preparation
- Specific in focus
  - Give positive feedback
  - Raise a straightforward issue
  - Discuss
  - Raise performance rather than personal issues
- Develop an action plan
  - Show what is required
  - Show how it can be achieved
  - Demonstrate your support
  - Provide progress reviews

Checklist 6.2 Appraisals

Action points

Objective factors
These are measures against key performance indicators that are primarily assessed in a quantifiable way.

Standards of performance
Measure against standards of performance set in key performance indicators for the trade outlets, e.g.:

- Call rate
- Call coverage
- Pioneer calling
- Display
- Market share
- Promotional activity
- Complaints
- Conversion ratio of orders to calls
- Distribution achievements
- Territory/area/customer profitability
- Sales value/volume targets
- Distributor/retailer sales performance

Skills
Objective comment in appraisals should refer to the key skill areas of: Selling; Product knowledge; Verbal and other communications; Numerical; Administrative; Organizational; Planning; Interpersonal

Subjective factors
Typically appraisals will cover commentary on subjective factors including those following.

Personal characteristics
Comparisons might be made with strengths and weaknesses of characteristics identified in a job holder profile, e.g.:

- Enthusiasm
- Integrity
- Reliability
- Sincerity/empathy
- Self-confidence
- Persistence
- Resilience
- Intelligence
- Appearance
- Adaptability
- Self-motivation
- Maturity
- Initiative
- Sense of urgency
- Loyalty
- Commitment

Attitudes
Comment on negative and positive attitudes to the job, company, customers and colleagues that relate to performance.

Development and training needs
Address development needs so meets requirements of current job, and is given opportunity to develop to meet future needs and responsibilities.

Potential
Comment on potential for promotion or assignment to new responsibilities within the sales force or elsewhere.

7

Communication in the sales force _____

The role and purpose of communications ▬▬▬▬

Good communications are a major source of motivation within a sales team – and bad communications are a major source of complaint, leaving open the opportunity for poor performance to be argued as the result of not knowing about something. The process of communication is the sending and receiving of signals that should have the same meaning to the recipient salesperson as to the issuing sales manager. The signals must be meaningful to the sender, the sales manager, and the receiver, the salesperson, otherwise they will not be acted upon.

Sales activity communications occur between:

- sales manager and salesperson
- salesperson and customers (whether key accounts or smaller customer accounts)
- customers and the head office
- head office managers and field sales managers.

In the sales environment a variety of means of communicating is commonly used within the communication chain (see Figures 7.1 and 7.2), e.g.:

- **verbally**, such as in face-to-face discussions, presentations, meetings
- **written communications**, such as letters, memoranda, sales literature
- **pictorially**, through product literature, advertisements, charts, graphs
- **numerically**, as with sales forecasts, performance data, computer printouts
- **demonstrably**, such as showing how to perform a task or use a product
- **physically**, through body language and facial expressions
- **attitudinally**, demonstrated or expressed by any of the foregoing.

Typically in first line sales management much of the communication with the sales team is on a one-to-one basis, communicating orally or demonstrably, supported with the occasional team (area) meeting. Senior sales management and sales office support functions usually have to rely more on written communications.

Purpose and means of communicating

The starting point of the communications process is for the communicator (sales manager) to clarify the purpose of communicating. Sales communications generally relate to:

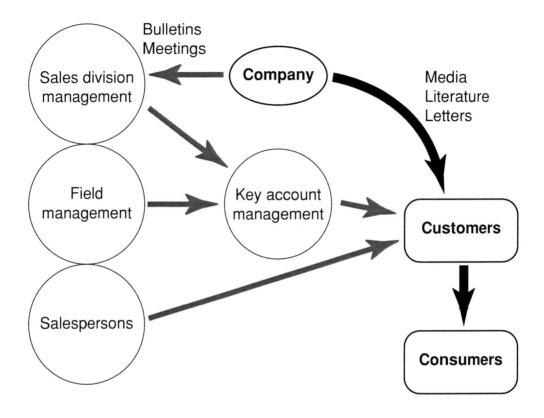

Figure 7.1 *A typical sales team communication chain*

- establishing new or existing policies of the company
- communicating the range of programmes, plans and strategies developed within the company
- advising on operational procedures and practices
- preceding actions, policies and programmes and their outcomes (feedback) or impact on the company or its environment, and relation to current policies, programmes and procedures.

Means of communicating _____

The means of communication selected in any situation will depend on such factors as:

- the amount of time available to you, the sales manager, to achieve your objective, and the degree of urgency of the subject matter
- the range of media available to both sales manager and the salesperson (e.g., telephone, electronic mail or computer, regular postal services)
- the complexity of the subject matter being communicated
- the ease with which face-to-face contacts can be made between the sales manager and his sales team (which will be influenced by the size and geographical spread of the sales team).

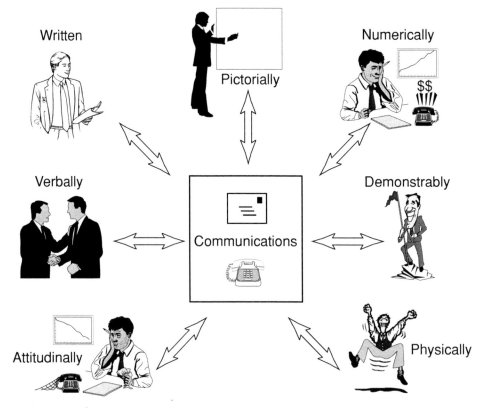

Figure 7.2 *Ways of communicating*

How to communicate

Common **communication media** are:

- face-to-face meetings (team meetings or one-to-one meetings)
- written or illustrative reports and documents
- computers (direct computer links or via modems using telephone lines, etc.)
- telephones
- telephonic data transmission services (FAX)
- audio or video tapes.

In most markets the main means of communications are still through **memoranda**, **bulletins**, **sales meetings** and **telephone**, and also during **field accompaniment** of salespersons. However, there is very rapid growth in computerization within field sales teams.

What to communicate

As the sales manager you have the choice in what to communicate, and should avoid overburdening your team with too much information or with too many requests for information. It is also important to prioritize requests for action, otherwise the salesperson will set his own priorities, which may not match yours and will normally result in easier requests or action being undertaken first. In considering what to communicate to the sales team you should clarify to yourself whether the content of the communication is **essential** or **optional** to the management of the sales operation.

Essential information

A range of information that both sales managers and salesperson would consider essential includes:

- everything the salesperson needs to know to perform basic job functions (e.g. product information, prices, promotions, etc.)
- everything that impacts on the sales team's ability to comply with procedures or implement programmes (e.g. instructions on administrative procedures)
- anything that affects their ability to perform responsibilities and duties (e.g. information of key account product approvals and promotional activity, or authorization for merchandising activity, details of above the line marketing programmes, etc.)
- information that provides feedback and measurement against standards of performance, forecasts, targets, goals and objectives (e.g. detailed monthly performance feedback based on analysis of order forms and daily activity reports).

Optional information

The range of optional information that could be provided (possibly on a 'need to know' basis) to members of a sales team is extensive, including anything that:

- adds to the salesperson's understanding of the company and its operations, or its results and achievements (e.g. financial accounts, market share data, product costing data for account managers, developments in other markets)
- improves the salesperson's understanding of the market place (e.g. company and competitive brand rankings and sector shares, data on trade channels such as their product category shares, trade channel and key account developments)
- provides a source of training and personal development (e.g. on the use of technology in the company or in retailing, tips on selling, subscriptions to relevant journals, etc.).

Communications should be restricted or limited where premature communication could be disruptive or lead to activity that might impact negatively on the subject of the communication (e.g. with new product launches, promotions, acquisitions and mergers).

Whom to communicate with

It is just as possible to send out too little information as too much, or to communicate with too few people as too many. In considering whom you should be communicating with it is often useful to make a list of:

- everyone who establishes a 'need to know' communication content in order to perform job functions in the sales organization (e.g. procedural practices, price changes, stock availability)
- persons required to take personal action on communications or to direct others to take action (i.e. if salespersons are to make certain recordings on daily reports then departments concerned with sales statistical preparation and analyses need to know)
- persons who need access to the content of a communication for information purposes (e.g. a personnel officer needs to see disciplinary notes).

Do not copy communications to everyone if they are not needed: they serve as a source of distraction, and while increasing the administrative burden reduce the management time available for planning.

Keep memoranda and bulletins to a minimum. Every time you write a memo, ask yourself: *'Is this memo really necessary to progress the management of the business, or is it just distracting from the key result areas, or serving as a defensive device to show I'm doing something?'*

Style of communications

There are two main formats in communications:

- **formal** communications, such as in letters, memoranda, bulletins and meetings
- **informal** communications, such as over the

telephone, in casual meetings at the office, or in kerbside discussion in the field.

Both **formal** and **informal** communications need to be:

- **empathetic**, demonstrating an understanding of the recipient's environment
- **sincere**, in content and expression
- **informative**, providing all the information the salesperson needs to fulfil functions effectively
- **clear**, in content, structure and format
- **concise**, homing in on the key issues – get to the point
- **meaningful**, in that the content should relate to the salesperson's (or other recipient's) environment
- **simple**, in structure and format, so that even complex data can be grasped.

Communication guidelines

- Where the subject of the communication is better treated as an informal matter, and not involving any data or detail, then it is better dealt with face to face or possibly on the telephone (if not about discipline or serious criticism).
- Where the subject of a communication is not good news, the first communication is better face to face.
- Where a communication sets out policies, procedures and practices, or relates to plans, forecasts, targets, performance feedback, standards of performance, product information, or anything that should be stored, etc., the communication is better in writing.
- Where the purpose of a communication is to recognize achievement, personal praise might be supported by mention in a bulletin or letter.
- Avoid the arbitrary issuing of orders, instructions or information without supporting explanation, otherwise there is the risk of non-compliance (as salespersons fail to see the need for, or benefit from, compliance) or of a poor standard of compliance.

In sales management poor communications or communication breakdowns can cost business or result in sub-standard service to customers, and communication problems must be identified and addressed.

Sales bulletins and other memoranda

The main uses of formal **sales bulletins** and **memoranda** to salespersons are to:

- issue instructions or guidelines for action, procedures, operating methods and systems
- inform of events, developments, plans, policies, programmes, targets, forecasts
- provide feedback on results and achievements against objectives, forecasts, targets, standards of performance
- motivate salespersons to improved productivity and performance
- confirm discussions and agreements, courses of action and projects
- give recognition to achievers of noteworthy results.

The purpose of sales bulletins is not just to convey factual information, but usually is aimed to provide a boost to sales team morale and motivation. It should therefore be **positive** rather than negative (as negative or critical communications are very demotivating to recipients). Bulletins might be issued periodically from the national sales office, and also from local field district managers.

Audio and visual (video) communications offer scope for flexibility and variety in communication media. The sales team should be familiar with all company public relations and advertising videos used in the market.

From a practical perspective the sales manager should be concerned with:

- who communicates with the sales force
- the frequency of communications
- the content of communications
- how information should be presented in sales bulletins, i.e. the structure.

Who communicates with the sales force

There is a particular danger in too many persons making direct contact with members of the sales force, in that the salesperson will have to decide whose communications to act on, and that may distract from the key selling priorities.

Typically several departments are involved in making direct communications, e.g.:

- **Customer service** – copies of order acknowledgements, delivery notes and invoices; payments chasing; customer queries
- **Marketing** – requests for data and feedback on activity; promotions and marketing programmes
- **Key accounts** – information on customer activity programmes; instructions on implementation of programme activity; requests for feedback data
- **Sales support departments** – instructions concerning display materials; administrative instructions

Communications other than routine copies of documents concerned with order processing and payments should be controlled through sales line management. Communications from individual persons or departments seeking help, information or promoting their own issues must be avoided and minimized, otherwise the salespersons will be distracted from selling and take the line of least resistance, devoting time to actioning either communications from those persons who exert most pressure, or those where the requests are easy or interesting to action.

The most efficient means of controlling communications is through periodic **bulletins**, issued from the sales office.

Frequency of communications _____

The second danger of distracting the sales force from its key selling activity is to have too much or too frequent communication. The frequency of issue of sales bulletins and memoranda should be controlled to minimize distracting the sales team from the task of generating business. The formal written communications should be sufficiently frequent to serve their purposes but not so frequent as to over-burden the salespersons with paperwork, information and instructions. As a general guideline, sales office bulletins are usually best issued monthly, although, of course, there are occasions when more frequent bulletins are justified. It is better to have material collected and issued centrally, say in a sales administration department, than to have a multiplicity of individuals communicating with salespersons, with resultant confusion in content and priorities.

Direct contact for feedback, training and motivational purposes, such as by field managers, is the most critical form of communication and should be the most frequent.

Sales bulletin content

The length, content and structure of a sales bulletin will depend on such factors as:

- its purpose (commented on previously)
- complexity of the subject matter
- experience and ability of recipients to assimilate data
- intended impact the communication should have on recipients
- the environment in which it will be received.

Typically **sales bulletins** communicate:

- current promotional or advertising activity
- key account (top customer) activity
- company performance data, e.g. feedback on sales performance against plans for latest month and year to date
- introduction of new recording systems or procedures
- new product developments
- changes in product specifications, packaging, etc.
- notable individual achievements
- competitive activity and general market information
- miscellaneous information.

Structure of sales bulletins ⸻

Before drafting a sales bulletin or memorandum the sales manager should clarify in his own mind what he wants to communicate and the purpose of the communication.

- **Group items with a common purpose together in a section**. All instructions or action points, or all performance feedback and recognition points, can be grouped in separate identifiable sections.
- **Clearly identify the sections**. Sections in bulletins, or types of memoranda, might be colour coded, e.g. red for action, green for information, etc.
- **Prioritize items for action within each section**. Where appropriate, list action points in a sequence representing the order in which action should be taken.
- **Give clear guidelines on when action should be taken or information submitted**. Ensure the recipient is clear on the nature of action to be taken. Normally sales managers should monitor and control that action is taken, such as by asking for confirmation that data has been supplied to the office, or that customers have been contacted on promotions, etc. In some cases a summary checklist attached to the sales bulletin will help the salesperson check he has read and actioned points.
- **Provide an overview summary of main activity** (see Table 7.1). This might include promotions, media, and major customer activity.

It is often practical to have a ring binder with sections in which current and recent bulletins can be filed. The field sales manager can then check this is up to date when accompanying each salesperson, and check the action and understanding of each section. It should not be assumed that receipt of a communication ensures reading and action. Similar formats to the examples in Table 7.1 and Figure 7.3 can be devised to suit a business-to-business or industrial product supplier.

Audio, visual and computer media communications ▬▬▬▬▬

While written and direct personal communications (including on the telephone) are still the most common communication means used in sales forces, some companies with specialist products and services have developed sophisticated communications using audio, video and computer-based communications. These can be developed with clients as a way of standardizing presentations, and demonstrating aspects of products hard to communicate effectively using traditional sales presentations and sales literature.

Sales managers know the benefits of communicating through a variety of media to keep interest, and involvement and motivation, higher within sales teams.

- **Audio cassettes** can supplement telephone contact where there is no need for complicated data to be communicated, or to accompany a sales bulletin. They are useful to motivate, and to communicate broad activity guidelines. They are particularly useful where direct personal field contact with line managers is lower than desirable.
- **Video cassettes**, while substantially more expensive to produce, provide an excellent medium for showing products in trial and use environments. They are also used most effectively to communicate a company perspective to customers, conveying the history and heritage, innovativeness, production processes, and so on, helping a customer (and salesperson) to relate to the supplying company. They also have great scope for development as a 'talking bulletin' where frequent sales meetings are impractical.
- **Computers** offer the scope to convey information directly by modem, or by disk, where complex data needs to be available and frequently updated and available to a sales team. Complex product data and pricing formulas can often best be held on a laptop computer. Compact disks can

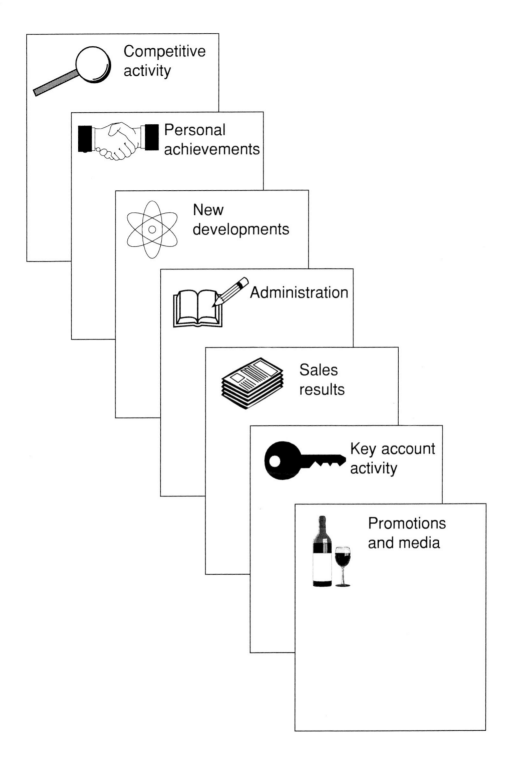

Figure 7.3 *A bulletin divided into identifiable sections*

contain complete product ranges in pictorial format, letting a buyer see each product in his own office.

The modern sales manager needs training and experience in the use of computers in the business environment, as they also offer the most effective way of maintaining contact and controlling field operations over the coming years. Complete sales communication, data transfer, customer account management and field sales reporting packages are all available now, although generally only used by major corporations. The use of computer packages greatly reduces the need for paperwork, and can reduce the time a sales team must allocate to paperwork processes and reporting, with a resultant cost benefit. Everything from customer records through pre-agreeing call objectives, and optimizing journey planning right through to sales reporting and performance monitoring can be managed with the use of computers.

Table 7.1 An example of a monthly activity summary

Monthly promotion activity summary	
Month: December	
Promotions	
Blue Mountain Bourbon	• Blue Mountain theme nights in key on-trade (clubs, bars, etc.) outlets. • Bar staff incentive: £1 for 5 bottle tops. • Free bourbon tumbler with 1 litre bottle in supermarkets – off-shelf displays
Media	
Blue Mountain Bourbon	• Press campaign: Sunday Globe, Sunday News (magazines), Daily News (Thursdays). • TV late evening spots (talk shows) • Magazine advertisements: entertainment pages – Out On The Town, The Scene, Evening Echo (Fridays).
Key account activity	
Continental Hypers	• Blue Mountain Bourbon off-shelf features in all A stores from 1/6 to 15/6. Free Glass Offer. All point of sale material approved.
Choice Supermarkets	• Blue Mountain Bourbon special price reduction 50p: on-shelf feature with display material.
Supasave	• Blue Mountain Bourbon off-shelf feature in all branches 16/6 to 30/6. 60p price reduction. Supasave feature cards authorized.
LoCost Cash & Carries	• Blue Mountain Bourbon case discount £2.90 all outlets 3/6 to 15/6. Off-shelf features. Point of sale material allowed.
Brady's Breweries	• Blue Mountain Bourbon theme nights to be agreed locally by salesperson, with promoters, and lucky draw for free bottle each night; one voucher given with each purchase. • 2 for 1 Happy Hour all outlets 7/6 to 21/6. Point of sale material supplied.

**Checklist 7.1
Communications**

Action points

What to communicate

Essential information:

- Everything the salesperson needs to know to perform basic job functions
- Impacts on the sales team's ability to comply with procedures or implement programmes
- Affects their ability to perform responsibilities and duties
- Provides feedback and measurement against standards of performance, forecasts, targets, goals and objectives

Optional information:

- Adds to an understanding of the company and its operations
- Improves the understanding of the marketplace and working environment
- Provides a source of personal training and development

Whom to communicate with

- Everyone who establishes a 'need to know' the contents of a communication in order to perform job functions in the sales organization
- Persons required to take personal action on communications or to direct others to take action
- Persons who need access to the content of a communication for information purposes

Style of communication

- Formal communications, such as in letters, memoranda and bulletins and meetings
- Informal communications, such as over the telephone, in casual meetings at the office, or in kerbside discussion in the field.
- Formal and informal communications need to be: empathetic, sincere, informative, clear, concise, meaningful and simple.

Communication guidelines

- Avoid the arbitrary issuing of orders, instructions or information without supporting explanation
- **Face to face communication is preferable:**
  - where the subject of the communication is better treated as an informal matter, and not involving any data or detail where the subject of a communication is not good news.

Checklist 7.1 continued	Action points

● **Written communications are preferable:**
  – where a communication sets out policies, procedures and practices, or relates to plans, forecasts, targets, performance feedback, standards of performance, product information, or anything that should be stored, etc.
  – where the purpose of a communication is to recognize achievement, personal praise might be supported by mention in a bulletin or letter.	

Action points

The main uses of formal **sales bulletins** and memoranda to **salespersons** are to:
- **Issue instructions** or guidelines for action, procedures, operating methods and systems
- **Inform** of events, developments, plans, policies, programmes, targets, forecasts
- **Provide feedback** on results and achievements against objectives, forecasts, targets, standards of performance
- **Motivate** salespersons to improved productivity and performance
- **Confirm** discussions and agreements, courses of action and projects
- **Give recognition** to achievers of noteworthy results.

Bulletin content and structure
The length, content and structure of a sales bulletin will depend on such factors as:
- Its purpose (commented on in previous section)
- Complexity of the subject matter
- Experience and ability of recipients to assimilate data
- Intended impact the communication should have on recipients
- The environment it will be received in

Typically **sales bulletins** communicate:
- Current promotional or advertising activity
- Sales activity priorities
- Key account activity
- Competitive activity and general market information
- Company performance data
- Introduction of new recording systems or procedures
- New product developments
- Changes in product specifications, recipes, formulas
- Notable individual achievements.

8

Sales meetings and conferences ─────────

Organizing and running sales meetings ▬▬▬▬▬▬▬

Sales meetings are usually organized periodically, often monthly, amongst a group of salespersons with common interests or issues to address, e.g. key account managers, field sales managers, territory salespersons, under the chairmanship of their line manager. Meetings are often planned to address:

- performance feedback, particularly deviations from plans
- product information (range, packaging, advertising, etc.)
- sales promotional activity
- sales targeting
- sales force procedures and operational matters
- sales skill training.

Sales conferences normally draw together all the various sections of the sales and marketing team, at a national gathering, often only once per year. Often conferences are designed to communicate more momentous developments than might be covered at local sales meetings, and provide a sense of focus and direction to a longer time period, such as the next year.

The purpose of meetings and conferences

A meeting should have a clear purpose (or a limited range of purposes) and agenda, established in advance in order that all the inputs focus on the purpose. The main purposes of sales meetings are:

- **participation** which promotes team building
- **problem resolution**, identifying and evaluating alternative options
- **instruction**, imparting new information, data, selling or marketing techniques, training, administrative systems and procedures, policies, programmes
- **motivation**, focusing on performance feedback, encouragement, productivity improvement ideas, and exchanges of experiences and ideas
- **exploration** of new ideas to improve productivity or performance, or promote the achievement of goals and objectives.

Sales meeting organization ─────────

If a sales meeting is to achieve its objectives and also to enhance the sales manager's reputation as a professional within his or her sales team it is essential that it be planned thoroughly. The main complaints of salespersons about meetings are usually that:

- they take too long
- subject coverage is repetitive
- they don't seem to achieve anything
- too much time is wasted on parochial (individual) issues not relevant to all the attendees.

The sales manager must avoid these criticisms within his or her own team, and can do this by thorough meeting planning and preparation, addressing each of the following points.

Conducting sales meetings

A sales meeting should be treated like a sales presentation, with the objectives of:

- gaining and retaining attention
- creating interest in the subject matter
- generating desire in the attendees to implement the content of the meeting in everyday work practices
- provoking appropriate action from the participants.

The sales meeting might make use of several formats, as listed in the following table, depending on its purpose and objectives.

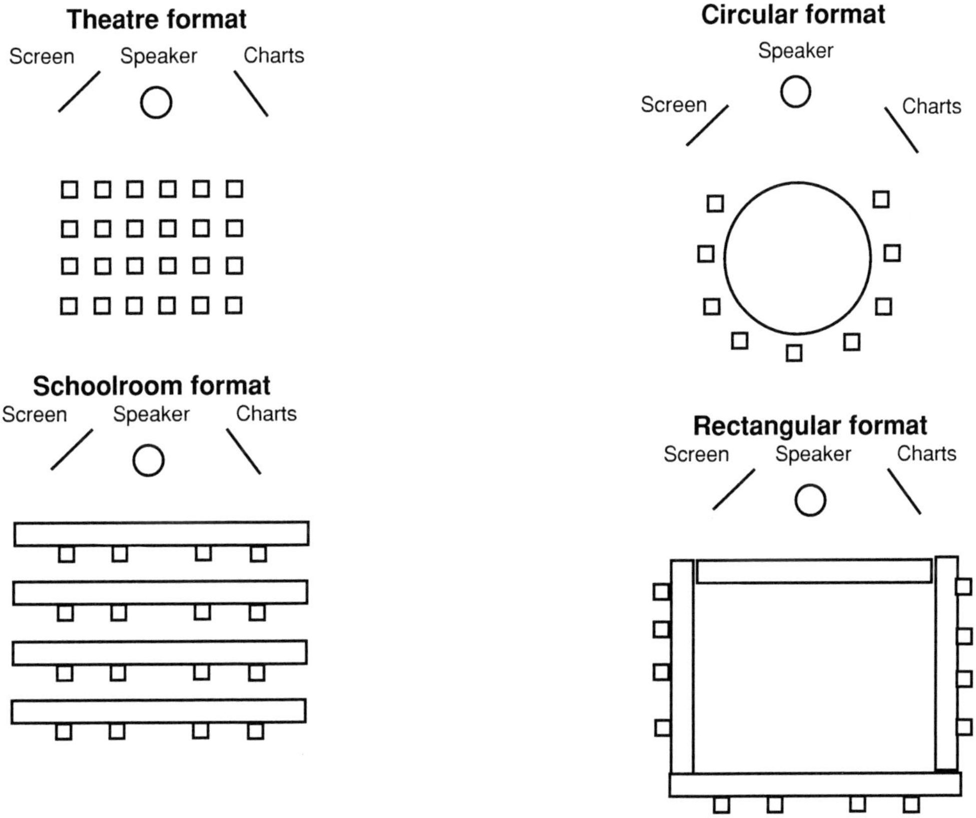

Figure 8.1 Example meeting room layouts

Meeting formats	
Presentations	On subjects of interest to the whole group
Group discussions	Related to the objectives, theme or content of the meeting
Planning sessions	Groups can turn general plans into specific area or territory plans
Role playing	New techniques or skills can be practised by the group
Case studies	An individual or team development exercise at meetings, related not just to sales and marketing matters but general management situations
Presentations by meeting attendees	Attendees should be encouraged to make presentations on special subjects or areas of expertise as a development and team building exercise

Guidelines for preparing and planning for meetings

- **Objectives** — Set and agree objectives and build the content round these.
- **Theme** — Ensure all speakers are notified of the core theme.
- **Responsibility** — Allocate planning, organizational and administrative authority for the meeting to someone competent to meet the demands of skill and time (that person might be you!).
- **Venue** — Identify and reserve a suitable venue. Major conferences often need to be booked a year ahead.
- **Length** — Set the length of the meeting to be no longer than necessary to accomplish objectives. Two to four hours is common for an area meeting of salespersons or field sales managers' meeting. An annual conference may occupy much of a day. Meetings should be run strictly to scheduled timings.
- **Agenda** — Prepare a full agenda round the objectives and theme, and organize topics and timings to maintain interest (Table 8.1).
- **Attendees** — Decide who should attend and notify early (with joining instructions, maps, etc., if necessary).
- **Communication aids** — Plan which communication aids to use. Be sure to use a variety to maintain interest, such as overhead transparencies, flip charts, slides, films or videos, and so on. Presentation aids should be legible to be read by the farthest participant. Speakers should rehearse with their communication aids to ensure fluency and competency on the day.
- **Handouts** — Prepare handouts where appropriate (and for guest speakers).
- **Review speaker presentations** — Obtain draft speeches for guest speakers and ensure they are in line with theme, objectives and time allocation (and well rehearsed).
- **Room layout** — Consider the most suitable room layout to match objectives, so that all attendees can hear and see presentations, in comfort, with minimal distractions (see Figure 8.1). Ensure that:
  - all attendees can see communication aids clearly
  - there are no distractions drawing attention away from the speakers and the focal point of the room
  - heating and ventilation are set to comfortable levels
  - water and beverages are within easy reach
  - natural and artificial lighting are adequate and balanced for a particular meeting room
  - the seating is comfortable, and room layout does not create a 'them and us', such as where all the bosses sit at a top table.

Chairing the sales meeting

At the beginning of a sales meeting the sales manager leading the meeting should:

- introduce the topics clearly and definitively
- define the purpose and objectives of the meeting
- limit the scope of the meeting and questions to matters which can be covered within the time span
- set the guidelines on rules and procedures for the meeting
- work to develop positive and receptive attitudes in the attending salespersons.

Table 8.1 *A sample agenda for a sales area meeting*

Sample area meeting agenda
Performance feedback
● Company/area/territory achievement against plans for the month and year to date ● Discussion on any problems or serious deviations from plan, with corrective action planning ● Feedback on any particular individual salesperson's achievements of note ● Brief commentary from each salesperson on his or her territory's progress against current plans ● Key account performance within the area or territories
Presentation on a project
● Personal presentation from an individual salesperson on progress against a particular personal project on his or her territory (e.g. the testing of a new display layout in a major store, or surveying the distribution and usage of certain office machinery in customers on a sales territory)
The new promotion plan
● Introduction to the next month's promotion plan ● Discussion on the promotion priorities and objectives ● Sales target planning and call objectives ● Special administration or recording requirements for the new sales period
Practical training
● Role playing how the new promotion can be sold into different types of accounts
Summary
● A motivational review and commitment to individual objectives

The sales manager, acting as the chairperson, should, in a participatory sales meeting:

● obtain views and opinions from participants
● gather information on the nature and strength of feelings on issues discussed
● get a reaction on the subject matter, discussion points and proposals
● develop the discussion so that it leads to the desired conclusion, action or acceptance of ideas and proposals
● produce the intended modification of attitudes, opinions, behaviour, activities, action or techniques
● demonstrate a neutrality or impartiality which earns the respect and co-operation of the group in the meeting
● encourage salesperson participation and involvement to retain attention and interest, drawing in people with a contribution to make.

The sales manager must remain in control of the meeting while involving each member of the team as appropriate. He must work to gain acceptance of ideas and a commitment to programmes introduced, communicating the benefits of change in a way the team understands and accepts.

Communication aids

In a sales meeting **communication aids** are generally used to:

● direct and retain attention and interest
● present often complex information in a meaningful and comprehensible fashion
● record salespersons' inputs and comments

- involve the sales team in a participatory meeting
- increase assimilation and retention of information
- summarize main points of presentations
- provide a focal point as the meeting develops into a practical planning and implementation session.

It is important to use a variety of visual communication aids to gain and retain attention. Typical **visual aids** you, the sales manager, are likely to use include:

- blackboards and flip charts, or other forms of 'white board' used for writing notes
- magnetic boards
- product samples
- films and video films
- prepared charts and graphs (possibly including some overlay charts)
- slides (possibly from a computer-based presentation programme, projected onto a screen), and overhead projector transparencies
- pictures and photographs
- models such as of products or projects
- sound recordings
- personal commentaries (from salespersons who have experience to contribute).

Check which visual aids will help you conduct the meeting, and ensure they are available at the meeting venue. Often you will want to do some preparation, such as writing notes on flip charts, in advance of the meeting. If any form of slides is being used you will need to check they are in correct running order (it helps to number them). If you are preparing visual aids in advance then consider how to maximize impact through design factors such as:

- size
- legibility
- originality
- simplicity
- clarity
- colour
- realism

- relevance to the meeting content and the audience.

Do not expect your audience to undertake mental gymnastics trying to comprehend your meanings and messages.

Making sales meeting presentations

The sales manager frequently has to make presentations to groups, including customers, colleagues or his area sales team. The key to successful presentations is preparation. Preparation starts with considering the **audience**, the **purpose** and the **subject matter** (see Figure 8.2).

The audience

In preparing for a sales meeting or presentation take account of:

- the present level of subject knowledge of the audience
- their experience in relation to the subject matter
- their likely interest level
- the attitudes of the audience
- their ability to assimilate the information being presented
- their familiarity and experience with participating in meetings or public presentations.

The sales team will normally have an interest in a level of detail about products and sales programmes that other groups, such as customers, may not.

The purpose

You, the sales manager, need to be clear on your objectives for the sales meeting or presentation. The format of the meeting should reflect its purpose, as should the preparation of notes and supporting materials. Typical purposes of meetings include:

- to give a background impression or overview of events, developments, programmes, etc.

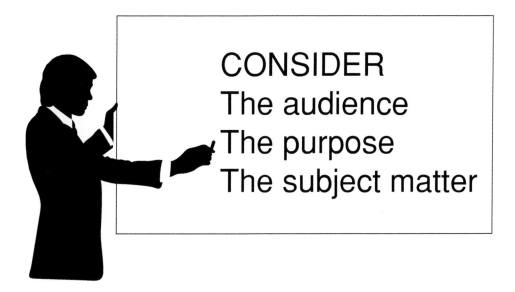

CONSIDER
The audience
The purpose
The subject matter

Figure 8.2 *Preparing for a presentation*

- to increase expertise or present detailed information
- to teach a new skill or modify participant behaviour
- to present a new point of view
- to present a programme or course of action.

A meeting that is designed to present detailed information (e.g. on product ranges, prices, targets, etc.) needs to have more comprehensive charts and supporting handouts than a meeting just giving background information (e.g. outlining label changes for next year). A meeting designed to modify selling behaviour (e.g. closing the sale, handling objections, addressing benefits of relocating shelf displays, etc.) needs to have role play scenarios prepared for active role playing in the meeting.

The subject matter

Once you are clear on the meeting's audience and purpose you need to prepare your notes for your own inputs, structure an agenda, and draft notes on points you want to ensure receive coverage in the meeting. Attention to detail at this stage will reduce the risk of a

meeting degenerating into a moaning or gossip session. Your sales team should leave each of your meetings feeling it was worthwhile and beneficial. Look at the subject matter to be covered and your agenda, and:

- jot down all your initial ideas on each topic on a sheet of paper
- group related points on each topic together
- identify the key points the talk can be structured around
- identify and research any additional sources of useful information that will help you cover the subject thoroughly:
  - your personal experience;
  - experience of colleagues or members of the sales team;
  - company literature or any other relevant published literature
- prepare any meeting presentation aids, e.g. charts, handouts, videos, etc., taking account of the ability of the team to absorb information (avoid using complex data unnecessarily)
- look for ways to involve the audience in a participatory fashion at this preparation stage, and plan how and when to draw them into active participation.

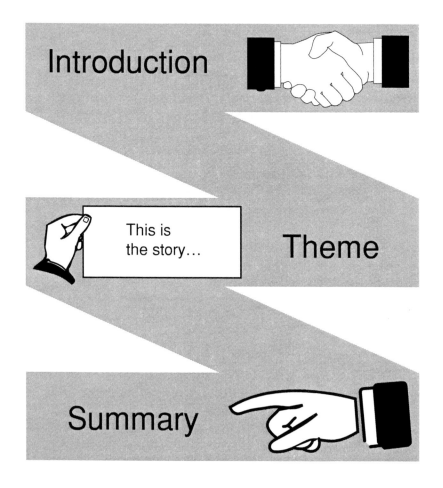

Figure 8.3 *Developing a presentation structure*

Structuring the presentation

Generally, if you are preparing a formal presentation on a topic, you should divide the presentation into (Figure 8.3):

- an **introduction**, presenting an overview of the topic and highlighting how team members can benefit
- the **core theme** of the subject matter, encouraging participation, discussion and questions
- a **memorable summary**, highlighting priorities and key action points.

Practical tips on making a presentation

Prepare comprehensive notes

- Jot down ideas on a sheet of paper
- Group related points on each topic together
- Structure the talk around key points
- Highlight how participants can benefit from the presentation

	● Research sources of useful information
	● Prepare any meeting presentation aids
	● Look for ways to involve the audience
Get to the meeting venue early and check facilities	● The environment
	● The room layout
	● Visual aid facilities
	● Lighting
	● Positioning of podiums or rostrums
	● Operation of any public address systems
	● Potential sources of distraction
	● Heating/cooling levels
	● Room ventilation
	● Availability of ashtrays
	● Positioning of sales team in relation to the speaker and visual aids
	● Water and refreshment breaks
Make an impact	● Don't be apologetic for subject matter or preparation
	● Speak clearly and audibly; use your natural voice
	● Address the whole sales team
	● Avoid flamboyance or distracting mannerisms.
	● Do not keep stopping to look at notes.
	● Repeat key points for impact and emphasis.
Positioning	● Position yourself where all can see you
	● Avoid moving round too much
	● Address yourself clearly to the whole of the sales team
	● Ensure your visual aids are within sight
Avoid distracting mannerisms	● Jingling coins in your pocket
	● Fiddling with a tie or earrings, etc.
	● Waving your notes or clipboard
	● Prowling all over the stage or room
	● Adopting awkward poses
Use available visual aids	● Blackboards/flip charts
	● Magnetic boards
	● Samples
	● Films/videos
	● Prepared charts and graphs
	● Slides and overhead projector slides
	● Pictures
	● Sound recordings
	● Product or other samples or examples
	● Personal testimonies (from concerned persons)
Timing	● Keep to a timetable
	● Use frequent pauses
	● Summarize regularly
Questions	● Allow time for questions
	● Do not embarrass or criticize questioners
	● Clarify facts promptly
	● Only delay answers where subject will be covered later
Handouts	● Give handouts where appropriate
	● Prepare summaries of key points
	● List action points
	● Motivate positive action

Checklist 8.1
Organizing a meeting or conference

Action points

- Set **objectives**
- Decide main **theme**
- Allocate organizational **responsibility**
- Select a **venue**, considering:
  - Geographical location
  - Accessibility
  - Accommodation/parking
  - Leisure facilities
  - Meal facilities
  - Available communication aids
  - Billing arrangements
  - Communications/message facilities
  - Meeting room facilities, e.g.:

Size	Audio facilities
Location	Rest rooms
Ventilation	Shape/layout
Lighting	Rest break services

- Confirm venue booking
- Prepare an **agenda** and circulate to speakers
- Invite **guest speakers** (confirm theme and subject of presentation)
- Invite audience, and advise of travel and accommodation arrangements
- Plan **room layout**
  Theatre/table or other format
  Water/beverages
  Ash trays, waste bins
  Lighting/audio
  Communication aids
  Theme displays
- **Review** all speakers' presentation scripts
- Prepare all **communications aids** and presentation handouts
- Prepare **conference folders** or manuals for audience (including writing materials, name tags, agendas, pre-conference reading)
- Plan **reception** for all attendees
  Accommodation check-in
  Welcoming committee
  Book meals and beverages for break intervals
- **Rehearse all** presentations, including the use and operation of communication aids

Checklist 8.2
Preparing a presentation for a meeting

Action points

The audience
In preparing for a sales meeting presentation take account of:
- The audience's present level of subject knowledge
- Their experience in relation to the subject matter
- Their likely interest level
- The attitudes of the audience
- Their ability to assimilate the information being presented
- Their experience at participating in meetings or public presentations.

The purpose
Clarify your objectives. Typical purposes of meetings include:
- Giving a background overview of events, developments, etc.
- Increasing expertise or presenting detailed information
- Teaching a new skill or modifying participant behaviour
- Presenting a new point of view
- Presenting a programme or course of action.

The subject matter
Structure an agenda, prepare your notes, covering points you want to ensure receive attention in the meeting, e.g.:
- Jot down all your initial ideas on each topic
- Group related points on each topic together
- Identify the key points the talk can be structured around
- Research any additional sources of useful information, e.g.:
  Your personal experience
  Experience of colleagues or members of the sales team
  Company literature or other relevant published literature
- Prepare any meeting presentation aids, e.g. charts, handouts, etc.
- Look for ways to involve the audience in a participatory fashion.

Checklist 8.3
Structuring the presentation

Action points

Divide the presentation into:
- an **introduction**
- the **core theme** of the subject matter
- a memorable **summary**.

Introduction
- Highlight aspects of the subject likely to interest the sales team
- Show how the sales team can personally benefit from the talk
- Arouse curiosity by the visual aids and style of presentation
- Relate the subject matter to the lives and experience of the sales team
- Project your personal enthusiasm, dynamism and commitment.

Theme
- Cover the detail matter of the topic
- Encourage participation and questioning within the sales team
- The pace should suit the sales team and the purpose of the talk
- Develop the theme in a step-by-step fashion; explain each point in a meaningful way; use examples the sales team can relate to; use visual aids liberally
- Involve the sales team in discussions, developing ideas and training situations
- Ensure your style is not too dominant, dictatorial, or suppressing serious comment or participation.

Summary
A good meeting summary helps pull a meeting together, confirm what is decided, and set action priorities. It should:
- be as brief as practical
- repeat the key points of the presentations
- highlight priorities for action
- draw conclusions from the material presented
- leave your sales team feeling motivated with your message.

Checklist 8.4
Practical tips on the presentation

Action points

Prepare comprehensive notes or a script
- Jot down ideas on a sheet of paper
- Group related points on each topic together
- Structure the talk around key points
- Highlight how participants can benefit from the presentation
- Research sources of useful information
- Prepare any meeting presentation aids
- Look for ways to involve the audience.

Get to the meeting venue early and check facilities
- The environment
- The room layout
- Visual aid facilities
- Lighting
- Positioning of podiums or rostrums
- Operation of any public address systems
- Potential sources of distraction
- Heating/cooling levels
- Room ventilation
- Availability of ashtrays
- Positioning of sales team in relation to the speaker and visual aids
- Water and refreshment breaks.

Make an impact
- Don't be apologetic for subject matter or preparation
- Speak clearly and audibly; use your natural voice
- Address the whole sales team
- Avoid flamboyance or distracting mannerisms
- Do not keep stopping to look at notes
- Repeat key points for impact and emphasis.

Positioning
- Position yourself where all can see you
- Avoid moving round too much
- Address yourself clearly to the whole of the sales team
- Ensure your visual aids are within sight.

Avoid distracting mannerisms
- Jingling coins in your pocket
- Fiddling with a tie or earrings, etc.
- Waving your notes or clipboard
- Prowling all over the stage or room

	Action points
Checklist 8.4 continued ● Adopting awkward poses. **Use available visual aids** ● Blackboards/flip charts ● Magnetic boards ● Samples ● Films/videos ● Prepared charts and graphs ● Slides and overhead projector transparencies ● Pictures ● Sound recordings ● Product or other samples or examples ● Personal testimonies (from concerned persons). **Timing** ● Keep to a timetable ● Use frequent pauses ● Summarize regularly **Questions** ● Allow time for questions ● Don't embarrass or criticize questioners ● Clarify facts promptly ● Only delay answers where subject will be covered later. **Handouts** ● Give handouts where appropriate ● Prepare summaries of key points ● List action points ● Motivate positive action.	

Part Three

Sales Recruitment and Training

9

Recruitment and selection in the sales force

Overview of the recruitment process and key steps ▬▬▬

While motivation is a key management function, the sales manager must have the right material, in terms of suitably qualified salespersons, to motivate. That means selecting and recruiting to rigid criteria that are demonstrably relevant to successful achievement and high performance as salespersons, and then training those persons to meet the standards and perform the selling job as suits the company's products and markets. In this chapter the aim is to develop a formalized framework that sales managers responsible for all or part of selection and recruitment can adapt or adopt to reduce the risk of inappropriate selection of unsuitable salespersons. Typically each sales line manager is responsible for his or her own final selection of new members to his or her team.

Sales recruitment is a costly process, and poor selection results in:

- under-performance in sales activities
- a distraction of management time as more supervision is needed
- additional training needs
- higher staff turnover with resultant repeat recruitment costs.

The basic recruitment process is illustrated in Figure 9.1, but a flowchart format of presenting the process is shown in Figure 9.8 at the end of the chapter.

Qualities and skills of salespersons

When selecting and managing salespersons we need to develop a clear view of what personal qualities and job-related skills we might expect to find in our successful salesperson. Here we can expand on some general qualities and skills. Larger corporations often make use of corporate psychologists to conduct job holder profiling based on study of persons considered demonstrably successful (and comparing for differences with persons found to be less than successful) that can give a perspective of what to look for when recruiting to sales positions in a particular company.

The range of characteristic **qualities and attributes** needed in the successful salesperson (and sales manager!) may be considered to include those priority qualities and skills illustrated in Figure 9.2.

In a number of these areas of personal qualities you will be called on to make subjective judgements during the stages of a recruitment, but these should be supported through questioning and evaluation of comments at the selection stage, and by subsequent observation on the job. A high rating for a mix of these qualities being exhibited by a salesperson, when viewed with the assessment of more objective skills and competency factors, will provide a sounder basis for judging job applicants for sales positions.

As was mentioned in the section on **appraisals** (Chapter 6), a range of skills is

The basic recruitment steps

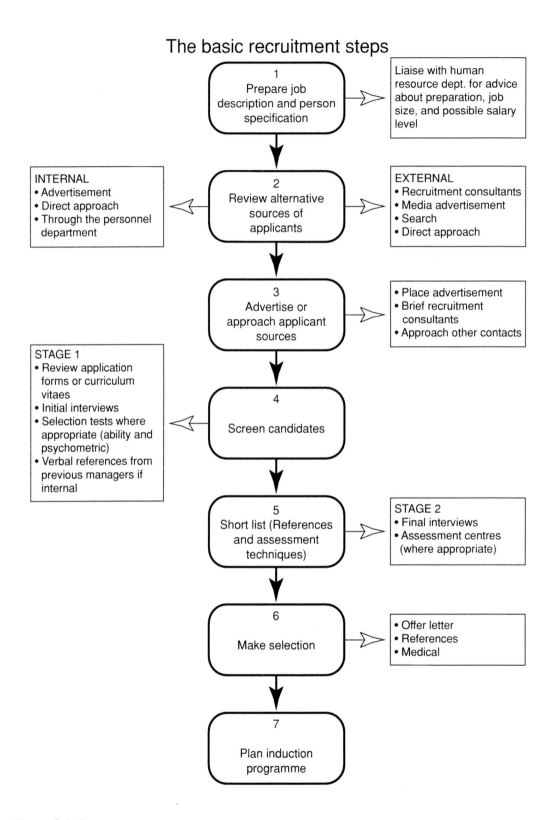

1
Prepare job description and person specification

Liaise with human resource dept. for advice about preparation, job size, and possible salary level

2
Review alternative sources of applicants

INTERNAL
• Advertisement
• Direct approach
• Through the personnel department

EXTERNAL
• Recruitment consultants
• Media advertisement
• Search
• Direct approach

3
Advertise or approach applicant sources

• Place advertisement
• Brief recruitment consultants
• Approach other contacts

STAGE 1
• Review application forms or curriculum vitaes
• Initial interviews
• Selection tests where appropriate (ability and psychometric)
• Verbal references from previous managers if internal

4
Screen candidates

5
Short list (References and assessment techniques)

STAGE 2
• Final interviews
• Assessment centres (where appropriate)

6
Make selection

• Offer letter
• References
• Medical

7
Plan induction programme

Figure 9.1 *Steps in a recruitment*

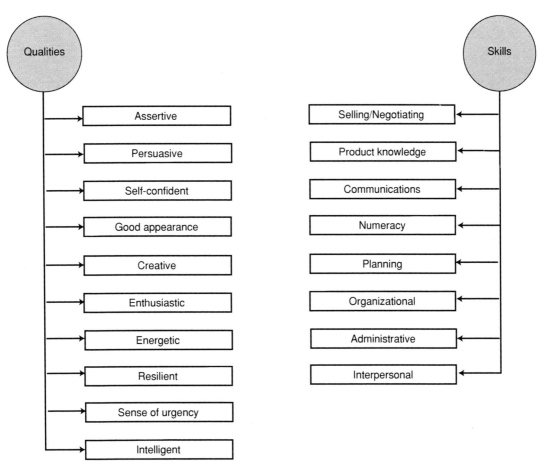

Figure 9.2 *Some key qualities and skills of salespersons*

needed by a salesperson, with additional skills needed by a sales manager. Typical skills needed by the salesperson include those listed in the following table.

In each of these areas we can form some objective measure of what is needed, and seek to identify a sufficient standard amongst job applicants during interviews, or to plan internal training of existing salespersons.

	Skills required of the salesperson
● **Selling**	An understanding of the selling and buying processes, and skill in the use of professional selling techniques is essential. A salesperson acquires these skills as a result of training and practice, not as an inherent talent, although a number of personal characteristics facilitate the process of acquiring skill.
● **Product knowledge**	Detailed product knowledge, and related company and marketing knowledge, is essential in selling. Without this the salesperson cannot match his products and programmes to the opportunities of the market place and needs of the customers.

● **Verbal**	The salesperson must be able to collect his or her thoughts and make clear, concise and logical presentations, using developed verbal skills, that hold the buyer's interest.
● **Numerical**	The necessary level of numerical skills will depend on the demands of a selling job. An account manager will need better developed skills than a territory salesperson. But all salespersons need sufficient numerical ability to understand data, prepare quotations or costings, calculate prices and volumes, etc.
● **Administrative**	Professional selling is not just about talking to customers, but needs an ability to keep good customer records and to handle and process the supporting sales force administrative paperwork (or manage information using computers).
● **Organizational**	The salesperson needs to be able to organize his or her workload, use of time, paperwork, promotional activities, etc.
● **Communicating**	Good communications skills are needed if the salesperson is not to experience problems resulting from communication breakdowns. Typically a salesperson must be fluent in verbal communications, and support that with skills in written communications, administrative and organizing aspects of the job as he or she liaises with customers, colleagues and the office support functions.
● **Planning**	Planning is a fundamental sales activity. Without good planning at the level of the territory and each customer, and the resultant implementation of plans, there will be an under-performance against targets and potential.
● **Interpersonal**	Selling and sales management are about inspiring and influencing people. This requires developing relationship building, people management, motivational and persuasive skills.

Job descriptions and person specifications

The starting point in the recruitment process is to develop a job description and person (job holder) specification.

Functions of a job description

A well-prepared job description serves several useful functions for the sales manager, including:

- as a basis for preparing personnel specifications
- clarifying job functions to sales managers and job holders
- providing a performance measurement base

- providing a base for appraisals and other formal and informal counselling
- aiding inter-job content comparisons
- facilitating job evaluations.

Poorly prepared job descriptions can produce demarcation disputes, cause interpersonal rivalries and jealousies, or result in unwarranted assumptions of authority by one person or another.

Content and coverage of a job description

Before you can recruit someone for a job you need to be clear on what the job is. It is important to be sure the job is quite distinct from jobs being done by other people in the sales organization, otherwise there is a risk of overlapping responsibilities, producing conflict or a failure by job holders to accept personal responsibility for actions or activities; for example, the salesperson's role could overlap with some responsibilities of key account managers, various managers in marketing or support functions, merchandisers or sales promoters.

Normally a job description should contain at least the information outlined in Table 9.1, although the style and format will vary between companies. The typical **job description** summarizes the nature of a job, its functions, responsibilities, duties and accountabilities, and key competencies of persons appointed to the position. The reader may already have job descriptions prepared in his or her company format, but if not should develop descriptions for all jobs within the sales organization.

Person specifications

Once you have a job description the next stage is to consider the kind of person you need to perform all the job functions. The qualities, skills and experience needed to fulfil the job can all be summarized in a **person specification** (or **job holder profile**), which is really just a pen sketch of the ideal job applicant. It can be used as a reference point when you are screening job application forms or conducting initial interviews.

When preparing person specifications some of the questions the sales manager should consider include the following.

- What are the present strengths and weaknesses of the team?
- What kind of personality will fit with the team?
- What skills/qualities in a new recruit will provide a better balance within the team?
- Do you need more graduate calibre salespersons?

- Do you need to increase the mix of salespersons with particular skills such as numeracy or familiarity with computers?
- Do you need a salesperson with established trade relations?
- Will special qualities and skills be needed to service any particular types of customer?
- Are there any special working hours for contacting customers that require particular flexibility or particular qualities/skills?

Some of the categories in which you might set **objective standards** include those illustrated in Tables 9.2 and 9.3, which show alternative approaches to designing personnel specifications.

The basic standards and requirements you include in the person specification should be factors that can be measured objectively, or where your personal assessment (if they are subjective factors) is critical in considering a job applicant. You really should only set a standard if the ability of an applicant to perform a particular job really may hinge on meeting that standard and an assessment can be made from application forms or at interviews. The minimum standards set in a personnel specification should be relevant to successful job performance, and optional standards can also be set in respect of qualities or skills that the ideal candidate additionally might possess. Persons who do not qualify in respect of minimum standards you set should not normally be interviewed or appointed.

Local laws relating to recruitment and employment vary round the world, and it is important that account is taken of these in developing job descriptions, person or job holder profiles, and the methods and manner of recruitment.

Table 9.1 Typical coverage of a job description

Information to be included in a job description	
Company name	The name of the local operating company
Operating divisions and/or department	e.g. Sales Division
Job title	Generally descriptive of the key function
Job holder's name	This can be inserted where appropriate
Reporting relationships	e.g. to the Regional Sales Manager
Purpose of the job	Provide a brief summary of the key elements of the job and what it is expected to achieve in the interests of the company. Key data that summarizes the size of the job might be inserted here, e.g.: ● numbers of direct and indirect subordinates ● numbers and sizes of sales accounts.
Job accountabilities	This section should describe the important end results (usually around 8 or 10 items) the job holder is expected to achieve. It should focus on stating what has to be achieved and why, not how it is to be achieved (which might be covered under the next section).
Job content and functions	Describe how the various accountabilities listed in this section are to be achieved. You could detail the main functions and activities, the main tasks of the job holder.
Job knowledge and competencies	Detail the main areas of experience, knowledge, skills and personal qualities needed to perform the job competently.
Decision making authority (this information should not be communicated at a candidate's first interview)	Describe the scope for decision making in the job, and the types of decisions the job holder is expected to make, and note any limits on authority. Any relevant quantitative factors should be noted, such as: ● sales and financial data ● expenditure, e.g. promotion budgets.
Relationships	Outline the key relationships with internal colleagues (e.g. line manager, colleagues in other departments, subordinates) and external contacts (e.g. customers). In some instances it will be appropriate to include an internal organization chart showing job functions, reporting relationships and other key functional relationships.
Additional information	This section can be used to add any additional information not covered in the other sections of the job description.

Table 9.2 *An example person specification*

Person specification		
Position:	*Territory salesperson*	
Reporting to:	*Area sales manager*	
Job requirements	**Essential**	**Optional**
Physical characteristics	● 1.70 metres ● Physically fit and able to merchandise product in company outlets ● No back problems or physical disabilities	
Attainments	● Secondary school education with certificates	● Completed education to 18 years with appropriate certificates ● Ideally with at least 2 years working experience in a sales position ● Formal sales skill training with consumer goods company
Special aptitudes		● Linguistic abilities
Personality/ Disposition	● Outgoing ● Persuasive ● Self-confident ● Enthusiastic ● Intelligent ● Determined/self-motivated	● Leadership qualities
Interests	● Social interests	● Preferably active, e.g. sports ● Preferably keeps up to date with current affairs, e.g. through reading
Circumstances	● Stable family background ● Mobile, with no restrictions travel ● Current driving licence	● Living close to territory ● Clean driving licence

Sourcing applicants for sales positions

Recruiting can be an expensive exercise in two respects:

1. the actual direct cost of seeking out suitable candidates and providing basic training
2. the resultant costs of mistakes if a person is wrongly recruited for a position for which he or she is unsuitable, or if he or she leaves for any reason within a short period after recruitment (where re-recruitment becomes necessary along with the repeat training costs).

At the stage of seeking suitable candidates you need to consider what alternative **sources** might produce suitable potential job candidates. Some of the more common sources to be considered include those illustrated in Figure 9.3.

Table 9.3 *An alternative person specification format*

Person specification		
Position:	Territory salesperson	
Reporting to:	Area sales manager	
Attribute	**Definition**	**Assessment technique**
Educational attainments	● School and college attendance and achievements ● Post full time education courses ● Professional training or courses related to career	● Application form ● Check documentation
Appearance and physical characteristics	● Smart, clean-cut look, with well-kept clothes ● Makes a good first impression ● Physical build suited to performing all job functions	● Observation at interview
Work experience	● Ideally with at least 3 years selling experience gained in a major international company servicing similar outlets ● Able to demonstrate positive contributions to progress and growth with previous companies ● Preferably with formal training in selling and negotiation techniques ● Used to dealing with senior-level customer contacts and clients	● Application form ● Interviews ● References checks
Abilities, skills, competencies	● Professional selling: can work to a structured sales sequence, use questioning techniques, make fluent rational presentations, handle objections, close the sale etc. ● Negotiation: able to develop a win-win scenario ● Verbal: speaks fluently and persuasively, and able to construct a reasoned presentation ● Numerical: able to analyse, compute, interpret numerical sales-related data ● Administration: able to understand and comply with all sales administration requirements ● Organization: well organized in use of time, materials, paperwork, etc. ● Communications: a fluent and effective communicator both internally (colleagues) and externally (customers), in both written and verbal forms ● Planning: thinks ahead, sets objectives and makes and implements plans to achieve them, and able to deal with crises in a positive rather than negative fashion	● Interviews and selection tests

Table 9.3 An alternative person specification format (continued)

Attribute	Definition technique	Assessment
Personality disposition	<ul><li>Assertiveness: persuasive and strong-willed in negotiating</li><li>Self-confidence: self-assured and willing to take the initiative</li><li>Creative: able to see other perspectives and to use imagination to try out new approaches</li><li>Enthusiastic: presenting a positive and zealous attitude</li><li>Persistent: continues firmly in the face of adversity or problems</li><li>Resilient: able to bounce back from unsuccessful negotiations with a positive mental attitude</li><li>Energetic: proactive in getting things done, and not easily tired from work activities</li><li>Intelligent: able to handle all the functional activities of the job, to reason rationally, to evaluate situations thoughtfully, and to propose creative courses of action</li><li>Good communicator: keeps all interested parties informed of developments through written or verbal communications</li><li>Business oriented: a hard-nosed profit conscious businessperson</li></ul>	<ul><li>Interviews and objective selection tests</li></ul>
Health	<ul><li>No physical disabilities limiting ability to perform job functions including carrying and driving</li></ul>	<ul><li>Observation at interview</li><li>Company pre-employment medical</li></ul>
Personal circumstances	<ul><li>Stable home environment</li><li>Mobility and freedom to stay away from home as the needs of the job dictate</li><li>Home location suited to work environment</li><li>Current driving licence</li></ul>	<ul><li>Application form</li><li>Interviews</li><li>Check documentation</li></ul>

Job application forms

Many companies develop a standard job application form. The advantage of using a standard form (either instead of, or to supplement, individual application letters and curriculum vitae) is that managers can see all the relevant information and responses in a standard layout, making it quicker to screen applications. Individual letters and curriculum vitae are prepared by the individual applicant and focus on telling you what they want you to know rather than what you decide you want to know about the person.

The basic information a job application might request include:

- full name of applicant
- date of birth, age

Figure 9.3 *Sources of applicants*

- nationality
- sex
- ethnic origin
- marital status
- children/dependants
- address and telephone number (and fax/electronic mail)
- medical history (including information on recurring ailments and disabilities)
- physical characteristics (height/weight)
- driving licence, driving record
- education
  - primary schools
  - secondary schools and examination results
  - higher education and examination
    results and qualifications achieved
  - other courses attended
- employment history
  - positions held
  - dates applicable to each position
  - summary of key functions and responsibilities
  - current income
  - reasons for wanting to change jobs
  - period of notice required at present employment
- trade or professional qualifications and membership of professional institutions
- personal interests
- personal references

- special aptitudes (e.g. languages spoken)
- supplementary (i.e. a space that invites applicants to comment on any relevant additional information).

Guidelines for press advertisements

While an advertisement is intended to attract a number of suitably qualified applicants it should not be so inviting as to encourage applications from persons clearly outside the limits of physical and personal characteristics and qualities contained in the person specification. The description of the skills, experience, personal characteristics and qualifications given in an advertisement should enable potential candidates to screen themselves in respect of their ability to match the criteria.

Coverage of advertisements

The actual content of the advertisement should give brief coverage to a range of information that helps the potential applicants decide if they have the qualifications and interest to pursue an application by sending in a curriculum vitae or requesting an application form. You should include:

- **The job title** e.g. Territory salesperson, key accounts manager, area sales manager, etc.
- **The company name and logo**. Identify who you are, with pride in your company and heritage. Some advertisers prefer to remain anonymous, possibly using post office box numbers or recruitment agencies. This tends to be preferred when there are strong reasons why you do not want others within the company to know about a recruitment.
- **The products**. Clarify the nature of your products, and the markets you are serving, possibly with a product illustration if appropriate (a useful way of attracting attention to an advertisement, particularly

if you have an established product).
- **The job functions**. State the basic key functions, accountabilities and responsibilities that help a potential applicant relate to his or her present experience.
- **Location or territory to be covered**. State clearly where the job will be based, as the issue of relocation can be a factor in attracting to, or detracting from, the job.
- **Candidate skill and qualification requirements**. State what minimum related sales or sales management experience, and other experience, you expect.
- **Rewards and benefits offered**. While in some countries, or within some companies, it is the practice not to disclose pay and benefits (e.g. 'An attractive package will be offered, commensurate with skills and experience'), most applicants prefer a clear statement of the range of rewards and benefits they might expect, as this influences a decision to apply.
- **Details of how to apply for the vacancy**. You might note if you want applicants to phone in for an application form or to send a curriculum vitae.

Screening applicants

Screening applicants is the process of comparing the various candidates for a position with the qualities, skills and experience judged necessary to fulfil the job functions satisfactorily. The usual screening stages are:

- issue job application forms
- study (screen) completed application forms, comparing them against the person specification
- reject unsuitable applicants (usually by letter)
- invite most suitable applicants to interviews.

Normally the first stage in the applicant screening process is to provide applicants with a **job application form**. The advantage of using a job application form is that all the basic information you require in deciding who to invite for interview, or what to pursue during the interview, is presented in a standard format, which saves you time hunting for relevant information. The alternative to asking for the completion of job application forms is to request the submission of a personally prepared **curriculum vitae**. Study the completed application forms, and invite the most suitable applicants for an interview, allocating time exclusively to the interviewing process.

In studying completed application forms it is normal to look at factors such as those listed below, and judge how these match your requirements.

- Applicant home location in relation to the job location
- Holding a clean current driving licence
- Age in relation to specified range
- Relevance of job experience
- Any evidence of formal training in selling skills
- Relevance of vocational education and professional qualifications
- Educational standards and achievements
- Comparison of educational achievements and job progression with successful company salespersons
- Health conditions (poor health is a negative factor, obviously)
- Personality and disposition
- Personal hobbies and interests
- Achievement relative to peer group norms
- Motivation and potential.

At the pre-interview stage of screening job application forms you should really be concentrating on **objective criteria** and trying to avoid rejecting applications for emotional or subjective reasons. As a rule you cannot attach much importance to handwriting or presentation unless it is apparent the applicant lacks sufficient literacy for the job.

The most suitable candidates can be invited to initial interviews either over the telephone or by letter. A rejection letter should be designed to leave rejected applicants (before or after interview) well disposed to the company – they are or might be customers!

Screening applicant interests

While it may be subjective to attach much importance to hobbies and interests prior to an interview, sometimes these can indicate special skills or attributes. For example: an applicant might be a youth group leader, or have intellectual interests such as chess or home computing, or pursue some other interest that indicates something about his or her personality, motivations or abilities.

Interests are particularly useful as an ice breaker in the opening minutes of an interview, and may provide some guidance to a candidate's motivations and disposition.

In the interview you can probe the **breadth**, **depth**, **pattern**, **commitment** (will the hobby conflict in any way with demands of the job), **stability/maturity**, **skills** and **knowledge** involved, **personal motivations** to pursue interests, and **relevancy** of interest to the job. Generally interests may be considered to fall into the broad categories of:

- social
- intellectual
- practical
- physically active
- artistic.

Communicating with unsuccessful applicants

As a matter of courtesy and goodwill you should communicate promptly with all unsuccessful candidates who have submitted a completed application form. It is important that rejected applicants still maintain a high degree of goodwill to the company as they and their contacts are all potential customers, and a well-conducted recruitment offers another excellent opportunity to promote goodwill for your business in the local community.

Conducting interviews ■■■■■■

The selection process will normally take more than one interview, possibly supported by other forms of assessment tests. Candidates you consider most suitable should be invited for interview (by letter or telephone) with you or a personnel manager as soon as possible, and if you plan to use other assessment techniques the candidates should be notified of that, and advised of the duration of the selection process.

The interview environment ——————

The interview stage of the recruitment process should be treated as systematically as each of the preliminary selection stages of exploring alternative applicant sources, advertising and screening applications (see Figure 9.4). It is unwise to try to slot interviews in between other appointments and management activities. Comparisons will be less meaningful and interviews less thorough if you see individual job applicants under widely divergent circumstances at different times.

- Allocate a specific time period (a day, morning, or whatever is needed) to the interviewing of applicants.
- Conduct all interviews without interruptions in suitably private locations such as your office or a hotel room.

Duration of the interview ——————

The time you need to allocate to an interview so that you can satisfy yourself you have formed an objective assessment of a job applicant will vary according to your personal interviewing skills. Generally you should expect to allow about 30 to 60 minutes per candidate at a first interview. Experience will show that a good proportion of candidates can be eliminated objectively within 15 to 30 minutes, where they fail to match the personnel specification for qualities, skills and experience.

Interview conduct and content ———

The way you conduct the interview and its general content is critical to obtaining relevant information to enable you to evaluate candidates in the minimum time.

The possible broad **structure** of the interview process could consist of:

1. **Personal introductions.** Introduce yourself by name and position so that the candidate does know whom he or she is talking to; candidates are frequently nervous and a smile always goes a long way towards relaxing a nervous interviewee.
2. **Introduction to the company, the products and the job.** Ideally this should take no longer than five minutes. Prepare notes on your introductory presentation to ensure you cover all the main points systematically. It is also useful to have some product samples and literature in the interview room.

The introductory commentary should cover:

- a brief history of the company and outline of main company philosophies
- a product range summary (best shown by photographs and examples)
- the job functions (you can provide a job description now or while the candidate is waiting for the interview)
- the main terms and conditions of employment.

3. **The actual interview.**

At this stage, as the objective is to interview the candidate rather than the reverse, it is unwise to permit yourself to wander off at a tangent in response to distracting questions or comments. If a question is raised which you will cover in your introductory commentary you can just delay response with a comment such as 'That is an important point, and I do plan to comment on that in a moment.'

Format of the interview ——————

The format of an interview will vary according to your personal experience and inter-

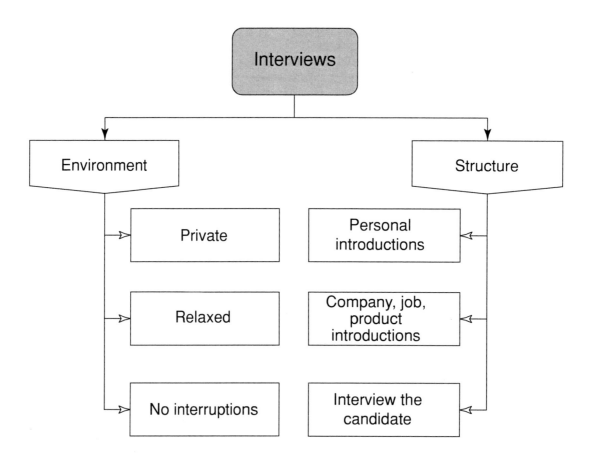

Figure 9.4 *The structure and environment of interviews*

view style, but some useful guidelines of **'do's and don'ts'** are shown in a checklist at the end of this chapter.

At the outset, in getting yourself into the interview frame of mind, ask yourself two questions:

'Do I know what I am looking for?'
'Will I recognize it when I do see it?'

You will find that the actual conduct of an interview is easiest if it follows a simple chronological pattern. Your objective is to elicit information on aspects of a person's experience, background circumstances and personality that will impact on his or her ability to integrate into the company team and effectively perform the job functions you assign to him or her.

The eight-point interview framework

This structured system encourages you, the interviewer, to ask questions and make objective observations about the candidate by eliciting relevant information in a number of key areas illustrated in Figure 9.5, and expanded in the checklist at the end of this chapter. Observations and judgements based on the interviews can then be supplemented by objective assessments and further judgements based on any other assessment techniques (e.g. aptitude tests, assessment centres, or personality profiles) used by the recruiting sales managers.

The simplest way for you to progress an interview is to work systematically through the information contained on the job applica-

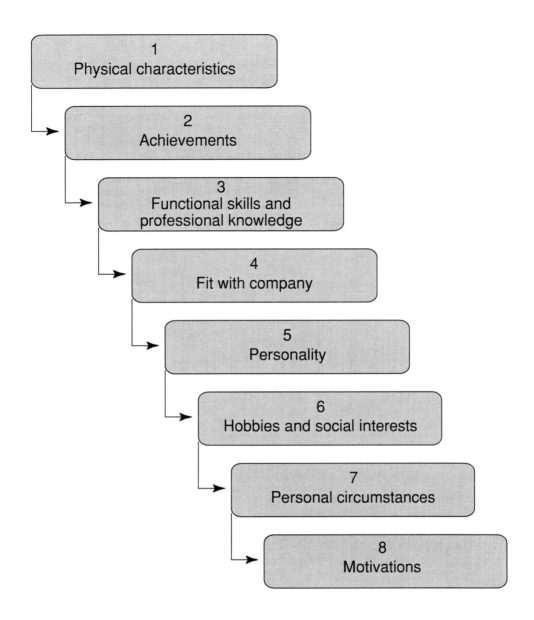

Figure 9.5 *The eight-point interview framework*

tion form and constantly use questions to expand on the facts contained in the form and to make observations and notes, to help you form judgements and opinions.

Notes at interviews

When conducting an interview you will need to make brief notes as a record of what you have discovered in addition to the information contained in the **job application form**, and to record your observations and conclusions. The notes will act as a pen picture later when you come to review the merits of each of the applicants you have seen.

It is useful to highlight on the **interview notes record** any points that might need further probing at the shortlist interview.

The selection shortlist

Once the first interviews have taken place, and objective decisions made about which candidates warrant further consideration, a second meeting with each of the shortlisted candidates should take place to further probe their suitabilities, skills and experiences. The shortlist interview can also provide additional information on the company and the specific job vacancy. This shortlist interview should be conducted within as brief a time interval as possible after the first interview. With an internal recruitment the first interview may be the only stage, or it may be supported by other tests. The typical shortlist process may be summarized as in Figure 9.6. The objectives of a short-list procedure are to:

- call back those candidates judged most likely to meet the requirements of the job and to elicit additional information about their suitability to the job and the company environment
- give other persons in the company team a chance to meet the candidates and provide an input to their suitability
- allow the candidate time to become more familiar with the company environment and team in order that he or she can

make fair decisions about joining the company if made a job offer. (It can be very useful to allow the candidates to meet other salespersons, and perhaps also to arrange for the most suitable candidates to spend some time with an established salesperson calling on a few customers.)
- provide an opportunity for company managers to meet a range of candidates, each of whom has been judged at the initial recruitment stages as having relevant skills, experience and personal attributes warranting their further consideration.

In most markets reliance will be upon selection through second interviews, often with a colleague involved, i.e. a personnel manager or senior sales manager.

At the shortlist stage it may prove appropriate, for certain positions, to support interviews with additional assessment techniques, such as additional intelligence or aptitude tests, group selection activities, or individual tasks. If these are appropriate then they should be discussed and developed with your human resource department, and administered by a person trained in their use and interpretation in the selection process.

Depending on the level of the position to be filled, and local recruitment practices, the shortlist procedure could include any or all of the stages outlined in the table on page 130.

In many markets it is found to be a very useful exercise to ask the final candidates, prior to a job offer being made or accepted, to spend a day with an established salesperson calling on trade outlets and observing the normal job functions. This serves to clarify to the candidate the real nature of the job and reduces the risk of successful applicants subsequently being dissatisfied with the job content.

Group selection tasks

While aptitude, personality and intelligence tests will normally be administered by trained professionals, when used as part of the selection process, the sales manager

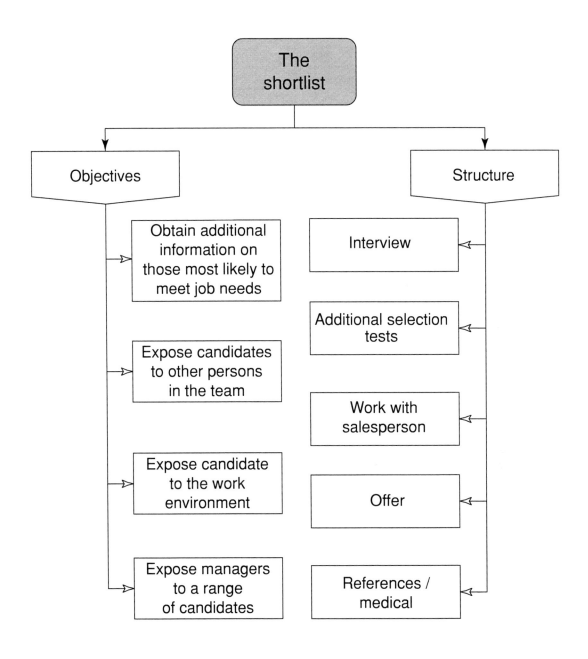

Figure 9.6 *Objectives and structure of a typical shortlist process*

would normally be involved as an observer in any other individual or group tasks that form a part of the selection process. Group tasks normally involve from four to eight candidates being brought together at a shortlist venue and being given a project or task to tackle for a defined time period. If this process is used candidates should be advised

---

Typical activity processes at the selection shortlist stage

Interviews	● Panel interviews with several company managers (usually from sales and human resource departments)
	● Individual interviews separately with sales and personnel managers
Additional selection tests	● Intelligence or aptitude tests
	● Personality tests
	● Group selection tasks
	(where a group of job candidates is invited to perform a group task together in order that interviewers can make objective interpersonal comparisons on the relative suitability of each for the company environment, and respective strengths and skills)
Individual tasks	● In some instances individual applicants might be asked to perform a skill-related task to assess their abilities and aptitudes. Some examples of individual tasks include:
	– placing merchandising materials in strategic locations
	– space management exercises
	– role playing sales presentations
	– analysing and interpreting sales data
	– drafting or constructing a letter to customers
Making a job offer	● At this stage the manager will decide the relative strengths and weaknesses of each applicant, and evaluate their respective qualities, attributes, skills and experience in relation to the needs of the job and the team
Taking references	● This is covered separately in the next section
Medical reports	● Most companies require all recruits to the sales team to undertake medical tests, just to ensure that they have no pre-existing conditions that might impact on ability to perform the job functions

---

of this before being invited to the shortlist selection process.

The group selection process is particularly valuable in external management recruitments where the candidates are unknown to the recruiting line managers. A group task might be as simple as giving the group a pile of paper and handful of paper clips, and asking them to design and construct a paper tower, or might just consist of the group being given a subject to discuss (either job-neutral or job-related) for a set time period, or a business case study exercise. It is not the specific task that is important in making group tasks valuable recruitment aids, but the content and process of inputs within the group.

The aim of group task observers is to evaluate the performance of each group participant, and to assess his or her contribution, qualities and skills as demonstrated in the task and in relation to those required of the appointee to the vacant job (see table on page 132).

When observing group tasks the panel members should make notes, and remain quiet during the group's activity, holding evaluatory discussions afterwards. Discussion should focus on **content** and **process** (see Figure 9.7) in the group activity, and relate those to the job and its environment. It is particularly worth noting that the group member who makes the most noise and

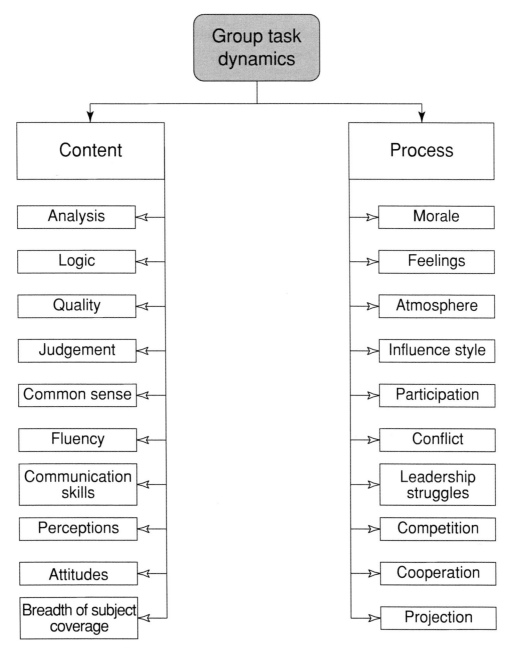

Figure 9.7 *Group task dynamics*

appears to be the most active might not be the most influential, effective in achieving a solution, or acceptable within the group.

Checking references

Prior to making a formal job offer, but after completing the selection process to the point where you have a favoured candidate, you should take references on the prospective appointee (with his or her consent). In some companies this may be undertaken by a human resource manager, but in others it will fall to the line manager. Where that is not the case the following guidelines will aid the sales manager in taking references.

Some behaviours to look for when observing group tasks

Participation	● Who exhibits high or low levels of participation?
Degrees of influence	● Who exhibits high or low degrees of influence?
	● Rivalries – do they develop and between whom?
Styles of influence	● Who are the autocrats?
	● Who are the democrats?
	● Who are the mediators?
	● Who takes a laissez faire attitude?
Task functions	● Who are the controllers?
	● Who are the strategists?
	● Who are the analysts?
Decision-making procedures	● Self-authorized decision taker?
	● Decision supporter?
	● Topic jumpers?
	● Majority decision (votes)?
	● Consensus of opinions?
	● Unrecognized contributions?
Maintenance functions	● Who involves others in the task?
	● Who blocks others' participation?
	● Who clarifies others' comments?
	● Who remains preoccupied?
	● How are ideas accepted/rejected?
	● How effective is each group member at communicating?
Group atmosphere	● Who avoids conflict?
	● Who prefers conflict?
	● Who resolves conflict?
	● Are participants involved and interested?
	● How relaxed is the atmosphere?
	● What is the pace?
Group membership	● What sub-groupings develop?
	● How do sub-groups relate to the rest of the group?
	● Do developing sub-groups reflect agreement/disagreement?
Group feelings	● What physical and emotional reactions are indicated by facial, verbal or other physical (body language) expression (e.g. anger, irritation, contempt, frustration, impatience, intolerance, pleasure, warmth, affection, friendliness, enthusiasm, excitement, boredom, competitiveness, sensitivity, etc.)
Group norms	● What group norms develop? (e.g. Are some topics avoided?)
	● Who reinforces avoidance and how?
	● Group formality/informality?
	● Group harmony/disharmony?
	● Open expressions of feelings or hiding of feelings?
	● Accepted styles of participation?

Sometimes a job offer is made orally in the first instance, but it should be made conditional upon satisfactory references being received. A conditional offer by letter avoids the risk of later misunderstandings. (Note that in some countries the taking of references from employers is not permitted.)

Personal references from friends acting as referees carry less weight than a reference from a current or former employer of a job applicant. Good sources of reference include:

- a former line superior, who can provide insight into a candidate's performance against objectives, job achievements, skills, abilities, strengths, potential, management style, etc.
- a peer group colleague, who may provide insight into how the candidate works within a team, interacting with colleagues, and earns and builds respect
- a subordinate, who may provide insight

into management style, team building and leadership skills, training and feedback skills, etc.

References are usually best taken over the telephone. Letters tend to be replied to slowly, if at all, and produce minimum factual information. Table 9.4 illustrates the who, what and how of taking references.

The person asked to give a reference will respond more positively if you identify yourself and confirm you call with the candidate's permission, and if the referee has been forewarned by the candidate to expect the call. Also, make a note of the key points. It is usually best to do this on a structured reference-taking form, such as that illustrated in Table 9.4.

During a reference-taking conversation it is always best to start with a few basic questions that are aimed to verify facts, as that usually will relax the referee more towards

	Telephone references: some pointers
Verify:	• relationship of referee to applicant
	• employment dates
	• job functions and responsibilities
	• present reported income
	• fringe benefits
	• job attendance record
	• time keeping record
	• sick leave and health record
Question:	• job performance, key achievements and progress versus colleagues
	• general job-related skills and competencies
	• planning and organizing competencies
	• management style (when recruiting for sales management jobs)
	• time management, including meeting deadlines
	• team spirit and ability to work with customers and colleagues
	• reasons for leaving
	• character assessment
	• integrity
	• reliability
	• independence
	• motivations
	• drive and energy
	• leadership
	• ability to influence others
	• adaptability
	• creativity

Table 9.4 *An example of a form for recording reference notes*

Reference notes	
Candidate:	
Position:	
Reference source:	
Employment history Probe with questions about: ● employment dates ● positions held ● job functions and responsibilities ● income and benefits ● health record ● time keeping	
Achievements and style Probe with questions about: ● job performance ● key achievements ● management style ● ability to influence and persuasiveness ● planning and organizing abilities ● time management ● creativity and promotion of change	
Personality and character assessment Probe with questions about: ● integrity ● reliability ● independence ● drive and determination ● motivations ● adaptability ● acceptability to colleagues ● team spirit	

Implications for company and summary
● Fit with the company
  – skills
  – experience
  – personality	

Date:	**Reference taken by:**

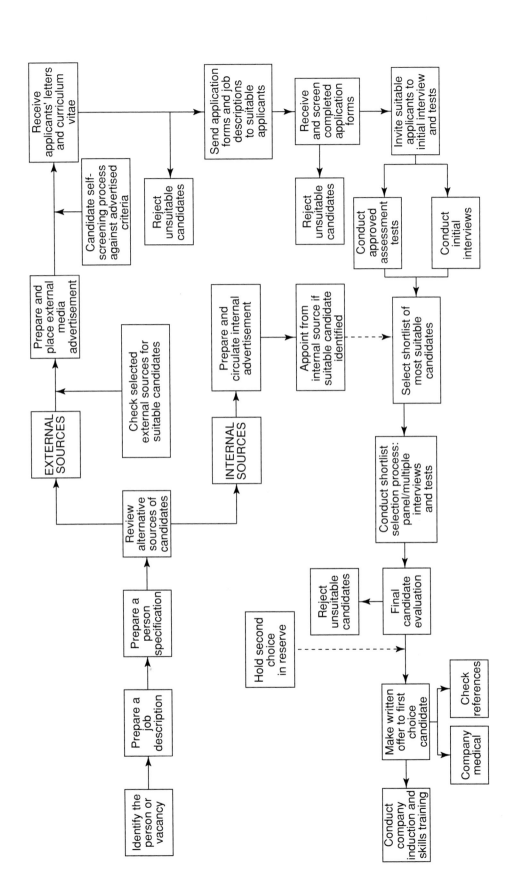

Figure 9.8 The recruitment process flow chart

you, and start the flow of information. Then you can proceed to elicit some additional information with **open questions**, e.g.:

- 'How would you describe his/her work and performance?'
- 'How does he/she get on with the other staff and supervisors?'
- 'Would you re-employ him/her?'
- 'What have you found to be his/her main strengths and weaknesses?'
- 'Is there anything else you think I should know about his/ her work, personality or background before offering a job?'

Making the selection

When the sales manager has made his or her decision on whom to offer a sales position to, and if all the references taken are judged satisfactory, then the last stages in the recruitment process are:

- sending a Letter of Appointment to the selected person
- sending 'No' letters to the unsuccessful candidates
- organizing the welcome and induction process and training for the new recruit.

Some or all of these actions might be under-taken by a human resource department in some companies, but where the sales manager is responsible for all stages of his or her own recruitment, it is very important in the interests of goodwill and professionalism that he or she communicates promptly with all unsuccessful interviewees as well as making a formal job offer in writing to the successful candidate.

The **job offer** letter should detail all the terms and conditions relating to employment with the company in the local market, and will normally include, either in the actual letter or in accompanying documents such as an **employee handbook**, details of:

- basic pay
- bonus and incentive schemes
- hours of work
- other conditions of employment, e.g. flexibility to travel
- expense allowances or claim procedures
- company vehicle
- other fringe benefits
- sickness benefits if applicable
- pension arrangements if applicable
- starting dates
- any other arrangements for joining the company
- detailed job responsibilities (i.e. a copy of the job description).

**Checklist 9.1
Recruitment stages**

	Action points

Job description
● Is it current?
● Has it been checked against functions of current job holders?

Job holder profile (person specification)
● Is it current?
● Has it been checked against successful job holders?

Sources of applicants
● What sources have been checked and researched?
Internal transfers and promotion?
   – Advertisements?
   – Other referrals?
   – Educational and professional institutions?
   – Trade competitors?
   – Employment agencies and recruitment consultancies?
   – Personal contacts?
   – Speculative applications?

Job application form
● Is it suited to sales recruiting?
● Does it ask relevant questions to facilitate pre-interview screening of applicants?
● Has it been sent to all applicants?

Job advertisement
● Does it:
   – attract attention?
   – arouse interest?
   – sell the benefits of the job?
   – provoke positive response from suitable candidates?
   – identify the company?
   – describe the job?
   – give the job location?
   – identify candidate qualifications?
   – state job rewards and benefits?
   – tell how to apply?
● Has the advertisement been placed with the most appropriate media?

Telephone screening of applicants
● Is it appropriate for the position?
● Has a screening question form been prepared?
● Does the advertisement give the phone-in details?

	Action points
Checklist 9.1 continued **Application screening** ● Have application forms been sent to all candidates? ● Has all screening been conducted objectively against the job holder profile? ● Have applications been acknowledged? ● Have invitations to interviews been sent? ● Have rejection letters been sent? **Initial interviews** ● Have dates and locations been arranged? ● Have all interviews been conducted? ● Have post-interview rejection letters been sent? ● Have shortlist invitations been sent? **Shortlist** ● Have dates and locations been arranged? ● Have any other interviewers been notified to attend? ● Have interviews been conducted? ● Have any additional selection techniques been completed, e.g. intelligence, personality or aptitude tests? ● Have rejection letters been sent to unsuccessful applicants? **References** ● Have former employers been contacted for references? ● Have other personal referees been contacted? ● Are references satisfactory? **Appointment letter** ● Has a letter of appointment been sent? ● Does it cover all the terms and conditions of employment? ● Has the offer been accepted?	

Checklist 9.2
Interview guidelines

Action points

Do adopt the following positive technique guidelines
- **Choose an informal interview environment**
  This is more likely to relax a candidate, e.g. possibly use a coffee table and easy chairs rather than across-the-desk interview.
- **Control the interview**
  Direct its contents along lines that help you to form objective assessments of each candidate's suitability to the company and the job.
- **Structure the interview round a framework**
  It is easiest to follow chronological events or circumstances using the job application form as a guide, and elicit relevant information about each candidate, e.g.
  - impact on other people
  - qualifications and experience
  - innate abilities
  - motivation
  - personality/disposition and adjustment
- **Project a friendly interest and atmosphere**
  The candidate should feel your warmth, empathy, sincerity, and interest.
- **Keep to a logical sequence**
  Avoid topic-jumping in a manner that seems irrelevant to the candidate.
- **Link questions to replies**
  By linking the next question to the last reply you will encourage the flow of information.
- **Ask open questions**
  Questions that demand more than just a simple yes/no answer will encourage the candidate to expand and give you more interesting information upon which to base judgements.
- **Give thinking time**
  Do not pressure the candidate to answer too quickly but relax him or her by waiting for answers.
- **Ask probing questions**
  Try to get to the issues behind the facts (e.g. 'Why did you choose to resign from your last job without another job waiting for you?').

	Action points

Checklist 9.2 continued
● **Use expansionary comments**
  More information can often be encouraged from a candidate by the use of expansionary comments such as 'and what happened then?'.
● **Do not be afraid of silence**
  This can be used as an effective tool to encourage a candidate to continue talking and to expand on earlier comments.
Avoid the following bad interview habits
● Do not project any prejudices during an interview
● Do not use exaggerated or distracting mannerisms
● Avoid projecting your own personality into the interview
● Avoid multiple questions
● Avoid leading questions
● Avoid technical jargon
● Avoid direct or implied criticism	

Action points

Physical characteristics
● Has the candidate any visible defects of health or physique that could present a problem in performing the salesperson's job functions?
● Is the candidate's appearance, bearing, presentation and speech suitable to represent the company?

Achievements
● What are the candidate's formal education achievements?
● Does the candidate's response to interview questions reflect educational/work achievements?
● How does the candidate respond to information you provide during the interview?
● Does the candidate appear to learn quickly?
● What type of formal education has the candidate had, and what standards did he/she attain?
● How well has the candidate progressed (in work)?
● Are there any distinguishing specific personal achievements versus the peer group?
● What occupational experience and training has he/she had, and is it relevant to the present vacancy?
● What are the candidate's personal contribution to change, business development, creativity, etc.?
● What have been his/her reasons for changing jobs (e.g. dissatisfaction with employers, seeking faster progression, etc.)?

Functional skills and professional knowledge
● Is the candidate able to sell?
● What relevant training and experience has the candidate had?
● Has the candidate negotiating skills?
● Has the candidate any special trade knowledge or relationships of value to the company?
● How good are the candidate's verbal communications?
● How good are the candidate's written communications?
● Has the candidate sufficient numeracy and analytical ability?
● How is the candidate's organizational ability and time management?
● Does the candidate demonstrate planning ability?
● Are the candidate's interpersonal skills suited to the job?
● What potential may this candidate have?
● Does the candidate have a broad business knowledge?

Checklist 9.3 continued	**Action points**
Fit with company ● Does the candidate have relevant knowledge about the company and its products? ● Has the candidate apparent networking skills? ● Will the candidate make a good team member, and enhance team spirit? ● Has the candidate any other cross-functional experience relevant to the position or the company? ● Will the candidate blend into a cross-cultural environment? ● Has the candidate any demonstrable linguistic abilities? ● How will the candidate fit into the existing sales/marketing team? ● How compatible are the candidate's skills, experience and personality with the company's values and principles? **Disposition/personality** ● Is the candidate committed to achieving results? ● Has the candidate an ability to motivate customers? ● Is the candidate a self-starter, demonstrating drive and initiative? ● How does the candidate work within a team? ● Does the candidate influence others? ● Does the candidate demonstrate a problem solving capability? **Hobbies and social interests** ● To what extent are the candidate's interests intellectual, social, practical, active or cultural? ● What motivates him/her to pursue interests? **Personal circumstances** ● Will the candidate's domestic circumstances impact on the job? ● Is the family background relevant? ● Does the candidate project any particular attitudes (religious, social, economic)? **Motivations** ● What have been his or her main motivations in life? ● What motivated particular courses of action at critical career points? ● Does the candidate exhibit obvious motivational drives? ● Why is the candidate interested in the job?	

Action points

Taking a reference on a candidate from a current or previous employer is the sales manager's opportunity to:
- **Verify**
  - Relationship of referee to applicant
  - Employment dates
  - Job functions and responsibilities
  - Present reported income and fringe benefits
  - Job attendance and time-keeping record
  - Sick leave and health record
- **Question**
  - Job performance, key achievements and progress versus colleagues
  - General job-related skills and competencies
  - Planning and organizing competencies
  - Management style (if recruiting for sales management jobs)
  - Time management, including meeting deadlines
  - Team spirit and ability to work with customers and colleagues
  - Reasons for leaving
  - Character assessment – Integrity; Reliability; Independence; Motivations; Drive and energy; Leadership; Ability to influence others; Adaptability; Creativity
- Identify yourself to the referee and confirm you call with the candidate's permission.
- During a reference-taking conversation it is always best to start with a few basic questions that are aimed to verify facts, as that usually will relax the referee more towards you, and start the flow of information.
- Elicit additional information with open questions, e.g.
  - How would you describe his/her work and performance?'
  - 'How does he/she get on with the other staff and supervisors?'
  - 'Would you re-employ him/her?'
  - 'What have you found to be his/her main strengths and weaknesses?'
  - Is there anything else you think I should know about his/her work, personality or background before offering a job?'
- **Record telephone reference notes on a reference form**

10

Basic sales training

The training of sales team subordinates is a fundamental responsibility of the sales manager. He or she can delegate that responsibility to a sales training manager or to individual field sales line managers, each of whom is accountable for the performance of their direct subordinate team. But the company sales manager cannot abdicate the sales training responsibility.

The role of training in the sales force

Why train?

The purpose of training is to improve the overall competence of members of a sales team, and this is usually tackled by sales managers working to:

- impart knowledge of the company, its products, and its markets
- create or change attitudes that affect performance
- develop skills that increase performance
- develop habits that contribute to improved performance
- reduce the level of field management supervision subsequently needed, or to

enable managers to widen their span of control and take on other duties or more subordinates
- increase job satisfaction (reducing sales force turnover).

Some of the basic competencies in a selling and sales management environment are listed below.

For these competencies to be exhibited it is essential that managers clarify the specialist and generalist skills that develop these competencies, and provide training. The skills should be supported by appropriate systems and procedures that aid implementation and use of the skills, and measure and monitor performance.

Figure 10.1 highlights the stages in developing training from concept through to performance improvement and measurement.

Managing to key result areas

The key to creating improved performance is illustrated in Figure 10.2, the model of the process for managing to key result areas. The sales manager can adapt this process model, identify the key sales result areas for the business, and focus each subsequent stage towards those, i.e.:

Some competencies in selling

- Influence (over people and performance)
- Interpersonal skills
- Teamwork

- Organization and planning
- Business and commercial skills
- Creativity

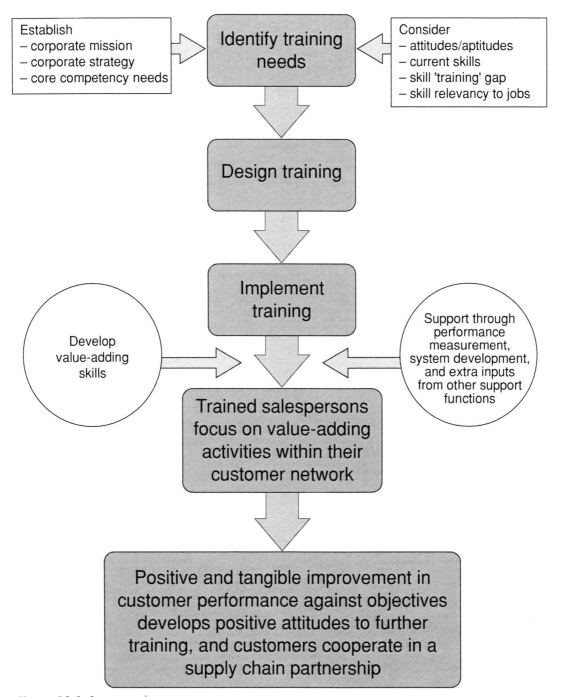

Figure 10.1 *Stages in the training process*

- by measuring current performance at each level that influences results (the store and down to the individual salesperson)
- setting standards and establish key result area goals and objectives
- training against the key result areas (quantitative and qualitative)
- then monitoring subsequent performance and providing frequent feedback

- linking the rewards and incentives to team and individual achievement against the factors that create improvement in the key result areas.

Figure 10.2 shows that we must start by identifying for any job activity the key result areas – the things that job holders influence or can do that contribute to quantitative or qualitative results. From that point we can move forward through the framework model to develop measurements, goals and objectives for the jobs, relevant training to improve performance, and packages of rewards and incentives that recognize performance improvements and achievements against the goals and objectives.

A loss of focus or under-performance will result if any stage of the process is not adhered to and followed through as part of the whole, for example:

- setting goals/objectives has little meaning if they are not related to measurable achievements, or if feedback does not show periodic achievement and foster corrective action for deviations
- training will be less effective if individual feedback is not given on resultant changes in performance
- rewards and incentives will not be motivational if individual measurements are not made and fed back, and if training is not geared primarily to improvement in the key result areas.

The focus of sales training

Sales training should be directed towards the following key result areas:

- better territory and account management, including identifying potential new customers and planning call coverage
- improved negotiating skills, including making presentations, handling customer objections and closing the sale
- improving the salesperson's adaptability to differing selling situations
- developing administrative, organization

and planning skills in order to improve territory management and administration
- setting call objectives and managing by objectives
- understanding basic marketing principles in order to improve field implementation of programmes
- improving the understanding of the buyers, their motivations, objectives and priorities
- more efficient time utilization
- post-call analysis resulting in self-appraisal of performance and self- development programmes
- developing greater expertise in aspects of human relations (interpersonal skills) relevant to selling
- customer care.

Training can have a major benefit in reducing the amount of supervision needed by salespersons, releasing management time for other key business development activities. It commonly also helps reduce sales team turnover (leaving rate), as performance and hence satisfaction with jobs (status, recognition, rewards, prospects, management) and work environments improve.

Assessing the training needs

No two members of the sales team can be expected to have the same training needs as each is likely to be a different mix of qualities, skills and experience. Sales managers need to respond with customized personal field training to support general structured training usually provided in core courses. The next chapter presents a model **training audit** form.

In designing training the sales manager needs to consider the level and mix of sales-related skills within the team. The amount of training needed by any individual is not necessarily a function of age, although field sales managers are often very sensitive to longer-serving members of the sales team. The training required by any individual is a function of:

- existing knowledge, experience and skills

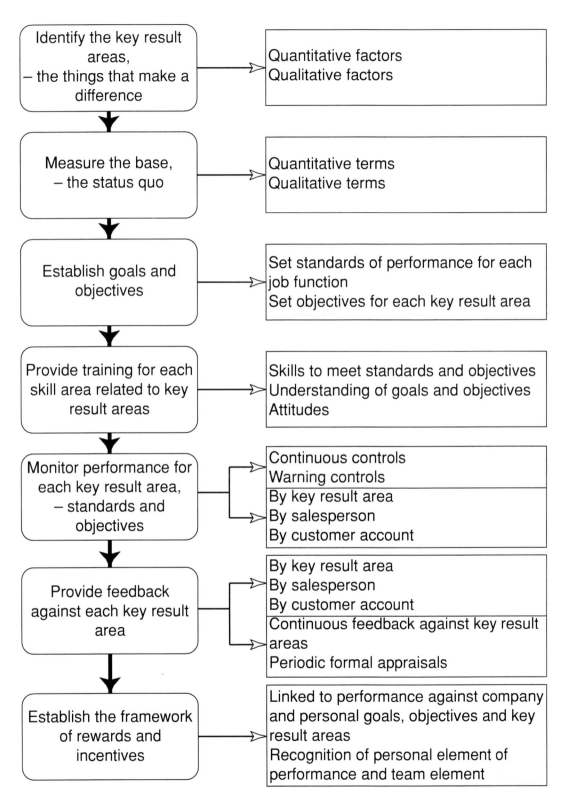

Figure 10.2 *Training in relation to the process for managing to key result areas*

- aptitude for the job
- attitude to the job
- adaptability and flexibility
- ambitions and motivations
- the 'training gap' between required standards and actual performance.

The sales manager should identify performance deficiencies of salespersons in order to focus training efforts, e.g.:

- achievement against objectives
- analysis of the conversion rate of orders to calls
- analysis of call rates compared with standards or average achievements
- identification of new potential customers
- success in obtaining new product listings, product displays, etc.
- effectiveness of sales presentations
- ability to overcome objections and objection handling techniques
- closing techniques and success rates
- customer relationships
- relationships between territory cost of operations and sales revenues compared with standards or averages
- compliance with administrative requirements and procedures.

Typical coverage of sales training ▪

If skills are to be increased, performance improved, and individuals to adapt to changing market conditions and work environments, then training must be an ongoing activity, with an ongoing review of needs. New salespersons need training in company orientation, products and basic selling skills. Established salespersons need ongoing training in developing new business, territory and customer management, advanced selling and negotiating skills, and ongoing personal development.

Basic training programme coverage ▁

Company knowledge

Most training programmes for new employees include a period of induction training during which they are familiarized with:

- company history and heritage
- the company's role in the industry
- management philosophies and style
- organization and management structures and reporting
- growth and performance

Typical focus of training

New salespersons
- Company orientation
- Company product knowledge
- The selling process, including basic customer care, professional selling skills and company administrative procedures, e.g.:
  - Developing a sales sequence
  - Selling techniques
  - Using the sales aids
  - Communicating effectively
  - Job administration
  - Pace control
  - Journey planning

Established salespersons
- Territory management
- Advanced selling skills
- Product promotion and merchandising
- Developing new business
- Refresher courses
- Communication skills
- Personal development planning
- Time management
- Key account management *
- Sales management *
(* Where appropriate to responsibilities)

- goals and objectives for the future
- personnel policies and practices
- factory production and office facilities (usually with organized tours and introductions of key persons).

Product knowledge

Under this broad heading training should give coverage to:

- product heritage and historical product development
- current product range, design aspects, packaging, specifications
- production methods and processes
- product range features and benefits
- new product innovations, developments, expansion plans
- legal aspects relating to products and markets
- competitors' products with comparisons
- the markets for the products
- marketing programmes and support.

Checklists at the end of this chapter highlight a range of training and information materials typically available within a company that could be provided to salespersons during induction and basic sales training.

Training in the selling process

Selling is concerned with satisfying the needs of customers and presenting solutions to their problems. As sales professionals we recognize that this involves communicating the product benefits to customers and not just listing product attributes and features. Whether the sales team is involved in high technology industries or mass market consumer goods, the basic steps of the selling process will include:

- identifying potential customers and their internal decision-making process
- analysing their product needs
- setting relevant and achievable objectives for the customer
- obtaining meetings with the decision makers

- presenting the products and product benefits in relation to customer needs
- responding to any objections in a manner that satisfies the customer's concerns
- negotiating terms and conditions within any prescribed limits
- closing the sales by asking for the order
- completing any post-sales administration and follow-up appropriate to the products and customer.

When training salespersons in selling skills it is usually best to work to a structured approach to selling (see Figure 10.3), and this structured approach can be modified to suit consumer products, industrial or business-to-business products, or sales through retail trade channels. The structured approach to selling in most companies is designed to provide skill training that suits your products and trade channels. It should be implemented to give broad but detailed coverage of **customer care, prospect identification** and the **seven steps to the call** identified here.

In Figure 10.3 we break down the selling process for **key accounts**, products distributed through **retail trade channels**, and **industrial products** to the **seven stages** each sales call should move through on the way to a successful outcome, the main **sales techniques** commonly adapted for use during the various stages, and a typical range of sales aids or **sales 'tools'**. As this text is focusing on sales management rather than selling skills, we can devote little space to selling skills here. Figure 10.4 does illustrate that there are three levels of activity, **pre-call activity, in-call activity** and **post-call activity**, that each sales call will encompass, and that every salesperson should be trained to progress through within a structured selling process. Figure 10.5 highlights the different key activity focuses of a salesperson selling into major categories of customers, namely for retail customers, trade distributors of products, and industrial users.

These diagrams can be used to provide a useful structure to the selling process, and as aids to developing appropriate selling skills training covering this structured approach to selling.

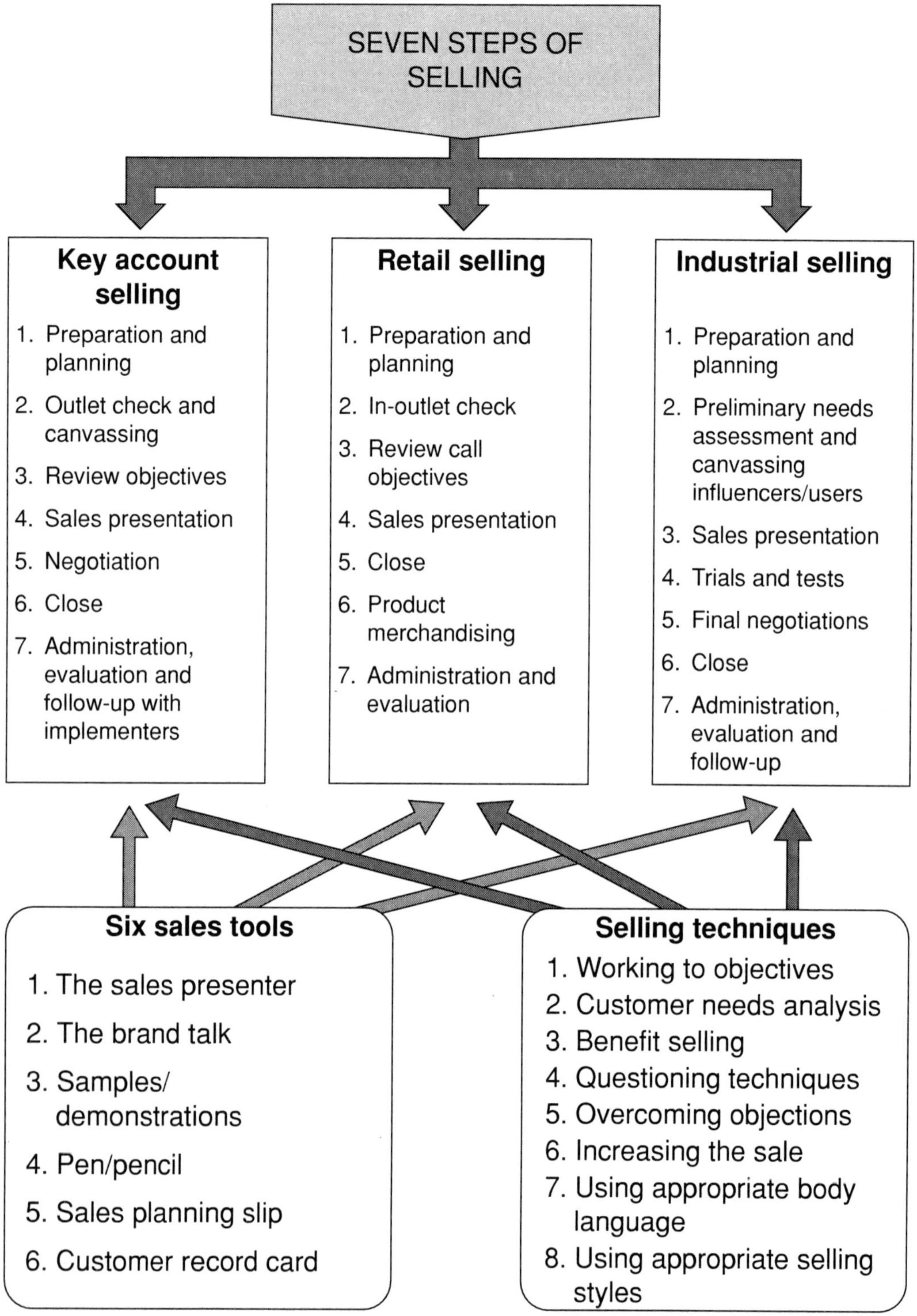

SEVEN STEPS OF SELLING

Key account selling

1. Preparation and planning
2. Outlet check and canvassing
3. Review objectives
4. Sales presentation
5. Negotiation
6. Close
7. Administration, evaluation and follow-up with implementers

Retail selling

1. Preparation and planning
2. In-outlet check
3. Review call objectives
4. Sales presentation
5. Close
6. Product merchandising
7. Administration and evaluation

Industrial selling

1. Preparation and planning
2. Preliminary needs assessment and canvassing influencers/users
3. Sales presentation
4. Trials and tests
5. Final negotiations
6. Close
7. Administration, evaluation and follow-up

Six sales tools

1. The sales presenter
2. The brand talk
3. Samples/ demonstrations
4. Pen/pencil
5. Sales planning slip
6. Customer record card

Selling techniques

1. Working to objectives
2. Customer needs analysis
3. Benefit selling
4. Questioning techniques
5. Overcoming objections
6. Increasing the sale
7. Using appropriate body language
8. Using appropriate selling styles

Figure 10.3 *The structured selling process – the professional selling road map*

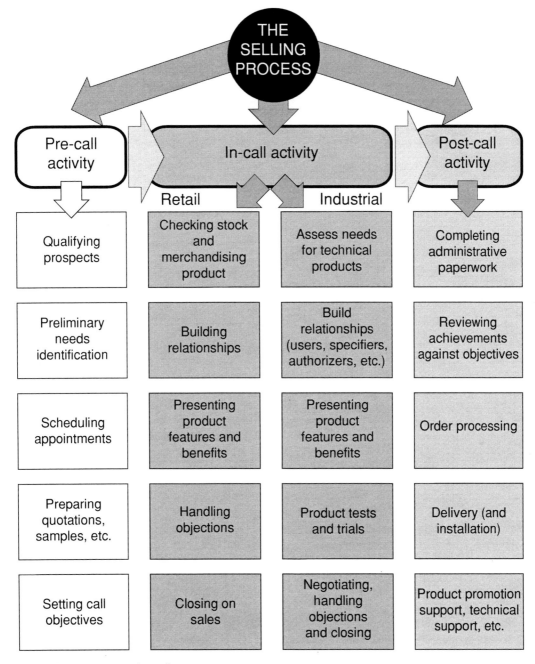

Figure 10.4 *Activity in the selling process*

Further considerations in industrial and business-to-business selling ■

As illustrated, a structured approach to selling can be developed for any selling environment, but there are differences between consumer and industrial selling and speciality markets that impact on sales training. An industrial or service salesperson is usually offering to supply:

● plant or equipment
● raw materials

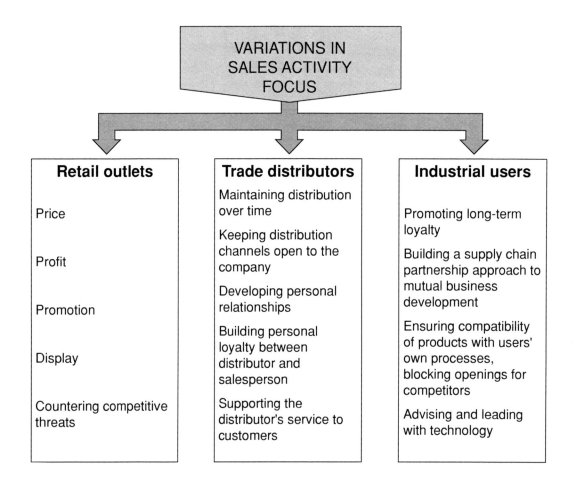

Figure 10.5 *Variations in sales activity focus*

- other components or inputs
- material supplies, such as packaging, stationery, etc.
- services (e.g. legal, financial, insurance, cleaning, security, etc.).

Some of these inputs are productive, used in the processing of a company's final products, and others are just seen as a cost or overhead to the business operation. There are several ways that industrial and commercial markets differ from consumer markets, and that impact on sales opportunities and therefore on training, as illustrated in the table opposite, and training programmes developed for

salespersons in any industrial or speciality markets need to take account of any particular market structure factors.

Conducting group training sessions

Chapter 8 dealt at some length with sales meetings and conferences. At this point a few additional points can usefully be made about running group training meetings. In general the principles for training individuals, discussed further in Chapter 11, should be applied to group training sessions, with the following points being taken into account.

Decision influencers	In industrial and business-to-business selling situations there is often a network of persons who will influence the decision. The salesperson needs to be trained to: ● identify all persons in the decision-making process ● develop a strategy for making initial contact with all influencers, and then to develop ongoing relationships ● develop presentations that address the particular needs of each separate person influencing buying decisions.
Transaction size	Industrial or service supply contracts often involve much larger transactions than consumer transactions, and not all salespersons are experienced in dealing with 'big ticket' sales.
Purchasing motives	The professional commercial buyer is often much less concerned with emotional factors in buying decisions than with rational factors, and salespersons may need additional training to focus on rational presentation factors.
Long-term supply agreements	Many industrial contracts involve scheduled deliveries over longer time spans. A prospective supplier will have to wait until an existing contract runs its course before having an opening to become a supplier to the customer and salespersons will need patience and diligence in pursuing opportunities.
Service support agreements	A manufacturer who buys or leases equipment from a supplier typically wants some form of maintenance agreement, and is often obligated to take this from the original equipment supplier as part of the contract.
Price negotiations	While in consumer product sectors customers may face fixed prices, in industrial sectors price is a very negotiable factor, dependent on quantities, specifications, distribution costs, and so on. Salespersons need training in managing negotiations to maximize profit.
Negotiation lead times	Commercial contracts can take considerable time to develop to fruition, through various stages of problem analysis, product specification, tests and trials, developing product costings, cost–benefit analysis, and negotiations. Some salespersons do not suit that, as they want immediate results and feedback on their own performance.
Special relationships	There may be 'favoured supplier' relationships the industrial or business-to-business salesperson needs to manage. Where a salesperson encounters situations where other parties have special relationships, this is a tough situation to break into as a new supplier, and requires great skill and patience, a quality not suited to all salespersons.
Technical assistance	Buyers of industrial equipment commonly need considerable technical assistance in testing and evaluating products in their own operating environment. This may involve specialists other than the salesperson working with specialists within the buyer's organization. Managing these specialist interactions is a skill that not all salespersons develop.
After-sales service	Most industrial supplies have an element of after-sales service, possibly as an additional add-on product, or included within original warranties. The salesperson may need training in ways

	of maximizing additional sales opportunities relating to such services.
Cash availability	With large-value commercial sales, extended credit that aids cash flow planning may be a key element in the choice of suppliers. Salespersons can be hampered by lack of flexibility to negotiate terms.
Cyclical fluctuations	While retailers may react quicker in curtailing ordering when there is a cyclical downturn, manufacturers may curtail production for longer, needing more time to build up production again. Salespersons need to understand the cycles in their industries, and the lead times in reacting to cyclical changes in demand and supply.
Market coverage	While consumer product outlets are both numerous and spread all over a country, manufacturers in particular product categories are often few in number and fairly concentrated in certain geographical regions that better suit an industry. This may mean that it is easier for an industrial salesperson to identify and service his or her customer network.

At the beginning of a group training meeting the trainer should:

- introduce the topic clearly and definitively
- define the purpose and objectives of the training session
- limit the scope of the training session and questions to matters which can be covered within the time span
- set the guidelines on rules and procedures for the training session
- work to develop positive and receptive attitudes in the attending audience.

In a participatory meeting the trainer should:

- obtain views and opinions from participants
- gather information on the nature and strength of feelings or experience
- get a reaction and group input on the subject matter, discussion points and proposals
- develop the discussion so that it leads to the desired conclusion, action or acceptance of ideas and proposals
- produce the intended modification of attitudes, opinions, behaviour, activities, action or techniques
- demonstrate a neutrality or impartiality

which earns the respect and cooperation of the group in the training meeting.

Variety in effective training

The experienced trainer recognizes the need to provide training information using a variety of means of communication (see Figure 10.6) in order to retain the attention and interest of participating trainees. Sales managers involved in presenting formal training courses are encouraged to use a multi-media approach.

Lectures

These are often an excellent method of involving an audience, if it is not too large. As an audience's attention span is limited it is usually advisable to change speakers every couple of hours, unless practical sessions can break the routine.

Demonstrations

The sales trainer should always be willing to demonstrate selling techniques and skills for his or her products in typical selling situations encountered during direct customer contact.

Some do's and don'ts of group training

DO

- Encourage questions and participant input.
- Praise and comment positively on input.
- Draw out relevant experiences from trainees.
- Encourage active participation through role playing and exercises based on the material.
- Encourage the group to feed back to each other on group activities.
- Demonstrate how to perform activities, tasks or functions.
- Monitor performance and provide group and individual performance feedback so that each participant can progress within his/her capabilities, skills and experience.
- Pay attention at all times.
- Involve everybody.

DO NOT

- Criticize input.
- Poke fun at participants, or cause them to become a butt of jokes amongst the group.
- Deliver material in a monologue with anecdotes which they cannot relate to their own experiences.
- Allow the pace to become monotonous or the group to become stale through lack of variety.
- Allow the group to become polarized into sub-groups.
- Expect the group to learn and improve performance without the trainer setting basic standards through demonstration.
- Sit on the sidelines allowing the group to drift along without clear support and guidance.
- Let your mind drift so that you miss key aspects of group dynamics or of the content or process of group/individual input.
- Develop favourites or be seen to focus more attention on particular trainees.

Role playing

Discussion, lectures, demonstrations, films and so on are no substitute in sales training for role playing, where each trainee is involved in simulated sales situations. Multiple role plays of any situation or any uses of a technique are usually necessary to develop skill and confidence, and those trainees watching the role plays of their colleagues are also learning.

Closed circuit television in role playing

This is a most useful tool in sales training, as each trainee can see himself or herself in simulated selling situations, and learn the skill of self-evaluation as well as developing specific sales-related skills and confidence. Closed circuit videoing of role playing scenarios provides one of the most powerful training tools, providing feedback, illustrating behaviour, and developing skill often at a much faster pace than could be accomplished without its use.

Films or videos

Many good sales training films are available for purchase or rent. Trainees are often more willing, initially, to comment on, or criticize, film or video role plays than live roles plays with colleagues. This medium can usefully communicate the development of sales objectives, use of sales presentation aids, presentation techniques, communicating features and benefits, questioning techniques, handling objections, closing techniques, body language and so on. The disadvantage is that they are usually fairly short, and have to focus on a few key messages designed for a multiplicity of selling situations. The skilled trainer can

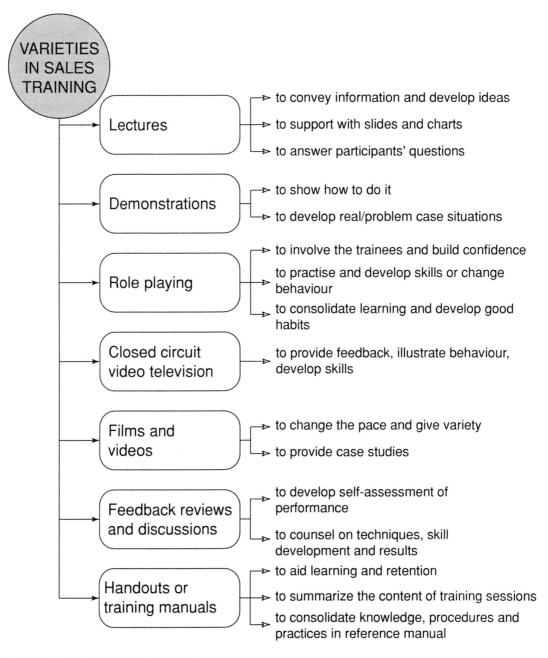

Figure 10.6 *Variety in effective sales training*

build on the film or video training messages in specific company-oriented role plays.

Feedback reviews and discussions

Feedback and discussion at each stage of training are essential tools in skill development and performance evaluation. If a posi-

tive attitude is to be developed feedback should not just be critical, but include a good proportion of praise and compliments.

Printed handouts

Participants in training programmes should have some materials to take from training sessions that provide a post-training reference point. Typical sales training manuals include coverage of essential information salespersons need on:

- the company
- the products
- job descriptions and responsibilities
- company personnel practices relating to the sales team operations
- practical and comprehensive guide to all the sales administrative and related procedures
- a summary of the sales skills and techniques covered in practical training.

The traditional training methods and media are now being supported by multi-media programmed texts suited to computer use. While these have a most useful role in training, they cannot substitute for role playing and practical experience.

Specialist training

Some product categories are very technical, and prolonged periods of product-oriented training may be necessary. Alternatively, it may be considered best to select persons with a high level of technical knowledge to become salespersons, and then to train them in professional selling. Whatever the scenario facing a company and sales manager, time devoted to training will reap dividends through increased sales and improved job performance and job satisfaction.

Use of training consultants

While larger companies may have internal resources to develop and run sales training to high standards, many smaller to medium-sized companies lack these human and financial resources. Such companies can, and should, still have a formal disciplined approach to sales training, but can do so making use of external consultants and train-

ing courses. A sales manager should carefully evaluate the available courses or consultants to ensure the proposed approach to selling suits company products and markets. If a particular training organization is favoured then that organization can usually develop programmes to be run internally with a client team, ensuring that all the case situations and role plays do apply to the products, and giving participants more confidence that the training is relevant to their customers and markets.

Length of training courses

The length of training courses is clearly very flexible. They need to be long enough to impart knowledge and give time to practise and consolidate skills, but not so long that participants become bored with material and repetition. Many companies favour an approach of conducting training through several shorter modules of two to three days in length, with interim 'on-the-job' training where sales trainers accompany salespersons in their field selling activities.

A typical induction training programme

New recruits should experience a professional approach to their induction to the company. This demonstrates both the company care and interest in staff and the professionalism of the sales organization. Basic induction should cover:

- company orientation
- product knowledge
- basic customer care, professional selling skills and administrative procedures.

Where a sales manager does not have the facilities or resources to place new recruits on a formal induction and selling skills programme as soon as they join the company, a typical sales force induction programme could consist of the following.

A typical induction programme

Days 1 and 2: Office-based training

1. Office tour.
2. Introductions to managers and colleagues based at the office.
3. Provide induction knowledge and sales administration pack (prepared in advance):
   - Company knowledge information
   - Product literature
   - Company accounts
   - Organization charts
   - Policy and philosophy statements
   - Terms and conditions of employment
   - Staff personnel handbook
   - Job description
   - Sales manual
   - Samples
   - Sample case/document case
   - Sales administrative systems (paperwork)
   - Sample head office performance feedback reports.
4. Take the new starter through all paperwork concerned with employment, e.g. terms and conditions of employment, staff personnel handbook, job description.
   - Ensure understanding and address all questions.
   - Allow reading time.
5. Take the new starter through all information relating to company knowledge.
   - Ensure understanding and address all questions.
   - Allow reading time.
6. Hand over all company equipment that goes with the job:
   - Car
   - Manuals
   - Administrative paperwork.
7. Take the new starter through all company sales administration documents.
8. Show the range of head office performance feedback reports, and illustrate how these are used in territory management.
9. Introduce the company's version of a sales manual.

Day 3: Demonstration day by field sales manager

The field sales manager should meet the new starter salesperson at the first call of the appropriate journey schedule day (or other suitable meeting point) at the normal start time. The field sales manager should then perform all the normal selling functions for the scheduled calls that day (he or she should not take specially pre-selected calls). This first day should be a 'model' of the company's selling practices as demonstrated by the accompanying sales manager. (Sales calls should not be specially selected as easy calls, as that is usually transparent to the trainee, and less of a learning experince.)

Days 4 and 5: Field practice day by new salesperson

Work to the normal journey cycle call schedule (do not use specially selected calls). The field manager usually should demonstrate the first call of the day. The salesperson should be left to do the second call alone, to build confidence.

Thereafter the manager can accompany the salesperson. After each call there should be a brief discussion on any matters that arose. The field sales manager should be providing feedback and training advice after each call, still focusing on the major points only, and personally demonstrating skills and techniques as necessary.

Week 2

During this week the field sales manager should expect and plan to accompany the new salesperson for at least two complete days, following the principles of field training outlined in the next chapter and in the related training checklists.
The field sales manager should continue to provide positive support, and to demonstrate personally in calls any key training points, not relying only on post-call discussion.

Week 3

As in Week 2 the field sales manager should plan to accompany the new salesperson for at least two days, possibly one complete day and two half days. By this time the salesperson should have a basic level of competence, and assessments of further training needs can be made on an individual basis.

Subsequent training

All salespersons should participate in formal product knowledge, professional selling skills and other courses as soon as possible after recruitment (either taking part in company organized internal programmes, or suitably evaluated external programmes).

Training sales managers

The sales manager needs all of the skills of the salesperson in professional selling and negotiation, and a lot more besides. The list below provides a summary in menu format of some of the skill areas in which a professional sales manager should expect to be able to demonstrate competency. The training of sales managers can be organized either on an internal basis, or through the broad range of excellent external courses available at leading business schools.

Skills and competencies of sales management

- Marketing and strategy development:
  - Market research
  - Marketing strategy development
  - Developing marketing plans
  - Marketing communications
- Legal aspects of trading:
  - Sales contracts
  - Customer rights
  - Intellectual property protection (trade marks, copyrights, patents, designs)
- Human resource management:
  - Leadership
  - Recruitment and selection of the sales force
  - Feedback and appraisal
- Sales planning and forecasting:
  - Sales strategy development
  - Developing sales plans
  - Sales forecasting
  - Sales performance measurement
- Category management
- Developing trade terms
- Planning market coverage
- Developing key accounts
- Use of information technology in the sales environment
- Selecting and managing distributors and sub-distributors:
  - Developing meaningful selection criteria
  - Identifying suitable distributors

- Developing sales training skills
- Developing motivational rewards and incentives
- Communication skills:
  - Making group presentations
  - Developing motivational sales team communications
- Financial management:
  - Budgeting principles
  - Financial controls
  - Costing/pricing principles
  - Cash flow management
  - Product and customer profitability management
- Managing distributors
- Selling and negotiating skills:
  - Professional selling
  - Negotiating with major accounts
- Organization and administration:
  - Organizing a sales force
  - Developing effective sales force controls and administrative systems

Checklist 10.1
Basic training for salespersons

Action points

Have the training needs and skills of new recruits been assessed?
Has an initial training course to cover needs been developed?
Does the initial training provide sufficient knowledge and skills in:
● **Company knowledge**
  Company history
  Role in the industry
  Management philosophies and style
  Organization and management structures and reporting
  Growth and performance
  Objectives for the future
  Market personnel policies and practices
● **Product knowledge**
  Product heritage and historical product development
  Current product range, design aspects, packaging
  Production methods and processes
  Product range features and benefits
  New product innovations, developments, expansion plans
  Legal aspects relating to products and markets
  Competitors' products with comparisons
  The markets for the products
  Marketing programmes and support
● **Customer care and professional selling skills**
  Does it give coverage of customer care, prospect identification,
  and the **seven steps** of the call, i.e.
  – Customer care
  – Prospect identification
  – Preparation and planning
  – In-outlet review
  – Reviewing the call situation against objectives, stock
  – checking, etc.
  – The sales presentation
  – Closing the sale
  – Merchandising
  – Call administration and evaluation
  Does it show how to use the basic **six sales tools**, of:
  – The sales presenter
  – The brand talk
  – Samples and the sample case
  – Pen/pencil

	Action points

Checklist 10.1 continued
    – Sales planning slip
    – Customer record card
Does it provide basic training in the **techniques of** selling, including:
    – Working to objectives
    – Customer needs analysis
    – Benefit selling
    – Selling styles
    – Questioning techniques
    – Using body language
    – Overcoming objections
    – Increasing the sale
What range of training materials is provided to salespersons participating in training programmes:
● Company knowledge information
● Product literature
● Company accounts
● Samples
● Organization charts
● Policy and philosophy statements
● Staff personnel handbook
● Sales manual
● Job description
● Administrative systems (paperwork):
    – Customer record cards
    – Order forms
    – Daily activity reports
    – Product uplift or credit notes
    – Territory journey plans
    – Sample request forms
    – Expense control forms
    – Stationery request forms
    – Display material requisitions
    – Customer invoices
    – Sales promotion control forms
    – Internal memo pads
Does the formal training programme use a variety of communication media, e.g.:
● Lectures?
● Films/videos?
● Role playing?
● Closed circuit television of role playing?
● Personal feedback?
● Discussions?
● Printed handouts?
Is feedback provided to all training course participants throughout the training process?
● Are participants encouraged to develop self-evaluation?	

11

Field sales training _____

The role and purpose of field training ▬▬▬▬▬▬

Field training of salespersons is probably the most important function of the field sales manager. Field managers commonly set particular field training objectives in the areas of:

- increasing marketing knowledge to sharpen awareness at the point of sale
- imparting product knowledge to increase expertise, enthusiasm and confidence
- improving personal selling and negotiating skills
- improving understanding of buyers' motivations, their organizations, role and objectives
- gathering market intelligence about customers and competitors
- increasing salespersons' adaptability to different buying and selling environments in changing markets
- developing administration and organizational skills (whether a paperwork-based system or computer-based system is in use)
- developing skills in interpersonal relationships
- developing expertise in customer needs identification and creation.

Assessing training needs ▬▬▬

Field training (see Figure 11.1) is particularly effective in focusing on:

> Every field visit by a sales manager with every salesperson should have **a training objective** and **training input, adding value** to the visit and sharpening the salesperson's skills.

- functional activities
- sales techniques
- organization
- personal attitudes.

Using a form such as the model **training audit**, shown later in this chapter, during field evaluation and training helps identify the specific key result areas the field sales manager might focus on in any field training session.

Functional activities _____

Quantitative or objective measures can be made of most aspects of a salesperson's functional activities. The field sales manager can observe each activity the salesperson undertakes during the selling day, and form judgements and conclusions on the satisfactoriness of performance in each area, while also making interpersonal comparisons with other team members. Most functional activities will apply in all selling environments, whether consumer, industrial or business-to-business, but their relative importance in the selling process may vary.

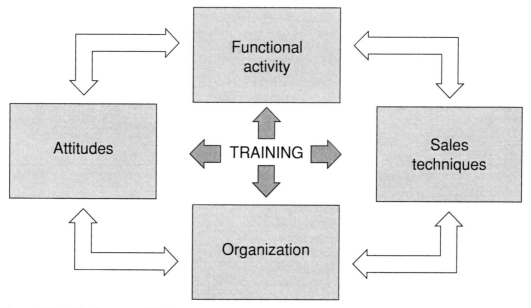

Figure 11.1 *The focuses of field training*

- **Selling activity – working to a structured selling process**. Does the salesperson work to a structured selling process? Observation will quickly show if the salesperson works to an appropriate structure to the selling process, such as the seven-step selling sequence proposed in this text. The manager is likely to want to focus on key stages that impact particularly on sales success and business development and profitability, such as identifying needs, effective presentations, negotiating and closing the sale.
- **Setting call objectives**. Does the salesperson establish realistic and achievable (but stretching) sales objectives in advance of commencing sales presentations, recognizing that managing to objectives is essential to growing business?

  Sales managers need to be alert to salespersons whose only objective is 'obtaining an order', and to develop a positive approach to setting quantifiable objectives in terms of volumes and turnover, or even other business-building objectives such as obtaining new listings, or new locations where the product can be displayed or used.

- **Use of time**. Does the salesperson manage his/her time effectively to maximize selling time?

  Time is a key limiting resource of the sales team, so analysis of use of time might consider the following points:
  - Time of first call
  - Time of leaving last call
  - Amount of time during the day spent driving and parking
  - Pre-call preparation and planning activities
  - Post-call administration
  - Lengths and frequency of inter-call breaks
  - Waiting time at calls
  - Time spent checking stocks
  - Time spent merchandising product
  - Time given to effective selling activities (e.g. the presentation)
- **Building relationships**. Are relationships with all buyers and decision influencers satisfactory and carefully cultivated over time? **Call rate**. Does the salesperson achieve a satisfactory daily call rate on customers, and how does this compare with the average for the sales team? **Conversion rate**. Does the salesperson have a satisfactory ratio between orders

and calls (compared with the average for the sales team), and if this varies significantly at times can causes be identified?

- **Administration**. Does the salesperson competently and promptly complete all administrative tasks associated with the selling activities?
- **Job description**. Does the salesperson comply with all the other responsibilities outlined in the appropriate job description, and with other job requirements established by the sales manager?

Sales techniques

Studying performance records does not give an indication of skill in using sales techniques in the face-to-face selling situation. That only comes through observation when the manager is accompanying members of his or her sales team. Field training can then be focused on areas of weakness or aspects of techniques judged as priorities in obtaining and building business.

Customer approach

- Is the approach professional, warm, confident and enthusiastic?
- Does the salesperson have the appearance and bearing to make a positive impression, commanding attention and respect as the buyer's equal?

Identifying/accessing decision makers

- Does the salesperson identify and gain access to the decision maker in the buying organization?
- Does the salesperson identify and recognize all the other decision influencers in the buying organization?
- Does the salesperson develop a programme of regular contact with the various decision influencers?
- Does the salesperson present product information to the decision influencers in ways that address their particular needs?

Working to call objectives

- Does the salesperson set overall objectives for the business with each customer account?
- Does the salesperson break down larger-scale objectives to specific objectives for each customer contact, and with each person involved in the decision-making process?

Identifying customer needs

- Does the salesperson establish the buyer's needs and problems in relation to the products being offered (including addressing the specific needs for each other person involved in the buying process, such as product specifiers, testers, users)?
- Do presentations recognize and satisfy needs, and address any buyer queries or concerns?

Benefit selling

- Does the salesperson highlight key benefits in relation to buyer needs, or just present a list of product features (leaving the buyer to judge the benefits)?
- Does the salesperson narrow down the range of features and benefits to focus on within a presentation, or run through the entire menu item by item?
- Does the salesperson approach each other decision influencer with a range of product benefits addressing their particular concerns and needs?

Objection handling

- Can the salesperson recognize real objections and clarify them?
- Can the salesperson respond to objections with appropriate objection handling techniques?

Increasing the sale

- Does the salesperson recognize and pursue opportunities to increase the sale (in value or volume) through product switching opportunities, selling up to higher value/profit items, or linking to sales of supplementary items (such as accessories, service contracts, etc.)?

Closing techniques

- Does the salesperson control the closing stage of the presentations?
- Does the salesperson present a positive request for an order (using the main closing techniques of positive close, assumptive close, concession close, fear close, alternative close)?

Use of sales aids

- Does the salesperson prepare all sales aids ready for sales presentations? (Check the salesperson has all available sales aids in their latest format, e.g. sales presenter and product literature, samples, customer records, order forms, other visual aids?)
- Does the salesperson make effective use of the range of sales aids to progress the sale and influence the buyer (or other decision influencers)?

Control of the call

- Does the salesperson control the pace, environment and content of the presentation (or is the buyer in control)?
- Does he work to influence the buyer's views, opinions and decision making (and similarly work to influence other decision influencers)?

Communication skills

- Does the salesperson exhibit suitable standards of communication skills (verbal fluency, skills in presenting data and information, questioning techniques, listening skills, responsiveness to voluntary/involuntary signals from the buyer, body language, etc.).

Use of product knowledge

- Has the salesperson adequate knowledge about the company, its heritage and products, and the markets served by the company and its customers?
- Can the salesperson effectively answer buyer questions and concerns based on knowledge (e.g. product specifications, performance, pricing, terms, servicing and maintenance, availability)?

Initiative in exploiting opportunities

- Does the salesperson network within the buying organization and demonstrate initiative in seeking opportunities for additional business?

Organization

The field sales manager's audit of training needs should encompass organizational aspects of the selling job. Any deficiencies can then be the focus of training according to how they are judged as impacting on sales performance.

Call records

- Does the salesperson keep all customer records completely up to date?
- Are all customer records carried by the salesperson (physically as record cards, or logged on to a laptop computer)?
- Does the salesperson make use of customer record information when preparing and planning for sales presentations?

Information retrieval

- Has the salesperson organized all files and data in a fashion that aids storage and retrieval of information during the selling day?
- Is all sales equipment (including records and sales aids) kept in tidy and accessible fashion in the vehicle? (It may be appropriate from time to time, where

salespersons work from a home-based office, for line managers to have access to check storage and management of company equipment and information.)
- Can all sales aids, paperwork, samples, equipment, etc., carried in any briefcase, be readily accessed by the salesperson during a sales presentation, and are they organized in some systematic fashion for use during sales presentations?

Sales aids

- Does the salesperson have a complete set of all current sales aids and related product and promotional material available throughout the selling day (i.e. in the car)?
- Does the salesperson check all necessary sales aids prior to making a call on each customer?
- Are appropriate sales aids taken into the call (or left in the vehicle)?

Journey planning

- Does the salesperson schedule sales appointments (where this is considered appropriate for the industry and market sectors)?
- Are appointments scheduled at intervals that maximize customer coverage during the selling day?
- Is the journey planning organized in the most cost- and time-effective manner?
- Are calls on customers made at frequencies that reflect their current sales performance with the supplier, or their potential (are some customers being over-visited, and others under-visited)?

Vehicle

- Is the vehicle kept clean and tidy to reflect a suitable image of the company and the salesperson's professionalism?
- Is the vehicle servicing up to date, with all aspects complying with relevant regulations?

Administration

- Are pre-call and post-call administration carried out promptly and efficiently?
- Are communications and correspondence with customers and other head office service functions and colleagues handled in a timely and efficient manner?
- Does the salesperson record, follow up, and honour all commitments made to customers and colleagues?

Personal attitudes

This is perhaps the most subjective area of all in preparing a training audit. Assessments of attitude may be influenced by personal feelings, prejudices and preferences. The field sales manager needs to attempt as best possible to make impartial assessments in this qualitative subject area, if only because it is often harder to train people to change attitudes than to improve performance of technical skills. For example, some salespersons become sceptical of a company's 'indoctrination style' of making sales presentations, mainly because they lack the confidence and skills to implement the recommended sales sequence and selling systems. The sales manager may recognize that skills training in the more objective areas of assessment will frequently produce a modification in attitudes, where the salespersons see that they can actually improve their sales performance. The attitude audit typically might cover the following aspects judged as impacting on sales performance.

Personal warmth

- Does the salesperson exhibit warmth and friendliness to all contacts in customer organizations?

Empathy

- Does the salesperson project empathy with the buyers when discussing their problems?

Enthusiasm

- Does the salesperson project enthusiasm, for the company, its products, policies and philosophies, and his or her job?

Loyalty

- Is the salesperson visibly loyal to the company, colleagues and management?

Positiveness

- Has the salesperson the right positive mental attitude to the job and life in general, and does this come over to customers in his or her contacts with them?

Team spirit

- Is the salesperson a good team person and participative at meetings and conferences (or is he or she more of a loner)?
- Will the salesperson voluntarily help colleagues in any practical ways that will help promote the development of the business?

Training stages

Field training by the sales manager should take the salesperson involved through the five stages of discussion, demonstration, explanation, practice and consolidation as illustrated in Figure 11.2.

The field training provided by the sales manager when accompanying the salesperson lays the foundations for progress and improved performance by the salesperson, but the salesperson must build on it through ongoing practice and self-evaluation. The sales manager must ensure that he or she does not simply disappear after a training session, only to reappear for another session some weeks later, but must maintain regular contact and provide support by specifically discussing progress and any problems arising with the salesperson.

It is normally necessary to break a training programme down to the five stages illustrated in Figure 11.2 in order to take participants through the chain of: unconscious incompetence – conscious incompetence – conscious competence – unconscious competence (see Figure 11.3). When we perform any task or function very regularly we get into a routine that includes developing many bad habits. Only when we recognize and identify the bad habits will we achieve conscious incompetence, and therefore be able to take the corrective action to move back to the stage of conscious competence.

The training audit

The first stage of field training is for the sales manager to **audit present skills and activities**, and form a judgement on the most immediate training priorities. The sales manager should develop a formalized approach to auditing or assessing his or her team, in order to be consistent on the criteria against which he or she is making assessments and judgements. Developing an audit form (an example is illustrated in Table 11.1), helps this process. The results and interpretation of the analysis should be shared with the salesperson being assessed and trained, and specific priority areas identified as the focus of practical field training and further self-development that will make tangible changes to performance.

If a standard audit assessment form is developed, an attempt should be made to standardize the terminology, measurement criteria and rating scales used by field managers preparing training audits and conducting performance assessments. A training audit should have a section where the trainer is required to report and comment on what training he or she has given the salesperson that day, and these notes can form part of an ongoing record of training and the salesperson's response to it.

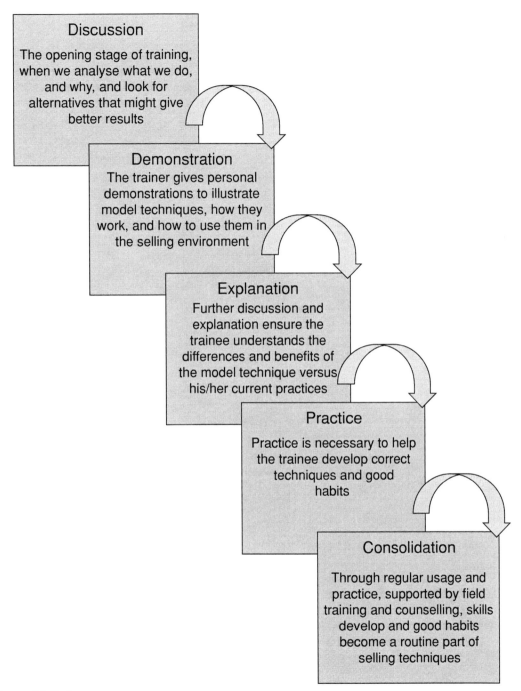

Discussion

The opening stage of training, when we analyse what we do, and why, and look for alternatives that might give better results

Demonstration

The trainer gives personal demonstrations to illustrate model techniques, how they work, and how to use them in the selling environment

Explanation

Further discussion and explanation ensure the trainee understands the differences and benefits of the model technique versus his/her current practices

Practice

Practice is necessary to help the trainee develop correct techniques and good habits

Consolidation

Through regular usage and practice, supported by field training and counselling, skills develop and good habits become a routine part of selling techniques

Figure 11.2 *Stages in training*

Conducting field sales training ▬

An assessment of sales performance and skills, strengths and weaknesses, and training needs should always be discussed promptly with the particular salesperson involved, and will generally be better received if it can commence with some favourable comment on strengths and good points in techniques and skills. The salesper-

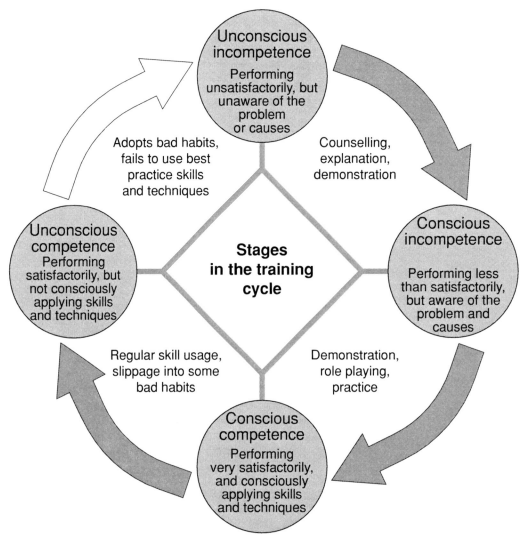

Figure 11.3 *The training process in relation to consciousness*

son should be clear that there is a difference between a training audit (and resultant corrective and performance-improving training) and a periodic formal appraisal. The training audit is based on analysis and judgement at a specific point of time, and is aimed at improving skills and performance over the short term in particular, and the longer term if possible. A formal appraisal will measure performance against agreed standards and objectives and other relevant criteria, based on an overview of all the data and events occurring between appraisals.

Priority training

The field sales manager's priority is to improve performance by change-creating training in areas of skill and attitude, and it is unlikely to be productive to spend long periods of time lecturing the salesperson on minor matters (in terms of impact on sales results). Field training should normally only focus on from **one** to **three** priorities on any visit to reduce the risk of confusion.

Training is a major route to improving sales performance and maintaining high levels of motivation, and needs time.

Table 11.1 A model training audit template

Training audit	Salesperson Date:	
Functional activities	**Rating**	**Comments**
● Sales sequence – Seven steps of the call – Preparation and planning – Outlet review (against objectives) – Stock check – Sales presentation – Closing the sale – Merchandising – Post call evaluation ● Setting call objectives ● Use of time ● Building relationships ● Call rate ● Conversion rate ● Administration/organization ● Other		
Sales techniques		
● Customer approach ● Identifying/accessing decision makers ● Working to call objectives ● Identifying customer needs ● Benefit selling ● Objection handling ● Increasing the sale ● Closing techniques ● Use of sales aids – Sales presenter – Brand talk – Samples/sample case – Pen/pencil – Sales planning slip – Customer record card ● Control of the call ● Communication skills ● Listening skills ● Use of product knowledge ● Initiative in exploiting opportunities		
Organization		
● Call records ● Information retrieval ● Sales aids ● Journey planning ● Vehicle ● Administration		
Attitudes		
● Personal warmth ● Empathy ● Enthusiasm ● Loyalty ● Positiveness ● Team spirit		
Training given: **Manager**		

> **Concentrate your field training on key result areas**

- Set time aside for sales team training to a formal programme.
- Do not move from one training subject to another until you are satisfied with progress.
- Work at the pace suited to the trainee. Time is not the priority in training: the standards you achieve are.
- Allow plenty of time for practice.
- Keep a record of training provided and progress made through the programme.

A training framework

The training framework developed by the field sales managers should take account of:

- individual differences
- individual needs of the trainees.

No two salespersons are the same, and therefore they must be recognized and treated as individuals by the sales manager if he or she is to succeed in motivating and training each of them. Table 11.2 highlights some pointers when training more experienced or less experienced salespersons.

Training must take account of:

Table 11.2 Training in relation to sales experience

Approaches to training experienced and less experienced salespersons	
Inexperienced (often younger)	**Experienced** (often older)
Common characteristics	**Common characteristics**
• open-minded • little personal experience to draw upon • more responsive to change • willing to try new techniques • keen to increase skills and knowledge • less reliant upon relationship selling • ambitious during early sales career • responds more positively to training and with a high rate of assimilation	• sceptical attitudes (seen it all before) • sensitive to criticism • reluctant to change • ingrained bad habits • more reliant upon relationship selling • less motivated by ambition than by recognition for experience, status, acceptance • responds more negatively to training in new skills and techniques, and with a slower rate of assimilation
Responds to:	**Responds to:**
• demonstration of general best practice sales techniques • logical explanation of selling techniques • guided practice • opportunities to increase knowledge and expand experience • variety in activity • job related goals and objectives • incentives related to sales performance • regular positive feedback (praise for progress)	• recognition for seniority and experience (e.g. in training younger salespersons) • demonstrations of alternative techniques to crack particular problems in specific accounts • training in small doses on very specific and relevant techniques, supported by a closely monitored personal development programme which rapidly yields tangible results • training which is non-threatening and not calling into question status, achievements or experience • projects which use experience and increase peer group recognition and acceptance • increased recognition, status, acceptance

- the salesperson's understanding and implementation of company policies and strategies
- the sales manager's previous experience of the trainee's
  - abilities to perform job functions
  - existing skill levels
  - rate of assimilation
  - attitudes
- previous experience of the trainee's response to training
- the different mix of needs and motivations of each salesperson.

At the end of this chapter is a useful summary checklist of guidelines for field training that will act as a practical framework for field sales management.

Training feedback

The intention of feedback is to improve or modify performance or behaviour. Giving frank, honest and open feedback serves several useful purposes:

- It lets salespersons see that their line manager is interested in them and their progress in the job.
- Salespersons recognize consistency in the behaviour of their line manager towards them, learn to expect and accept counselling and training, and come to realize that the line manager does not expect perfection, but does expect effort and improvement
- It helps the salespersons improve self-analysis in selling situations, and therefore to develop self-improvement programmes.
- It leads to awareness that changes in behaviour and performance improvement lead to greater acceptance, respect and satisfaction exhibited by line managers.
- It aids maintenance of high morale, as it can, and should, refer to the positive as well as the negative aspects of behaviour and performance, with praise being a more common input from line managers than criticism.

A checklist of guidelines for giving training feedback is included at the end of this chapter.

Judging the trainer's effectiveness

The effectiveness of a sales manager as a trainer can be judged through progress against a mix of objective and subjective factors. In the sales environment the results and benefits of training are often quickly apparent, often more so during periods of economic recession when the general level of sales activity is lower.

Some factors where change provides a measure of training effectiveness

Objective factors
- More time allocated to productive business building activities during the normal working day (better time management)
- Salespersons' call rate
- Sales to calls (conversion ratio)
- Size of orders (cases/value/range)
- Display activity
  - shelf layouts
  - promotional features
  - use of point of sales material
- Expanding distribution
- Market share versus competitors.

Subjective factors
- Higher team and individual morale (less cynicism, fewer complaints)
- Increased participation in meetings
- Increased flow of creative ideas
- Evidence of improved networking within customer organizations (targeting a broader range of decision influencers)
- Lower sickness rates (less lost time)
- Less time spent at home on non-selling activities
- Less time spent during the working day on non-selling activities (e.g. breaks, waiting).

- Prices controlled within guidelines in distribution channels
- Territory and account profitability
- Implementation and effectiveness of sales promotion programmes
- Increase in identification of (and tackling) new business opportunities
- Staff turnover (reducing)
- Compliance with administrative procedures (fewer problems)
- Fewer customer complaints and expressions of dissatisfaction with sales service

- Less management time needed for routine supervision
- Salespersons actively seeking field training time with the sales manager
- Observations or other evidence of improving levels of job satisfaction
- Team members gaining promotion

Checklist 11.1
Guidelines for field training

Action points

Develop a consistent framework to your approach to field training, e.g.
- Relax the salesperson to your presence
- Observe performance
- Identify current training needs
- Assess skill levels
- Concentrate on priorities:
  - Using the information from the training audit, recognize and concentrate on priorities
  - Concentrate on key result areas
- Provide training, giving attention to the stages:
  - Discussion
  - Demonstration
  - Explanation
  - Practice
  - Consolidation
- Review different techniques
- Obtain agreement and acceptance of benefits of change
- Demonstrate the techniques
- Encourage practical application
- Provide feedback:
  - It lets the salesperson see you are interested in him
  - Consistency in your style creates an expectation of training and counselling, and builds confidence
  - Feedback sharpens self-analysis
  - The salesperson realizes he earns favour by modifying performance and behaviour, increasing satisfaction from respect, achievement and acceptance
  - Feedback improves morale
  - Regular feedback gains acceptance as counselling not as criticism.
- Maintain contact
- Provide frequent supportive training
- Maintain progress records
- Take account of:
  - The salesperson's understanding and implementation of company policies and strategies
  - Previous experience of the trainee's abilities to perform job functions, sales techniques, and attitudes
  - The salesperson's previous responses to training

Action points

The intention of feedback is to improve or modify performance or behaviour.

- Field training feedback should be given generally in a relaxed informal environment
- Avoid interruptions and distractions
- Allow plenty of time so that the neither you nor the trainee feels pressured
- Establish your rapport with the trainee
- State any issue clearly, concisely and in comprehensible terms to the trainee
- Develop a two-way exchange of communications, views, comments, opinions
- Let the trainee see, understand and agree his or her actual performance in relation to agreed standards
- Check that the trainee agrees the training need exists
- Seek to develop a mutual understanding of why the training need is arising
- Obtain agreement that changes would be beneficial to the trainee (use questioning techniques)
- Seek a commitment to work for a change in behaviour, skills or performance
- Ensure the trainee learns your views of his or her performance
- Demonstrate your commitment to assist the trainee achieve the desired results
- Advise the trainee how to realize his or her potential through further training and personal development
- Increase the trainee's personal motivation to improve his/her productivity and performance through agreed objectives and personal development programmes
- Monitor progress, provide regular feedback in relation to the agreed programmes and changes, and develop further corrective action training as necessary

Part Four

Planning, Forecasting and Performance Monitoring

12

The planning process

Why plan?

Planning is a core management function, although one that often attracts too little time within a busy marketer's schedule. While planning is perhaps the most important function of the sales management and marketers it need not be the most time consuming, but is critical in reducing the risks associated with investing in sales and marketing activity.

The time given to planning is less critical than the quality of the planning, and with that in mind this chapter will attempt to present a framework for the planning process. My companion volume, *The CIM Handbook of Export Marketing*, provides more extensive coverage of the topic. Planning gives a sense of purpose and direction to subsequent activities, by:

- setting objectives
- identifying priorities
- recognizing key result areas
- developing strategies and tactics
- monitoring results.

Key result areas are those aspects of the business that impact on the outcome of a plan, but which might not always appear in the shortlist of primary objectives. Typical key result areas within the selling organization can include:

- use of professional selling skills and techniques
- product knowledge
- sales call rates (average number of

customer calls being made by salespersons)
- customer coverage (customers on the database receiving scheduled visits at prescribed intervals)
- conversion ratio of sales to calls
- product distribution
- the effective use of point of sales material
- obtaining display siting in the most visible and accessible position in an outlet.
- accessing the end user of a product within an organization (usually a different person from the buyer)
- effective networking with influencers in customer organizations
- the selection of key exhibitions to target specific user groups.

In any form of selling activity, critical key result areas include the level and use of professional selling skills, and product knowledge, and these are core training topics for initial and ongoing training (see previous chapters on basic sales training and field sales training). The sales manager should take a little time to identify and list those key result areas that demonstrably impact on his or her performance and ability to achieve market objectives in order that appropriate programmes are developed to improve performance in the key result areas.

Stages in the planning process

The full planning process in most companies will encompass the stages of:

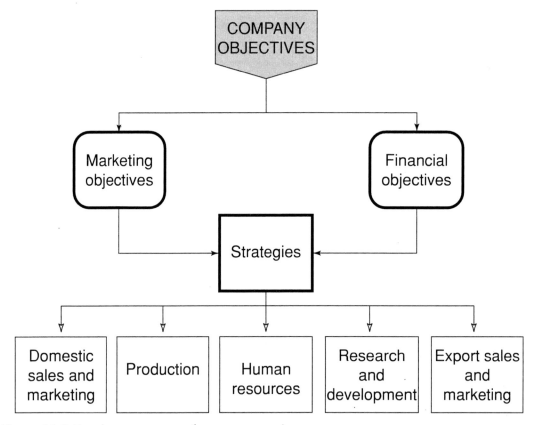

Figure 12.1 *Developing strategies from company objectives*

- developing an overall company corporate plan
- setting objectives for each market sector or target market (including export markets)
- developing specific strategies to achieve objectives
- developing market sales and profit forecasts
- making specific programmes (tactics and plans) to achieve objectives (e.g. breaking down market sales forecasts by outlet or customer and setting sales targets, identifying new business opportunities such as targeting specific potential outlets or users, developing supporting promotional activity)
- developing controls to monitor results and ensure the implemented strategies and tactics produce results in line with plans
- taking corrective action where deviations from plans occur.

The sales manager and his or her marketing colleagues must look to identify what information is needed to assist the planning process as well as considering how he or she can measure progress against plans and towards achieving objectives. Making a market plan means having access to **historical data** on each market sector and using that historical data to project market trends, and then making reasoned **assumptions** about factors that are outside the control of the marketer and other players in his or her market (such as economic conditions and regulatory controls). Figure 12.2 illustrates the stages in the planning process.

An alternative way of illustrating the planning process is shown in Figure 12.3. This presents planning rather like a road map, working from a starting point, with a clear destination in mind, planning the route, and having landmarks to check you remain on course.

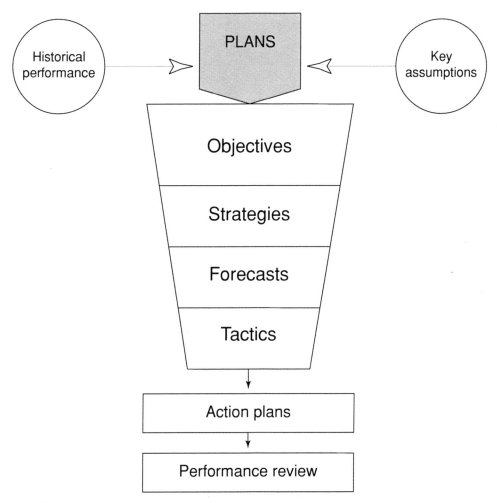

Figure 12.2 *Stages in the planning process*

Decision areas in strategy development ▬▬▬▬

Figure 12.4 summarizes the key areas where the sales managers and marketers will be involved in taking decisions and which will impact on performance of the products in the target market sectors. At the end of this chapter a checklist breaks down these key considerations to specific points that need addressing in developing the sales and marketing strategy.

Inputs to market sales planning ▬

Contributions to market planning ___

The key to planning is **market knowledge,**

and some general market knowledge is required in respect of the following factors:

- The economic and social environment external to the company:
  - Incomes
  - Prices
  - Interest rates
  - Currency movements
  - Employment levels
  - Production
  - Distribution
  - Demographic factors
  - Lifestyle trends
- Legislative and regulatory environment
- Competition (domestic and foreign)

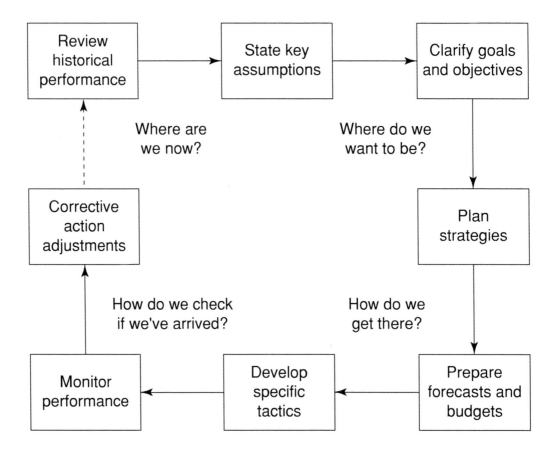

Figure 12.3 *The planning road map*

- Political considerations
- Distribution channel factors (e.g. changes in patterns of distribution)
- Trend and product preference patterns and changes
- User attitudes, perceptions and expectations
- Company human resources and training
- Company financial resources and controls.

In preparing market plans account must also be taken of your own company resources in respect of:

- plant production capacity and flexibility to vary any product mix to meet changing opportunities
- limitations resulting from a need to modify products to suit certain customers

- availability of input supplies to meet expanding production
- product innovations and technology (how your own innovations and range changes will impact on the market, or how they will compare with competitor product developments)
- sales and marketing resources (i.e. sales force resources to cover the potential customer base, marketing budgets for marketing communications support)
- financial resources to fund growth (i.e. as more of the limited resources are tied up in input supplies, goods in process, inventories, and trade credit).

Many sales managers find that the market opportunities are greater than they can tackle within their limited resources of product,

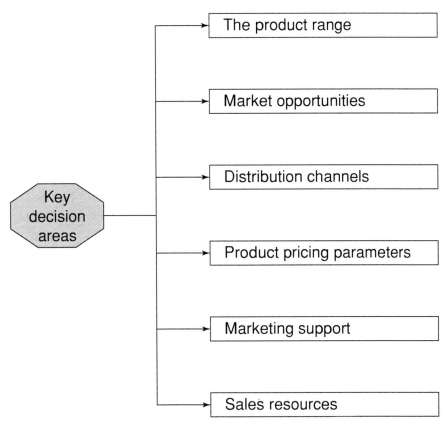

Figure 12.4 *Key considerations in developing sales strategies*

finances and staffing levels. That means assigning priorities to opportunities, or diverting internal resources from other activities, which in turn can impact on quality and service in support functions.

Historical market and performance data in planning

Earlier Figure 12.2 referred to the importance of using available historical market and performance data in market planning. This is expanded in Figure 12.5, which shows a typical range of market data that might be available and useful in framing the sales and marketing plan.

Estimates should be made or obtained (from desk research) into the total market for the product category, so that you have estimates of the total market for your products, rather than looking at your own sales in iso-

lation.

Your own distribution should be compared with that of your competitors, as a measure of the effectiveness of your sales team, and as a guide to the suitability of your products and prices to market needs.

You will want to know about market pricing structures to ensure your competitiveness and positioning correctly in relation to competitors' products and your strategic marketing objectives. It is essential to know trade margins at each level of the distribution chain if you are to control market prices. Many suppliers do not have much influence over the market pricing of their products, in part because of lack of knowledge of market pricing structures and in part because of the absence of any control over their trade distributors (where a product is re-sold rather than purchased for use directly by end users).

Your historical performance in sales and

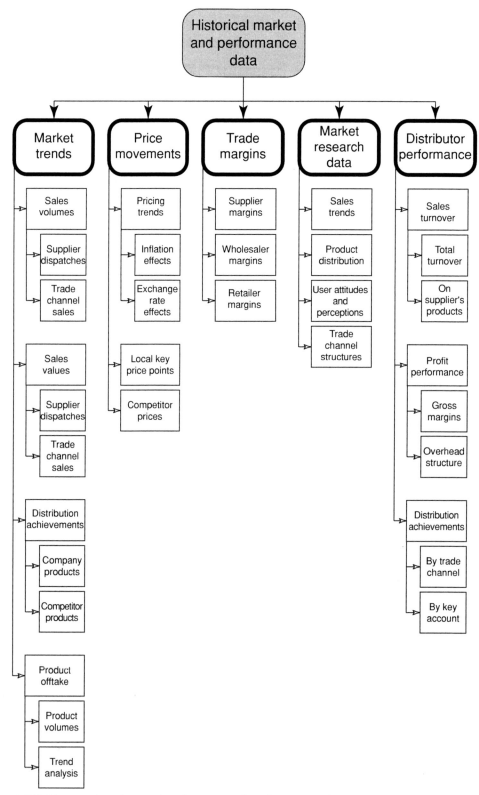

Figure 12.5 *Historical market and performance data for use in planning*

distribution achievements may provide an important insight as to how you might perform in the future, and how effective your sales team might be in implementing your marketing strategies and plans.

Key planning assumptions

There are a number of aspects of planning where we might make assumptions, as illustrated in Figure 12.6.

Market size

Under this heading, when making assumptions or projections based upon assumptions, the marketer will be looking for information relating to product volumes and values within relevant product categories or substitute products. Also he or she will want any information about distributors of the product category, such as how many distributors or distribution points are estimated to cover the market, and their estimated sales volumes. It

will also be useful to know the numbers of users or consumers in the target market segments, and their likely level of use or demand for the product.

Market dynamics

This is about the changes that are taking place in the product sector and distribution channels, independently of the supplier. For example, users or consumers may be demanding higher quality products with greater reliability and lower servicing needs. Or there may be a move towards higher (value-added) or lower (basic commodity type) priced products. Consumers might be pressuring for more variety in products (such as car models with a greater range of options), or there might be movements in user or consumer product preferences, such as the move in recent years towards more environmentally friendly and natural products.

Looking at distribution channel dynamics, these are constantly changing. Suppliers

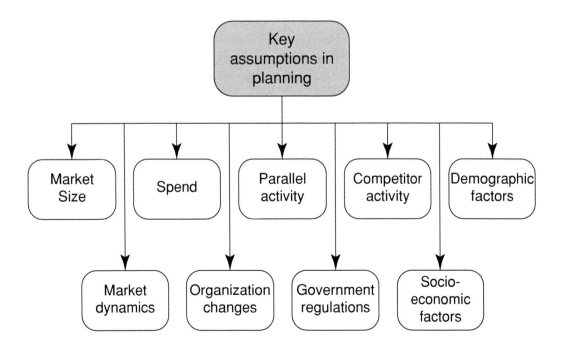

Figure 12.6 Key assumptions in planning

merge with other suppliers, with objectives of strengthening market positions. New suppliers enter markets to service niche needs. In consumer goods the retail market is dynamic, with new outlet formats servicing customer needs, e.g. the move to out of town shopping locations.

Spend

The market plan must make assumptions about the users' or consumers' spending power. Some products are essential either as industrial components or consumer necessities, and others are discretionary if funds permit purchase. The availability of disposable funds to use on the products may be a critical factor in purchase decisions. High interest rates may discourage investment in capital goods. High unemployment may discourage consumer spending on non-essentials. Knowledge of the state of the local market economy will assist in making sensible planning assumptions.

Organization changes

In some situations there may be a need to consider likely changes in either the marketer's own company organization, or in that of his or her market distributors. Internal company re-organizations might impact on markets and planning. Whatever company organizational changes occur, if they are likely to impact on performance then assumptions must be made at the planning stage and factored into plans.

Parallel activity

In some product categories it is quite common for marketers to find a significant level of parallel trade. This is trade that is not officially sanctioned or managed by the supplying company, normally by-passing official distribution channels, and possibly even including smuggling operations. Parallel trade normally develops where there are onerous duties or taxes or where a company fails to supply (for whatever reason) suffi- cient goods to meet market demand, or where there are significant price differentials between markets. Goods exported from the home market may return through opportunistic traders if they can be purchased abroad and re-imported more cheaply.

The effect of parallel trade is quite disruptive to orderly marketing, particularly of branded goods, and can often result in the same products selling at differing price levels through the alternative distribution channels.

When it comes to market planning, if the marketer's products or markets attract parallel trade then this must not be ignored, but factored into plans, and estimates made both of its magnitude and of its effect on orderly marketing.

Government regulations

Government involvement in trade can cover a number of situations:

- control of sales through authorized trade channels (where the government wants to collect taxes or limit persons permitted to purchase products)
- advertising and promotion of products
- control of imports though an import licensing or quota system
- labelling regulations
- specifications and quality standards.

The plan should normally summarize regulations applying to trade in a market and must then make assumptions as to whether these will remain consistent or change during the period of the plan.

Competitor activity

Markets are dynamic not static, and it is dangerous to plan without taking account of competitors' achievements and activity, and their responses to your plan. Continuous monitoring of competitors' marketing programmes, their product ranges (particularly noting innovations and changes), and their product pricing and target market positioning all add to the base of knowledge that helps the marketer make a better plan. With this knowledge the marketer must then make assumptions about what the competitors will do in the future, during the planning period and in response to his or her market activities.

Socio-economic factors

The stability of the political environment, levels of income and employment, and consumer/user attitudes may impact on sales of many products, but in some markets the degree of industrialization may also have an impact on sales volumes or the product mix suited to local needs. The market plan should consider any socio-economic factors that will affect the implementation of the plan and present the assumptions on which the plan is developed.

Demographic factors

The marketer needs to identify what demographic factors affect his or her planning process, and factor in assumptions on developments and their likely impact on sales potential. Planning assumptions for many products need to consider market demographics. Consumer products can be influenced by population age, the sexual balance, size of average family unit, birth rate and other factors affecting population growth, trends in population location, and education of the population and resultant increase in incomes and lifestyle sophistication can all impact on sales potential for many products.

With the wealth of market knowledge the marketer acquires over time, the planning process should become more sophisticated and accurate in its predictions about trends and sales volumes.

Checklist 12.1
Decision areas in sales strategy development

Action points

The product range
- What product sectors to target product at
- Company brand versus private label brand
- What product range to offer
- How to differentiate company products from competitors

The markets
- Customer mix, target customers or market segments
- Domestic sales versus export opportunities
- Geographical spread
- Cultural factors in marketing the products

Distribution channels
- Distributor networks
- Direct user/consumer sales
- Retail outlets
- Physical distribution
- After-sales service product support needs

Pricing parameters
- Marketer's quoted prices to distributor or customer
- Market price positioning
- Market trade terms (discounts, rebates, minimum orders)
- Distribution costs, sales taxes, other levies or duties

Marketing support
- Advertising and promotional budgets
- Advertising media selection
- Promotional activity
- Public relations/sponsorship
- Sales promotion literature and sales aids
- Consumer trial and loyalty building programmes

Sales resources
- Size of direct sales force
- Geographical spread of sales force
- Sales management structure
- Key account management structure
- Financial resources of marketing unit
- Training resources
- Distributor network
- Sales promotion budgets
- Rewards and incentives in sales organization
- Key sales functional activities with customers
- After-sales service support

Checklist 12.2
Planning – the planning framework

Action points

Develop a formalized approach to market planning:
- Establish corporate objectives:
  - Marketing objectives
  - Financial objectives
- Set objectives for market sectors
- Develop specific strategies to achieve objectives
- Develop market sales and profit forecasts
- Develop specific market tactics and plans
- Develop controls to monitor performance
  - Allow for corrective actions to counter deviations

Develop a portfolio of market knowledge to use in market planning, e.g.:
- The market economic and social environment, e.g.
  - Incomes
  - Prices
  - Interest rates
  - Currency movements
  - Employment levels
  - Production
  - Distribution
  - Demographic factors
  - Lifestyle trends
- Legislative and regulatory environment
- Competition (domestic and foreign)
- Political considerations
- Distribution channel factors
- Trend and product preference patterns and changes
- User attitudes, perceptions, expectations
- Company (and distributor) human resources and training
- Company (and distributor) financial resources

In preparing market plans take account your own company resources limitations, e.g.:
- Plant production capacity
- Flexibility to modify products to suit customers
- Availability of input supplies to meet expansion
- Product innovations and technology
- Marketing and sales resources
- Financial resources to fund growth

Action points

Note historical market and performance data, e.g.
- Market trends
- Price movements
- Trade margins
- Market research data
- Distributor performance

Make planning assumptions about changes that might occur during the plan period and impact on plan implementation and performance, e.g.:

Market size
- Volumes: demand and product availability
- Values: prices and product mix
- Distribution outlets: number, locations, throughputs
- Users/Consumers: numbers, levels of use, frequency of use

Market dynamics
- Sector dynamics: trends on price, quality, variety, taste, etc.
- Distribution channel dynamics: numbers and locations of suppliers and outlets

Spend
- Incomes
- Interest rates
- Employment
- Proximity to product

Organizational changes
- Changes in resource allocation to sales and marketing
- Changes in product portfolio
- Change in production or distribution logistics
- Changes in management control (ownership)

Parallel activity

Government regulatory actions
- Importation; restrictions, duties, etc.
- Products: labelling, composition, advertising, use control

Competitive activity
- Distribution: achievements, trade channels, strengths/weaknesses
- Marketing; advertising and promotion, ranges, pricing, positioning

Socio-economic factors
- Employment: levels, income, stage of industrialization
- Government and politics; stability, free market or controlled economy
- Attitudes: social, religious, political

Demographic factors
- Population trends
- Location trends

13

Sales forecasting ──────────────

This chapter will look at some of the issues that sales forecasters might consider in developing their market sales forecasts. It is not intended to turn them into statisticians, and therefore the focus is on practical approaches using data that most sales forecasters can find internally or through basic desk research. Those readers whose companies are already using more advanced statistical forecasting techniques, which experience shows are few, can refer to more specialized texts.

Sales forecasting is all about:

- estimating the total size of the potential market for a product or group of related products
- estimating the current level of total market demand (normally lower than the market potential)
- estimating the supplier's current share of the total market demand (i.e. company demand)
- forecasting forward the level of sales the company would expect to achieve in each market sector based upon particular marketing strategies.

As we will attempt to show in this chapter, simply taking last year's sales and adding a set percentage is not a forecast in any sense that a sales forecaster would find acceptable. The forecast growth of the company must be benchmarked against external data, to ensure that the company is keeping pace with the market and competition. Table 14.6 in the next chapter shows a situation where a company was very happy with its percentage

growth year on year, until it compared sales with the total UK product category and found that it was in relative decline. Later examples in this chapter also highlight how sales can be lost through poor forecasting. Sales managers responsible for forecasting and achieving sales must satisfy themselves that the market demand is not rising faster than the demand for their own products.

The issue of poor data availability can be addressed through:

- desk research into markets and customers
- market research into total product category (and substitute product) sales, including local production and net Imports to estimate total local demand in each market.

Terminology associated with sales forecasting ████████

A useful starting point in looking at the subject of sales forecasting is probably to develop common understanding of the standard terminology used, and an approach to developing working definitions follows.

For simplicity and clarity here we will use the term **forecasts** to refer to any figures aimed at assessing demand for a product at either the market or the company level.

In many companies the common practice with respect to sales forecasts and marketing plans and budgets is to make an estimate of sales, and then to develop marketing plans and supporting marketing expenditure bud-

Forecasting terminology

Market potential	The **potential market** for a product is the total of all those persons or businesses with the means, need and opportunity to buy.
Market demand	The **market demand** can be considered as the total volume of the product that would be purchased by a qualified customer group in a prescribed time period, in a known marketing environment. The known marketing environment is assumed to include an established political/economic/legal/social environment, an established distribution infrastructure, and predictable levels of marketing activity – advertising, promotion, etc. Changes in the marketing environment will prompt changes in the level of demand (i.e. variations in industry marketing expenditure, and stages of an economic cycle are two key variables that typically influence market demand).
Company potential Forecasts	This will normally be limited by the demand that can be created as the company increases its marketing activity relative to its competitors. These can be defined as projections of **expected sales** over a particular time period based upon known parameters.
	Forecasts are normally prepared for each market sector at the **industry** and **company** level. The **industry** forecast will make assumptions about industry marketing support for the products in the market. The **company** sales forecast should be based upon a defined marketing strategy and assumed level of marketing expenditure in pursuing that strategy.
Targets	These can be defined as a statement of what the sales manager wants to achieve in the way of market sales, and may be based mainly on data external to the company, such as competitors' known sales, market volume data, etc.
	Achievement of targets is heavily dependent on developing and implementing suitable strategies and tactics, including promotional activity.
Budgets	These really are a projection of revenues and expenditure, and the term 'budgets' is really an accounting term that has been adopted into the language of marketers in many companies through its use in annual company plans that are largely financially based and prepared by accountants.
	Budgets may or may not be based on sales performance history, and are just as likely to be a target of sales revenues, volumes and profits needed from sales operations to achieve overall company financial projections.

gets. This is logically erroneous, in that the earlier sales forecast definition clearly indicates that the sales forecast is derived from the marketing strategy, which assumes a level of marketing expenditure to support the programme aimed at pursuing the strategy. To base marketing plans on sales forecasts may seem reasonable where the marketer does not expect the company's demand in the total market to be capable of expansion, but it is patently wrong where company demand is capable of expansion and influenced by marketing expenditure.

Another common scenario is that where sales run behind forecasts, the response is to cut back on the marketing budgets. If for any reason in any market the sales forecast is not being achieved then before cutting marketing expenditure the marketer should seek to establish the reason for any shortfall. If there have been changes in the marketing environment (such as imposition of import restrictions, changes in duties or taxes, etc.) then it may be reasonable to re-forecast sales and prepare new marketing expenditure budgets at the same time as making any appropriate changes to the marketing strategy. If shortfalls arise for other reasons, such as poor performance by members of the sales team, then, on the assumption that the strategy was appropriate and the forecasts were realistic, attention must be given to improving the performance of the sales team – cutting marketing budgets will only prove a short-term saving and will do nothing to help you to achieve your forecasts or potential.

Planning time spans

Companies vary in the time spans they apply to their planning process. Forecast time spans might be defined for practical purposes as in the following chart.

Apart from the accuracy of forecasting depending on the stability and maturity of the overall product markets, consideration must be given to the security of access to individual market sectors (or export markets, if included in the forecasting process) when forecasting. If a company's trade in a market sector is under threat then this should be reflected in forecasts (e.g. if new sources of similar products are likely to start supplying the market, or innovation by competitors will make company products obsolete, or changes in rules and regulations will block company sales opportunities).

What to forecast

The starting point for any forecasting is to attempt to estimate the **total market size** for the product category (or near substitutes), and then to make an estimate of the share of the total market that the company can expect to achieve, through a proactive marketing programme.

Typical considerations in forecasting

Sales forecasting is primarily about predicting **sales volumes** and **sales values** (revenues). The strategies the company plans to adopt in pursuing its marketing objectives are key considerations when forecasting volumes and values, along with the product mix, and expectations of market price movements. Figure 13.1 illustrates the two sides of the forecasting equation, as seen from the perspective of the marketer and the financial planner.

It is common for the sales forecaster to focus primarily on estimates of sales-related figures, such as volumes and revenues. In

	Planning time spans
Short-term forecasts	These usually cover the period immediately ahead, such as from three to six months. Short-term tactical decisions, such as promotional activity, are based on the short-term forecasts.
Medium-term forecasts	These are usually projecting sales volumes and values at least a year ahead, and sometimes for 18 months to two years ahead, with a greater input of detailed marketing strategy than long-term forecasts.
Long-term forecasts	These typically attempt to forecast three to five years ahead, with limited accuracy, and often with coverage of the longer-term diversification or expansion strategies of the company.

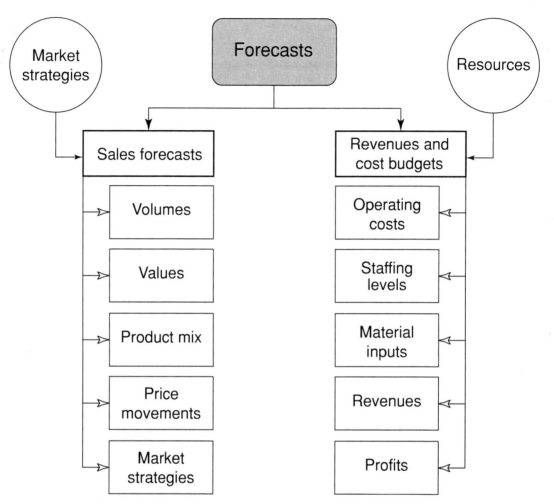

Figure 13.1 *The forecasting equation*

looking at these, clearly attention must be given to the product mix expected to be sold, as variations in product mix will affect volumes, revenues and resultant profits. Also, since in good forecasting practice the forecast is derived from the marketing strategy (and not vice versa), account must be taken of strategies and marketing expenditure, and as these change so must the forecasts be modified to reflect the expected impact of the changes on sales volumes and values.

When the forecasts are developed from the marketing strategy, the marketers need to be involved with the accountants in preparing the budgets, taking account of any resources limitations (human, physical and financial).

The values of sales should match up with the revenue budget, and estimates should be made of the operating costs, material inputs and staffing levels need to achieve the forecasts. If the marketer is estimating market potential and market demand, he or she can benchmark performance and forecasts against these.

Main methods of developing forecasts

There are a number of approaches to forecasting, at the macro level of the total market or industry, and at the micro level of the com-

On the sales forecasting side of the equation account must be taken of:

Volumes	● By product
	● By customer or distributor
	● By market sector
	● By foreign market (for exports)
Values	● By product
	● By customer or distributor
	● By market sector
	● By foreign market (for exports)
Product mix	● Variations in the marketer's product portfolio and price mix may change the levels of sales volumes or values, with resultant effects on product or total profits for markets
Pricing levels and movements	● Regionally/nationally/internationally (versus competition)
	● Changes in product costs (inputs, etc.)
	● By market sector
	● By product type
	● Currency movements (if these impact on market prices)
Marketing strategies	● Product positioning
	● Pricing
	● Distribution
	● Advertising and promotional activity
	● Product ranges
	● Quality
	● Presentation
	● Consumer attitudes/preferences
	● Changes in the market environment
	● Regulatory controls
	● Market dynamics/distribution channels
	● Consumer attitudes/preferences
	● Employment/incomes
	● Competitive activity and marketing strategies

Sales forecasts should be supported by resource/cost estimates, e.g.:

Operating costs	● **Sales departmental costs**
	Wages and wage increases
	Sales training
	Recruitment
	Support department costs
	Travel and subsistence
	Sales force expenses including vehicles
	Bonus and incentive payments
	Sales promotional activities (off sales budgets)
	Customer service/shipping
	Order processing
	Sales planning
	Transport and distribution of goods
	Export distribution (where applicable)
	Export travel and subsistence costs (where applicable)

	● **Marketing costs**
	Advertising and promotion budgets
	Promotional and display materials
Staffing levels	● Sales management
	● Sales office support staffing
	● Marketing management
	● Export marketing management (where applicable)
	● Shipping / customer service staff levels
	● Expansion / contraction to meet market coverage needs
	● Natural wastage
	● Retirement
	● Sickness / holidays
	● Changes in required qualifications, experience, skills
Material inputs	● Capabilities of the company to source / produce competitively.
	Breadth / depth of company range
	Exchange rate movements (for imported inputs)
	Input supply availability (labour & materials)
Revenues	● By product
	● By customer or distributor
	● By market sector (and by foreign market for exports)
Profits	● By product
	● By customer or distributor
	● By market sector (and by foreign market for exports)

---

pany down to the individual customers. Forecasting normally needs to be undertaken at both levels, and then a considered approach by the sales manager to the outcomes of macro forecasting and micro forecasting should help come to a reasoned view of realistic and achievable sales forecasts or targets. These can be looked at in relation to the overall goals and objectives for the market, and the range of marketing and sales strategies and tactics to be employed in a marketing plan to ensure their achievement.

Figure 13.2 illustrates a number of the major macro and micro forecasting techniques, split under two headings that group those dealing with **future demand** separately

Macro forecasting	Macro forecasting involves looking at the overall market for a product or category of products. It is about: ● studying company historical performance in relation to the environment (political, economic, social, legislative), industry performance, demographic factors related to company or market performance, and product demand ● relating industry demand to national levels of production, income levels, interest rates, employment, imports, demographic factors.
Micro forecasting	The typical approach to market micro forecasting is to: ● study the performance of each existing and potential customer account on a product-by-product basis over the past few years or recent sales periods and preparing forward sales estimates for the next forecast period ● build up to territory, area and national sales forecasts for comparison with the independently prepared macro forecasts.

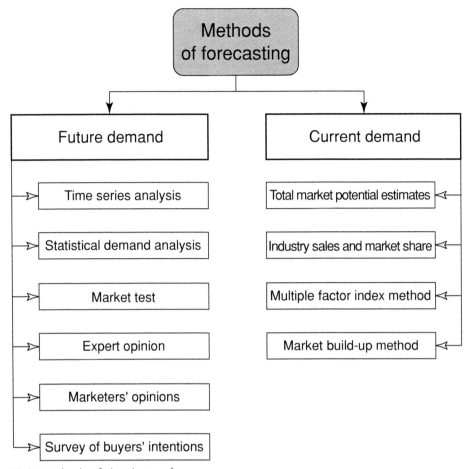

Figure 13.2 *Methods of developing forecasts*

from those dealing with **current demand**. Some of the techniques are **quantitative**, in that there are often accessible statistical records that will form a firm basis for estimates and forecasts, and others are **qualitative**, in that they rely heavily upon the judgement of the forecasters and their market knowledge and assessments of trends. The quantitative techniques would mainly be compiled using appropriate computer programs and spreadsheets.

Current demand

The starting point should be to make some estimate of market potential for each market sector and the overall market for company products, and then see how this is being satisfied, i.e. current levels of demand, and the

company share of the current demand can then be factored in to develop marketing strategies to develop the company's sales and market share.

Total market potential

The market potential is basically an estimate of the total sales potential for all industry suppliers in a market (a macro market forecast). This will invariably be a larger number than current actual levels of demand. Quantitative techniques can lead to estimates of volume or value being made. First the forecaster must make some assumptions about what qualifies a person as a prospective buyer.

It is always difficult to make a reasonable estimate of the number of prospective buyers for a product. The target market should be profiled or qualified in any practical way that relates to product consumption or use, in order that estimates of the number of potential buyers have some rational basis.

For example, a basic profile of the scotch whisky drinker might be a male, over 35, with certain levels of income. If we have knowledge of the average consumption of the typical whisky drinker we can then add this to the equation, and find a first estimate of market potential as in the following table.

Estimating whisky market potential

Market potential (litres volume) =
Number of males meeting the profile criteria (over age 35 years and earning at relevant income level)
times
average consumption (litres) per whisky consumer

Market potential (value) =
Number of males meeting the profile criteria (over age 35 years and earning at relevant income level
times
average consumption (expenditure) per whisky consumer

With industrial products this kind of macro market estimate is often difficult to develop with any accuracy, although some good estimates can be built up from micro-level data (discussed shortly).

A starting point is often to attempt to establish the number of persons employed in an industry or market sector that uses the products, and apply a ratio of usage based on experience or rational criteria.

A supplier of computers might obtain market estimates of numbers of persons employed in industrial and commercial activities (excluding agriculture) and apply a reasonable ratio (possibly based on experience in similar markets) of computers to employed persons (say one computer per 20 persons) to estimate maximum likely market potential.

A more refined approach to estimating total market potential involves taking a base number considered to represent the maximum possible level of consumers, and then applying a sequence of percentage ratios (**chain ratio approach**) that narrows down the market and to which some value or volume factors can be applied. Readers interested in this technique will find it explained in detail in more specialist texts on forecasting methodology.

In many developed countries government organizations monitor industry statistics of production and consumer expenditure, and desk research to access this data can help in developing estimates of market potential and market demand for products.

Manufacturing companies are normally classified by *standard industrial classification* (SIC) codes, and if a company's industrial products have applications in certain industries then accessing government statistics and lists of companies in appropriate SIC classifications will assist the sales manager in estimating market potential and in subsequent sales forecasting.

Industry sales and market shares

Making quantitative estimates of industry sales and market shares is often easier for consumer goods producers than for industrial products suppliers. There are some starting points in developing industry sales estimates, and competitor shares, including from the following sources:

● trade association data
● company accounts for competitors, suppliers and customers
● market research studies (e.g. A. C. Nielsen market audits, and the numerous other sources of published market research into product categories and industries)
● import and local production statistics
● user surveys (a ratio of usage can be developed for survey respondents that might then be applied to other non-respondents).

Multiple factor index method

This approach to forecasting regional demand is most commonly used by consumer goods companies wanting to break down national forecasts to regional forecasts, or trying to build national forecasts from known regional data about a product category. It involves having access to a reasonable range of relevant demographic data on a population, in order to build an index relating to demand and potential for growth. The method is probably a little more complex than most sales forecasters will normally choose to involve themselves in, unless for markets where a lot of relevant index data is readily available (often to be purchased or developed by a market research company), and, once again, those readers with particular interest can refer to other specialist texts on forecasting methodology.

In some markets where government departments monitor consumer expenditure (as in the UK), statistics may be available to show national expenditure on a range of product categories and regional variations in expenditure, and sales forecasters may be able to use this data to make forecasts of regional sales as a percentage of national forecast sales.

Market build-up method

This approach to forecasting is commonly used for both industrial and consumer goods as a quantitative technique, building up from the micro level to give an overall macro assessment of sales or forecast. It does require the sales forecaster to have access to lists (e.g. from trade directories) identifying the potential buyers for a product.

With an industrial product, an initial profile can be developed for typical potential users, and use might be made of any listings of companies by *standard industrial classification* (SIC) codes to identify other companies matching the user profile. If there are a large number of potential customers in the product category then data obtained from a sample of users can provide broad criteria to build mar-

ket demand estimates (see the earlier section on *user surveys*).

Future demand

When forecasting the future, a much more difficult period to forecast, many more variables come into play, not least of which must be technological change and changes in consumer or user preference.

Much future forecasting activity is directed to macro market forecasts, using both quantitative and qualitative techniques.

Time series analysis

Bearing in mind the target readership for this text, practising sales managers, we will not attempt lengthy expositions of complex statistical forecasting techniques, most of which are based on analysing data over a longer time period (time series analyses) but refer interested readers to more specialist texts. We will look briefly at some of the main macro forecasting quantitative techniques.

Time series data studies, which would normally make use of computer facilities such as spreadsheets, include the following main statistical techniques.

- **Trend fitting** is a technique where historical actual data is plotted and the trend projected.
- **Moving annual totals** or **moving annual averages** are practical techniques that smooth data in a time series, showing a trend that is not distorted by serious seasonal, cyclical or random fluctuations. An example of constructing a moving annual total trend follows in this chapter. A disadvantage of moving annual or moving average techniques is that they do not respond quickly to unexpected or significant changes in the pattern of sales.
- **Exponential smoothing** is where extra weighting is given either to earlier or to more recent data (depending on which data is seen as more likely to be representative of the future sales pattern), in an attempt to take account of more

significant changes in the pattern of sales.

- **Forecasting from time series data using standard deviations**. Again, this quantitative technique, which can be used at the level of industry or company sales, is probably unlikely to be used by most sales forecasters except possibly within major corporations serving major market sectors. But it is a technique that can be developed quite easily using a computer spreadsheet package, and also it is a technique most suited where there is a repetitive seasonal sales pattern (i.e. monthly or quarterly). The objective is to measure the seasonal fluctuations, typically by month or quarter of the year, in terms of their deviation from the average trend, then to project the trend forward, adding back in the seasonal deviation factors for each quarter.

Statistical demand analysis

The weakness in time series forms of analysis and forecasting is that it treats sales only as a function of time, taking no account of any other demand-influencing factors that affect sales, such as the effects of price and promotion, income levels, changes in population (or the mix of population where relevant, e.g. age structures, sex mix, education levels, and so on) or the introduction of new technology or product varieties. Various statistical demand techniques (often referred to as **causal analysis techniques**) are available, for those with access to computers and sufficient interest and expertise, but we will only mention them here by way of an introduction, leaving the reader to study specialist texts where appropriate.

These **causal studies**, often found in use only in the largest companies, include:

- **regression analysis**, where equations are developed that relate the volume of sales to a number of independent variables known to impact on sales performance (such as: advertising, salesperson call rate, number of distribution points, promotional expenditure, display activity,

etc.) and a line of regression (line of 'best fit') describes in quantitative terms the underlying correlation between any two sets of data
- **econometric models**, which look at the interdependent relationship of a number of factors that affect sales and profits
- **input/output models**, which might be very useful for ingredients or component forecasting where projections will encompass the demand for inputs in relation to outputs in user industries. This technique requires some knowledge of the expected level of output from users of the forecaster's products.

Market sales tests

Normally in market sales tests for new consumer products, the products are distributed into a limited geographical sales area whose consumer profile matches closely the national pattern, and where it is judged that sales performance can be monitored closely while any marketing communications can also be tightly focused to the target audience. National forecasts can be extrapolated from the test market results in this quantitative technique.

Expert opinion

In this mainly qualitative approach to macro forecasting, panels of experts on the industry (both internal and external) give their reasoned opinions on trends and estimates of market volumes in this qualitative technique.

From the perspective of the sales forecaster, an expert panel might include himself/herself, trade distributors, trade dealers or retail stockists, major end users (for industrial products), marketing consultants, international market researchers, and possibly trade association representatives.

However small or large the panel is, it will have a weakness in that each participant will have limited market exposure and knowledge. That does not mean the approach should be discarded, but does suggest that it should be only one of the approaches to forecasting adopted by a company, and not the only one.

Any known historical market or company data should be shared between all the panel of experts, and each expert will add to this from his or her own perspective of market knowledge or insight. The experts should all state the assumptions upon which they are basing their estimates. The sales forecaster can then take account of panel inputs in planning marketing strategies and developing sales forecasts.

In some markets local research firms or specialist economic forecasters will develop macro market models of expected trends and demand levels for certain industries, and larger companies often avail themselves of data from these sources.

Marketers' opinions

In this approach the sales forecaster uses his or her experience to make a primarily qualitative **judgement** of demand in, or sales to, each market sector based upon the known data and historical performance, and a considered view of the trading environment. In some instances, particularly with major branded consumer products, market research reports may indicate consumer attitudes, buying patterns, and product preferences, thereby providing help in observing or predicting trends.

The weakness in relying only on judgemental estimates in practice is that they often rely too much on the marketer's own recent sales data, taking little account of the total market and competitive activity. If an agent or distributor is under-performing against the overall market this may be missed, or even if recognized, might not be addressed through a corrective action plan. A sales manager may be more influenced by his or her distribution or sales limitations in estimating sales potential or demand than by independent data on the market.

Another factor that produces a weakness in basing forward forecasts on sales team opinions is that the team usually have no reasonable basis to anticipate trends that will emerge from significant technological changes.

The more data that sales forecasters have available on markets and existing and potential customers, the more meaningful will be any sales estimates they produce. Later in this chapter we will look at an example of building up sales estimates from customer sales records.

Surveys of future buying plans

Surveys of future buying plans are also a key means of obtaining information that can be used in preparing future forecasts of market demand and potential. This is a qualitative technique commonly used for industrial products or larger consumer products (such as household appliances and cars), where users are asked about expected product category purchases to meet their own company needs, and the company estimates its likely share of these user estimates. Most industrial products have a certain life in use, and users will need to replace equipment over time, either with an identical item where it is purely a consumable product in production processes or a wearable part, or usually with more recent technology where it is equipment. With industrial products advance knowledge of likely buying intentions and patterns can be important to plan market coverage and marketing strategies.

Other considerations in forecasting

Apart from the foregoing commentaries there are other factors that may warrant consideration when preparing a forecast, such as:

- inflation
- seasonal trends
- cyclical trends
- random fluctuations
- product life cycles.

Inflation

Normally forecasts of cost factors need to allow for inflation, and if an allowance is made in costs then a similar assumption should be made about the effect of inflation on prices. In some companies they prefer to avoid taking a view about inflation in the medium- to longer-term plans, forecasting all values at constant costs/prices applicable at the time of forecasting, and they would then take a similar approach as they roll forward the plans to further years. However, for the short term (one year) it is normal to attempt to judge the levels of inflation and its effect on both costs and prices.

Seasonal trends

Many industries and their products experience seasonal sales trends, such as in holiday and leisure goods, home improvements, gardening equipment, toys, cosmetic products, etc. If the manufacturer of the finished goods experiences seasonal sales trends, then generally the suppliers of components and other inputs will face similar trends.

Seasonality of sales affects the organization of production and the organization of the sales effort. If goods can be produced seasonally to meet demand, there may be better cash flow positions, but there may be other problems in finding suitable labour or other input supplies at short notice. The sales manager faced with seasonal products will not only need to forecast market sales with a good degree of accuracy, to ensure adequate stock is produced and available for shipment, but also will need to work with his or her sales team and any distributors to ensure that seasonal coverage of all current and potential outlets or users is at a high enough level to maximize sales during key selling seasons.

Cyclical trends

Industries serving the building, construction and agricultural products markets are familiar with the cyclical nature of these markets. Sales volumes and resultant revenues and profits are often erratic, but in some instances there is a cyclical trend that can be monitored and included in planning, so that costs (and possibly investment) can be reduced in a downswing, and expansion planned early in the upswing. If the cycles are occurring at different times in different markets supplied by the company there may be a sufficient spread of markets so that the overall sales are less disruptive to the planning process and the company's profit performance.

Random fluctuations

Typical unpredictable events that cause random or erratic fluctuations in markets can include industrial disputes, natural catastrophes, conflict and political upheaval. Random fluctuations can have **positive** or **negative** effect on sales, and as they are not normally the result of predictable events they are not normally allowed for in the market planning process.

Product life cycles

In longer-term planning the sales forecaster should consider where each of his or her products lies on their product life cycle for each market sector when developing forecasts. All products have a life cycle (see Figure 13.3), where sales will rise for a period after launch, eventually reach a peak, and thereafter decline. What differs between products and markets is the length of the life cycle, the rate of growth and decline, and the levels of peak sales; in other words the shape of the life cycle graph is not identical between products and markets.

Not all markets move at the same rate, and in some instances sales managers and marketers may find that an obsolete product in sophisticated markets may have clear functional benefits, and therefore a longer life, in less developed markets.

Developing a practical market forecast

Having looked at the issues in market forecasting, at this point it is worth taking time to look at developing a practical sales forecasting process based upon the available data. In

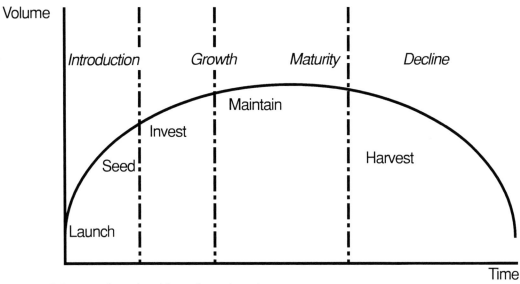

Figure 13.3 *Typical product life cycle and marketing strategies*

this section we will develop tables and graphs using a consistent set of figures through the examples given in Tables 13.1 and 13.2 and Figures 13.4 to 13.7.

Information inputs for forecasting

Most historical sales performance data can play a role in forecasting. In many companies a basic problem arises over how data is recorded and presented. It is quite common for performance data to be prepared by the department responsible for financial control, and, quite naturally, that department is sometimes more interested in monitoring costs and profits than in monitoring unit sales by product and by market. The starting point in market planning is to ensure that sales performance is monitored for the volumes and values of each product shipped to customers on a month-by-month basis.

Where sales are through a network of distributors, it becomes important to receive monthly reports of the distributor's sales from his or her stock in volume terms, as this provides the real measure of sales performance in the market. This local data is essential if the final forecasts (or targets) are to be broken down to the level of targets for individual customers in the market. A macro

(market level) forecast is much less likely to be achieved, or even if the forecast is achieved it might represent an under-achievement against real sales potential, where it is not broken down to the micro level on an account-by-account basis. A multi-product company will need to forecast or target separately for each product.

The basis for a simple practical forecasting process can be as follows:

- use recorded historical data to provide a base for measurement against plans and forecasting
- fit a trend line (using judgement or more sophisticated statistical techniques if practical)
- plot total industry data, and project trends similarly
- build up forecasts by product, market sector and account, summarizing to give sales territory and national estimates (this micro-level build-up of account sales forecasts can be compared with the macro forecasts).

Forecasts should include any appropriate adjustment for any significant developments that are expected to affect sales more than a forward projection of historical sales might suggest, e.g. innovative new technology that might open the market to more consumers through price, availability, ease of use factors, etc., such as we have seen in the computer and mobile telephone industries.

While the sales forecaster will normally have access to data on his or her own market sales, industry data for the total product category (in volume or values) or sub-categories might be available through national trade associations, market research sources, government statistical publications, or other identifiable sources. Industry estimates might not always be very accurate for any single market sector, but they should not be ignored as the sales manager should benchmark his or her performance against the total market and individual competitors (where any data is available on their sales performance).

Tabulating data and projecting trends in moving annual formats

The sales forecaster can compile a simple table of market sales data, as illustrated in Table 13.1, where we have assumed the data used is sourced from the company's sales reports. The illustrative graphs in Figures 13.4 to 13.7 are based upon the data in this table.

From the reported **actual monthly sales**, entered in the left-hand column under each of the three year's data, the **cumulative sales data** can be tabulated (shown in the second column under each year's data) as a simple numerical summation, producing the total of the full year's sales in the last row for each year. The monthly sales data illustrated in this example shows a wide variation in local monthly sales, likely to indicate a seasonal sales pattern or possibly some stock management problems.

The cumulative sales for 1995 show an increase over 1994 of 6.5 per cent, with a further increase in 1996 compared with 1995 of 5.5 per cent. So, in this example, there is real growth in unit sales of the company's widgets in the national market, albeit with a very irregular monthly sales pattern. To use this basic data to see a clearer overall picture of sales trends we can tabulate what is termed **moving annual data.**

Moving annual data

As was referred to earlier in the chapter, when introducing some of the quantitative forecasting techniques, tabulating **moving monthly averages** of monthly sales data

Table 13.1 Market sales data, units sold

Market sales performance data, company sales of widgets (including monthly sales, cumulative sales and moving annual data)											
Units	**1994**				**1995**				**1996**			
	Actual	Cumulative	Moving monthly average	Moving annual total	Actual	Cumulative	Moving monthly average	Moving annual total	Actual	Cumulative	Moving monthly average	Moving annual total
Jan.	25350	25350			27960	27960	17648	211770	25560	25560	18365	220390
Feb.	30010	55360			30260	58220	17668	212020	47520	73080	19804	237650
March	13560	68920			12170	70390	17552	210630	16800	89880	20190	242280
April	13090	82010			11830	82220	17448	209370	7080	96960	19794	237530
May	18040	100050			14260	96480	17133	205590	8420	105380	19308	231690
June	13600	113650			16670	113150	17388	208660	16190	121570	19268	231210
July	8470	122120			16180	129330	18030	216370	14280	135850	19109	229310
Aug.	22890	145010			10880	140210	17030	204360	12360	148210	19232	230790
Sept.	28760	173770			25560	165770	16763	201160	29740	177950	19580	234970
Oct.	15480	189250			25130	190900	17568	210810	26390	204340	19685	236230
Nov.	8270	197520			12330	203230	17906	214870	11420	215760	19610	235320
Dec.	11640	209160	17430	209160	19560	222790	18565	222790	19240	235000	19583	235000

Moving annual totals	This data is a useful measure of trends and performance on a year-on year rolling basis. Once data for a full year on a monthly basis is available, the moving annual total can be developed and updated each month.
	Starting from the total for the base period of 12 months, a calendar year in Table 13.1, you add the actual monthly sales figure for the next month (for volumes or values, as appropriate) to the 12-month total, and deduct the monthly sales figure for the same month in the previous year, i.e. the MAT for January 1995 is
	$$209160 + 27960 - 25350 = 211770$$
	This is continued for each subsequent month, so that you are always looking at a rolling year total, including all seasonal or monthly sales patterns, highlighting positive or negative sales trends.
Moving monthly averages	In the example, this figure is purely a division of the moving annual total by 12, to show the average monthly sales on a rolling year basis. That smoothes out wide fluctuations between the sales for individual months.

smoothes out wide fluctuations in actual monthly sales patterns, and tabulating **moving annual totals** (MAT) of sales smoothes out wide fluctuations in seasonal sales, showing the longer-term underlying sales trend more clearly. Moving annual data is developed as shown above.

In Figure 13.4 alternative ways of plotting data are illustrated, and each can be used in the forecasting process to project sales trends into the future.

The graph in Figure 13.4(a) shows the actual monthly sales, with wide fluctuations between months but the main seasonal peak around December to February, with a lesser peak in the late summer. By plotting the moving monthly average the underlying trend is more apparent, and can be projected forward from the point where actual data finishes, indicated by the arrow on the graph, fitting a line by inspection or through calculation (in this case into 1997). The moving monthly average projected to a point in time can be multiplied by 12 to give the estimate of moving annual total sales to that point if the sales continue to follow the projected trend. In this example we are not looking at any more sophisticated techniques but just projecting a trend line by eye and judgement. We will look at some of the many ways of projecting the trend line, using the

same base data, through calculation later.

The graph in Figure 13.4(b) plots the moving annual total of the data from the preceding table, and from the point marked by the arrow this has been projected forward, fitting a trend line by inspection based on a similar percentage sales growth pattern.

So far the data recorded, and projections made, look at the market sales of the supplier's widgets in isolation, without any cross-reference to what is happening in the total market for widgets. The marketer should seek out any data on the total market for widgets, plot this and compare his or her own performance with the total market performance. It is not usual to get meaningful total market data on a month-by-month basis, but annual data may be available (or calculated from local production statistics if available, plus imports, minus exports). Figure 13.5 illustrates how data might look when total market sales of widgets are plotted, with our supplier's widget sales also plotted for comparison, and some sales trend projections added in for the next five years, fitted by judgement.

Plotting the total market compared with company product sales can highlight aspects of the marketing strategy that might need

(a) Actual monthly widget unit sales and moving annual average of unit sales

(b) Moving annual total of widget sales and trend projection fitted by inspection

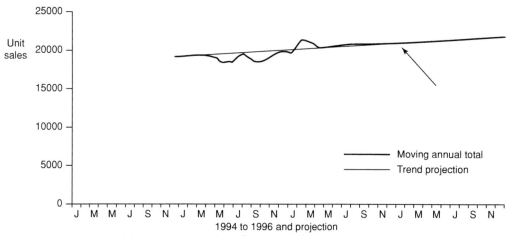

Figure 13.4 *Fitting trend lines to historical performance data to aid forecasting*

attention. In our example of widgets, the company widget sales have grown much faster than the market rate of growth, to the point where the company has approximately 25 per cent market share at the end of 1995. While this may be the result of good marketing and sales activity, with product advantages communicated effectively to customers, the supplier's high share may need to be looked at in relation to potential competitors who might erode that share, and in relation to the total widget market that might be growing at a slower rate than the company's sales. The resultant considerations, taken with regard to all the other information and variables, might prompt marketing strategies aimed at:

- defending the existing share, building further on customer loyalty,
- reinforcing perceptions of points of brand differentiation,
- price positioning strategies aimed at stealing a larger share through aggressive pricing, or of harvesting profit from the product possibly by confident upward pricing,
- or of diversifying the marketing effort to build other products in the portfolio.

The 'Z' chart in monitoring performance

Another way of depicting sales data is as illustrated in the **'Z' chart** of Figure 13.6, which plots actual monthly, cumulative and

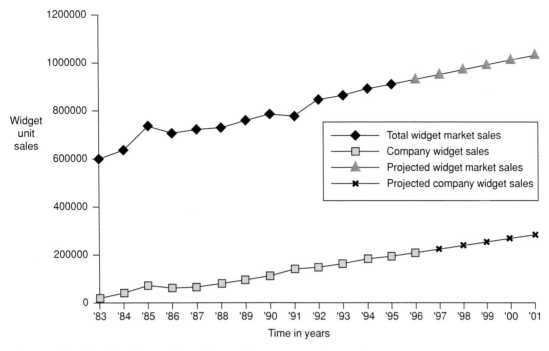

Figure 13.5 *Total market widget sales and company widget sales*

moving annual data for a year, in this case 1995 sales of the company's widget.

In this example, where we have plotted the marketer's forecast for 1995 along with the subsequent actual sales, we should question:

- the accuracy of the forecasting process, since the forecast cumulative sales were less than was achieved in the previous year (shown from the moving annual total at the start of the year)
- the pattern of monthly sales forecast, which bears little relationship to the actual monthly sales.

In some cases there would be valid reasons for forecasting a downturn in sales, but with our additional data in this instance, it is suspect, possibly with a forecast being submitted by a cautious forecaster rather than calculated rationally and negotiated between the marketers and the sales management team as part of a joint planning process for the market. Also, if production were scheduled to match the forecast monthly sales pattern, without sufficient account of the apparent

seasonal nature of sales, then it is likely that there would be stock problems at certain points in some months, or sales rationed, and in either case actual company product sales would then have been below potential sales.

Figure 13.7 shows some of the data from Table 13.1 plotted over recent years with the addition of sales forecast data for the market, and in this example we can see that the marketer has taken action in the latest year, 1997, to improve the forecasting and narrow the gap between actual and forecast sales.

When sales data is being recorded the sales forecaster should note any particular events that cause unusual fluctuations in sales that might affect forecasting. For example, the widget sales for February 1996 in this example jumped to an extremely high figure of over 47,000 unit sales, some 50 per cent over previous February sales, even though this is a peak selling month. If this represents a serious and lasting increase in sales, it is reasonable to continue to forecast at that sort of level for future months of February. If, however, it was a freak month's sales for any reason, possibly in anticipation of an expected

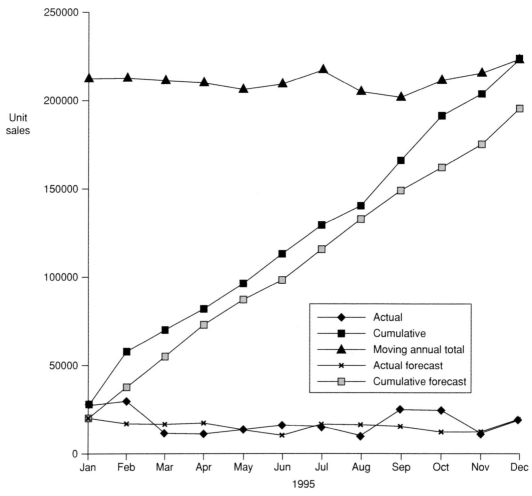

Figure 13.6 *'Z' chart – sales performance of company widgets*

price increase, or there was an unusually heavy burst of advertising, then future forecasts should reflect the more normal level indicated using average monthly deviations in this example.

Forecasting from moving annual total data

An alternative to just projecting a trend line on a graph of tabulated moving annual total data is to take the moving annual total at a point in time, and to project it forward by a factor expected to represent the achievable growth (this factor possibly being higher than that shown by plotting the trend line forward by eye and judgement). Normally spreadsheet packages are used in forecasting

calculations, which enable variations to be incorporated easily.

In the example here we have taken the actual data from Table 13.1, and made two forecasts (see Table 13.2) at the level of five per cent and ten per cent on the moving annual total at December 1996 (235,000 widgets). We have arbitrarily assumed straight line growth in the moving annual total for both calculations, and can use the projected moving annual totals to calculate the monthly sales that would be necessary to achieve those moving annual totals.

The reader may note that one problem in forecasting by projecting a moving annual total in a straight line, and using that to calculate the monthly sales, is that it will project

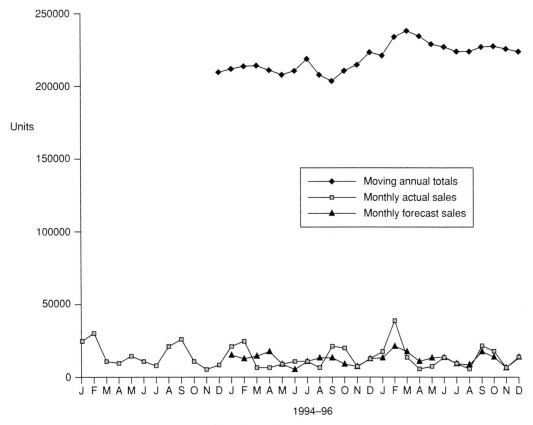

Figure 13.7 *Continuous monitoring of market sales*

a pattern of sales representing the last year, which may not be fully representative of the longer-run seasonal pattern. In this example we would be projecting extremely high February sales followed by low April and May figures, as per the 1996 pattern. The alternative way to build the forecast this way is to estimate the monthly sales first, and build these into the moving annual total to see what projected growth (or decline) pattern of sales is predicted.

Forecasting as in this example adds more weight to recent months and the last year than to earlier years, again producing a possible bias.

Problems in using trend data based on past sales

Whenever trends are identified and plotted they are, quite obviously, based on history, and do not allow for strong current trends,

particularly when based upon averages of longer time periods. Any forecasts based on moving annual data, moving monthly averages, moving quarterly averages or other past data must be tempered with the sales forecaster's inputs of judgement to allow for current trends or anticipated developments. A weakness in using moving averages is that all the time periods being analysed are weighted equally, and information from the oldest periods are just as important in the forecasting as information from the newest periods – which is often inappropriate in real-life marketing, where recent events should have more weight attached to them.

In essence, what we are saying is that there is no simple ideal and accurate way of producing a forecast, particularly with all the complexity of factors to be considered in product marketing. If there is additional market knowledge the sales forecaster might decide to apply his or her judgement to this

Table 13.2 *Using moving annual totals in forecasting*

Month		Forecast moving annual total (5% growth)	Forecast monthly sales (5% growth)	Forecast moving annual total (10% growth)	Forecast monthly sales (10% growth)
1996 base	Dec.	235 000		235 000	
1997	Jan.	235 958	26 518	236 880	27 440
	Feb.	236 919	48 482	238 775	49 415
	March	237 885	17 765	240 685	18 710
	Apr.	238 854	8 049	242 611	9 005
	May	239 827	9 393	244 552	10 361
	June	240 805	17 167	246 508	18 146
	July	241 786	15 261	248 480	16 252
	Aug.	242 771	13 345	250 468	14 348
	Sept.	243 760	30 729	252 472	31 744
	Oct.	244 754	27 383	254 491	28 410
	Nov.	245 751	12 417	256 527	13 456
	Dec.	246 753	20 241	258 580	21 292

knowledge, and alter the growth factor accordingly from that indicated by historical sales data. Other information might also be available suggesting the forecasts should be adjusted from the moving monthly average or moving annual total trend approaches to forecasting (including surveys, expert opinions or panels, or through statistical quantitative techniques).

In summary of this section, the sales forecaster should attempt to gather and plot data on his or her product sales in total and for each market sector, and comparable data for the total market for his or her product category. Actual monthly and cumulative (year to date) sales statistics can be tabulated and graphed, along with moving annual total data and moving monthly average data that smoothes out major fluctuations and helps in identifying trends and developing more accurate forecasts.

For readers interested in developing forecasts using actual data and calculations of seasonal deviations I would refer them to Chapter 14 on Export Sales Forecasting in my companion volume, *The CIM Handbook of Export Marketing*. That text extends the coverage of this chapter, which is aimed more at practising sales managers probably with lim-ited data and resources to devote to the forecasting process.

Building forecasts from local market sales data

Apart from using the overall data of sales to, or in, the market to monitor progress and provide a basis for market forecasting, forecasts can also be built up from the micro level by looking at the historical sales for each current customer account and potential sales to each prospective account, and comparing the two to come to a reasoned, realistic and achievable (within the forecast period time frame) figure. To build forecasts in this way it is necessary to have sales data on individual customers kept for each product.

The importance of key accounts

For most suppliers, and in most markets, a few key accounts dominate purchases (for local distribution and re-sale) or direct use of a supplier's products. The sales manager should be monitoring sales to and through these accounts. If they are being supplied by direct shipments from the supplier, it is easier to access the direct shipment records. If they are being supplied through locally appointed distributors, it will be necessary to obtain data from the distributors, and that will be more forthcoming where distributors see the need for the data in forward planning, and the benefits of accuracy in forward planning to their sales throughput, cash flow and stock management.

The sales manager might design some simple form (or computer spreadsheet) that summarizes sales history and contains an estimate (ideally based on discussions with the key account) of its likely purchases in the next planning period. A well-designed form, provided the information can be collected, can provide useful insights into the relative growth of major customers, and provide information useful to developing market sales tactics.

Table 13.3 illustrates a form that can be used in key account planning. Experience of

the account and judgement of its progress and prospects will play a role in forecasting its future demand for the supplier's products.

In Table 13.3 we have assumed that the product is an industrial component sold to manufacturers of other products for incorporation in their own products. The example shows the key widget accounts, with their purchases from our widget supplier, and their estimated total widget purchase requirements for 1997. With this data the sales manager can judge the importance of accounts in the market and to his or her company in particular, and plan particular sales tactics to develop business with individual key accounts. In this example the top ten listed accounts represent 42.5% of the 1997 projected total market for widgets, and the higher share of 47.8% of our supplier's projected widget sales to the market, so key

Table 13.3 Forecast of widget sales to key user accounts

Top accounts' share of markets and forecasts					
Unit Sales		Company sales history		Company sales forecast	Total volume estimate
Year	1994	1995	1996	1997	1997
Key accounts	Volume	Volume	Volume	Volume	
1 Acme Toy Factory	2 470	7 970	8 230	9 000	45 000
2 Car Spares Incorporated	14 690	18 930	16 500	17 500	40 000
3 Wing Electronics	13 780	15 780	15 900	16 000	38 000
4 Lee Mechanical Toys	7 500	9 560	8 900	10 000	36 000
5 A & B Accessories	6 490	9 670	10 350	11 500	30 000
6 Chan Radiophonics	-	-	-	4 000	30 000
7 Oriental Lighting	8 240	12 530	13 420	15 000	35 000
8 Asian Electronic Industry	11 420	7 420	9 460	10 000	60 000
9 Photo Accessories Ltd.	6 900	13 600	12 630	14 000	50 000
10 Intelligent Toys Ltd.	5 640	8 360	10 200	12 000	46 000
Total key accounts sales	77 130	103 910	105 590	119 000	**410 000**
% share of company total	36.9%	46.6%	44.9%	47.8%	
TOTAL COMPANY SALES	209 160	222 790	235 000	249 000	
Company share of market	23.4%	24.5%	25.0%	25.8%	
TOTAL MARKET SALES	893 600	910 750	940 000	965 000	965 000
Key account % share of market					**42.5%**

account relations and development are clearly critical in that market category.

Once the overview of the key account market is prepared, and targets or forecasts established, sales tactics must be developed and implemented to turn these targets into reality. Since not every customer may want the identical format of widget the supplier can plan production to suit customer requirements, and minimize stock holding of product variants.

If it is helpful to the planning process the sales manager may want to summarize his or her sales history and forecasts or targets by category of end use, as illustrated in Table 13.4. This might be particularly useful where there are differences in the product variants needed for each industry sector or outlet type.

Building targets for a larger customer base

Since most products are sold to a larger number of users or outlets (i.e. retail outlets or other sub-distributors for re-sale), if forecasts or targets are being built up from the market base then a more comprehensive listing of current and prospective customers will be needed. The sales manager can design some suitable forms for data tabulation, or a simple computer spreadsheet data record, but typically data is needed that shows the expected pattern of sales across the year, or the expected sales by product variant.

Typical example forms, on which computer database spreadsheets can be modelled, for developing market targets or forecasts are shown in Tables 13.5 and 13.6. Whether the sales manager is marketing industrial or consumer products, the same approach to building forecasts or targets can be applied.

Most sales forecasters can improve their market sales forecasting. If the only current approach to forecasting is either taking last year's figures for shipments and aiming to better it by a certain percentage, or just developing an annual sales 'target' and dividing it into 12 equal portions, then there will be additional information available from some source that can improve upon that, and reduce the risks of a hit or miss forecasting style. As we have seen in this chapter, apart from making better use of company sales data, having an external benchmark, such as industry data on market sales, will provide an additional dimension further refining forecasting. Identifying trends and incorporating them into forecasting (whether seasonal or cyclical) improves the meaningfulness.

The medium-term annual forecasts will need to be monitored frequently, at least monthly, and updated short-term forecasts prepared as necessary, often quarterly, to ensure production and sales plans are adjusted to meet demand or potential.

Table 13.4 Sales analysis and forecasts by market sector

Widget sales by market sector				
Units Market sector	1994	1995	1996	Forecast 1997
Toys	41 320	47 400	48 175	49 800
% total	19.8%	21.3%	20.5%	20.0%
Electrical and Electronics	118 080	121 630	133 715	141 930
% total	56.5%	54.6%	56.9%	57.0%
Car Accessories	49 760	53 760	53 110	57 270
% total	23.8%	24.1%	22.6%	23.0%
TOTALS	209 160	222 790	235 000	249 000

Table 13.5 Market sales target product summary sheet

Market: UK					Product variant: Wall coverings (10 metre rolls)						Year 1997				
Customer	**1996**	**1997**													
	Sales	**Target**	**Jan.**	**Feb.**	**Mar.**	**Apr.**	**May**	**June**	**July**	**Aug.**	**Sept.**	**Oct.**	**Nov.**	**Dec.**
Khan Stores	340	355	15	15	20	20	50	70	40	30	35	25	20	15
Acme DIY	460	535	20	20	25	30	100	70	110	60	40	20	20	20
Decor City	900	980	40	60	60	70	130	160	200	100	60	40	30	30
TOTALS	20 960	22 990	1020	1 170	1 340	1 900	2 560	2 980	3 100	2 420	19 60	1 800	15 40	1 200

Table 13.6 Market annual product sales targets, unit sales and values

Market: UK		Product group: Hand cut crystal						Year 1997	
	Royal Windsor		**Buckingham**		**Westminster**		**TOTALS**	
Customer	**Volume**	**Value**	**Volume**	**Value**	**Volume**	**Value**	**Volume**	**Value**
Astel Dept Store	560	6 160	380	4 560	470	6 110	1 410	16 830
Royal Dept. Store	350	3 850	620	7 440	720	9 360	1 690	20 650
The Wedding List	290	3 190	430	5 160	370	4 810	1 090	13 160
TOTALS	21 300	234 300	49 000	588 000	47 500	617 500	117 800	1439 800

Checklist 13.1
Forecasting and planning

Action points

Sales forecasting
  Decide on forecast period
  - One year (short term)
  - One/three years (medium term)
  - Three/five years (long term)

Check data sources relevant to planning and forecasting
  - Internal sales records:
    - Volumes/values
    - Month by month data
    - Product data
    - Trade market sector data
    - By customer/distributor
    - (Unfulfilled order enquiries)
  - External relevant data:
    - Published data on potential markets
    - Import and local production data
    - Competitive foreign market activity

Choose the approach to forecasting current or future demand:
  - Statistical approaches (time series analysis such as moving annual totals and moving monthly averages, demand analysis, multiple factor index method)
  - Surveys of buyers' intentions or market tests
  - Marketer's judgement, distributor's judgement, sales force opinions or expert opinions
  - Estimates of market potential
  - Industry sales and market share analysis
  - Market build-up methods

Develop your sales forecasts at macro and micro levels:
  - Product volumes/values
  - Market/product group profitability
  - Target market share
  by relevant categories such as:
  - Monthly
  - Annually
  - Market sector
  - Product or product group

Consider:
  - Market knowledge
    - Competition
    - Economic and trading environments

	Action points
Checklist 13.1 continued	

Checklist 13.1 continued
   - Political factors
   - Distribution channel factors
- Trends in market sales/production/imports
  Regulatory factors
- Consumer (changing) attitudes, perceptions, etc.
- Product innovation
- Seasonal or cyclical factors
- Product life cycles
- Company resource limitations
   - Production capacity
   - Flexibility to modify products
   - Availability of inputs
   - Financial resources for sales and marketing activity
   - Human (marketing) resources
- Adaptations or specialist products for customers (or export)

Set overall company objectives for each market
- Market volumes/values
- Distribution
- Market shares

Take account of:
- Product mix
- Pricing levels
- Marketing strategies

Set objectives for each level of sales activity in the market:
- Trade market sector
- Product/product group
- Key account
- Customer
- Salesperson/territory

Revenue and cost budgeting
Support forecasts with department budgets, taking account of costs of:
- Order processing and physical distribution costs
- Marketing communications
- Advertising and promotion
- Travel and related expenses
- Customer service
- Department salaries
- Sales training and recruitment

Plan staffing levels required to achieve objectives and forecasts:
- Marketing management
- Sales personnel
- Clerical and administrative support
- Changes in the needs and mix of skills

Establish availability of material inputs enabling the company to source and produce competitively, with consideration to:
- Breadth/depth of product range

	Action points

Checklist 13.1 continued
  ● Exchange rate movements (for imported inputs)
  ● Input supplies availability
Develop revenue forecasts by:
  ● Trade market sector
  ● Product/product group
  ● Key account
  ● Other customers
  ● Salesperson/territory
Develop profit contribution forecasts by:
  ● Trade market sector
  ● Product/product group
  ● Key account
  ● Other customers
  ● Salesperson/territory	

14

Performance monitoring

Monitoring sales performance ▬

Professional sales managers or marketers will want a broad range of performance monitoring data to enable them to measure their progress and benchmark performance in respect of:

- company forecasts or targets (sales values, volumes and profitability)
- national sales of similar products to their markets
- the activity and progress of competitors (both domestic producers and importers)
- the share of each product category or market sector that they supply
- product distribution within the company's customer base, and within all companies buying or using products in the appropriate product categories
- the effectiveness of any distributors in expanding market share, distribution and sales volumes (versus competitors)
- sales progress with individual accounts or customers (particularly key accounts)
- effectiveness of sales promotions
- effectiveness and responses to advertising programmes.

Figure 14.1 illustrates diagramatically some of the levels of activity and information that the sales manager may want to measure and monitor on an ongoing basis, depending what is available or relevant to an individual company. The diagram emphasizes the need to monitor both company performance against itself, i.e. current performance com-pared with performance in previous comparable periods, and company performance in relation to an outside benchmark, such as the performance of the industry sector.

If the company is exporting, then measurements, where possible, should be for each of the categories illustrated in Figure 14.1 on a:

- market-by-market basis
- company sales versus national export sales (obtained from Customs & Excise published data) for each product type identified
- company sales versus the total foreign market sales for each product or category (i.e. imports to the foreign market from all sources, plus local production, minus any exports or re-exports).

> A company's performance should not just be looked at in isolation, but always monitored or benchmarked against external or industry data to give a measure of comparative performance.

In the sub-sections below we will take a broader look at sales performance monitoring, and examples of how performance monitoring data might be constructed.

Analyses of sales despatches

Most companies will be using computer spreadsheets and databases to monitor sales

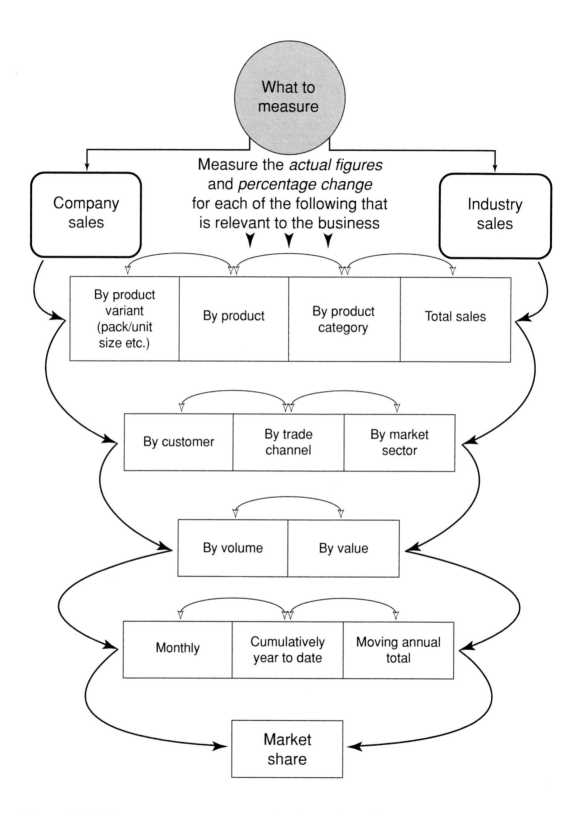

Figure 14.1 *What to measure – company and industry sales to the market*

performance, but we can illustrate here with tables some data that can be recorded as part of the sales monitoring process. First identify the performance criteria that can beneficially be measured. More usually you will want to establish progress and measurement against some or all of the following criteria.

- Compare the individual performance of your company against **industry national total sales** of the relevant product categories. Figures can compare volumes, values and percentage share of each itemized product category.
- Your company's **share of market sales** in the relevant category, monitored by volume, value and percentage share of each market sector.
- Your company's **month-by-month sales performance** in volume and value, recorded for total sales and by product or

product type. This data can be compared with, say, the same month last year. This generally should be done both for total sales covering product categories or market sectors you supply, and on an individual sector-by-sector or category-by-category basis. It is also useful to measure the percentage change of this year (TY) versus last year (LY).
- **Cumulative performance** in total, and sector by sector or category by category, for the current year to date (updated monthly) versus last year to date, both by volume and value.

If you are starting an information recording process you could design simple sales despatch records, as in Tables 14.1 to 14.4, in which the sales of some electrical products are monitored. It is always useful to note the sales forecast or target wherever you are

Table 14.1 Monitoring current year despatches

Market despatch record: UK				Year 1997	
Product				Electric razors	
	Date	Customer no.	Invoice	Units	Value
Forecast				10 000	150 000
JAN.	01/01	Khan Ltd	0001	50	750
	15/01	Acme Ltd	0004	25	375
	19/01	Capitol Ltd	0011	100	1 500
Month				175	2 625
YTD				175	2 625
FEB.	03/02	Acme Ltd	0019	40	600
	09/02	Astra Ltd	0023	50	750
	15/02	Capitol Ltd	0027	75	1 125
	26/02	Disco Ltd	0031	100	1 500
Month				265	3 975
YTD				440	6 600
MARCH					
Month					
YTD					
%TY/LY					

Table 14.2 Comparison of current year despatches with previous year

Market despatch record: UK				Year 1997	
Product				Electric razors	
	Date	**Customer no.**	**Invoice**	**Units**	**Value**
Forecast				**10 000**	**150 000**
JAN.	01/01	Khan Ltd	0001	50	750
	15/01	Acme Ltd	0004	25	375
	19/01	Capitol Ltd	0011	100	1 500
Month				175	2 625
YTD				175	2 625
LYTD				200	2 800
%TY/LY				87.5%	94%
FEB.	03/02	Acme Ltd	0019	40	600
	09/02	Astra Ltd	0023	50	750
	15/02	Capitol Ltd	0027	75	1 125
	26/02	Disco Ltd	0031	100	1 500
Month				265	3 975
YTD				440	6 600
LYTD				430	6 020
%TY/LY				102%	110%
MARCH					
Month					
YTD					
LYTD					
%TY/LY					

recording performance data, as that keeps you conscious of progress against objectives. Table 14.1 records individual despatches to customers for each month, and total them to give a month and year to date (YTD) figure.

Alternatively, the same individual data for despatches can be tabulated, but additionally we could enter the despatch figures for the previous year, shown as last year to date (LYTD), and a comparison of the performance this year versus last year in percentage terms (%TY/LY). Table 14.2 shows that, while January was not a good month compared with last year, shipments picked up in February, and by the end of February despatches for the first two months were ahead of last year by two per cent on units

and ten per cent on values.

For each separate month, say February, you can then extract the total by product, sold through each trade channel sector, and the grand total for each individual product, and place these figures on a **monthly market summary** covering all products or sectors (see Table 14.3). This chart shows monthly, year to date (YTD) and a comparison with the last year to date (LYTD). Additionally, you can make a percentage comparison of this year versus last year (TY/LY).

Using the same format, you can transfer the month-by-month totals from the bottom of the market despatch summaries for each separate month and build these to give month-by-month comparisons (see Table

Table 14.3 Monthly market shipments summary

Market sector record: ALL SECTORS						Year: 1997 Month: February			
Products	Razors		Toasters		Hair dryers		Electric irons		
Units/ £ 000's	**Units**	**Value**	**Units**	**Value**	**Units**	**Value**	**Units**	**Value**	
Forecast	43 200	6 48K	24 000	288K	13 000	135K	17 000	272K	
Electrical specialists	265	3 975	140	1 680	120	1 248	160	2 560	
YTD	440	6 600	310	3 720	190	1 976	280	4 480	
LYTD	430	6 020	300	3 360	180	1 728	265	3 975	
%TY/LY	102%	110%	103%	111%	106%	114%	106%	113%	
Department stores	330	4 950	300	3 600	160	1 664	290	4 640	
YTD	560	8 400	500	6 000	280	2 912	410	6 560	
LYTD	540	7 560	480	5 376	300	2 880	400	6 000	
%TY/LY	104%	1115	104%	1125	93%	101%	103%	109%	
Catalogue suppliers	110	1650	90	1 080	20	208	150	2 400	
YTD	150	2 250	130	1 560	40	416	250	4 000	
LYTD	260	3 640	140	1 568	40	384	240	3 600	
%TY/LY	58%	62%	93%	99%	100%	108%	104%	111%	
YTD									
LYTD									
%TY/LY									
TOTAL FEBRUARY	**3 000**	**45 000**	**2 000**	**24 000**	**900**	**9 360**	**1 050**	**16 800**	
YTD	4 750	71 250	3 000	36 000	1 400	14 560	1 650	24 600	
LYTD	4 500	63 000	2 900	31 900	1 450	14 210	1 800	27 000	
%TY/LY	106%	113%	103%	113%	97%	102%	92%	91%	
% F/cast	11%	11%	13%	13%	11%	11%	10%	9%	

14.4). This example shows the overall company sales position to the latest month, and in the format illustrated here the sales manager can see at a glance his or her overall performance against the annual forecast. Table 14.4 indicates that sales values are increasing at a faster percentage rate than volume, but this basically reflects inflation, in that there was a product price increase.

This format could be re-designed to show a separate forecast for each month of the year, and subsequent performance against that monthly forecast. That might be more useful where there were strong seasonal variations to sales, and therefore it could be necessary to monitor each individual month more closely to ensure the performance in key months matches expectations.

Table 14.4 shows that while the year did not start off well, indicated by the January figures for all product sectors (possibly despatches or orders were late in the post-Christmas period), February showed an upturn, and by the end of the second month there is real growth.

Looking at any single month usually tells us little in monitoring sales performance. Year-to-date versus last-year-to-date comparisons are generally important in sales analyses because there are so many distortions to affect any single month, such as delays in despatching resulting from production prob-

Table 14.4 *Company summary: cumulative sales data for all market sectors*

Market Despatch Record: ALL MARKETS									Year: 1997	
Products	Razors		Toasters		Hair dryers		Electric Irons		TOTAL COMPANY	
Units/ £000's	**Units**	**Value**	**Units**	**Value**	**Units**	**Value**	**Units**	**Value**	**Units**	**Values**
Forecast	43 200	648K	24 000	288K	13 000	135K	17 000	272K	97 200	1 379
JAN.	1 750	26 250	1 000	12 000	500	5 200	600	9 600	3 850	53 050
YTD	1 750	26 250	1 000	12 000	500	5 200	600	9 600	3 850	53 050
LYTD	1 800	27 000	1 100	12 100	530	5 194	620	9 300	4 050	53 594
%TY/LY	97%	97%	91%	99%	94%	100%	97%	103%	95.1%	100%
% F/cast	4%	4%	4%	4%	4%	4%	3.5%	3.5%	4%	3.8%
FEB.	3 000	45 000	2 000	24 000	900	9 360	1 050	16 800	6 950	95 160
YTD	4 750	71 250	3 000	36 000	1 400	14 560	1 650	24 600	10 800	146 140
LYTD	4 500	63 000	2 900	31 900	1 450	14 210	1 800	27 000	10 650	136 020
%TY/LY	1 06%	113%	103%	113%	97%	102%	92%	91%	101.4%	107.4%
% F/cast	11%	11%	13%	13%	11%	11%	10%	9%	11.1%	10.6%
MARCH										
YTD										
LYTD										
%TY/LY										
% F/cast										

YTD = Year to date   TYTD = This year to date   TY/LY = This year/Last year comparison

lems, or late ordering by customers in one year versus another.

This detail of analysis draws the sales manager's attention to potential problems where plans are not being met, may assist in identifying seasonal patterns not previously taken into consideration (if, say, you simply allocated the same plan volume to each month), and enables future planning and forecast preparation to be more accurate and sophisticated as you build up a historical database. If you have a relevant budget figure, this should appear at each point of measurement on each of your analysis sheets and you can show achievement by individual salesperson and/or customer, month by month, total sales month by month, and percentage achievement and cumulative achievements against the budget or plan.

As more data becomes available over a longer time period you will benefit by preparing **moving annual total** analyses of market sales (discussed in Chapter 13). These will provide a measure of the longer-term trends that the sales manager should monitor. As shown in the previous chapter, moving annual totals (MATs) and/or moving monthly averages (MMA) can usefully be tabulated and updated monthly for:

● the total sales of company products (turnover, volume sales, profit performance)
● individual products and/or product categories (turnover values and volumes)
● market sectors or trade channels supplied by the company (turnover values and volumes)

- by sales territory where it would be an additional longer-term meaningful measure.

Do constantly bear in mind that there is no benefit in producing data just for the exercise of statistics. Production of statistical data is worthwhile only if it:

- measures performance against comparable relevant criteria (forecasts, targets, budgets)
- helps in identifying underlying trends and aids the planning process
- gives warnings of significant variances from plans and programmes in sufficient time for corrective action to be implemented to impact on results within

the plan's time frame
- aids the planning process
- aids the sales team in the performance of its functions and assists in the recognition and acceptance of training needs.

Market share analysis

The first estimate of performance that in any way relates to a share of a market is generally to **monitor your share of total sales** to the market, which gives you a simple comparison of your performance against other suppliers. That may be broken down further to market shares by particular trade channel sectors or market segments, or even to your share of category purchases for particular customers (e.g. key accounts). Table 14.5

Table 14.5 Market share analysis

Share of UK sales: clocks by trade channel Period: Jan.–June 1997						
Trade channel	Company		National – all suppliers		Company % of National	
	Vol.	Val.	Vol.	Val.	Vol.	Val.
Independent jewellers						
TY	9 100	38 000	18 800	66 000	48%	58%
LY	8 500	34 000	18 000	60 000	47%	57%
%TY/LY	107%	112%	105%	110%		
Department stores						
TY	4 800	20 000	13 300	60 000	36%	33%
LY	4 700	19 000	13 600	59 000	36%	32%
%TY/LY	102%	105%	98%	102%		
Catalogue companies						
TY	14 600	61 300	48 600	168 000	30%	36%
LY	13 700	54 600	46 500	153 600	29%	36%
%TY/LY						
Others						
TY	6 600	27 700	21 700	74 600	30%	37%
LY	6 300	25 100	22 000	72 300	29%	35%
%TY/LY						
All sectors						
TY	35 100	147 000	102 400	368 600	34%	40%
LY	33 200	132 700	100 100	344 900	33%	38%
%TY/LY	105.7%	110.8%	102.3%	106.9%		

illustrates one simple analysis of a company's share versus industry national sales. The example shows that, while both the company and industry are showing growth versus the previous year (comparing TY/LY figures), our supplier is growing faster than the industry for both volume and value sales, and gaining slightly in market share.

As an alternative in the example, clock sales could be monitored by market sector rather than trade channel, such as:

- personal household users
- commercial users

or by type of clock, possibly with further subcategories, e.g.

- digital clocks
- analogue clocks
- wall clocks
- desktop/ mantel clocks.

Total market sales data may be available from:

- industry trade associations
- feedback from major users or customers, building up an estimate from individual purchases
- government monitoring data, such as household expenditure surveys production output surveys import/export (Customs & Excise) data.

If the sales manager can obtain data for industry sales of key product categories to major customers some useful analyses can often be prepared to compare company performance with the industry. In the example of Table 14.6, if the company looked at its sales in isolation the performance might seem satisfactory, as the bottom line shows it has year-on-year growth over 11 per cent and over 12 per cent for 1995 and 1996 respectively. But by looking at individual key accounts we see that in some it has grown in value and in share, in some it has grown in value but declined in share of UK product category sales, and to some major customers it does

not supply at all. The company's sales market ranking in the second to last (from right) column reasonably parallels the UK sales to the main customers ranking of the last column, but there are some glaring differences, which would warrant investigation or commentary if this chart were part of the marketing strategy plan.

- Company sales to Welcome are negligible, yet it is the second largest customer in the industry.
- The company has no sales to Argosy, Khans and Altons.
- Company sales to Morrisey and Delmon are well below the users ranking in the industry.
- Company sales to Mangels and Aisher & Aisher indicate an unusually high variation in share and ranking from the industry, possibly resulting from too much attention to these accounts to the neglect of some of the others mentioned.
- The top 20 accounts represent 87% of industry offtake, but only 72.7% of company sales, suggesting scope for more key account development.
- The company has grown consistently at 11.7% and 12.7% year on year, but in the latest year industry sales grew 18.2%.

Monitoring profitability of sales activity

Good sales management practice should require that attempts are made to measure the profitability of all sale transactions. This can be done:

- on a customer-by-customer basis, possibly consolidated into sales territories (suited to situations of ongoing regular supplies to the customers, such as with consumer goods, industrial consumables, components and inputs)
- on a shipment-by-shipment basis (often more suited to products or services that are subject to irregular orders with no regular market supply pattern, as with heavy equipment, tenders, etc.).

Table 14.6 Ranked UK sales of widgets to major accounts 1994–6 (£000s)

Account £000s	UK Widgets sales totals and company share										
	Total 1994	Company 1994	%	Total 1995	Company 1995	%	Total 1996	Company 1996	%	Company rank 1996	UK rank 1996
Intermart	36 700	2 459	6.7%	40 958	2 867	7.0%	48 421	3 480	7.2%	1	1
Welcome	22 035	115	0.5%	20 815	100	0.5%	22 161	110	0.5%	20	2
Trade Centres	13 034	1 538	11.8%	13 439	1 626	12.1%	13 900	1 750	12.6%	2	3
Argosy	4 100	-	-	6 922			11 868	-	-	-	4
PriceLo	9 095	637	7.0%	10 574	634	6.0%	11 187	696	6.2%	6	5
Morrisey	6 529	286	4.4%	7 963	320	4.0%	9 634	340	3.5%	11	6
Superbuy	5 478	696	12.7%	7 456	764	10.2%	8 926	896	10.0%	4	7
LoCost Centres	2 749	102	3.7%	6 475	259	4.0%	8 440	346	4.1%	10	8
Delmon	5 913	151	2.6%	7 909	183	2.3%	8 176	196	2.4%	16	9
Selections	6 965	620	8.9%	6 800	639	9.4%	7 402	720	9.7%	5	10
Top 10 Sub Total	112 598	6 604	5.9%	129 311	7 392	5.7%	150 115	8 534	5.7%		
% UK sales	69%	52.6%		71%	53.0%		70%	54.3%			
Wells & Wallace	2 596	125	4.8%	1 676	84	5.0%	5 850	305	5.2%	13	11
Uptown Discount	3 029	60	2.0%	2 560	70	2.6%.	5 109	80	1.6%	23	12
CenterPoint	2 379	92	3.9%	4 374	108	2.5%	4 593	120	2.6%	18	13
Deco-Art	3 849	331	8.6%	3637	331	9.1%	4 102	405	9.9%	8	14
Mangels	2 884	662	31.6%	3 069	994	32.4%	3 602	1 280	35.5%	3	15
Khans C & C	2 095	46	2.2%	3 188	-	-	3 151	-	-	-	16
Rite Group	902	110	12.2%	2 342	138	5.9%	3 103	140	4.5%	17	17
Altons	1 605	-	-	2 348	-	-	2 554	-	-	-	18
Aisher & Aisher	3 179	345	10.9%	2 137	370	17.3%	2 487	420	16.9%	7	19
Waltons	2 664	47	1.8%	2 211	190	8.6%	2 201	150	6.8%	16	20
Top 20 Sub Total	137 780	8 422	6.1%	156 853	9 677	6.2%	186 867	11 434	6.1%		
% UK Sales	84%	67.1%		86%	69.4%		87%	72.7%			
UK TOTALS	163 290	12 551	7.7%	182 447	13 948	7.6%	215 683	15 720	7.3%		
% Change				11.7%	11.1%		18.2%	12.7%			

Some typical performance measures that the sales manager should monitor and that relate to profitable customer management include:

- the average order size by customer (in volume and value terms)
- the average costs of servicing an order (e.g. order processing, physical distribution, and any other relevant and measurable costs)
- the break-even order size (taking account of costs of order processing, delivery, and related directed selling costs)
- the pattern of orders, in total and by customer, by size and profitability, to provide a measure of the number of orders that are serviced unprofitably.

Where the sales manager cannot get a good measure of transaction processing costs,

some rough measures are usually available (quite simply, for a specific time period, say one month, or the last year, taking all the related sales, order processing and distribution costs in total, dividing by the number of transactions processed, as separate invoiceable transactions or separate deliveries, will give an average processing cost that can then be compared with the gross margin per order). Table 14.7 illustrates a calculation of average profitability for a company that can then be compared with the performance for individual customers (see Table 14.8). This is a more sophisticated analysis than an earlier illustration shown in Table 2.2.

From the calculations in Tables 14.7 and 14.8 we have figures that show an average order value of £402, average order gross contribution of £161, and an average order gross transaction processing cost of £118. If we only

Table 14.7 *Example of analysing customer profitability*

Average order profitability analysis		
Company turnover (12 months)		£14 650 000
Gross profit contribution	40%	£5 860 000
Number of active customers	845	
Average turnover per customer		£17 337
Average gross contribution per customer		£6 935
Number of orders processed	36 400	
Average order value		£402
Average contribution per order		**£161**
Costs of processing orders		
Estimated portion of sales and marketing budgets allocated to order processing	£728 000	£20
Carriage and packing at cost	£691 600	£19
Cost of marketing and field sales operations	£2 875 600	£79
	£4 295 200	
Average sales, marketing and distribution costs per order		**£118**

want to consider the direct order processing costs (paperwork processing and delivery, excluding the share of overall sales and marketing costs) on average, then this would be £39.

With an average gross margin of 40%, we can see that on the basis of direct transaction processing costs (paperwork processing and delivery) we would have a break-even order size of £98. If we were to include the average sales and marketing costs (£79) which gave a full average sales, marketing and distribution average of £118 per order, then the break-even average order size would rise to £295.

What we are saying is that on average, any order shipped that has a value lower than £295 is losing money for us, and certainly any order shipped at under £98 value does not even generate the gross contribution to cover the average costs of paperwork processing and distribution.

In the analysis of the top 50 customers for the case example (Table 14.8), we see that in a very basic calculation, where gross contribution is set in standard costings at an average 40%, we have 5.9% of the customer base (i.e. 50 out of 845 customers) accounting for 59% of turnover and gross contribution, and 48% of order transactions. What is particularly

apparent for this company is that it has a very high number of low value transactions (common to many suppliers of small items and consumables). Of particular concern to the sales manager will be the two top 50 customers who have average gross contributions per order at £38 and £39, approximating the level of contribution that hardly covers average direct transaction costs of paperwork processing and delivery. In addition, there are 11 other customers that contribute less than the average of £118 that we would expect to cover the full sales and marketing, processing and distribution costs per average order. In other words, we have clear signs that a number of our major accounts are making unsatisfactory profit contributions. Without a doubt, this sales manager would be very interested in the remaining 795 customers' pattern of orders and contribution!

There are many situations where customer profitability can be eroded in a way that can be easily missed by the busy sales manager, and a few are noted here.

- Where there are many buying and use points for a supplier's products in a customer organization, a multiplicity of small order transactions can result

Table 14.8 Analysis of Top 50 customers by sales and profitability

Customer	Cum. %	Cum. sales	Sales value	Gross margin	Orders	Cum. orders	Cum. orders %	Ave value	Ave margin
A	6	846,350	846 350	338 540	607	607	2	1 394	558
B	**10**	**1 386 100**	**539 750**	**215 900**	**56**	**663**	**2**	**9 638**	**3 855**
C	14	1 904 700	518 600	207 440	1 190	1 853	5	436	174
D	18	2 380 080	475 380	190 152	1 135	2 988	8	419	168
E	20	2 688 800	308 720	123 488	110	3 098	9	2 807	1 123
F	23	2 996 434	307 634	123 054	1 097	4 195	12	280	112
G	25	3 291 910	295 476	118 190	1 920	6 115	17	154	62
H	27	3 566 977	275 067	110 027	996	7 111	20	276	110
I	29	3 839 979	273 002	109 201	106	7 217	20	2 575	1 030
J	31	4 073 435	233 456	93 382	499	7 716	21	468	187
K	32	4 299 135	225 700	90 280	357	8 073	22	632	253
L	34	4 504 854	205 719	82 288	487	8 560	24	422	169
M	36	4 699 763	194 909	77 964	264	8 824	24	738	295
N	37	4 882 ,103	182 340	72 936	140	8 964	25	1 302	521
O	38	5 053 492	171 389	68 556	229	9 193	25	748	299
P	39	5 217 290	163 798	65 519	29	9 222	25	5 648	2 259
Q	41	5 370 746	153 456	61 382	34	9 256	25	4 513	1 805
R	42	5 518 589	147 843	59 137	698	9 954	27	212	85
S	43	5 663 958	145 369	58 148	178	10 132	28	817	327
T	44	5 806 314	142 356	56 942	347	10 479	29	410	164
U	45	5 942 814	136 500	54 600	460	10 939	30	297	119
V	46	6 076 468	133 654	53 462	276	11 215	31	484	194
W	47	6 210 011	133 ,543	53 417	71	11 286	31	1 881	752
X	48	6 339 541	129 530	51 812	1 356	12 642	35	96	38
Y	49	6 465 941	126 400	50 560	146	12 788	35	866	346
Z	50	6 591 583	125 642	50 257	275	13 063	36	457	183
AA	51	6 712 383	120 800	48 320	136	13 ,199	36	888	355
BB	52	6 832 728	120 345	48 138	341	13 540	37	353	141
CC	52	6 943 468	110 740	44 296	124	13 664	38	893	357
DD	53	7 043 768	100 300	40 120	265	13 929	38	378	151
EE	54	7 141 124	97 356	38 942	26	13 955	38	3 744	1 498
FF	55	7 233 878	92 754	37 102	198	14 153	39	468	187
GG	55	7 326 111	92 233	36 893	109	14 262	39	846	338
HH	56	7 418 115	92 004	36 802	306	14 568	40	301	120
II	57	7 509 615	91 500	36 600	342	14 910	41	268	107
JJ	57	7 594 175	84 560	33 824	56	14 966	41	1 510	604
KK	58	7 677 715	83 540	33 416	234	15 200	42	357	143
LL	59	7 760 815	83 100	33 240	198	15 398	42	420	168
MM	59	7 844 375	83 560	33 424	91	15 489	43	918	367
NN	60	7 926 842	82 467	32 987	360	15 849	44	229	92
OO	61	8 008 187	81 345	32 538	396	16 245	45	205	82
PP	61	8 088 587	80 400	32 160	167	16 412	45	481	193
QQ	62	8 167 037	78 450	31 380	417	16 829	46	188	75
RR	62	8 242 393	75 356	30 142	56	16 885	46	1 346	538
SS	63	8 313 380	70 987	28 395	238	17 123	47	298	119
TT	63	8 382 385	69 005	27 602	24	17 147	47	2 875	1 150
UU	64	8 448 838	66 453	26 581	51	17 198	47	1 303	521
VV	64	8 510 602	61 764	24 706	155	17 353	48	398	159
WW	65	8 571 455	60 853	24 341	617	17 970	49	99	39
XX	65	8 631 215	59 760	23 904	107	18 077	50	559	223
Top 50 totals			**8 631 215**	**3 452 486**	**18 077**				
			59%	59%	48%				
Company total			14 650 000	5 860 000	36 400				
Company average			17 337	6 935					
Order average			402	161					

Information requests and feedback in selling
1. **Keep information requests to a minimum**
2. **Provide feedback**
   - Ensure when you ask a salesperson for data that he or she understands why you need it and how you use it.
   - Provide the salesperson with feedback on data use and interpretation or analysis resulting from his or her data inputs, e.g.: table of comparative performance with other salespersons (for products, market sectors or trade channels), or his or her own performance historically presented (sales over time).

- Where a supplier of equipment that needs consumables or spare parts has customers that order on an item-by-item-as-needed basis
- Support engineers may need to go to meet a customer, to provide training or installation assistance
- Over-calling by the salesperson, in relation to sales volume and potential
- Overlooked costs of financing the major sales transactions (goods in process or store, insurance, credit to the customers, bank charges, etc.)
- Special promotional materials provided to a customer to support promotional activity.

Customer profitability should be monitored (ideally net profitability, but otherwise, at least, gross profitability), and corrective action taken where problems are identified. The answer is not normally to discontinue supplies, but to look for changes in the ways of servicing the customer that will return it to profitability.

Monitoring salesperson performance

If the company sells through a network of **salespersons** who either sell on direct to end users/consumers, or who supply various levels of trade stockists, then there is benefit in establishing measures of **salesperson performance**.

What to measure

The company can measure the salesperson's performance by monitoring:

- salesperson's share of total company sales
  - by volumes/values
  - by product/ trade sector
- product/brand performance
  - by volumes/values
  - versus competitive brands
- trade sector sales
  - by product
  - by volume/ values
- key account sales (where the salespersons/distributors have local key accounts to service)
  - by volumes/ values
  - by brand
- salesperson's share of category sales on his or her territory or through his or her accounts.

Monitoring monthly sales against territory sales budgets

The next example illustrates a simplified form (Table 14.9) of an **annual sales budget** typical of the format (normally logged on a computer) that might be used in monitoring the performance of an individual territory salesperson. **Monthly totals** for actual **sales against budget** and for **percentage achievement**, as well as **comparisons with the same time last year**, can all be monitored on the same table.

In this example the budget was closely based on the previous year's actual sales,

Table 14.9 Territory salesperson's market sales records

Territory sales performance record (Product units)	Salesperson: Tommy Wilson Territory: Central											Year: 199-	
	January	February	March	April	May	June	July	August	September	October	November	December	YEAR
Electric razors													
Target	250	150	150	100	100	100	150	200	250	300	400	600	2750
Actual sales	**254**	**146**	**143**	**94**	**110**	**115**	**167**	**190**	**273**	**320**	**420**	**615**	**2847**
% Target	101.6%	97.3%	95.3%	94%	110%	115%	111.3%	95%	109.2%	106.7%	105%	102.5%	103.5%
Last year actual	240	140	140	92	95	96	130	180	230	280	360	550	2533
% TY/LY actual	105.8%	104.3%	102.1%	102.2%	115.8%	119.8%	128.5%	105.6%	118.7%	114.3%	116.7%	111.8%	112.4%
TY cumulative	254	400	543	637	747	862	1029	1219	1492	1812	2232	2847	
LY cumulative	240	380	520	612	707	803	933	1113	1343	1623	1983	2533	
% TY/LY cumulative	105.8%	105.3%	104.4%	104.15	105.7%	107.3%	110.3%	109.5%	111.1%	111.6%	112.6%	112.4%	
MAT actual TY	2547	2553	2556	2558	2573	2592	2629	2639	2682	2722	2782	2847	
MAT actual LY	2406	2412	2409	2447	2442	2462	2473	2472	2499	2508	2515	2533	
MAT % TY/LY	105.9%	105.8%	106.15	104.55	105.4%	105.3%	106.3%	106.8%	107.3%	108.5%	110.6%	112.4%	
Electric toasters													
Target	140	100	60	60	60	60	80	100	150	200	300	460	1770
Actual sales	**130**	**90**	**83**	**74**	**50**	**54**	**76**	**97**	**152**	**220**	**366**	**470**	**1862**
% target	92.9%	90%	138.3%	123.3%	83.3%	90%	95%	97%	101.3%	110%	122%	102.2%	105.2%
Last year actual	140	95	55	62	55	59	75	90	135	180	276	430	1652
% TY/LY actual	92.9%	94.7%	150.9%	119.4%	90.9%	91.5%	101.3%	107.8%	112.6%	122.2%	132.6%	109.3%	112.7%
TY cumulative	130	220	303	377	427	481	557	654	806	1026	1392	1862	
LY cumulative	140	235	290	352	407	466	541	631	766	946	1222	1652	
% TY/LY cumulative	92.9%	93.6%	104.5%	107.15	104.9%	103.25	103.0%	103.6%	105.2%	108.5%	113.9%	112.7%	
MAT actual TY	1642	1637	1665	1677	1672	1667	1668	1675	1692	1732	1822	1862	
MAT actual LY	1624	1631	1632	1634	1639	1636	1640	1642	1638	1642	1648	1652	
MAT % TY/LY	101.1%	100.4%	102.0%	102.6%	102.0%	101.9%	101.7%	102.0%	103.3%	95.5%	110.6%	112.7%	
Electric irons													
Target	160	120	80	50	50	50	80	100	130	200	300	400	1740
Actual sales	**153**	**147**	**93**	**41**	**63**	**72**	**56**	**103**	**171**	**210**	**327**	**480**	**1916**
% target	95.6%	122.5%	116.3%	82%	126%	144%	70%	103%	114%	105%	109%	120%	110.1%
Last year actual	146	115	75	50	46	55	72	96	120	182	269	380	1606
% TY/LY	104.8%	127.8%	124%	82%	137%	130.9%	77.8%	107.3%	142.5%	115.4%	121.6%	126.3%	119.3%
TY cumulative	153	300	393	434	497	569	625	728	899	1109	1436	1916	
LY cumulative	146	266	336	386	432	487	559	655	775	957	1226	1606	
% TY/LY cumulative	104.8%	114.9%	117.0%	112.4%	115.0%	116.8%	111.8%	111.1%	116.0%	115.9%	117.1%	119.3%	
MAT actual TY	1613	1645	1663	1654	1671	1688	1672	1679	1730	1758	1816	1916	
MAT actual LY	1525	1545	1550	1558	1563	1560	1565	1570	1562	1574	1586	1606	
MAT % TY/LY	105.7%	106.5%	107.3%	106.2%	106.9%	108.2%	106.8%	106.9%	110.8%	111.7%	114.5%	119.3%	

TY = This year, LY = Last year, MAT = Moving annual total of unit sales with a budgeted growth of between seven per cent and nine per cent, depending on product. However, each product actually exceeded the local sales budgets (forecasts). If we look at the individual months, there are some months where sales of products varied greatly from budgeted figures. An unusually high month's sales would presumably have depleted company reserve stocks, possibly contributing to a lower following month through stock shortages (e.g. electric irons in June/July).

The example territory figures in Table 14.9 illustrate the use of moving annual total analysis in territory measurement (the concept of moving annual totals as a trend measure is explained in Chapter 13). In our example, where we are looking at unit sales rather than sales values (i.e. real growth versus monetary growth), the percentage change in the moving annual total comparison for this year versus last year is increasing as the year moves through the months, indicating a faster rate of growth presumably through greater sales activity (possibly a new salesperson on the territory). Moving annual totals provide an additional longer-term trends measure to supplement the normal sales measures of comparing monthly actual data and cumulative annual data.

Those readers who have limited direct sales operations, but who work through a network of specialist distributors (either in the domestic market or in export markets) will find useful extension coverage of the topic of measuring and monitoring performance of distributors in my companion volume, *The CIM Handbook of Export Marketing*, and are recommended to read that source.

Continuous monitoring

Chapter 12 dealt with the basic principles of developing a formalized approach to sales and marketing planning. Once a strategy plan is developed it is essential to **monitor** both its **implementation** and the **performance outcome** at every stage, as these are very much within the sphere of responsibility and control of the sales organization. You must also set in process a programme of monitoring the key aspects of both the **market environment** and **competitive environment** that impact on the plan, as illustrated in Figure 14.2, as both of these are dynamic and will not stand still unchanged for the duration of the planning period.

Competitive benchmarking

The sales manager should establish (possibly with the marketing department) a system of monitoring indicators of **competitive performance** versus his or her company and its distributors in the markets **qualitatively** and **quantitatively**. This serves to **benchmark** factors considered important to trade users and consumers in buying or promoting a company's products versus the competition. Both for industrial and consumer products the marketer can prepare a list of factors (see Table 14.10) that are important in influencing the decision to make a purchase, at the level of the trade channel and at the level of the consumer or user.

You can obtain periodic qualitative or quantitative data by:

- personal observation while in the market and when calling on customers
- asking questions of trade stockists, consumers and users
- developing a system of recording key points on salesperson daily reports or customer record cards
- obtaining data from periodic market audits (including some government monitored data such as household expenditure on items).

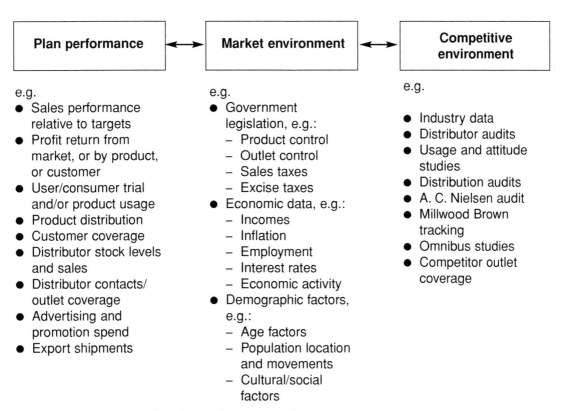

Figure 14.2 *Monitoring the plan performance and the market environment*

Presenting sales monitoring data

As a general rule all marketing monitoring data should be shared with your sales team to help improve sales performance and market planning.

- Data should be presented in a meaningful format that highlights trends and encourages corrective action where there are deviations from plans.
- Do not assume the salesperson will take time studying and analysing copious statistical reports, but focus on only providing performance reports that are meaningful and useful in the context of managing local distribution.
- Where statistical reports are being presented these should be accompanied by an explanation of the interpretation that the salesperson should attach to them, along with suggestions for action. Some data may be presented graphically, such as moving annual data.
- Do not make the salesperson (or your distributors) produce information and tables that will neither give any measurement of progress or marketing programme effectiveness, nor aid in future planning.

Table 14.10 Typical factors to bench mark in monitoring competition

Some factors for bench marking

Consumer factors (consumer goods)
- Trade channel in-store service
- Demonstrations
- Merchandisers
- Promotional support
- Marketing support
- Media selection
- Media weight
- Advertising executions (positioning/targeting)
- PR and sponsorship activity
- Promotions

Industrial user factors
- Product tests and trials
- Availability from local stock
- Local spare parts and service facilities
- Product training (and installation)
- Product reliability in service
- Service costs
- Speed of delivery from ordering
- Product pricing
- Payment terms
- Product promotional support
- General user friendliness

Trade factors
- Product pricing
- Product distribution
- Display
- Delivery system and reliability
- Distributor stock levels/availability
- Trade channel stock levels
- Distributor sales force structure
- Quality of sales representation
- After-sales (trade customer) service
- Accuracy of invoicing/paperwork
- Order cycle frequency and suitability to trade channel/customer needs
- Communications on stock/order status
- Cooperative advertising and promotion activities

Checklist 14.1
Sales performance measurement

	Action points

Performance measurement
- Have you identified key result areas?
- Do quantitative measures exist for them?
- Is data presented meaningfully?

Do analyses measure:
- variances from your plans and forecasts?
- trends?
- promotional and advertising effectiveness?
- profitability by:
    - market sector?
    - trade channel?
    - product group?
    - major customer account?

Specifically, is it relevant to monitor company's sales performance (volume/value/share – TY/LY) versus:
- total industry product category or market sector sales?
- competitor sales performance (market share)?

Do you monitor performance in actual volume/value terms and against forecasts
- monthly (This year/Last year)?
- cumulatively?
- on a moving annual basis?
- other (note)?

Do you measure change (i.e. % TY/LY):
- by market sector?
- by product or product group?
- by volume/value?
- by trade channel?
- by customer (particularly key accounts)?

Are moving annual total (MAT) analyses prepared for:
- sales volumes?
- sales values?
- profitability?
- market shares?
- distributors' sales performance?

Is each item of data analysis being presented in the most meaningful and easily interpreted format for action?

**Checklist 14.2
Competitive benchmarking**

Action points

Develop a survey to benchmark your own marketing and distribution expenditure and performance in relation to competitors (Agencies can assist in some of markets, or compile a confidential outlet panel.)

Trade factors to be benchmarked in regular surveys include:
- Product pricing
- Product distribution
- Display
- Delivery system and reliability
- Distributor stock levels/availability
- Trade channel stock levels
- Distributor sales force structure
- Quality of sales representation
- After-sales (trade customer) service
- Accuracy of invoicing/paperwork
- Order cycle frequency and suitability to trade channel/customer needs
- Communications on stock/order status
- Cooperative A & P activities

Consumer products marketing support factors that can be benchmarked in regular surveys include:
- Trade channel in-store service
- Demonstrations
- Merchandisers
- Promotional support
- Marketing support
- Media selection
- Media weight
- Advertising executions (positioning/targeting)
- PR and sponsorship activity
- Promotions

Industrial user factors to be benchmarked include:
- Product tests and trials
- Availability from local stock
- Local spare parts and service facilities
- Product training (and installation)
- Product reliability in service
- Service costs
- Speed of delivery from ordering
- Product pricing
- Payment terms
- Product promotional support
- General user friendliness

Part Five

Management and Control of the Sales Force

15

Territory management ─────────

Management of resources ▬▬

The salesperson has three key resources to manage:

- time
- company resources
- himself or herself.

Some of the typical activities within these resource categories are illustrated in Figure 15.1.

Managing selling time ─────────

Selling time is the one irreplaceable resource the salesperson controls, and is often the most difficult to manage. There are many demands on the salesperson's time, some less critical or important than others, yet still a necessary part of the workload. The efficient salesperson recognizes the importance of good time management. In most markets the typical salesperson spends only two to three hours daily in front of customers, conducting negotiations. The rest of the day goes in travel, pre-call preparation, waiting at calls, administration, breaks or contacting the sales office.

A simple **salesperson use of time analysis** form, illustrated in Table 15.1, can be adopted by field sales managers to conduct an audit of the use of time by salespersons. It is usually best to use the form discreetly during the course of a day with the salesperson, ticking the appropriate box for the main activity that uses the time within each 10-minute interval. The sales manager wants to get a fair representation of how time is normally used, rather than a distorted picture if the salesperson is aware of being monitored, and changes work habits as a result. The results of this time audit can then be fed back to the salesperson to create awareness of where time is going during the working day, and training can focus on more productive use of time.

Sales activities ▬▬▬▬

The typical range of activities of the salesperson can be allocated generally to one of the functions identified in Figure 15.2.

Planning ─────────

The planning functions of the salesperson include the following.

- Prospecting for new customers
- Journey planning
- Appointment scheduling
- Travel plans
- Longer-term account planning
- Call objectives
- Sales presentation strategies
- Preparing sales aids
- Post-call evaluation and future planning.

Selling ─────────

Typically the selling activities will cover at least the following stages, depending on the nature of the products being offered to the customer.

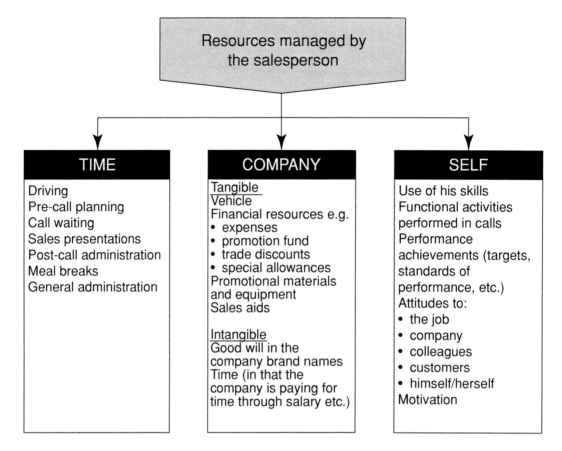

Figure 15.1 *Resources that the salesperson manages*

- Identifying decision makers
- Access to decision makers
- Analysing customer needs
- Making effective presentations
- Overcoming objections
- Closing sales
- Product merchandising
- Promotional activities
- Post-call follow-up.

Communicating

Much of a salesperson's activity involves communicating, in person, by telephone, or through correspondence. Skill training may be beneficial in each of these areas. There is a risk of misunderstanding in any communication, and brevity, clarity and simplicity are basic guidelines that reduce the risk. A typical salesperson will be communicating with:

- customers
- sales line managers
- head office support departments
- distribution depots
- wholesale distributors or other trade dealers.

The range of communication tasks will encompass:

- arranging appointments with customers
- communicating journey plans
- reading, interpreting, understanding and implementing communications from head office and line managers, which frequently relate to matters such as: customer payments, marketing and promotional activity, new products and initiatives, price changes, trading terms, performance analysis of sales with

	Making the most of time in selling
Extend the selling day	• Avoid start of day or end of day visits to the office • Schedule the first call to start by 9.00 a.m. • Avoid lengthy breaks (including business lunches)
Plan the sales itinerary	• Determine optimum call frequencies in relation to potential volumes • Schedule calls logically to minimize driving and callbacks • Have alternative calls ready to fill spare time (regular accounts or new prospect calls)
Organize your sales aids	• Check all sales literature is collated in the order of best reference for use in the call • Check you have appropriate samples for the customer • Plan call objectives by reference to customer records
Utilize call-waiting time	• Check sales aids • Plan strategies • Make contacts within the account
Utilize travel time	• Re-set objectives • Plan strategies • Make phone calls to customers as appropriate
Use the phone	• Make appointments • Follow up on previous calls or promotions • Book repeat orders • Liaise with the sales office

accounts, deliveries, production issues (scheduling of product production), product specifications, and so on

• distilling relevant aspects of communications originating from head office into a local territory action plan, or relaying communications in a digestible form to customers

• communicating the contents of sales presentations and marketing and promotional activity effectively to buyers

• liaison with head office support services on aspects relating to particular customers, such as order lead times, product availability, and payments.

Administering

Sales administration puts a significant time burden into the lives of most salespersons, whether systems are still paperwork based or computer based, and therefore managers should work to keep administration to a minimum and as simple as effective management control will permit. The use of standard forms and recording systems will aid efficient and effective administration, and reduce the risk of neglect. The next chapter will examine some typical standard sales administration, but a few key controls include:

• customer call records
• journey planning reports or programmes
• order forms and other order processing paperwork
• daily activity reports
• contact reports (for major accounts)
• credit notes (for goods uplifted or exchanged)
• internal memos to internal departments
• sales promotion control forms (for managing sales promotional activity)
• sales invoices

Table 15.1 Monitoring a salesperson's use of time

Salesperson's use of time analysis Salesperson						
Tick main activity box for each interval	Travelling	Preparation and planning	Waiting time at calls	Active selling	Administ-ration	Breaks
09.00–09.10	✔					
09.10–09.20			✔			
09.20–09.30				✔		
09.30–09.40				✔		
09.40–09.50					✔	
09.50–10.00						✔
10.00–10.10	✔					
10.10–10.20	✔					
10.20–10.30		✔				
10.30–10.40				✔		
10.40–10.50				✔		
10.50–11.00				✔		
11.00–11.10					✔	
11.10–11.20	✔					
11.20–11.30	✔					
11.30–11.40	✔					
11.40–11.50		✔				
11.50–12.00			✔			
12.00–12.10				✔		
12.10–12.20				✔		
12.20–12.30				✔		
12.30–12.40					✔	
12.40–12.50						✔
12.50–13.00						✔
13.00–13.10						✔
13.10–13.20						✔
13.20–13.30						✔
13.30–13.40	✔					
13.40–13.50	✔					
13.50–14.00		✔				
14.00–14.10				✔		
14.10–14.20				✔		
14.20–14.30				✔		
14.30–14.40					✔	
14.40–14.50	✔					
14.50–15.00	✔					
15.00–15.10	✔					
15.10–15.20		✔				
15.20–15.30			✔			
15.30–15.40				✔		
15.40–15.50				✔		
15.50–16.00					✔	
16.00–16.10	✔					
16.10–16.20			✔			
16.20–16.30				✔		
16.30–16.40				✔		
16.40–16.50				✔		
16.50–17.00					✔	
TOTALS	120 mins	40 mins	40 mins	160 mins	60 mins	60 mins

Figure 15.2 *Key selling activities*

- letters and forms chasing payments/credit control.

Decision making

While the decisions that a salesperson has to make may not be as large in impact on company performance as those of the sales director, they are probably as frequent, and require the same processes in arriving at a judgement on a course of action. Some of the typical subjects of decision making at territory level include:

- alternative account development strategies
- sales presentation strategy and tactics
- trade channel product mix priorities
- product portfolio mixes in customer outlets
- display space utilization advice (for consumer products)

Market Intelligence

Competitors
- Competitive sales activity
- New products and packs
- Sales team staffing levels
- Prices
- Competitive promotional activity
- Distribution
- Products on trial with customers
- Product specifications
- Organization structure management

Customers
- Financial status and performance
- Changes in key contacts
- Changes in ownership/management
- Buying plans and budges
- Creditworhiness
- Investment plans (new facilities etc.)
- Changes in layouts or outlet format
- New branch openings/closures
- Promotional activity

- alternative promotion opportunities
- choice of product to offer to an industrial or business-to-business client
- trade terms to individual customers.

Market intelligence

An important function of every salesperson is to collect market intelligence about customers and competitors. This might cover a range of topics such as those in the following table. The sales force should collect information and submit a (weekly) report on all relevant market intelligence in order that evaluations can be undertaken by sales management.

Territory planning

Territory management is basically about adopting normal management principles at the level of the territory, e.g.:

- **setting goals and objectives** (see Chapter 4)
- **preparing targets and forecasts**
- **developing strategies and tactics for each account**
- **implementing the sales and marketing programmes at the level of each account.**

Territory sales forecasting

In Chapter 13 we explored sales forecasting in some detail. One approach to forecasting favoured by many sales managers is the **market build-up method**. The salesperson should be involved in the planning process, even if the main targeting or forecasting is done at the sales office. The salesperson can be involved in either of two ways:

- in building up his or her own territory forecast by account, by product, by volume/value to produce his or her overall territory forecast
- by taking the head office territory forecast and breaking that down to the level of

each individual account, and allocating a product mix target for each account which at least equals the overall company target for the territory.

Periodically the sales manager should work with each of his or her sales team to explore their views and knowledge and to build local sales forecasts for each territory and account based on knowledge of:

- existing customer account sales history
- existing customer account assessed potential
- potential for additional new business from unexplored (or unexploited) pioneer calls (pioneer calls being those we have not previously developed to active sales)
- knowledge of the local economic environment
- competitive activity
- wholesale distributor's or other trade dealer activity
- company marketing initiatives and programmes
- trends in product preference.

Developing sales strategies

There are two sets of factors to take account of in developing a successful sales strategy aimed at maximizing sales:

- brand strategy factors
- sales strategy factors.

Sales strategies, aimed at achieving volume, value and share of spend objectives with customers (see Table 15.2) typically will encompass a range of issues, including:

- the product range (range extensions, product modifications, product customization, etc.)
- pricing (price positioning in relation to competition for retail products, and in relation to relative value-adding benefits versus competitors for industrial products)
- trade terms
- trade marketing and promotion

- building supply chain partnerships and customer loyalty.

Within any single customer, strategies typically can focus on:

- strategies to increase share of the customer's expenditure
- strategies to increase buying requirements
- strategies to influence the customer's growth rate.

These are expanded on in Table 15.2.

Territory call coverage and journey planning

Companies in developed markets tend nowadays to seek to identify the actual or potential customer base within each postal code district. The outlets can then be classified by appropriate criteria into groupings that reflect differing sizes and potential. All sales managers will have heard of the 80–20 rule, which postulates that around 80 per cent of sales (and profits) will come from around 20 per cent of customers. On this basis, companies commonly develop three customer classification grades, **A**, **B** and **C**. Customers classified as **A** customers would typically be those whose sales potentials would place them in the top 15 to 20 per cent of customers by volume. The **B** classification customers would then typically fall into the next 30 to 35 per cent by volume potential. The **C** classification customers will typically be the lower 50 per cent or so, by volume potential.

When all actual and prospective customers are identified, and classified according to volume potential, the frequency of calling on customers can then be assigned in relation to

Table 15.2 *Account strategies for increasing sales*

Strategies to increase share	Strategies to increase consumption or buying requirements	Factors that influence the rate of growth of the account
<ul><li>Improved price competitiveness</li><li>Quantity discounts</li><li>Performance rebates and allowances</li><li>Lower delivery costs</li><li>Increased or improved technical support</li><li>Product customization</li><li>Improving service</li><li>Enhancing product benefits</li><li>Enhanced customer value perceptions from products</li><li>Improved networking amongst decision influencers</li><li>Improving communications with customer</li></ul>	<ul><li>More intensive product usage</li><li>New usage points within customer organization</li><li>New applications for established products</li><li>New products for new applications</li></ul>	<ul><li>Demographic factors</li><li>Economic factors</li><li>Competition</li><li>Government regulatory factors</li><li>Changing tastes/preferences within the account's customer base</li><li>Innovativeness</li><li>Range of markets and market sectors served</li><li>Effectiveness and productivity of the customer's sales and marketing organization and programmes</li></ul> NB: These are not generally under the influence of the supplier

their sales potential – the higher the potential the greater the calling frequency. From this information a collection of sales territories can then be built up to give balanced workloads (and also, ideally, sales potential) between the sales territories.

Territory call coverage _____

Coverage

Coverage is the planned calling on customers and prospects, with regular calls scheduled according to the needs and potential of each customer or retail outlet (for products resold through trade distributive channels).

Planning coverage requires information on:

- outlet locations
- outlet turnover/potential
- outlet requirements
  - delivery frequencies
  - stockholding practices
  - merchandising support
- company sales resources.

Sales call rate

The call rate that a salesperson can be expected to achieve is a function of:

- distance between calls (i.e. allowance for driving and parking time)
- pre-call preparation
- in-call functions to be performed, e.g.:
  - stock checking
  - merchandising
  - networking amongst other decision influencers
  - selling
- average length of presentation
- post-call administration.

A salesperson for a consumer products company or supplier of business-to-business products (e.g. office stationery) might be able to manage 12–15 calls a day if sales calls are in close proximity to each other or grouped into tight clusters. If sales calls are being made on larger volume customers, such as high street shops, where some product merchandising is required, then the call rate expectation might fall to around 6–8 calls. A key account executive or salesperson for industrial products, such as machinery, might only find it practical to schedule 2–4 calls per day.

Journey planning principles

- Each trade call in a geographical area should be classified according to the frequency of call it requires.
- The length of a journey cycle will be governed by the minimum frequency of call needed to maintain and develop business.
- All the calls in a geographical area can be tabulated on a list to estimate the time needed to service the call on each visit, and in total over a journey cycle (i.e. the time per visit multiplied by the number of calls with a journey cycle).
- The requisite size of a national sales force can be calculated from the workloads for each territory and the national call universe.

In the example of Table 15.3 a journey workload analysis is illustrated for a consumer products salesperson calling on food outlets. In this example, where call durations for many smaller outlets are short, typically 20 minutes, and calls are also normally close together, we have allowed a minimum call time of 30 minutes to include driving time. We show in the example 240 customers on the territory, with 380 selling calls over the eight-week journey cycle. The planning principles apply to any product category where a regular customer base exists for repeat orders, and use of a computer database or spreadsheet can speed the planning process. Driving time can be factored into the calculation either as an average per call (as in our example) or as a separate calculation.

Table 15.3 *A journey workload analysis example*

Journey Workload Analysis		Territory: Northern Region 1				
Customer details	Annual potential sales volume	Expected call frequency (weekly)	Calls per cycle	Minutes per call visit	Minutes per cycle	Cumulative time (mins)
1. J & J Superstore, Newtown	1 000	1	8	60	480	480
2. Acme Hypermarket, Hightown	1 500	1	8	60	480	960
3. Micro C & C, Anytown	2 800	1	8	60	460	1 440
30. Wilson's Market, Newtown	900	2	4	30	120	4 420
31. Save-All Supermarket, Hightown	600	2	4	30	120	4 540
32. Johnson Wholesale, Newtown	1,700	2	4	40	160	4 700
108. The Corner Store, Newtown	280	4	2	30	60	7 680
109. Khans Store, Hightown	240	4	2	30	60	7 740
110. Alpha Grocery, Hightown	180	4	2	30	60	7 800
156. Hightown Coop, Hightown	100	8	1	30	30	14 600
157. Moon Grocery, Newtown	80	8	1	30	30	14 630
158. Star Grocery, Anytown	60	8	1	30	30	14 660
240. Jason's Mart, Anytown	60	8	1	30	30	15 900
TOTALS			**380**			**15 900**

Journey cycle planning

Once each call has been allocated a call frequency and the territory workload assessed, the territory salesperson should then prepare his or her **territory journey cycle schedule**. The next stage with a regular journey cycle is to plan each day's work activity. A simple format such as the journey cycle planning sheet illustrated in Table 15.4 can assist in planning daily journey routing.

Journey scheduling

The calls listed on a **journey cycle planning sheet** can then be scheduled in correct, logical, call order, as illustrated in Table 15.5, just giving brief name and address details. On a territory with an eight-weekly call cycle eight forms would be completed, copies kept by the sales person and the appropriate field sales manager. The only calls not appearing would be new prospects visited on journey.

Weekly journey plan

A weekly **journey plan** may not be necessary where salespersons are working set territories and have a pre-set journey schedule detailing calls and the sequence of calling on accounts. Where this is not the case, such as with a salesperson doing relief work on various territories, or where a salesperson does not have regular customers and prepares contacts and appointments only a short time in advance of meetings, there must still be a control. That can be provided by having a **journey plan** completed each week in advance, as for an insurance salesperson, illustrated in Table 15.6. It can either be completed in full, or, where a relief salesperson is doing a set journey schedule day of a vacant territory, may just use a short note, say against Monday, showing '*Journey Schedule Day 11 on Territory 4*', which would be enough for a sales manager to locate a salesperson on journey, and the subsequent daily activity report can be compared with the

Table 15.4 Journey cycle planning sheet

Territory 6		Journey cycle day 11	
Outlet	Time allocation (mins)	Special calling times	Frequency of calls per cycle
J & J Superstore, Newtown	60	Mornings	8
Micro C & C	60	Mornings	8
Wilson's Market, Newtown	30		4
Johnson Wholesale, Newtown	30		4
Acme Hypermarket, Hightown	60		8
Khans Store, Hightown	30	Not Wednesday	2
Alpha Grocery, Hightown	30		2
Save-All Supermarket, Hightown	30		4
Hightown Coop, Hightown	30	Afternoons	1
Moon Grocery, Newtown	30		1
Totals	390		
Prepared by: Territory salesperson		**Approved by:** Sales manager	

appropriate journey schedule day to check that all customers scheduled for calls and coverage that day did receive a sales call by the salesperson.

Segmenting a territory for coverage

The sequence of calling on customers will in large part depend on the geography of the territory. For urban areas the preferred style

of calling is more of a circular motion, as illustrated in Figure 15.3. Many salespersons adopt an approach of starting either at the closest point to home, or at the farthest. It is not normally a good practice to start closest to home, as that does mean that as the day progresses the salesperson is getting farther from base, while also becoming more fatigued. Usually it is better to make the longer drives early in the day, while the sales-

Table 15.5 An example of a weekly territory journey schedule

Territory Journey schedule		Journey cycle Territory 6 week number 3			
Monday	Tuesday	Wednesday	Thursday	Friday
1 J & J Superstore				
2 Wilson's Market				
3 Micro C & C				
4 Save-All				
5 Moon Grocery				
6 Kahns				
7 Alpha				
8 Acme				
9 Johnson				
10 Hightown Coop				

Table 15.6 *A weekly journey plan for an insurance salesperson*

Alpha Insurance Group Weekly journey plan		Week commencing: 1 December 199-		Territory Southern	
	Monday	**Tuesday**	**Wednesday**	**Thursday**	**Friday**
9.00 a.m.	Minster Accountants Acton, W3		Office	Dunn's Engineering Wolverhampton	Office
10.00 a.m.		Portaglass Ltd Brighton			
11.00 a.m.	Mrs Wilson Ealing, W5		Nuttal & Skinner, Accountants Wembley	Alpertons Plastics West Bromwich	*Review meeting*
12.00 p.m.		Mr Fotheringay Hove			
13.00 p.m.				Fred Brown Lunch Birmingham	
14.00 p.m.	Brown & Brown, Solicitors, Ealing W5		Mr Dunstable Alperton		*Telephone appointment scheduling*
15.00 p.m.		Mr Devlin Brighton		Dr Johnson Birmingham	
16.00 p.m.	Office				
17.00 p.m.					
18.00 p.m.		Dr Rothman Worthing		John Etherington Stratford	
19.00 p.m.			The Askews Birmingham		
20.00 p.m.					
Night contact point	Home	Home	Minster Arms Hotel Birmingham 0121 123 4567	Home	

person is fresher, with a plan to arrive at the first call at their opening time. What should be avoided is frequent doubling back over the same route, as this is wasteful of both time and petrol.

Daily calls should be sequenced to minimize driving time and distances, and to facilitate call-backs if a customer is missed for any reason (such as a buyer being unavailable for a short time). Many salespersons mark customer locations on territory maps to aid journey planning. The general principles of journey planning are:

- tours should be circular
- sales tours ideally should never cross
- do not use the same route to and from a customer whenever possible
- visit customers in neighbouring areas in sequence.

Segmenting a territory for coverage: mapping

A. Divide the territory into five main segments, as in Figure 15.3, if you work a five-day week, one for each weekday in a

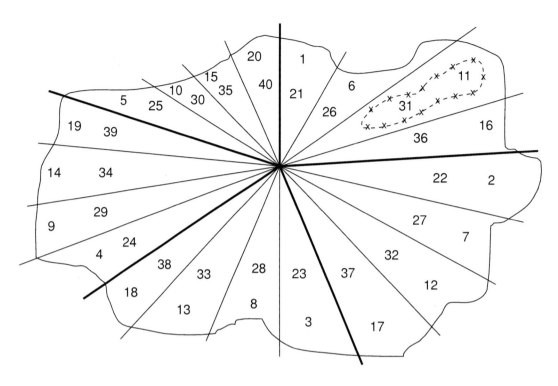

Figure 15.3 *Segmenting a territory for sales coverage*

week, and subdivide each segment into four further segments. This aids call planning on a 20- or 40-day journey cycle (the numbers indicate the journey day).

B. Each weekday the salesperson should be in a different segment of the territory, and if any customer is missed on the pre-set journey day the salesperson will be back in that vicinity within a week, able to pick up the missed call.

C. Customers with differing call frequencies can be factored into the daily schedules in the way discussed in the previous sections.

Cold call prospecting ▬▬▬

Purpose of cold call prospecting ___

The main reasons a salesperson would call on a new prospect are:

- to identify and qualify prospective customers for products to evaluate sales potential, possibly with a view to providing a regular call and supplying the customer directly if sales volume warrants that approach
- to promote the brands, possibly introducing new brands or promotional activity
- to identify outlets suitable for supply through a local wholesale distributor (where the usage volumes would not warrant direct supply from the company).

Prospecting is a more important activity where sales territories have too low a call load, or where the company does not have adequate brand representation in some or all categories of trade outlets, or where the nature of the products or services is that they are one-off sales without serious repeat purchase potential (such as with home improvements).

Sources of new prospects _____

Apart from observation while on journey, some **sources** of new prospect leads include:

- personal contacts, e.g. existing customers, friends
- listings in directories, e.g. trade directories, appropriate Yellow Pages sections
- journals, particularly advertisements such as in entertainment sections, professional directories
- exhibitions, e.g. approaches from visitors to exhibitions where the company is participating
- referrals from existing customers or suppliers of other products
- enquiries responding to advertisements in trade journals
- callers to the company
- local market research aimed at customer identification.

Priority should be given to pursuing leads from sources most usually found to be productive, possibly referrals from other customers, and to those that are 'qualified' as matching profiles of existing customers on established criteria.

Customer targeting ▬▬▬▬

At the core of field sales activity is customer targeting. The role of customer targeting is to ensure the cost-effective deployment of sales resources by identifying and classifying customers, and scheduling call coverage on those meeting specific relevant criteria, such as those illustrated in Table 15.7.

The sales manager should chart the sales levels of product categories in which the company competes and company business through local trade channels or categories of product users (for industrial type products), and look for areas of coverage weakness, often indicated where there is a wide difference between the trade channel pattern for the product categories and company pattern.

Table 15.8 is illustrative of where there are potential coverage problems.

In this example it would seem the company performance is poor in the restaurant, bar and nightclub sectors, probably resulting from poor coverage of those sectors (absence of evening sales activity, perhaps), and that there is a heavy company concentration of sales through the larger volume outlets of supermarkets, grocery stores and hotels. This is typical of situations arising where one sales force covers all trade channel outlets. The various trade channels may have different coverage needs, i.e. certain outlets may need evening coverage to match their opening hours.

Study the relationship between your share of each trade channel and the general market pattern to look for coverage weaknesses, either nationally or locally by area.

The questions in targeting customers

The sales manager should address the questions:

- How many outlets or customers do we cover?
- What proportion of the respective trade channels, or product category users, do they represent (volume/value)?
- Are they the best outlets or users to cover within our resource limitations?
- Do we call often enough?
- Do we call too often?

Surveying for outlets

The market outlet database needs to be comprehensive before strategic marketing, distribution and organizational decisions can be made. Data can be collected by various means, including:

- local government agencies (controlling company registration or reporting by business classification)
- trade associations
- trade directories
- telephone directories
- wholesaler customer lists (rarely released)

Table 15.7 Criteria for targeting customers

Criteria for targeting retail outlets	Criteria for targeting industrial companies	Criteria for targeting individuals as customers
• Type of outlet • Type of products sold • Volume or potential • Compatibility of retail customer profiles • Creditworthiness • Location • Cooperativeness with product promotional programmes	• Type of industry • Type of product produced or service offered • Suitability of supplier's standard products or services • Opportunities for customized products building supply partnerships and loyalty • Volume or potential • End customer profiles of producer • Creditworthiness • Prospective customer profiles match those of existing customers	• Income • Creditworthiness (access to sources of finance) • Employment and/or profession • Age • Sex (male/female) • Family situations (single, married, children) • Home location (urban/rural) • Home style (house, apartment, etc.) • Lifestyle factors
Results of poor outlet targeting	**Results of poor customer targeting**	**Results of poor prospect targeting**
• Brands sold into inappropriate outlets • Hard-won distribution being quickly lost or eroded by competitive activity • Scatter-gun approach draining valuable management time and sales force resources • Poor performance in wrong outlets leading to negative trade perceptions • Poor sales force morale resulting from poor sales performance, earnings against sales targets, wasted effort, etc.	• Products that do not meet performance expectations lead to customer disillusionment and negativity • Time wasted organizing product tests and trials • Limited product development resources misused • Standard products do not meet prospects needs • Misuse of scarce development resources attempting to customize products	• Time wasted making selling calls where no need is established • Unproductive use of limited sales and sales management resources • Customer dissatisfaction where products are wrongly sold

Table 15.8 Model of outlet categories in relation to distributor business

	Trade channel share of all soft drinks	Trade channel share of Company's soft drink sales
Supermarkets	30%	45%
Grocery stores	12%	18%
Hotels	10%	20%
Restaurants	9%	5%
Bars	20%	8%
Night-clubs	14%	3%
Others	5%	1%

- market surveys and questionnaires
- trade press advertisements requesting response if interested in product categories.

Once prospective customers are identified by name and address location it will be necessary to survey them to check how they match ideal call criteria. Contacts identified can then be surveyed (by direct personal contact, or through telephone contact) as appropriate using:

- existing sales resources
- specialist market research agencies
- other resources, such as students.

Some special considerations in coverage planning

Van sales

Car or van cash sales may have a place in company distribution in some markets or to some trade channels. Van selling:

- provides an opportunity to minimize out-of-stocks of standard brands or promotional products through instant off-the-car replenishment for cash, usually focusing on certain specific trade channels (e.g. smaller independent stockists)
- supports advertising and promotional campaigns by ensuring distribution is achieved or maintained along with the

placement of relevant POS material.

Factors to consider in operating a car sales programme include:

- stock security
- salesperson security while carrying cash
- stock record controls
- cash handling, invoicing and banking
- sourcing stock (if it is not always available from the supplier's own warehouses), e.g. from wholesaler distributors
- range to be carried, with a focus on
  - major brands
  - focus brands
  - promotional brands
  - new packs/varieties.

Tele-sales

Telephone sales operations may have a role in a sales strategy to provide sales support in:

- making initial cold contacts with new outlets
- replenishing stocks with existing accounts where field support is not essential
- providing emergency cover during lapses in field coverage
- soliciting orders from small, geographically remote, or some seasonal outlets
- focused blitz activities, e.g.: rapid distribution of new packs/varieties countering competitive activity with pipeline filling deals.

Relief salespersons

When systematic coverage is planned to a regular pre-set journey schedule (i.e. all customers are to be visited at pre-set frequencies) it is essential to budget additional sales resources in the form of **relief salespersons** to allow for:

- sickness
- holidays
- training days and meetings
- public holidays
- resignations
- promotions
- blitz activities.

Estimates should be made for the average time lost, or days' coverage lost, for each of these factors if a set coverage schedule is to be maintained, as illustrated in the following calculation.

Calculation of relief salesperson needs

Days available for work (365 – 104 weekend days)	**261**
Less:	
Holidays per year at 20 days per persons	20
Public holidays at 8 days per person	8
Average sickness at 5 days per person	5
Training/meetings at 12 days per person	12
Net days available for field coverage of customers	216
Annual coverage gap per salesperson	**45**

Relief salesperson can fill the gaps unless alternative arrangements are made (such as tele-sales calls).

The costs of selling

The sales force is a major cost centre in most companies, but also one of its major assets. Sales managers should recognize the costs of selling, and work to improve salesperson productivity through the use of technology, systems and training. Obviously costs increase over time, but an example of an approximate costing for a salesperson is shown in Table 15.9. This highlights that a salesperson costs a lot more than just basic salary, and what the sales manager should be particularly aware of is the average cost per sales call made (and the average cost per order obtained, which will usually be a higher cost figure – see the example illustrated in Table 14.7 in the previous chapter).

Table 15.9 *The typical costs of selling*

	UK £
Direct costs	
● Salary, commissions/bonuses	25 000
● Fringe benefits (life assurance, pensions, etc.)	5 500
● Company vehicle: depreciation and running costs	8 000
● Subsistence expenses: hotels, meals, entertainment	5 000
● Telephone and postage	1 300
Total direct costs	**44 800**
Indirect costs	
● Sales support services: samples, literature, stationery	
● Management and central overheads	
Total indirect costs	**20 000**
Typical total costs per salesperson	**64 800**
Net working days per salesperson	216
Average sales cost per day worked	300
Average daily call rate	5
Average sales cost per customer call	**60**

Checklist 15.1
Resource control

Action points

Time

- Is driving time minimized (effective journey planning)?
- Is pre-call planning thorough?
- Is call waiting time at customers' premises used effectively?
- Is stock checking and merchandising efficiently and quickly completed?
- Are sales presentations conducted with an awareness of time?
- Is post-call administration completed promptly and accurately?
- Are breaks too long or too frequent?
- Is contact with the sales office excessive?

Company
Tangible

- Is the vehicle well maintained and effectively organized as a mobile office?
- Are financial resources managed cost-consciously?
  Are expenses reasonable?
  Are promotion funds used to generate maximum sales?
  Do trade terms reflect turnover without favouritism?
  Is customer credit controlled within prescribed terms?
- Are promotional materials and sales aids used to maximum effectiveness?

Intangible

- Is goodwill in the company brand names developed?
- Is company working time well used (see above)?

Self

- Are the skills present to perform all the functional requirements?
- Are all functional activities performed in calls?
- Are performance achievements against targets satisfactory?
- Are standards of performance being achieved?
- Are attitudes (to the job, company, colleagues, customers and himself/herself) positive?
- Are morale and self-motivation high?

Checklist 15.2
Managing selling time

Action points

Extend the selling day
- Avoid start of day or end of day visits to the office
- Schedule the first call to start by 9 a.m.
- Avoid lengthy breaks (including business lunches)

Plan the sales itinerary
- Determine optimum call frequencies in relation to actual or potential volumes
- Schedule calls logically to minimize driving and call-backs
- Have alternative calls ready to fill spare time:
  regular accounts
  pioneer calls (preferably previously qualified)

Organize your sales aids
- Check all sales literature is collated in the order of best reference for use in the call
- Check you have appropriate samples for the customer
- Plan call objectives by reference to customer records

Utilize call-waiting time
- Check sales aids
- Plan strategies
- Make contacts within the account

Utilize travel time
- Re-set objectives
- Plan strategies
- Make phone calls

Use the phone
- Make appointments
- Follow up on previous calls or promotions
- Book repeat orders
- Liaise with the office

**Checklist 15.3
Functional activities**

Action points

Planning
- Are potential new customers identified, contacted and developed?
- Is journey planning efficient?
- Are appointments scheduled in the most time-efficient manner?
- Are travel plans produced on time?
- Are longer-term account development plans produced?
- Are call objectives set for each customer and visit?
- Are presentation strategies pre-planned and objections anticipated?
- Are sales aids prepared for each call?
- Is post-call evaluation undertaken and is call planning adjusted to reflect call outcomes?

Selling
- Are decision makers identified?
- Is access obtained to key decision makers?
- Are customer needs correctly analysed and considered in setting objectives and preparing call strategies?
- Are sales presentations effective?
- Are objections handled competently?
- Is there a close to every presentation?
- Is product merchandising completed satisfactorily?
- Are promotional opportunities pursued, and promotional activities properly supported?
- Is post-call follow-up thorough?

Communicating
- Are telephone communications effective?
- Are communications with the sales office timely and effective?
- Are communications with the sales manager thorough, informative, accurate and sufficiently frequent?
- Are communications with customers timely, efficient and mutually beneficial?

Administering
- Do you train in the correct use of administrative procedures?
- Are all administrative procedures correctly complied with? E.g.
  - Are customer call records accurate and kept up to date?
  - Is journey planning efficient and timely?
  - Are order forms correctly processed?
  - Are daily activity reports completed after each call, accurate and correctly submitted?

	Action points

Checklist 15.3 continued
   – Are contact reports prepared, informative, and submitted on time (for major accounts)?
   – Are sales promotion control forms correctly used?
   – Are outstanding payments pursued with priority?
● Are incoming mail and bulletins read promptly and actioned?
Decision making
● Are decisions taken promptly?
● Does the quality of decisions show good judgement?
● Is the eight-point decision-making cycle understood and adhered to?
   – Recognizing the problem
   – Analysing and identifying causes
   – Identifying alternatives
   – Evaluating alternatives
   – Deciding on a solution
   – Implementing
   – Monitoring outcome
   – Take corrective action
Market intelligence
● Does a formal system of gathering and reporting on market intelligence exist?
● Is it effectively operated and complied with?
● Does it cover:
   Competitors, e.g.:
   – Competitive sales activity
   – New products and packs
   – Sales team staffing levels
   – Prices
   – Competitive promotional activity
   – Distribution
   – Products on trial with customers
   – Product specifications
   – Organization structure and management
   Customers, e.g.:
   – Financial status and performance
   – Changes in key contacts
   – Changes in ownership/management
   – Buying plans and budgets
   – Creditworthiness
   – Investment plans
   – Changes in layouts or outlet format
   – New branch openings/closures
   – Promotional activity
● Are report inputs reviewed, studied and considered in relation to their impact on company market plans and activities?	

Action points

Key focus of territory management is on:
- Setting goals and objectives
- Preparing targets and forecasts
- Developing strategies and tactics for each account
- Implementing the sales and marketing programmes at the level of each account.

Agree **personal objectives** with each territory salesperson or account manager, for all categories of trade outlets. E.g.
- Call rate
- Outlet coverage
  - Current accounts
  - New prospecting (pioneer) calls
- Sales conversion rate
- Personal development
  - Additional personal development programmes, i.e. reading or college courses
- Skill development training
  - Formal courses
  - Field training by line manager
- Set account objectives
  - Sales volume/value
  - New product listings
  - Existing range extensions
- New accounts

Territory forecast/targets should be prepared taking account of:
- Existing account sales history
- Existing account assessed potential
- Potential from new prospect/pioneer calls
- Knowledge of economic environment
- Competitive activity
- Wholesale distributor's activity
- Company marketing programme
- Trends in product preference

Territory call coverage
Coverage is the planned calling on accounts and prospects, with regular calls scheduled according to the needs and potential of each account or outlet.

Planning coverage requires information on:
- outlet locations
- outlet turnover/potential

Checklist 15.4 continued	Action points
<ul><li>outlet requirements<ul><li>delivery frequencies</li><li>stockholding practices</li><li>merchandising support</li></ul></li><li>company sales resources</li></ul>**Call rate** is a function of:<ul><li>distance between calls</li><li>pre-call preparation</li><li>in-call functions to be performed, e.g.:<ul><li>stock checking</li><li>merchandising</li><li>networking amongst decision influencers</li><li>selling</li></ul></li><li>average length of presentation</li><li>post-call administration</li></ul>**Journey planning**<ul><li>Each regular sales call should be assigned a call frequency related to sales volume or potential.</li><li>Typical journey cycle length relates to the minimum call frequency judged necessary to maintain distribution.</li><li>Calculation of coverage needs enables the size of a national sales force to be calculated.</li><li>**Segmenting a territory for coverage: guidelines**<ul><li>Tours should be circular</li><li>Sales tours ideally should never cross</li><li>Don't use the same route to and from a customer whenever possible</li><li>Visit customers in neighbouring areas in sequence</li></ul></li></ul>**Customer targeting** Issues to consider in targeting customers include:<ul><li>How many outlets or customers do you cover?</li><li>What proportion of the respective trade channels, or product category users, do they represent (volume/value)?</li><li>Are they the best customers to cover within your resources?</li><li>Do you call often enough?</li><li>Do you call too often?</li></ul>	

10

Sales force administration _____

Basic administrative controls ▬

Each company will need to develop certain minimum administrative records and procedures in standardized form to aid in managing sales operations. The needs may vary company by company, and industry by industry (consumer product selling traditionally requiring more standard reporting and control documents than larger value industrial product sales within smaller customer bases). Records and reporting may be developed using traditional paperwork systems, or may be computer based within sales forces that make use of computer technology in field selling. These days several computer packages already provide comprehensive sales management programmes that can be modified to meet the needs of most selling environments.

Sales administration occurs at two levels:

- field sales administration, normally completed by the salesperson
- sales office administration procedures and controls, designed to control order processing and monitor field activity.

Field sales administration _____

The typical range of sales force field paperwork or computerized administrative reporting systems, used by the salesperson in controlling and managing his or her work and territory, includes at least the following items:

- customer call record cards

- daily activity report
- journey plans (examples shown in Chapter 15 under section on journey planning)
- order forms
- credit/product uplift notes
- contact report forms
- sales planning slips
- sales promotional activity forms
- expense forms
- quotation forms
- internal memo pads.

Model examples, just for illustrative purposes, of the main control forms follow in the text, and these may be adapted to suit particular company requirements depending on the nature of the industry or markets.

Sales office administration _____

While in this chapter we will only review typical field sales administration controls, the sales office will provide a lot of sales support, and is also likely to have a range of standard documents that may be routed to field sales personnel, including all or some of the following:

- order acknowledgement
- invoices
- despatch advice notes
- product uplift notes
- credit notes
- overdue payment advice notes (including computer printouts giving the payment status for each customer's account).

Customer call records

These might be in the form of a double-sided record card, or a record folder into which the salesperson puts other paperwork concerning an individual customer, or might form a computer record within a database. The basic information required for the customer call record would include:

- trading name of the company

- ownership/affiliations (if relevant or not otherwise apparent)
- full postal address, telephone and fax numbers (and e-mail if appropriate)
- buyer's name (and job title)
- names of other contacts influential in buying decisions
- any special buying times (or times to be avoided) and other relevant call notes
- sales history

Guidelines for building a customer profile

Who owns the buying company?	• Is it a sole proprietorship, partnership, private corporation, public corporation, government agency?
Who are the key persons in the organization?	• Are any of them known to you (directors, key department managers)?
Who might be involved in the buying process?	• Who is involved in specifying, evaluating, or using product, authorizing purchases or paying for them from budgets?
What market does the buying company serve?	• Trade sectors, e.g. industrial companies, retail, customers, trade buyers, etc.?
	• What is its image to its customers (quality, reliability, market positioning, product pricing)?
	• How does it distribute its products?
	• Is it subject to seasonal trends or changes in consumer fashions?
	• How does it promote and market its products?
	• Who are its competitors and how are they reacting to the buying organization?
	• Is it expanding or contracting?
	• What are its present sources and consumption patterns of similar or alternative products?
Who are its customers?	• Are they industrial companies, service companies or retail distribution channels?
	• How does the customer profile match those of your company products or brands?
	• What socio-economic groups do the majority of its customers fall in (e.g. social class, income, education, employment, etc.)?
	• What lifestyle characteristics do the majority of customers pursue or share?
What is the financial status of the buying organization?	• Is it creditworthy?
	• Is it profitable?
Is there an established need for company products?	• What problems are there with existing sources of supply and their products?
	• Can you create a need for your products?

Table 16.1 *Individual prospect record*

Individual prospect record	**NuGlaz Conservatories**
Contact name William Evans	**Address:** 100 Acacia Avenye Hampton Vale
Tel: 01234 567 8910 **Fax:**	**Best visit times:** Evenings after 7 pm, on Saturdays
Finance available: £1000 deposit	**Finance needed:** £700

Method of financing:
Bank loan for house improvement on re-mortgage house (not keen on NuGlaz nance schemne

Lifestyle indicators:
Four bedroomed, detached property well maintained with one third acre garden. Two cars, Main house double glazed, with recently tted kitchen. Garden pond.

Substitute products in use:
Small existing conservatory attached to kitchen, not functional axcept as storage. Propose removing this and replacing with NuGlaz model that would link behind the house to French windows from the dining room.

Key persons

Name	Age	Occupation	Education	Interests	Image/aspirations
Bill Evans	42	Accountant	Chartered Accountant	Gardening Golf	Wothaholic, conservative, ambitious
Linda Evans	39	Teacher	University	Home, Art and Design	Creative outgoing, committed to career
Frankie Evans	14	Student	Secondary	Sport, Friends	Outdoor type, likes entertaining friends

Table 16.2 Company prospect record

Company prospect record	Process Controls Limited
Customer name FlowLine Foods Ltd	**Contacts** Jim Wilson – Engineering buyer
Address Unit 99, Newtown Industrial Estate Newton	**Tel:** 01234 567891 **Fax:** 01234 567892
Best visit times	By appointment – Wednesdays or Friday mornings
Ownership Division of Multi-Foods Ltd.	**Nature of business** Food production packaging
Key managers John Briggs – Production Director Alan Evans – Head of R & D	**Persons with authority to buy** Frank Nuttall – Chief Engineer (budget holder)
Budget period Company year starts in May	**Finance available** Funds available from May
Credit rating Good – division of listed Plc.	
Key suppliers to the company Takes input supplies from Del Norte Foods, European Fresh Foods Ltd, Clearview Packaging Ltd	
Current suppliers of alternative products Electra Controls Ltd Foodline Systems Inc. (USA)	

Trading history		Date incorporated	1982
	Turnover	**Profit**	**Employees**
1994	£35m	£1.1m	220
1995	£37m	£1.5m	210
1996	£42m	£2.3m	195

Trading prospects
Sales and pro ts growing during a period of market stagnation. Increased use of technology resulting in improved productivity per employee. Well managed.

Product opportunities		
Standard products	**Modified products**	**Potential sales volume**
In-line metal detectors Check-weight controls	Computerized production line management control systems	Four production lines producing pre-packed foods

Other special product requirements
Once established as reputable supplier, future potential for customized systems.

Delivery arrangements By agreement	**Billing arrangements** FlowLine attention Jim Wilson
Training needs On-site training of production, engineering and R&D personnel and operatives	**After-sales service needs** Annual maintenance contract covering parts and labour

Table 16.3 *Reverse of a customer record card showing stock, orders, objectives*

Customer stock record					Customer Acme markets							
Call date	15 March		12 April		10 May							
Product	**S**	**O**	**S**	**O**	**S**	**O**	**S**	**O**	**S**	**O**	**S**	**O**
Kopi Kola												
2 litre	2	5	1	6	2	5						
1 litre	3	9	3	10	4	10						
Cans	3	12	2	15	3	15						
Sunset Orange												
1 litre	1	4	2	3	2	3						
Cans	1	4	2	3	1	4						
'Arundel'												
2 litre				4	2	6						
1 litre				5	2	10						
330 ml bottle				5	1	10						
Objectives/Notes Notes	Obtain launch order for 'Arundel'		Re-position cans on shelf fixture		Promotion 'Arundel'							

- stock and order records (for repeatable products)
- notes on display or merchandising (for retail products)
- customer objectives.

Figure 16.1 and Table 16.2 illustrate basic example designs for customer call records, showing the type of information that might be collated for products sold direct to individuals (e.g. conservatories) and products sold to companies (in this case, a process controls supplier, with the customer being a food packaging company). Table 16.3 illustrates the reverse of a record card where stock and orders are recorded.

These forms illustrate the importance of building customer profiles, and some guidelines for that activity follow.

Daily activity reports

Some form of **daily activity report** should be required from all levels of salespersons including territory salespersons, key account managers and field sales managers, partly as a record of activity and partly for management control purposes.

A key account executive is likely to fill in a

Table 16.4 An example of a daily activity report

Daily activity report	Order	Volumes					Facings					Promotions		
Territory salesperson: Opening mileage: Closing mileage:		A	B	C	D	E	I	II	III	IV	V	X	Y	Z
1														
2														
3														
4														
5														
6														
7														
8														
9														
10														
11														
12														
13														
14														
15														
Total daily sales														
Cumulative sales														
Daily target														
Cumulative target														
Variance														

Alpha Products Ltd — Date: — Time of first call: — Time of last call: — Customer

form of **contact report**, which is basically a brief record of who was met, points discussed, agreements reached, and subsequent action required (including a note of who should progress the action).

Any field sales manager working with a subordinate with the objective of monitoring performance and providing training and motivation should prepare a brief training review record noting strengths and weaknesses observed and training given. This record should be kept as part of ongoing performance review and development programmes.

If a field sales manager is making visits to retail or other trade customers with a view to establishing levels of display and distribution, his or her observations should be recorded on a simple form to be reviewed with the appropri-ate salesperson as soon afterwards as practical. Prompt feedback is an essential element of training and development processes if the feedback is to have current relevance to activities and performance.

When a field sales manager is conducting a **follow-check audit** on a recent day's work by a territory salesperson (which is particularly appropriate in many consumer goods markets), the best recording aid is to use the manager's copy of the relevant daily activity report, and mark observations on the copy as appropriate.

At the level of the territory salesperson, the daily activity report is most important to:

- identify the salesperson and territory
- identify who was visited: customer name and address

- provide a statement of daily work activity and achievements
- summarize orders taken on journey
- summarize special in-call activity (product merchandising, promotional activity, etc.)
- provide a post-call control to line managers
- assist in monitoring performance and training needs
- enable actual calls made to be compared with scheduled calls in the territory sales journey schedule (i.e. to check the scheduled call coverage)
- monitor pioneer calling activity (i.e. contact with new prospective customers, where all such contacts should be recorded on the daily report)
- enable field audit checks to substantiate reports based upon the salesperson's reported activity.

Daily activity reports can also be designed to record information covering:

- time of first and last calls
- time spent in each call
- in-call activity
- contacts made
- objectives
- orders received
- mileage
- use of time (time of entry to first call – exit from last call).

There is no ideal format for a salesperson's daily activity report. Design and layout (whether in paperwork form, or using a computer reporting system as now used in many selling organizations) should be suited to the information and management control needs of the business. What is important is that every salesperson has an obligation to record relevant daily activities and achievements as a personal discipline and management control. Some companies do tend to adopt the approach that their salespersons are well known to the company, and can be trusted to be working. The purpose of a daily report is not to show distrust: it is to provide a means of accurate measurement of activity that can

then provide a focus on ways to improve skills and productivity, to improve returns from that very valuable company resource – the sales team. A simple design format is illustrated in Table 16.4.

The advantage of a daily activity report is that it focuses attention over a relatively short time span, and adds a sense of urgency to selling as the salesperson is faced with writing his or her results down as the day progresses. Some information should **always** be recorded, such as the customers visited and the orders taken (with a note of value or volume, such as bottles sold, if that is easier to record against target). The information recorded in the other columns can focus attention on priorities in any month, such as distribution, display and promotional factors.

Using the daily activity report

There are many variations on this format that might suit a company, but most will be similar in content.

- Calls should be recorded in the order in which they are made.
- If a duplicate form is used, then the back copy can be used as a pre-planning (journey plan) copy, where the salesperson submits his or her proposed daily itinerary in advance, in calling order, and a field sales manager should be able to pick the salesperson up on journey.
- Also, where a pre-planning copy is made, this can be cross-checked with calls actually made (calls not made will not show entries under the category headings).
- The column headings can either have permanent recording categories preprinted in, or can be varied monthly according to priorities for recording and monitoring. In the example of Table 16.4, particularly suited to retail selling:
  - the volume headings, A to E, might be used for the top five brands, or top four plus one brand on special promotion;

- the facings heading, which in this case is intended to measure the number of display facings of product on the standard shelf fixtures, similarly can be used for a regular set of products, or varied to note special products of interest to the company;
- the promotions heading leaves room to record up to three special promotional activities, such as demonstrations, off-shelf feature displays, point of sale material, etc.
- The salesperson can record his or her daily and cumulative progress against targets at the bottom of the sheet.
- New prospects (pioneer) calls can be entered on the daily activity report from the bottom upwards, so that they are noted separately.
- Monitoring mileage and time into first call and out of last call acts as a control on salesperson productivity.
- Inter-salesperson comparisons can be made on:
  - call rates
  - sales to calls ratios and average sales values and volumes per call
  - average time spent in call, etc.

Journey plans

A journey plan should be submitted in advance of a day's work or week's work to the sales line manager as a control that the salesperson has a specific work programme, and to enable the line manager to plan his or her own work schedule in choosing when to work with any individual salesperson, or to conduct any post-call field audits.

In an industry where set journey cycles are not possible or practical, or for an account executive who is calling on major accounts, the journey plan may simply be an advance list of the calls or contacts to be made the following week (as illustrated in Figure 15.3 in the previous chapter).

As a general rule, the principles of submitting journey plans are:

- they should be submitted weekly/monthly in advance;
- they should clearly identify calls to be made, in planned calling sequence;
- pre-set journey scheduling (for markets where repeat product sales are normal) simplifies weekly journey planning;
- a pre-planning copy of the daily activity report can be used for journey planning;
- line managers should plan their field work using salespersons' journey plans (field follow checks, training days).

A more comprehensive example of a journey plan is illustrated in Table 16.5, where the calls are identified in advance, along with a statement of the main focus of sales objectives for that particular visit. This enables the sales manager to check:

- that the salesperson does set specific and meaningful objectives
- the effectiveness of a salesperson in working to and achieving objectives.

Order forms

It is normal practice for companies to have standard order forms, either with products pre-printed, or with blank spaces left for salespersons to enter products, prices and quantities. The style and format will vary with the nature of the products, size of product range and pack variations, and company and customer needs for information. Essentially order forms should detail:

- customer's name and full delivery address
- invoicing address
- customer reference (order) number
- company reference (order) number
- salesperson's name and territory reference
- special delivery instructions
- list of goods being ordered (varieties, pack sizes, quantities)
- prices of goods being ordered
- total order quantities and values

Table 16.5 An example of a comprehensive journey plan

Salesperson: Fred Wilson		Week commencing: 1 December	
Customer name and address	Appointment time	Objectives/notes	Overnight location
Monday			
1 United Controls, Hightown	9.00	Present new model to buyer and chief engineer. Try for test.	Home
2 ABC Motors, Hightown	10.30	Final price negotiation	
3 Tendex Ltd, Newtown	12.00	Review test results, and move to full production trial.	
4 Alpha Controls, Newtown	14.00	Negotiate new lease	
5 Foster & Co, Anytown	15.30	New contact. Establish buying organization.	
Tuesday			
Wednesday			
Thursday			
Friday			

- terms and conditions of sale (these may be standard, or may be subject to individual negotiation with each customer).

Credit notes and product uplift notes

Salespersons sometimes have occasion to issue credit notes or arrange for the uplift of product and transfer of goods, perhaps because of wrong delivery or faulty merchandise. Some companies prefer the salesperson to request the uplift of goods using an appropriate form, with the subsequent issue of a credit note (see Table 16.6) from head office once the returned goods are processed back into the system. This reduces the risk of abuse of credit note systems and provides a good control.

Contact reports

These are usually used by sales managers and/or key account executives calling on major customers. In that type of organization there are often several persons involved in the buying process: the titular buyer, and other decision influencers (sifters, authoriz-

Table 16.6 *An example format for a credit note and product uplift note*

Product uplift/credit note Customer name Address Tel. No.			Alpha Products Ltd Account number **To be collected*** **Collected by salesperson*** *(delete as appropriate)	
Product	**Pack size**	**Quantity**	**Reason for uplift/credit**	
Salesperson		**Store manager**		**Date**

ers, testers, users, influencers, etc.). Negotiations are often protracted over a series of meetings and stages, often including product tests and trials before final price and terms negotiations. This selling scenario makes it especially important that notes and records are kept of the various meetings and contacts in contact reports (see Table 16.7) that summarize:

- dates and times of meetings (and locations)
- persons present at meetings (salesperson and contacts from buying organization)
- meeting objectives
- discussions and agreements reached
- notes on action required (and by whom), with deadlines
- note on any subsequent meeting dates and objectives.

The sales planning slip

The **sales planning slip** is a very simple but versatile tool to aid the selling process, being particularly useful when discussing order quantities and closing the sale. Its use is not limited to consumer product salespersons,

and it can be designed to suit most industrial and business-to-business selling environments.

A **sales planning slip** has several useful functions, such as:

- providing a focus of attention when talking specifics about products and quantities
- outlining a suggested order when starting to close on a sale
- discussing concessions in relation to suggested quantities
- highlighting recommendations for additional quantities to support promotional activity
- highlighting key promotion dates or buy-in periods
- adding authority to a discussion on products and relative order quantities
- providing a neutral point of reference when discussing products and quantities (including range extensions), as the closing of the sale can often be an emotional point in the presentation when decisions must be made
- it can be used to highlight information specific to a dealer, such as particular special prices, discounts, retail price in relation to cost, margins, etc., which might

Table 16.7 Contact report example format

Contact report	Account:
	Date of meeting Location
Meeting objectives	
Points discussed and agreements reached	
Action resulting from meeting	**Actionable by (person/date)**
Pre-agreed objectives and discussion points for next meeting	
Next meeting scheduled for:	**Signed: Account manager** **Date**

not be so clearly expressed on general price lists or literature

- it shows a very personal input to the sales presentation, where the salesperson hand-writes key quantities or data on the sales planning slip
- acting as a reminder for an indirect customer (who purchases from a wholesaler) to place an order, or it can sometimes even serve as a transfer order form for the salesperson to take an order to a trader's normal wholesaler.

There is no special format for designing a **sales planning slip**, but a typical model would look like the examples in Tables 16.8 and 16.9, for consumer or industrial products.

Sales promotion control forms

Sales promotions are used in many companies, in consumer sectors, industrial product markets, and business-to-business environments. Sales promotion monitoring should focus on:

- costs
- quantities
- commitments
- performance.

Sales promotions are a major cost factor in most companies and markets. However, they are not always controlled and monitored to ensure a benefit is achieved in terms of an

---

Using the sales planning slip in selling situations

- The particular information it is being used to communicate can be written alongside the product.
  (e.g. suggested order quantities, promotion quantities, recommended retail prices, promotion prices, dates, profit margins, display facing agreements, etc.).
- Key points can be highlighted by using a pen as a pointer, possibly circling any key data such as a suggested promotion quantity or new brand listing.
- Concessions, when agreed, can be written alongside the original suggestion, which makes a buyer feel more comfortable that he or she is being listened to and points noted.
- When giving a concession it is useful to draw attention to another point on the sales planning slip and gain an agreement on that as a trade-off for a concession.
- A copy of any information on the sales planning slip can be left with the buyer as confirmation or a record of an agreement.
- Sometimes it can be useful to add authority to a deal by asking a buyer to sign or initial the information on the sales planning slip.
- Using coloured pens to highlight key points (e.g. red as well as black) can add impact.

---

increase in sales giving incremental profits greater than the cost of the promotion. A form can be designed, as in Table 16.10, that can be used by territory salespersons and sales managers in planning and negotiating special promotional programmes with customers.

The promotion can be evaluated against its objectives, and a calculation made as to whether the total costs of the promotion are more or less than the incremental contribution from the extra case sales over the normal level of sales.

be dealt with quickly and firmly according to a company's disciplinary procedures). The common alternative approaches to controlling sales expenses are to:

- state fixed daily allowances for approved expense items (where the allowances are realistic and at such a level to permit the fulfilment of responsibilities)
- establish standard guidelines for meals/accommodation, and reimburse expenses against receipts.

Expense control form ▰▰▰

Reporting and control of sales force expenses (see example Table 16.11) is essential if a manager is to keep costs within budgets, and is also required for auditing purposes. At the same time, integrity is a vital quality in the sales force, where there can be more scope for abuse of systems than in many office based positions (and any abuses identified should

Quotation forms ▰▰▰

In industries where it is customary to quote to supply goods or services, the suppliers may want to design simple standard quotation forms to be prepared at the buyer's location by the salesperson. The form is likely to contain blank spaces for products, quantities, prices and delivery (or installation) dates.

Table 16.8 An example of a sales planning slip for a consumer product

National Soft Drinks Co.	Acme Markets		
	Regular order	*Promotion*	
Kopi Kola			
2 litre	5 cases		
1 litre	10 cases		
Cans	15 cases		
Sunset orange			
1 litre	3 cases		
Cans	4 cases		
' Arundel' Natural Mineral Water			
2 litre		6 cases	Off shelf
1 litre		10 cases	Demonstrator
330 ml bottle		10 cases	Price reduction
		(5 cases free)	

Basic information normally needed on a quotation form includes:

- supplier's name and address, and other contact details (telephone, fax)
- name of the person preparing the authorized quotation
- date of the quotation
- period of validity of the quotation
- products quoted on:
  - description and specification
  - quantity or volume involved
  - prices of units of packs
  - any discounts, rebates or allowances
- method of accepting the quotation (i.e. signing the quotation form)
- guarantees or warranties attached to the goods or services (although these may be referred to in other documents associated with the sale, such as an order confirmation)
- general terms and conditions of trade or related to the specific offer (also possibly included separately in an order confirmation)
- timing and terms of shipment and delivery, or installation of plant and equipment
- payment terms, including deposits required on acceptance of the quotation.

Guidelines for designing forms ▬

Each company will develop paperwork systems to meet internal needs for information and control, and to assist in managing sale force operations. However, all documents (whether for manual completion or for use in computer-based sales controls and reporting systems) should be designed with ease of comprehension and administrative compliance in mind, to minimize time given to administration, to facilitate/promote action, and to standardize systems and procedures internally.

Table 16.9 *An example of a sales planning slip for a commercial product*

National computer supplies company	The Graphic Design Co.	
Computer models		
Magnus Pentium XL1	2	
Magnus PC DL2	2	
Magnus Laptop	1	
Hard drive options		
1000 MB (laptop only)	1 Laptop	
2000 MB		
4000 MB (4 gigabyte)	2 / DL2	
5000 MB (5 gigabytes)	2 / XL1	
Other hardware options		
CD-ROM	1 / XL1	
Tape Streamer	2 / XL1	
Fax Modem (int./ext.)	2 / XL1	
	Full sound, etc. XL1	
Support options		
Standard warranty only		
1 year on-site warranty		
3 year on-site warranty		Group contract
Hot-line support service		Group contract
Installed software options		
Note preferences from list		Full standard package on XL1/DL2
Software training		2 days on-site

1. List prices less 10% for hardware.
2. Support & software options at list.
3. Prompt settlement within 7 days of delivery

Basic guidelines for developing forms

- Keep the layout simple.
- Do not ask for information that will not be used in measuring or monitoring performance, planning or control.
- Note special recording instructions on the form if possible, along with any routing instructions for originals and copies.
- Ensure the design encourages completion after the activity to which it relates (i.e. particularly that the customer record card and daily activity report are completed during or immediately after the customer visit).

Table 16.10 *An example of a sales promotion control form*

Account promotion programme: Control form					Cost factors						Post-promotional analysis		
Brand/Pack	Promotional activity	Promotion dates	Normal period case sales	Target promotion case sales	Normal case cost	Promotion case cost	Other fixed costs e.g. adverts	Budge promotion case cost	Normal retail price	Promotion retail price	Actual sales	Actual total costs	Actual cost per case
Supasoap – large	Buy 1 2nd half price	14–28 March	100	200	£30.00	£24.00	£100.00 = £0.50 per case	£6.50	£4.50 each	£6.75 for 2 packs	250 cases	£1600	£6.40
Wondawash – large	On pack coupon: collect 3 coupons plus £3 for beach towel	1–14 April	50	100	£33.00	£33.00	£200.00 end of gondola fee	£2.00 excluding towel cost (self-liquidating)	£4.65 each	£4.65	110 cases	£200	£1.82

Table 16.11 An example expense control form

Expense report form				Salesperson:			
Week				Function:			
Date							
	Sunday	Monday	Tuesday	Wednesday	Thursday	Friday	Saturday
Lunch							
Other meals							
Accommodation							
Entertainment							
Car maintenance							
Petrol and oil							
Parking							
Other travel							
Telephone							
Postage							
Other: (specify)							
Signed:				Approved:			
Attach all receipts to the top copy of this form. Top copy to line manager. Bottom copy to be retained by salesperson.							

Essential customer communications

At this point some brief commentary is appropriate on the essential company literature that is generally supplied to customers in standard format:

- product price lists
- product specification sheets
- catalogues and brochures
- advertising and promotional information sheets.

Each of these documents is intended to communicate information important in the selling process, and should be designed to create interest and gain attention, encouraging a buyer to pursue contact with the salesperson to the point where an order is placed.

Product price lists

These need to include information on:

- product names and/or descriptions, along with any item codes that facilitate ordering
- pack or unit sizes (volumes, weights, dimensions)
- number of units in a shipping pack
- price quotes per shipping unit to the point of ownership transfer (customarily delivery to the buyer's specified location for domestic transactions)
- standard terms of sale, payment terms and conditions
- warranties and exclusions
- periods of validity of the quoted prices.

Specification sheets

These will normally include comprehensive technical data concerning the structure and performance of the products, with illustrations, drawings, technical data, wiring diagrams (if appropriate), servicing and maintenance data, etc.

Catalogues and brochures

These are intended to show the product to a prospective buyer, but cannot substitute for a sample or demonstration. Illustrations should be photographic wherever possible, as this makes more impact than line drawings, although those can usefully aid a presentation where they show the workings or functions of a product.

Companies are now looking at other media to carry catalogue information, such as video tapes and computer systems (on CD-ROM disks). Without a doubt the use of computer and associated media will grow rapidly, as companies can download latest prices and catalogue data via modem links. This will link with direct ordering over computer links as we move more towards a paperless business environment. But the salesperson will not become redundant, still having a key role in promoting consumption growth, communicating about products to prospective customers.

Advertising and promotional programme information sheets

These are most commonly issued by suppliers of consumer products and products sold through trade dealer networks as they alert their distribution outlets and trade dealers to the forthcoming marketing communications supporting products. Typically a leaflet will summarize the times and dates of media advertisements, to encourage trade purchase and display in order to maximize the impact of advertising on sales and profits through distribution outlets. Salespersons would normally use this information during presentations to obtain orders and increase sales, selling up on the strength of media support generating additional demand through increased consumer awareness.

The reader may find some of the principles and guidelines expounded in Chapter 7 relevant to the presentation of information to customers.

Checklist 16.1
Sales force administration

Action points

Have you conducted an audit to identify:
- all administrative documents used by the sales force?
- all administrative documents originated by the office and copied to salespersons?
- all sales related literature despatched to salespersons?
- what performance feedback data is: relevant to doing the job?; needed?; used?
- which persons at the office contact salespersons?

Guidelines
- Keep paperwork to a minimum
- Control through formal reporting those parts of the job that impact on the sales performance and profitability
- Design customer record cards and daily report forms that:
  - require completion at the time of the call
  - focus on key result areas and priorities of the job.
- Minimize the number of head office staff with authority to contact salespersons with requests for information, etc.

Typical sales force field control documents:
- Customer call record cards
- Daily activity report
- Journey plans
- Order forms
- Credit/product uplift notes
- Contact report forms
- Internal memo pads
- Sales planning slips
- Promotional activity control forms
- Expense forms
- Quotation forms

Head office administrative documents copied to the sales force typically include:
- Order acknowledgements
- Invoices and despatch advice notes
- Product uplift notes and credit notes
- Overdue payment advice notes
- Responses to customer queries
- Price lists
- Promotional literature
- Marketing information
- Sales bulletins
- Target setting documents
- Performance feedback reports
- Correspondence from a variety of departments

17

Sales management control

The need for control

An assumption is often made that salespersons are all highly motivated work-horses, who, because they are frequently rewarded by substantial commissions or bonuses, need very little active management and control. That assumption is erroneous. A sales force without proactive hands-on management is like a missile without a guidance system – a device full of energy but with no sense of direction, drifting along aimlessly through space. In managing a sales force **controls** are needed to:

- ensure performance and results relate to plans, programmes and policies
- maximize the productivity from the available resources, e.g.
  the sales team
  time
  sales aids and promotional materials
  financial resources allocated to budgets
  for sales and marketing activities.

Controls cannot exist in a vacuum. If controls are to be implemented in the sales force then as prerequisites it is necessary for sales managers to:

- identify key result areas
- establish standards of performance against which productivity and activity can be measured.

Controls can be implemented either by the **sales office** or by the **field sales managers**.

- Sales office controls normally focus on monitoring sales performance at the company level down to the level of the individual territory, against company objectives, e.g. sales targets in terms of volumes and values of products sold.
- Field management control normally focuses on monitoring and controlling:
  - work activities
  - skills
  - achievements and standards of performance covering aspects of the job not easily monitored from paperwork controls, or where reporting through paperwork controls needs to be verified (e.g. claims about display and promotional activity).

Types of controls

Control, like training, is on ongoing management function. There are three main forms of control.

- **Continuous controls** are designed to:
  - monitor tasks and duties, reducing the risks of problems occurring;
  - monitor objective factors (quality, quantity, cost, time).
- **Warning controls** are designed to:
  - recognize and identifying deviations from plans;
  - identify the direction and magnitude of variations, usually in numerical form analysis of performance measurements

operating in key result areas. Warning controls typically take the form of:

- computer printouts
- graphs
- tables of comparative performance.

● **Self-control** is promoted through skill training and feedback, where the salesperson monitors his or her own performance against standards of performance and requirements of the job. The salesperson is the best guide to problems and deviations from standards of performance and plans.

It is particularly important to concentrate control in the sales force on key result areas because of the natural tendency we all have to concentrate effort on those aspects of the job that are noticed or are emphasized in training, bulletins or other verbal or non-verbal communications.

All personnel should be familiar with their standards of performance so that they can check their own performance against objective factors and criteria. It is useful to encourage salespersons to keep their own basic records in key result areas, such as call rates, or sales against targets, and to ask for these to be summarized (possibly on the daily report). Self-control is fostered where salespersons make commitments as to how a territory target will be broken down and achieved through each individual customer at a monthly area sales meeting.

Managing time

Time is the one irreplaceable sales force resource. Time lost or wasted cannot be recovered, and is rarely made up subsequently, with a resultant loss in overall business. The field sales manager must recognize where time goes to in the selling day. Most objective surveys show that little of the day is actually spent in productive selling activities, with often only from two to three hours being spent on business generating activities such as selling and merchandising.

Sales managers must control and manage the use of time at two levels:

● salesperson use of time
● managers use of their own time.

Salesperson use of time

It is useful for a sales manager, as well as a salesperson, to have a good understanding of where time goes in the field sales force. One simple form, illustrated previously (Table 15.1), suggested occasionally measuring time used in 10-minute intervals against main activities in the selling day. An alternative approach, illustrated in Table 17.1, possibly undertaken as part of a more serious sales engineering project, is to measure your sales force's use of time under the categories of:

● preparatory work
● productive or selling activities

Two basic rules in sales management

1. Practise **management by exception** to monitor **management by objectives**.
   That means you focus on monitoring and controlling against key result areas of the job where there are deviations from standards, objectives or plans, either within the whole team, or with one individual.
2. **Good managers** see, know and note everything going on within their team, and control many of the activities through their system of formal continuous and warning controls. But they overlook many of the non-critical situations, focusing on correcting, through training and counselling, a few key points that particularly influence results in key result areas of the job.

Table 17.1 *Sales activity time management analysis*

Sales activity time management analysis (time recorded in minutes)												Salesperson John Smith			Date 5 Jan. 199-
Call	1	2	3	4	5	6	7	8	9	10	11	12	Total	Average	%
Preparatory															
Customer record checks		2	3		2	1	2	2	2	3			17	1.7	3%
Objective setting			1	2		2		2		2			9	0.9	2%
Proposal preparation			2	2	2		3		1	2			12	1.2	2%
Selling activities															
Contact making		2	4		3		5			3			17	1.7	3%
Stock checking		3	4	3	2	3			4				19	1.9	4%
Sales presentations	16	10	9	15	10	20	16	30	20	12			158	15.8	31%
Merchandising	5		5	3	4	2	3	5	3				30	3.0	6%
Non-selling activities															
Driving	20	10	6	8	12	11	7	14	9	17			114	11.4	22%
Waiting at calls	5	5	2	3		2		3		7			27	2.7	5%
Administration	5	3	5	4	6	2	4	3	1	2			35	3.5	7%
Meeting attendance															
Office contact			2			5				10			17	1.7	3%
Call management															
Post-call account servicing															
Evaluation of programme results					4								4	0.4	1%
Processing queries			3		2			5		4			14	1.4	3%
Personal															
Meal breaks, etc.				10			30						40	4.0	8%
TOTAL (in minutes)	51	35	46	50	47	48	70	64	40	62			513	51.3	100%

- unproductive or non-selling activities
- call management
- personal time.

By sales managers becoming more aware of how time is used in relation to priority functions, field management time should be more effectively directed to management of key result areas, and to focusing training on those aspects of the job that make a difference to sales performance.

Sales manager's time use analysis

A similar time management exercise can be conducted for each sales manager. The sales manager should monitor his or her use of time to ensure its use is focused on priority and key result areas. In the format illustrated in Table 17.2 time use can be monitored over a typical 20-working-day month, using a monitoring form such as the example shown in this section. Standards of performance for use of time in major and priority functions can be set, such as training, and managers can measure themselves against those standards.

Table 17.2 A sales manager's use of time analysis

Sales manager's use of time analysis

Day	1	2	3	4	5	6	7	8	9	10	11	12	13	14	15	16	17	18	19	20	Total	%	Plan %
ACTIVITY																							
Management																							
Field training																							
● Territory 1	4																				8	4	6
● Territory 2			6																		10	5	6
● Territory 3				4							4			4		6					14	7	6
● Territory 4																8	8				24	12	6
● Territory 5								6										8			9	5	6
● Territory 6						4									4				3		8	4	6
Field audits																							
● Territory 1	2									2											4	2	2
● Territory 2			2									2									4	2	2
● Territory 3										2											2	1	1
● Territory 4									3												3	1	2
● Territory 5								2													2	1	2
● Territory 6				2										2							4	2	2
Recruitment		8																			8	4	3
Customer queries				1		1				1										2	5	3	2
Bulletin preparation					1											1				1	3	1	1
Sales meetings					2		4														6	3	3
Counselling									2				1								3	1	3
Personal accounts	1					2												2	2		7	3	4
Distributor contacts	1			1					2	1				1					1		7	3	2
Administration																							
Report preparation	.5		.5	.5	.5	.5		.5	.5	.5	.5	.5	.5	.5	.5	.5		.5	.5	.5	6.5	3	3
Correspondence	1				2	1	1	.5	.5	2		1			3	.5	1	1		2.5	16.6	8	5
Journey planning				.5						.5					.5	.5				.5	2	1	1
Personal expenses				.5	.5				.5	.5						.5				.5	2	1	1
Credit control	1												1					1			3	1	1
Driving/travel	1		1.5			1.5	3	1	1.5	1.5	1.5	2	1	2	1	2	2	2	2	.5	29.75	15	15
Planning																							
Sales forecasting	1				1					1				.5						1	3.5	2	2
Promotion planning	1			1	1											1	2			1	5	3	3
Territory objective setting	1			1	1													.5			4.5	2	3
TOTALS	10.5	11	10	9.75	10	9	8	10	10	10	10.5	10.5	9.5	10.5	11.5	11	11.5	11.5	9	9	203.75	100	100

Obviously not all management activities occur at regular intervals or with the same frequency. There are certain tasks the sales manager might perform only at infrequent intervals. As a useful time control it might be worth preparing a list of the main occasional tasks that are time bound, noting in which months or weeks action is needed. An example is illustrated in Table 17.3, and most sales managers would log this onto a wall planner, or into their computer diary planning system. Key periodic tasks can then be built into the short-term monthly detailed time planner.

Field controls

Identifying key result areas and setting performance standards

Once overall company plans, forecasts or targets, and objectives have been established and communicated, these need to be broken down to territory and customer forecasts, objectives, strategies and tactics. Then measurement and achievement bases can be agreed for each salesperson, with standards of performance set and agreed for each key result area, where objective measures can be made in terms of quantity, quality, cost or time.

The main key result areas where sales managers should set standards of performance and make control measurements are:

- standard daily call rate (i.e. minimum acceptable)
- average daily call rate (measured over a longer period, such as a month)
- minimum order size (volume/value)
- average order size (volume/value)
- total daily, weekly, monthly sales achievements (against targets, forecasts)
- calls on new prospects
- conversion ratio of calls to orders
- distribution by product
- product display achievements (quality observed from field audit checks; quantity possibly measured through daily report recordings)

Table 17.3 Sales manager's key task diary planner

	Annual key task planner											
---	J	F	M	A	M	J	J	A	S	O	N	D
Annual sales forecast									x			
Annual cost budgets									x			
Annual sales force objectives										x		
Annual sales promotion plan											x	
Annual sales conference	x											
Manpower planning schedule										x		
Regional sales conferences				x					x			
National trade convention							x					
Field sales managers' meeting	x	x	x	x	x	x	x	x	x	x	x	x
Sales force appraisals												x
New starters' course	x			x			x			x		
Salary reviews						x						x
Vacations	x							x				
Quarterly performance review & plan update			x			x			x			x

- achievement of scheduled call coverage
- pre-call objective setting.

By monitoring each of the objective criteria for each member of the sales team a good measure of interpersonal differences in productivity can be made. The manager's personal judgement can be used where there are particular differences in the potential or trade channel structure of territories.

A standard of performance can be expressed as an absolute number, such as 'to achieve 10 calls per day and 100 per cent scheduled call coverage over a journey cycle', or in ratio terms, such as 'to convert 40 per cent of calls made to active customers'. If standards of performance are to have credibility with the sales team responsible for achieving them, they must have a basis in historical performance and achievement. They must be seen as realistic and achievable by all, and only work as motivators within the team where they are subject to measurement and regular feedback. It would be of little benefit setting a standard for, say, new customer prospecting, if there is no measure of new calls made and the outcomes of those calls.

Sources of control data and performance information

Sources of information that the sales manager or head office sales department can use for analysis should include the **daily activity report** and the **customer order form**. If well designed and properly used in sales management these two documents contain a wealth of information for analysis as measures of activity and effectiveness. In addition, any of the standard forms and control documents used by the sales force provide sources of control data to the field sales manager. Some of their control uses are illustrated in the following table.

Developing sales force controls from available information	

Daily activity reports	● This can be used for:
	  – coding and sorting of information to monitor against overall plans and objectives;
	  – exception analysis to identify trends and deviations from plans;
	  – comparison of calls made with journey cycle schedules, and exception printouts of missed calls
	● Monitor effective coverage.
	  – Have scheduled calls been made?
	  – Why are scheduled calls missed and will they be picked up?
	● Monitor call rates and sales conversion ratios and prepare inter-territory comparisons.
	● Monitor sales volumes and values against targets.
	● Monitor special display or promotional activity where a special recording is requested (self-reporting of achievements).
	● Monitor new prospect pioneer calling (new calls to be identified on report).
	● Check seasonal outlet coverage.
	● Monitor car mileage.

Customer order forms	● Analyse volumes and values of orders, and average order sizes by customer, territory, area, and each higher tier to national sales force total. ● Make comparisons of actual sales to targets and forecasts, and percentage changes over time, e.g. by – week or month

	– this year/last year analysis
	– actual values and percentages
	– cumulative and moving annual totals
	– geographical area (territory/area)
	– trade channel sector (outlet type).
	● Develop exception printouts of customers who have not ordered on a journey cycle.
Journey plans	● Are calls made to schedule?
	● Are appointments made?
	● Are calls planned to fill the working day?
	● Do calls made match the master journey cycle schedule?
	● Are pre-call objectives being set and pursued?
	● Is the salesperson giving contact point details?
Customer call records	● Do call record cards exist for all customers?
	● Are records current?
	● Are call objectives being set?
	● Are special reporting requirements being complied with?
	● Are all product ranges and items being fairly represented?
	● Are additional volume and distribution being actively sought?
Credit notes	● Obtain copies of all product uplift and credit notes.
	● Set guidelines for the issue of notes.
	– If goods are credited ensure they are withdrawn from the outlet.
	● Check uplift/credit note books when working with salespersons.
Expenses records	● Check receipts.
	● Monitor for reasonableness.
Discounts and allowance levels	● Monitor for abuse of discretionary trade allowances.

Supplementary analysis
- Supplementary analysis of **daily activity reports** and **customer order forms** can also focus attention on:
  - product-by-product analysis to show gains and losses in distribution by customer, territory, area, etc. (often using self-reporting by salespersons);
  - to identify and highlight new distribution achievements;
  - to measure achievements against established standards of performance;
  - to conduct analysis of special recordings or data of short term interest;
  - profit performance by area/territory/salesperson.
- When working with salespersons in the field the sales manager should take the opportunity to check that all **customer call records** maintained by the salesperson are up to date, and that they are used by the salesperson during the selling day for call planning and management purposes. Managers often find it useful to check the call records for accounts that have not been active in recent sales periods. Also, surveys of call records can often highlight weaknesses in product distribution or usage, and if stock levels are entered it may be possible to spot where sales are below potential from recorded stock levels on entry to calls.
- Managers can look to see if calls being missed follow a pattern, such as the more remote customers, or where buyers are considered less cooperative.
- Salespersons should be encouraged to log on the **daily activity reports** their daily and

cumulative sales against targets, to create a self-awareness of achievement against territory targets.

- Managers must closely monitor salespersons who have authority to vary terms and prices, to ensure that best prices are being achieved, and that profitability is not being eroded unnecessarily. A commission salesperson normally will be more motivated by his or her personal earnings than improving company profitability.

Where data is monitored using computers, the sales manager should develop exception printouts to monitor:

- that all scheduled calls per cycle are being made
- which scheduled visits did/did not produce orders
- which customers have ceased to be active (i.e. customers who have not ordered within the journey cycle)
- where customer orders deviate significantly from customer targets
- customer payments, i.e. overdue payments, monitored by territory
- new customers opened in the latest sales period
- orders taken but not delivered within the sales period (watching for production and stock management problems).

Sales performance league tables

One of the most commonly used tools for providing performance feedback against key result areas is the **sales territory league table**. An example of this is illustrated in Table 17.4. Where practical, this might be prepared by data logged on to computer performance-measuring spreadsheets or databases, but in many companies the sales performance league table is found to use summary data from several different data recording sources, and may need to be prepared manually as a summary. Analysis should be used to highlight any variations in patterns between territories. By providing feedback in a league table that covers a range of key result areas it provides an opportunity for different salespersons to lead in the various measurement categories, and it is rare for one salesperson to lead in all categories. A league table makes individual performance public, and provides a source of motivation.

Another example of how performance data might be presented at the sales territory level is shown in Table 17.5, which can also be totalled to give similar charts by sales area (groups of territories) or nationally for the company. This example looks at performance for individual products against a range of performance measurement criteria.

Monitoring performance against territory sales target

If the sales manager wants a closer monitoring of territory performance against targets, the control form illustrated in Table 17.6 can be developed for each territory. This will:

- show a running territory performance against target
- help to plan the following month's targets (adjusted to take account of the latest market situation)
- show up interpersonal (inter-territory) anomalies
- flag danger signs of serious shortfalls (indicating training needs, corrective action marketing/promotional programmes, market trends)
- provide a basis for re-allocating target shortfalls over the balance of a month or even to other (better performing) territories.

A summary sheet, accumulating the sales and performance against target for each sales area grouping of salespersons, can also be prepared along the same lines. All this control data can be produced manually or using computers, with automatic updates as new data arrives daily. Experienced sales managers know that it is critical to monitor target achievement daily in most industries, as shortfalls are very hard to rectify the further you go through any sales period.

Table 17.4 Example of a territory league table comparing performance

Monthly territory performance comparisons												Sales area: North		Date March 199-					
	Territory 1		Territory 2		Territory 3		Territory 4		Territory 5		Territory 6		Area		Area average	
	Month	Year	Month	Year	Month	Year	Month	Year	Month	Year	Month	Year	Month	Year	Month	Year
Days worked	17	56	19	58									114	324	19	54
Total calls made	172	588	187	616									1345	3564	224	594
Average daily calls	10.1	10.5	9.8	10.6									11.8	11.0	11.8	11.0
Total scheduled calls	228	684	220	710									1380	3880	230	646
Scheduled calls made	160	540	175	586									1259	3560	210	593
% scheduled calls made	70%	92%	80%	95%									91%	93%	91%	93%
Total orders	95	356	106	398									798	2300	133	383
% orders/calls	55%	61%	57%	65%									59%	65%	59.%	65%
Average daily orders	5.6	6.4	5.6	6.9									7.0	7.1	7.0	7.1
Case target	1320	5460	1460	5980									8250	29500	1375	4916
% of area target	16%	19%	18%	20%									100	100		
Case sales	880	4620	1240	4830									7100	25430	1183	4238
% territory target	67%	85%	85%	80%									86%	86%	86%	86%
% area case sales	12%	18%	17%	19%												
New prospect calls	12	24	4	16									86	170	14.3	28.3
% new prospects to total calls	7%	4%	2%	3%									6%	5%	6%	5%
% new prospects to Area total	14%	14%	5%	9%												
Holiday promotion % outlets committed	25%		30%												31%	
Average total category shelf facings	60	58	65	63											59	60
Ave. company shelf facings per Off trade outlet	21	19	25	24											24	23
Distribution on entry																
• Brand X	76%	78%	81%	82%											79%	815
• Brand Y	17%	16%	24%	23%											20%	19%

Note:

1. Any other factors can be listed here where local recordings are made, e.g. on daily activity reports, where special recordings may monitor display or distribution.

2. Data on this table comes from customer orders and daily activity reports (whether in hard copy format or computer logged with hand computer terminals).

In the example of Table 17.6, the territory target has been divided equally across each selling day. While that is a common practice where companies operate in repeat consumable product categories, it is not normally appropriate in many industrial or business-to-business patterns. In such situations, a daily target monitoring system may be less meaningful, and perhaps monitoring is on a weekly basis. In our example, we show that by 14 July the territory salesperson is 118 cases behind target, about a half-day's selling time. If the territory forecasting was accurate, the territory salesperson would have some catching up to do, and the sales manager would need to be working with the salesperson to seek ways of correcting the deficit.

Field checks or audits

Field checks (or **field audits**) by sales managers offer an excellent opportunity to keep in touch with customers and the market, and to monitor the performance and activities of the sales team. While this is a more common form of management activity in consumer

Table 17.5 An example territory report for product performance

Territory performance report			Territory: 6 Month: July 1997			
	Brand W	Brand X	Brand Y	etc.	etc.	TOTAL: ALL BRANDS
Current month July 1997						
● Value	50 000					
● Volume	833					
Month last year July 1996						
● Value	46 000					
● Volume	793					
% This year/ last year						
● Value	108.7%					
● Volume	105.0%					
Cumulative this year to date						
● Value	370 000					
● Volume	5 970					
Cumulative last year to date						
● Value	360 000					
● Volume	6 000					
% This year to date/ last year to date						
● Value	102.8%					
● Volume	99.5%					
Month target						
● Value	48 000					
● Volume	800					
% Month target						
● Value	104%					
● Volume	104%					
Year target						
● Value	600 000					
● Volume	10 000					
% Year target						
● Value	61.6%					
● Volume	59.7%					
Moving annual totals (volumes)						
This year to current month	9 210					
Last year to same month	8 905					
MAT This year/ Last year %	103.4%					

Table 17.6 *Example of a territory target control sheet*

Monthly sales target control sheet							
Territory 1		Total target 4774		Working days 22		Month July 199-	
Day	Day target	Day sales	+ or −	Cumulative target	Cumulative sales	Cumulative + or −	Danger zone
1/7	217	220	+3	217	220	+3	
2/7	217	196	−21	434	416	−18	
3/7	217	239	+22	651	655	+4	
6/7	217	240	+23	868	895	+27	
7/7	217	165	−52	1 085	1 060	−25	*
8/7	217	145	−72	1 302	1 205	−97	*
9/7	217	306	+89	1 519	1 511	−8	*
10/7	217	147	−70	1 736	1 658	−78	*
13/7	217	278	+61	1 953	1 936	−17	*
14/7	217	116	−101	2 170	2 052	−118	*
15/7	217			2 387			
16/7	217			2 604			
17/7	217			2 821			
20/7	217			3 038			
21/7	217			3 255			
22/7	217			3 472			
23/7	217			3 689			
24/7	217			3 906			
27/7	217			4 123			
28/7	217			4 340			
29/7	217			4 557			
30/7	217			4 774			
31/7	Meeting						

product companies, where managers can discreetly visit a range of stores or trade dealers, it also has applications in some industrial and business-to-business sales, possibly in the guise of a **service quality audit**. The sales manager should conduct regular checks of field activity on each territory under his control.

Two types of field check or audit, each with a different emphasis, are:

- general field check audit, i.e. taking a limited geographical area and calling on all outlets to make and note observations
- follow check audit, i.e. using a recent daily activity report as the base, and calling on all outlets listed to observe the salesperson's work activity and achievements.

An example of a **field audit notes** form is illustrated in Table 17.7. While this illustrates a retail audit check, the format might be adapted for use in other selling environments.

The sales manager conducting a field audit should make notes of observations and comments, for subsequent feedback to the appropriate salespersons. An audit should focus on a few key current priorities, such as the implementation of current promotion programmes, effective use of point of sales material, or distribution achieved with the launch of a new product.

If a sales manager is planning to work with a salesperson later in the day it can be good practice to visit briefly a couple of customers who would have received a sales call earlier

---

Field checks or audits

Use of general checks
- Establishing levels of distribution and outlet coverage (visiting outlets called on by the sales team and uncalled on outlets)
- Monitoring display achievements (regular display and promotional display)
- Checking effectiveness of prospecting for new customers
- Checking wholesale distributor effectiveness in maintaining distribution
- Checking use of promotional aids by sales team (e.g. point of sales material)
- Monitoring competitive activity (display, distribution, pricing, product range, staffing levels, coverage, promotions)
- Monitoring customer satisfaction with sales service and customer service (including any after-sales service or technical support)

Use of follow checks
- Monitoring the accuracy of daily activity report recording: assess training needs
- Monitoring the understanding of, and compliance with, instructions

---

that day by the salesperson about to be accompanied. The sales manager then has immediate knowledge of activity, and may form views about what to focus training attention on during the period with the salesperson.

It is important to provide **feedback** on both general checks and follow checks as soon as practical after these have been conducted. The salesperson should learn how you view his or her territory, both with praise for good standards and achievements, and constructive criticism and advice where problems are identified. If the sales manager meets a salesperson soon after a field audit of his or her work then it is not wise to rush into giving feedback, as that makes an audit look like a policing action. Usually a little time to relax the salesperson to your presence, and some positive feedback on observations in any customers visited, can provide a basis for more comprehensive feedback and some specific counselling and training.

Focusing performance measures on key result areas

Sales managers should devote their limited resources and time available for performance monitoring to monitoring and measuring against the main key result areas for their particular business. Some of the typical key result areas that can be the subject of measurement over time are outlined here.

Table 17.7 An example of a basic field audit form

Field audit form Newtown	Salesperson/Territory John Smith – Territory 6					Date 5 January 199-	
Outlet details	Call on journey	Holiday promo	POS material	Brand X	Brand Y facings	Compet- itor Brand Z	Notes
J & J Superstore	✓	✓	✓	✓	26	✓	Good display
Acme C & C				✓	4	✓	Poor company representation
Khans Store	✓	✓		✓	8	✓	Good range, poor Brand X facings
Alpha Grocery	✓			✓	10	✓	Good display limited range
Save-All Supermarket	✓	✓	✓	✓	9	✓	Excellent
Hightown Coop.	✓	✓	✓	✓	15	✓	Good range, relocate display
Wilson's, South St	✓			✓	5		Lower income clients

Scheduled call coverage	● Are calls being made as scheduled? Missed calls may mean missed orders, and irrecoverable loss of sales as consumers or users switch to alternative products or sources.
Sales to calls ratios	● This can give a measure of: – presentation and training effectiveness; – efficiency in identifying and qualifying new prospects (pioneer calls). ● Standards of performance should relate to historical levels and relate to the industry or market place (high sales to calls are normal with fast moving consumer goods products, but much lower sales to calls are normal with many products such as home improvements, insurance, services). ● A low conversion ratio for new prospect calls may suggest: – training needs in screening and qualifying leads; – training needs in basic selling skills, if ratios are good for established customers, as skills may be rusty;

	– incorrect targeting through marketing communications;
	– poor information on, and identification of, target market group.
Distribution	● This is a key measurement in assessing the impact of a sales force on markets and customers (impacting on market share analysis).
	● It may be measured from sales force reporting data, or, more accurately, from independent data from research sources covering all potential uses or stockists.
	● Managers should be alert to any loss of distribution or product usage within the established customer base.
Sales volume and values	● This is a key result area normally subject to direct measures from order processing data, and compared with targets/forecasts.
Display achievements	● This is a key result area in fast moving consumer goods market sectors, where products are re-sold through retail stockists and trade dealers.
	● Salespersons can be requested to enter display recordings for major brands or special activities, e.g. sale promotions, in allocated spaces on daily activity reports, for tabulation and comparison over time.
Trends in performance	● Analysis of longer-term and underlying trends is a critical sales management performance monitoring activity. Moving annual totals (see Chapter 14) provide one useful trend analysis tool.
	● Trend analysis is useful in evaluation of promotions, advertising, marketing programmes, training, pricing policies, product range preferences.
Pioneer calling (identifying new prospective customers)	● Are new prospective customers being identified and called on to assess potential and to solicit orders or promote product trial?
Response to advertising and promotional activity	● This should be measured to:
	– measure response
	– assess cost effectiveness
	– impact of particular types of promotion and marketing communications.
Gross profit contributions	● Where products can be costed on a contract basis, or standard costing system, profitability at gross or net levels should be assessed for:
	– each salesperson/territory
	– each customer
	– each product or product category.
	● Managers will be aware that profitability may not be the same for all products in the portfolio, and measurement will highlight opportunities to improve profitability by varying the focus of attention within the product mix (i.e. highlight more profitable products in the mix).

Action points

Types of control
- Continuous controls, designed to:
  - monitor tasks and duties, reducing the risks of problems occurring;
  - monitor objective factors (quality, quantity, cost, time).
- Warning controls, designed to:
  - recognize and identify deviations from plans;
  - identify the direction and magnitude of variations
- Self-control
  where the salesperson monitors his or her own performance against standards of performance and requirements of the job

Have key result areas been identified?
Focus analysis on key result areas of the selling job, e.g.:
- Scheduled call coverage
- Sales to calls ratios
- Distribution
- Sales volume and values
- Display achievements
- Trends in performance
- Pioneer calling
- Response to advertising and promotional activity
- Gross profit contributions

Have standards of performance been established, e.g.
- Standard daily call rate (i.e. minimum acceptable)
- Average daily call rate
- Minimum order size (volume/value)
- Average order size (volume/value)
- Total daily, weekly, monthly sales achievements (against targets, forecasts)
- Calls on new prospects
- Conversion ratio of calls to orders
- Distribution by product
- Product display achievements
- Achievement of scheduled call coverage
- Pre-call objective setting

Secondary factors for sales managers to monitor are:
- Compliance with administrative systems and procedures
- Maintenance and updating of customer call records
- Timely submission of journey plans

	Action points
Checklist 17.1 continued	

Checklist 17.1 continued
- Salesperson appearance
- Care and maintenance of vehicle and sales equipment
- Pre-scheduling of customer appointments
- Frequency and handling of customer complaints
- Staff turnover

Information should:
- measure actual performance against plans, forecasts, targets, budgets or standards of performance
- help in identifying and monitoring underlying trends
- give warnings of significant variations from plans and programmes in sufficient time that corrective action can be taken in key result areas
- help the sales organization perform its functions more effectively, and contribute to identifying training needs

Performance statistics usually measure and report on performance at two levels:
- The overall company (macro) level
- The territory or account (micro level)

At the macro and micro levels performance statistics usually monitor:
- Sales volume by product and in total
- Sales value by product and in total
- Distribution by product and market sector
- Market share data
- Company turnover
- Company profit performance
- Profitability by account

Do analyses relate to figures of comparative reference points, such as:
- The appropriate plan or forecast achievement due by the point in time
- Performance over the same comparable period last year (This year/Last year comparisons)

Supplementary analysis can also focus attention on:
- Product-by-product analysis to show gains and losses in distribution by customer, territory, area, etc. (often using self-reporting by salespersons)
- Identifying and highlighting new distribution achievements
- Measuring achievements against established standards of performance
- Conducting analysis of special recordings or data of short-term interest
- Profit performance by area/territory/salesperson.
- That all scheduled calls per cycle are being made
- Which scheduled visits did/did not produce orders
- Which customers have ceased to be active

	Action points

Checklist 17.1 continued
● Where customer orders deviate significantly from customer targets
● Customer payments
 	
Is all data presented in the most meaningful and easily interpreted way?
 	
Sources of control data and their use
Daily activity reports
● Coding/sorting information to monitor against plans and objectives
● Exception analysis to identify trends and deviations from plans
● Effective coverage: comparison of calls made with journey cycle schedules, and exception printouts of missed calls
● Analysis of conversion ratios
● Call rates
● Sales volumes (in total and average per order)
● Special display or promotional activity where a recording is requested
● Seasonal outlet coverage
● Analysis of display and promotion achievements
● Car mileage.
● New prospect contacts.
Customer order form
● Analysis of volumes and values of orders, and average order sizes by territory, area, etc.
● Comparisons of actual sales to targets and forecasts, e.g. by:
  – week/ month
  – this year/last year analysis
  – actual amounts and percentages
  – cumulative and moving annual totals
  – geographical area (territory/area)
  – trade channel sector
● Printouts of customers who have not ordered on a journey cycle
Journey plans
● Are calls made to schedule?
● Are calls planned to fill the working day?
● Do calls made match the master journey cycle schedule?
● Are pre-call objectives being set and pursued?
● Is the salesperson giving contact point details?
Customer call records
● Do call record cards exist for all customers?
● Are records current?
● Are call objectives being set?
● Are special reporting requirements being complied with?
● Are all product ranges and items being fairly represented?
● Are additional volume and distribution being actively sought?
Credit notes
● Obtain copies of all product uplift and credit notes	

	Action points
Checklist 17.1 continued	

Checklist 17.1 continued
- Set guidelines for the issue of notes
- If goods are credited ensure they are withdrawn from the outlet
- Check uplift/ credit note books when working with salespersons

Expenses records
- Check receipts
- Monitor for reasonableness

Discounts and allowance levels
- Monitor for abuse of discretionary trade allowances

Feedback using territory league tables
- Do you use data in summary format to feed back performance on key result areas and standards of performance to the sales team?
- Use analysis to highlight variations in patterns between territories

Sales management territory target control sheet
- Used to monitor daily territory performance against target
- Helps to plan the following month's targets
- Shows up interpersonal (inter-territory) anomalies
- Flags danger signs of serious shortfalls
- Provides a basis for re-allocating target shortfalls over the balance of a month

Field checks
Are regular field checks conducted to monitor field activity, performance, programme implementation, and the focus of priorities?

General field check audit
Conduct general checks of the territory to:
- establish levels of distribution and outlet coverage
- monitor display achievements
- check prospecting
- monitor wholesale distributor effectiveness
- check use of promotional aids
- monitor competitive activity (display, distribution, pricing, product range, staffing levels, coverage, promotions)
- assess customer satisfaction with service

Follow check audit
Conduct follow checks on recent work to:
- monitor the accuracy of daily activity report recording
- assess training needs
- monitor the compliance with instructions

Budgetary control
Items to monitor against budgets include:
- Salaries, commissions, bonuses and fringe benefits
- Field sales expenses
- Purchase or lease and maintenance of vehicles and other equipment

	Action points
Checklist 17.1 continued ● Sales promotion costs ● Trade term allowances **Are moving annual totals relevant and prepared for key result areas:** ● Product sales volumes and/or values ● Distribution by brand ● Market share ● Company turnover ● Company profit. **Time management** Is the use of time regularly monitored? ● Salesperson use of time? Preparation, selling and non-selling activities, call management. ● Managers' use of time?	

Part Six

Developing the business

18

Trade development _____

Mapping trade channels ▬▬▬

Marketing and sales management overlap considerably, the sales organization being charged with field implementation of the marketing strategy. As a starting point to discussing an approach to trade channel mapping, the sales manager should recognize that selection of suitable trade channels and management of distribution through trade channels are critical to strategy implementation. That means considering aspects of market segmentation illustrated in Figure 18.1.

The sales manager has responsibility for identifying and prioritizing those trade channels that the company has the best chance of supplying and servicing profitably. Distribution to the priority segments will be obtained through some or all of the trade channels serving the network of users and consumers.

Trade channel mapping is just a term for plotting the structure of the trade channels in a market, and noting which market segments they serve and their relative importance in the market place. It is essential that the sales manager understands the structure of distributive trade channels in each of his markets, as this knowledge influences strategic decisions on where to target products. Not every company has the resources to target either all market segments or all of the trade channels serving the market segments, and decisions need to be taken that reflect the most profitable opportunities and the distributive strengths and expertise of the supplying company. Sales managers frequently demon-strate limited knowledge about the structure and size of trade channels, their relative importance in supplying market segments, and their sales volumes in the product category.

The objectives of trade channel mapping are to:

● identify the trade channels for the exporter's products
● identify the key accounts in each trade channel
● develop a trade channel strategy.

The sales manager will want to know:

● how many trade channels there are serving each market segment
● who are the main customers in each trade channel, the key accounts
● where they are located
● how many outlets they have
● what share they have of any trade channel.

This information is essential to planning the correct allocation of sales resources, and marketing and promotional budgets. It can be illustrated diagrammatically as in Figure 18.2.

Typically, in consumer goods markets (and for some industrial products) one of the trade channels in each market segment would be wholesalers, and the other would be direct customers of the supplying company. For example, if trade channel **A** is a wholesaler trade channel, then the wholesalers would

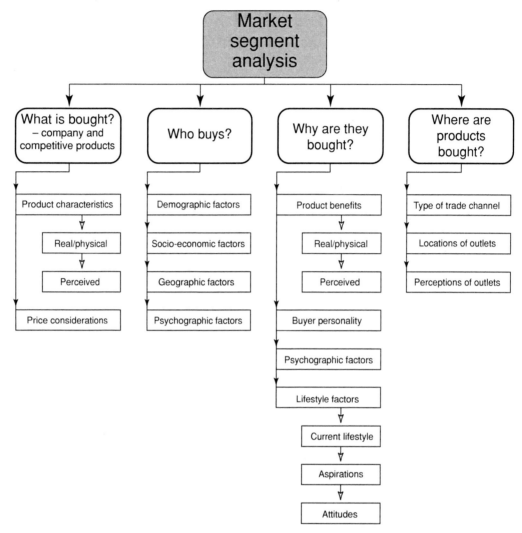

Figure 18.1 *Some issues in market segmentation*

normally service a certain range of larger (key) accounts where they have special relationships or provide a special service, such as a broader product range than just your company's products, and a bigger network of smaller customers who might not be able to purchase the minimum quantities set by suppliers for direct supply.

There is no standard format for a trade channel map. It is just a device for presenting data on the respective volumes of a particular product, or category of products, and shares of sales through the various trade channels distributing the product. An illustrative trade channel map for a supplier of soft drinks

might look something like Figure 18.3.

Here the map shows two main market segments: the '**on** trade', where product is served for consumption on the premises; and the '**off** trade', where product is sold for later consumption at home.

Figure 18.4 gives an outline trade channel structure for an industrial product, industrial cleaning fluids. Two of the trade channels served directly by suppliers are also acting as wholesalers into other trade channels, illustrated in the subordinate diagrams, and the supplier would ideally want to know their split of sales into these channels if any data is available.

Figure 18.2 *Trade channel mapping*

At the very least a trade channel mapping exercise, done on a market sector by market sector basis, should:

- identify and highlight the trade channel structure
- give approximate shares or turnover in the product category
- identify the key accounts within each trade channel with an estimate of their product category turnover that can be compared with the exporter's sales through the respective accounts.

Using trade channel data

A schematic diagram showing the trade channel structure needs to be supported by estimates of the values of the product category sales going through each trade channel to assist in taking decisions on where to focus sales effort, particularly in targeting key accounts.

In most market sectors, whether for industrial or consumer goods, there will only be a handful of key accounts in each trade channel. It can then be useful to prepare a list that highlights the relative importance of each of these to your business over time, such as by using a simple form as in Table 18.1. This is the type of data that a sales team should assist in collecting or developing, within whatever limits of accuracy available data impose on you.

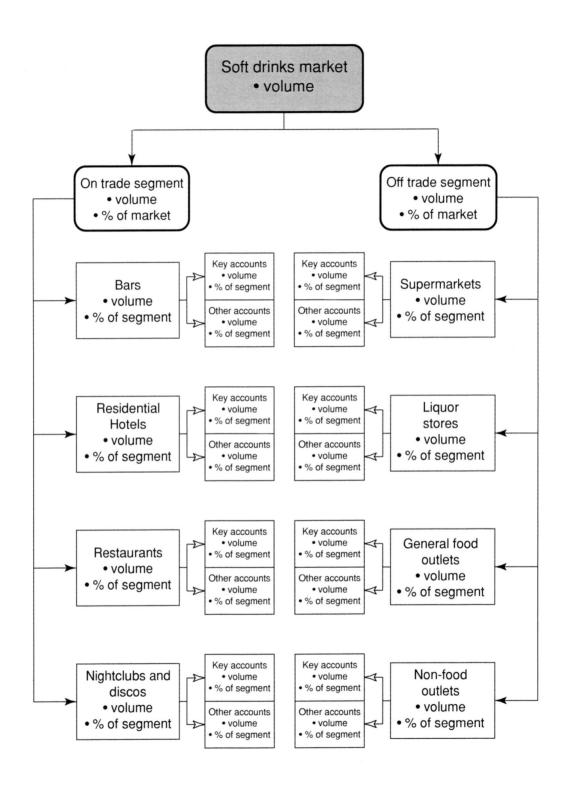

Figure 18.3 *Soft drinks market – trade channel mapping*

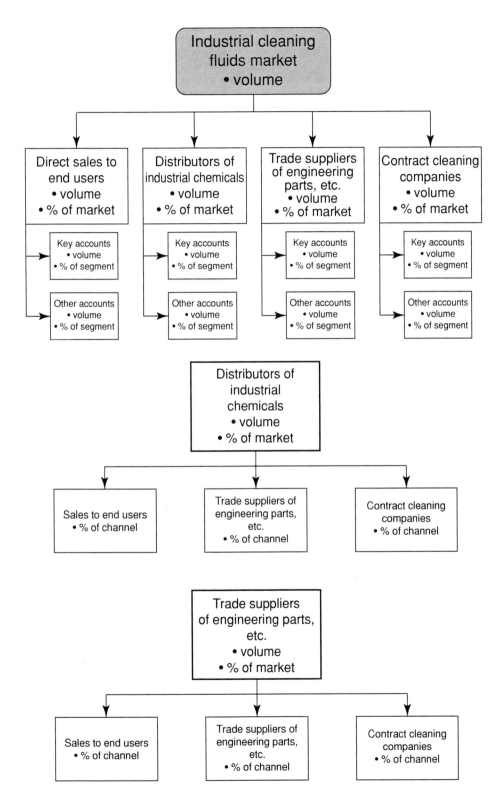

Figure 18.4 *Trade channels for an industrial product*

Table 18.2 illustrates how data can be tabulated in a simple format that highlights the relative importance of the various trade channels distributing to a market segment. This example shows a company supplying table glassware to the two main market sectors, retail outlets for sale to households, and food service sales into businesses providing food and drink for consumption on the premises.

While our example company has a decent overall market share of 16 per cent, compared with only 12 per cent coverage of outlets in each sector, indicating a perfectly reasonable deployment of sales resources, there are some opportunity areas.

In the retail sector the supplier is performing well in the major channels of department stores, hypermarkets and supermarkets, but

Table 18.1 *Tabulating key account share of market data*

Top accounts share of markets				
Market sector: Turnover				
	Year	19—	19—	19—
Key accounts: Trade channel A 1 2 3 4 5 6 7 8	Number of branches			
Total trade channel A turnover. % share of total				
Key accounts Trade channel B 1 2 3 4 5 6 7 8	Number of outlets			
Total trade channel B turnover. % share of total				
TOTAL KEY ACCOUNT TURNOVER – ALL TRADE CHANNELS				
TOTAL MARKET SEGMENT TURNOVER				
Key account % share of segment turnover				

Table 18.2 *Analysing the relative importance of trade channels to a supplier*

Trade channel share of segment analysis						
Table glassware products	Number of outlets	Trade channel turnover 000s	Trade channel % share of segment turnover	Supplier's turnover 000s	Trade channel % share of supplier's turnover	Outlets covered directly by company
Retail trade segment						
Department stores	20	7 000	17%	1 420	24%	15
Hypermarkets	22	10 600	25%	1 690	29%	16
Supermarkets	310	14 000	33%	2 090	36%	150
Gift and speciality stores	460	3 850	9%	290	5%	130
Sundry other retailers	3 260	6 650	16%	320	6%	190
TOTAL RETAIL TRADE	**4 072**	**42 100**	**100**	**5 810**	**100**	**501**
Retail trade share of total glassware market			75%		66%	12% sector outlet coverage
Food service segment						
Hotels	820	1 648	12%	1 160	40%	410
Restaurants	4 650	3 790	27%	820	27%	670
Bars	2 620	5 460	40%	700	23%	420
Clubs	270	940	7%	220	7%	50
Others – Snack bars	4 500	1 960	14%	90	3%	30
TOTAL FOOD SERVICE TRADE	**12 860**	**13 798**	**100**	**2 990**	**100**	**1 580**
Food service trade share of total glassware market			25%		34%	12% sector outlet coverage
TOTAL MARKET: GLASSWARE TRADE	**16 932**	**55 898**		**8 800** 16% market share		**2 081**

is weaker in outlet coverage and sales to gift and speciality stores and the sundry retailers' categories. Those weaknesses might be addressed by developing a network of wholesaler distributors (if sales resources are not available to expand direct coverage), as this analysis currently indicates the company does all its sales direct.

The company is achieving 34 per cent of its sales into the food service sector, compared with 25 per cent of total glassware sales to that sector. Clearly it is using its resources well there. It has an unusually high share of the hotel trade (40 per cent), clearly to be envied and defended. It is weak, however, in bars and in the others and snack bar sector. These weaknesses could be addressed either by developing sub-distributors (wholesalers) to service those channels, or by improving its own coverage. Its weakness in bars could result from salespersons calling when buyers are unavailable, and some evening sales calls might be necessary to increase sales to that channel. Snack bars are likely to be small and busy, in key locations where it can be difficult to park, and also purchasing in limited quantities, so they might be a good trade channel to service through distributors, who will supply a multiplicity of products meeting their needs.

By building a picture of the trade channel structures and developing data that enables you to know the pattern and relative volumes of trade through the various trade channels you can compare your own performance to the overall pattern, and take informed decisions on your relative strengths and weaknesses.

Developing and using trade terms

Any company that is selling through a network of sub-distributors, dealers or retail stockists will have to develop a local pricing structure that matches trade terms on offer from other suppliers to the market. In the same way, industrial and business-to-business product suppliers will need to compete through the package of trade terms, as this is one of the key factors influencing buyers' decisions, along with price, quality, availability, warranties, after-sales service support, training and technical support, product functionality (benefits addressing needs) and design.

It is part of the sales manager's role to establish that any local trade terms are both competitive with other suppliers and consistent with the market pricing and distribution policies of his or her company. Hence we will provide some commentary on the typical role of trade terms in influencing market activity through the distributor.

What the trade looks at

There are various typical forms that trade terms take, outlined in Table 18.3, which also highlights the particular concerns of the local dealer or buyer, and the supplying company.

Credit

The credit a company will give is normally influenced by:

- local custom and practice of the trade
- competitive terms of trade
- cost of credit from the company versus alternative sources (e.g. bank)
- credit provided to the company from the sales manager's own network of input suppliers (and at what cost)
- state of the local economy, including:
  - need for stockists to extend credit or hold stock
  - employment
  - interest rates and inflation
- strategic marketing considerations, e.g.

Guidelines for credit

There are a few basic guidelines that the sales manager might like to bear in mind, when being pressured to extend the credit to any distributor or direct customer even further (perhaps from 30 to 60 days).

- Do not extend credit if you do not have to – encourage the distributor or direct customer to look for other sources of local finance.
- Credit-check before you extend credit (to end users, retail customers, distributors, and particularly for exports).
- Take trade references.
- Avoid extending credit beyond the normal level of stock cover carried by the trader.
- Credit-check distributors/customers before extending credit.
- Enforce your payment terms.

– expanding distribution and/or product usage
– pipeline stock pressure
– expanding display
– building market share
– blocking competition.

The sales manager will be concerned that his or her company is providing adequate trade credit where that influences performance against marketing strategies and objectives, such as expanding product trial and distribution, or improving display for retail products.

The sales manager should recognize the time value of money in all transactions that extend credit at any level of the distribution chain.

Table 18.3 Trade terms and their objectives

Trade term factor	Dealer's or buyer's concerns	Distributor's or company objectives
Credit		
● Trade credit	Obtaining maximum supplier credit. Comparing of credit terms from alternative suppliers. To finance inventories from supplier credit.	To provide minimum trade credit. To offer trade terms consistent with local trade custom and practice.
● Prompt payment discounts	Discount should be at a higher level than local bank interest to encourage early payment.	To motivate payment as early as possible and within payment terms.
Discount		
● Volume discounts	To have a bonus for volume purchases. Discounts should reflect cost savings on bulk deliveries.	To motivate larger volume purchases. Particularly applied to major accounts. To reduce the likelihood of out-of-stock positions in the trade. To increase trade order sizes. To reduce out-of-stock situations.
● Sliding quantity rate scale	Net price to reduce according to the volume purchased.	
● Retrospective performance discounts	A reward paid in arrears for achieving agreed volumes of purchases. A reward for loyalty. An incentive to push the supplier's products.	To provide an incentive to develop an annual plan with the company, attracting more promotional activity to company products.
Minimum order quantities		
● Fixed quantity (units/cases, etc.) minimum order	To avoid buying any more stock than necessary, i.e. smaller orders and more frequent deliveries.	To cover minimum costs of servicing an order (sales and distribution costs). To maintain stocks in the pipeline, rather than allowing the trade to run out through placing small orders.

Discounts

Discounts are a tool for use in trade dealer and account management and are normally related to:

- the need for improved cash flow
- influencing sales volumes through
  - maintaining distribution
  - expanding the base of distribution
  - minimizing out-of-stocks
  - building market share
  - dealer or account stock holding policies.

Many suppliers offer discounts not related to any of the above, but as:

- an incentive to buy (not specific to volume performance or marketing objectives)
- custom and practice for a particular account.

Discounts given without specific contractual performance conditions are hard to remove and non-motivational in building sales volume and market share.

Types of motivational discounts

There are two main types of motivational discounts (with various application formats)

used by suppliers in many markets, designed either to improve the cash flow or to encourage increased sales and loyalty.

To be controllable and motivational discounts and rebates should be for specific performance achievements, and retrospective rather than 'off invoice' except where related to a sliding case rate scale.

Minimum orders

The basis of calculating a minimum order is normally to set it at a level where the margin contribution will at least cover the direct costs of distribution and servicing the customer account. It is very common for companies not to know servicing and distribution costs, and therefore to set minimum orders too low, with the result that many orders are actually loss making.

Guidelines for establishing minimum orders

From the practical perspective the sales manager might develop an approach to minimum orders using the following guidelines.

- Calculate the cost of distribution, order processing, and related sales and marketing costs, and estimate the optimum minimum order to cover these.

	Types of motivational discount
Prompt settlement discounts	• Designed to improve cash flow. • Will not produce the desired result unless it is greater than the alternative source of financing trade credit, i.e. the customer's bank interest rate.

Performance discounts	• Decreasing price with increasing order volumes: this recognizes the savings on distribution and marketing costs and should not normally be higher than these savings as otherwise you are sacrificing margin.
	• Performance rebates at pre-agreed rates geared to annual performance:
	  – at fixed absolute levels
	  – or an increase on the previous year's sales
	  – as an achievement against target.
	• Sliding scale quantity discounts, e.g.
	  0 – 49 cases £100 per case
	  50-99 cases £ 98 per case.

- Set call frequencies at time intervals to justify orders of the optimum minimum.
- Smaller outlets will need to review stock cover in line with prescribed minimum orders.
- Trade credit can be used to finance an increase in stock holding.

The objective is to use trade terms fairly and equitably to motivate growth in volume and distribution.

Managing wholesale distributors ■

For every one salesperson a company has servicing a market there are probably several wholesaler salespersons or other types of trade dealerships covering the same market base of customers. This is an enormous resource available to help us build our businesses if we can develop and exploit it to mutual advantage – that is, to the benefit of both the supplying companies and the wholesalers or other trade distributors.

The role of the wholesaler or trade distributor

In most market sectors wholesalers exist at two levels:

- as traditional order taking and delivery wholesalers, calling on a network of customers in a geographical area or a particular trade sector
- as cash and carry warehouses, where customers call to select and collect their merchandise.

The typical key functions of the wholesaler or trade distributor in the distribution chain include:

- to carry stocks of a supplier's products so that the products are available to the trade customers not covered directly by the supplier's own sales team
- to extend credit to the customers serviced by the wholesaler

- to generate volume sales through the multiplicity of smaller customers in the various market trade channels
- to cooperate with the supplier in
  - maintaining market distribution;
  - introducing products to suitable trade customers (where the brand's target consumers match the outlet's typical customer profile);
  - generating a regular pattern of orders from the trade customers covered by the wholesalers;
  - promoting the brands through local promotional activity developed and organized by the suppliers.

In some market situations it might be advantageous for a supplier to form special relationships with a few key wholesalers who can act as sub-distributors, supporting your efforts to develop the brands and the market, including:

- providing display and merchandising support for products in the retail outlets he or she covers
- working to achieve agreed objectives in respect of:
  - sales volumes
  - brands distribution
  - market share
- providing you with competitive market intelligence reports
- providing period sales performance and stock data reports
- training their staff in your product knowledge and professional skills in sales, marketing and management
- participating in the annual sales and marketing planning process, providing local expertise and input, and subsequent performance reports on their progress
- providing an organization structure, both in quality and numbers, capable of working to achieving agreed objectives and implementing agreed plans
- running the business efficiently, including using modern technology and management systems to develop a high standard of customer service (since the

trade customers buying from your distributors will associate their quality and standards of service with your good name).

If the supplier expects his or her key wholesalers to match this outline of their role, then his or her first priority will be to address the main concern of most wholesalers, that the supplier is in direct competition with the wholesalers in supplying products to what they see as their traditional customer base. When working through a network of wholesale distributor or trade dealers who you expect to support your products, complement their activities rather than compete head-on for sales to the same customer group.

Auditing the wholesalers

Since it is highly unlikely that all wholesalers will add value to the product development and distribution activities in the market, the supplying company should start by auditing the wholesalers, with a view to identifying:

- how many wholesalers are in the market?
- how many outlets does each cover?
- what are their particular strengths in supplying geographical areas or trade niche sectors?
- how many salespersons does each of the wholesalers have?
- how are their sales teams rewarded?

And to this we should add one more key question:

- how do our competitors service and develop wholesalers?

The sales manager can use the earlier principles of trade channel mapping to help him understand the wholesale structure for his or her market. Table 18.4 illustrates a scenario for a supplier of electrical products into various trade channels in the two main market sectors of retail and trade sales.

In this example, the company is looking to expand sales and distribution in its southern area, which has 40 per cent of all national outlets (according to the company's best information). The company, in turn, only covers with direct selling calls some 1198 customers from 2707 in the southern area, i.e. 44 per cent outlet coverage. The objective is to increase that by developing relationships with a number of specialist wholesale distributors. Data could be collected by direct contact with the distributors, and asking for cooperation.

Obviously, there would normally be a significant overlap with often more than one distributor servicing the same customers. That aside, the overall information did show just how important the wholesale sector was in terms of the outlet universe it served, and highlighted some key wholesalers worth special attention to develop cooperation.

The analysis shows the supplier's sales manager that the 10 wholesale distributors covering the southern area have a total of 63 salespersons, and the 2707 outlets in the southern area are receiving a total of 8764 calls from the various wholesalers – meaning an average of 3.2 wholesalers were calling on each outlet. Since the supplier covers only 1198 outlets (those he views as the more important outlets) with his eight salespersons in the southern area, the opportunity to expand distribution and outlet coverage by working more closely with some of these wholesalers is apparent.

The example analysis also shows that some wholesaler distributors are relatively stronger in servicing particular trade channels, and that kind of knowledge is useful to a supplier's sales manager in deciding which wholesalers to focus his or her attention on and in developing programmes to support individual wholesalers.

In this example, since the supplier covers all the DIY superstores, and is strong in covering the category A and B outlets in the other trade channels, he might want more support in covering high street multiples (smaller, local chains), independent hardware stores, and the multiplicity of small trade dealers who supply trade electricians. With that objective, while he might decide not to

Table 18.4 Collating information on wholesale distributor coverage

	Salesmen	Outlets	DIY super-stores	High street mulitple	Independent hardware stores	Sundry stores	Trade dealers tors	Major contrac-ies	Local aluthorti-ies
			Electrical products **Market outlet coverage**						
			Retail outlets				**Trade and contractors**		
Total market		6 740	160	2 102	2 498	848	862	96	174
Southern area		2 707	91	780	928	389	387	61	71
Supplier	8	1 198	91	362	296	220	148	36	45
Wholesalers									
Distributors									
A	6	849	18	460	130	98	124	7	12
B	9	1 328	24	524	320	168	236	24	32
C	6	922	12	216	298	130	212	28	26
D	5	563	6	176	180	84	93	8	16
E	8	1 322	38	562	260	228	174	21	39
F	3	495	11	162	149	74	66	6	27
G	10	1 253	29	417	412	142	196	16	41
H	5	604	14	246	172	97	48	5	22
I	7	834	6	128	306	216	146	11	21
J	4	594	9	266	137	109	47	9	17
Southern area total	63	8 764	167	3 157	2 364	1 346	1 342	135	253

restrict the sale of products to any creditworthy wholesaler, he might focus on developing special relations and customized support activity with **wholesalers B, E and I**, but C and G might be worth some additional effort to develop as they have some niche trade channel strengths.

The sales manager looking to improve his or her market distribution and management through wholesale distributors and trade dealers can:

● develop a similar table that will help analyse the structure and importance of the wholesalers, and understand the opportunities to develop in partnership with some, or all, of them
● clarify how competitors work with and through the wholesale trade to supply their brands to the various market sectors and trade channels
● study the relative strengths and weaknesses of each wholesaler.

Problems in managing wholesalers

The problems a supplier normally sees in managing wholesalers arise at two levels:

● the attitudes of the wholesalers to the supplier
● the limitations on the supplier's ability to manage the wholesaler because of the nature of wholesalers' business.

Attitudes of wholesalers

The main concern of most wholesalers – that the supplier is in direct competition with them – is usually expressed in two ways:

● that the supplier, in supplying direct to customers, is reducing their opportunities to generate additional sales volume and profits and eroding the loyalty of their traditional customers
● that the supplier is only interested in supplying higher volume, more credit-

worthy outlets, leaving the wholesalers to supply the lower volume outlets who often are also more of a credit risk.

Any programme to develop and manage wholesalers must address these wholesaler concerns, and we will look at ways of doing this in a later section.

Limitations on the supply company's ability to manage wholesalers

Wholesalers in general will have limited resources and a lower level of management and selling skills than supplier operations and sales personnel. Some of the typical problems encountered by suppliers in managing wholesalers are given below.

- Suppliers do not have direct control over the wholesaler's staff and operations, and have little scope to influence their activities.
- Wholesalers stock and sell a very broad range of products, and cannot be experts in all of them.
- There are conflicting pressures on wholesalers from other suppliers who are also seeking a dominant share of time and mind.
- Wholesalers frequently distribute their own agency brands, usually smaller and less well-known brands (some of which they may be importing), and which they see as their priority and main opportunity to make a larger profit margin.
- Wholesalers are reluctant to disclose any sales and market information to suppliers,

usually keeping details of their sales volumes and customer base to themselves.
- Wholesalers' salespersons are normally more interested in collecting orders than in brand selling. This results in part from a lower level of selling skills than in manufacturing supplier organizations, and in part from reward systems that normally relate earnings to sales turnover.
- Wholesalers often have a lower quality of management personnel, and may be less sophisticated in using modern technology in their businesses.

For manufacturing suppliers to progress their relations and develop their business through wholesalers they must recognize and tackle these problems.

Developing the partnership and motivating distributors

Suppliers will only achieve their objectives for the brands in the wholesale sector by directing efforts to helping wholesalers achieve their own business goals.

Both supplier and wholesaler have a common interest in developing sales volume. The supplier is well placed to help the wholesaler generate more volume, and also has the expertise to contribute to the other areas of wholesaler interest.

In many markets, where a manufacturing company does supply wholesalers, the traditional relations between supplier and wholesaler is largely based on long-term familiarity with each other, what we might term 'personal relations', but the wholesaler's feeling

---

Focus of objectives

Distributor	Wholesaler
● Profit (longer term)	● Profit (short term)
● Volume	● Volume
● Distribution	● Cost control
● Market share	● Building customer loyalty
● Brand awareness	● Risk spreading (through a broad product base)

that the supplier is also the 'competition' is not reduced. In large part this is because the supplier sells products to the wholesaler, but then does little to support its products through the wholesalers, but does have its own active sales force out promoting direct. We can build on traditional personal relationships and focus on an **adding-value** approach to developing and managing wholesalers (see Figure 18.5). This is the **partnership approach** to motivating and managing wholesalers. Supplier and wholesaler each focus on what they can do best in the partnership.

The focus of value-adding activities

The manufacturing supplier's sales team should focus on those selling activities that add most long-term value to trade development and management, and therefore require greater skill and product knowledge, such as:

- developing outlet presence
- selling in new brands
- building brand images consistent with brand positioning and brand communication messages
- working to gain an increased share of mind in trade customer outlets
- developing customized promotional activity for key outlets
- building trade customer loyalty to the supplier's company and products.

The wholesalers can focus on those activities that may seem to require less specialist skill and add less long-term value, but are very important in building the market, such as:

- acting as the order takers and order processors to satisfy the volume needs of the multiplicity of smaller customer outlets, both those called on by a supplier's salesperson and those not receiving a call from the supplier
- meeting the trade needs for credit, and managing the process of collecting payments from the numerous outlets in the market
- maintaining and expanding brand distribution (particularly in outlets not receiving direct calls from the supplier's salespersons)
- communicating product knowledge to non-direct outlets
- supporting brands in non-direct outlets by implementing manufacturing suppliers' promotions (giving the many smaller customers a change to pass on benefit down the chain to their own customers).

The focus of activities with key wholesalers must be aimed towards building **trust, commitment** and **cooperation**. The manufacturing supplier will do this by:

- demonstrating an understanding of the wholesalers' business and trading

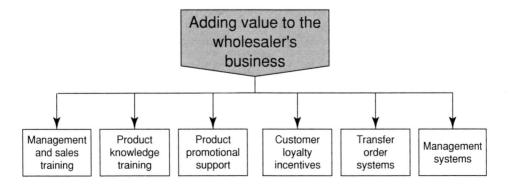

Figure 18.5 Adding value in the supply chain

environment, supporting them and not treating them as 'competition'
- developing specific wholesaler development strategy plans
- developing a trade marketing structure within the supplier's organization that can focus on trade development
- ensuring the seniority of the salesperson calling on any wholesaler matches the importance of the account
- sharing information on customers and markets.

Practical ways to add value to wholesaler relations

Once you have taken action to demonstrate this commitment to developing your wholesalers, there are some specific activities you can take to add value to your relationships with your wholesalers. These include:

- developing an active **transfer order system**
- passing new outlet leads to wholesalers
- letting the wholesaler supply some of the better volume accounts, so that he has some of the 'cream', and they will become his key accounts

- providing **training** to wholesaler's sales teams covering
  - basic selling skills
  - product knowledge
  - product merchandising
  - using point of sale material effectively
  - selling in brand promotions
  - tele-sales training
- improving management information systems and order processing systems within wholesaler organizations
- improving journey planning for wholesaler salesmen
- matching the calling cycle of supplier's salespersons to the delivery cycle of wholesalers, so that transfer orders can be delivered promptly
- supporting wholesalers with promotional packages that build outlet loyalty to them
- developing sales incentive schemes to encourage effort and loyalty amongst wholesaler sales teams
- developing preferential support packages for key cooperative wholesalers that can additionally motivate and bind them to the manufacturing supplier.

Five rules for developing and managing wholesalers

Rule 1   In many product categories developing the role of the wholesalers is critical to success in developing the market in view of the diverse size and nature of outlets, and requires building a 'partnership' through an active account management policy towards wholesalers, building mutual trust and commitment.

Rule 2   Complement the wholesalers' activities; do not compete in a way that produces conflict.

Rule 3   Only when you understand the wholesaler's business can you begin to develop a strategy for partnership and growth.

Rule 4   Motivating a wholesaler or trade distributor to push your products means doing something for him that he sees adds value to his business.

Rule 5   Focus on what the wholesaler can do with his resources that supports what you do, and focus your resources on what he can do less well.

**Checklist 18.1
Trade channel mapping**

Action points

The objectives of trade channel mapping are to:
1 **identify the trade channels serving the market segments for your products;**
2 **identify the key accounts in each trade channel;**
3 **develop a trade channel strategy.**
- Has a trade channel map been prepared for each market sector?
- How many trade channels are there serving each market sector?
  – List the trade channels for each market sector
- Who are the main customers, the key accounts, in each trade channel?
- Where are the key accounts located?
- How many outlets have each of the key accounts?
- What is the total turnover of each key account?
- What is the market segment or product category turnover of each key account?
- What share do you have of product category sales in each key account?
- What share does each key account have of its trade channel (or total market)?
- What are the sales servicing needs of each key account?
  e.g. consumer products
  – Head office calling
  – Branch selling calls (retail branches or business units)
  – Retail branch merchandising calls
  – Retail sales promoters
  e.g. industrial products
  – Networking amongst decision influencers
  – Product installation
  – Product training
  – Regular product servicing
- Does the sales force organization need to be modified in any way to reflect the trade channel structure or key accounts within any trade channel, and if so, what changes are needed to provide best service and maximize sales through key accounts?

Action points

Trade credit
Do current company trade terms take account of the following:
- Local custom and practice of the trade?
- Competitive terms of trade?
- Cost of credit from the company versus alternative sources?
- State of the local economy? E.g.
    - Need for stockists to extend credit or hold stock
    - Employment
    - Interest rates
- Strategic considerations? E.g.
    - Expanding distribution
    - Pipeline stock pressure
    - Expanding display
    - Building market share
    - Blocking competition

Discounts
- Are you using discounts as an effective tool in account management and in relation to:
    - The need for improved cash flow?
    - Building sales volumes?
    - Expanding the brands' distribution base?
    - Minimizing out-of-stocks?
    - Building market share?
    - Account stock holding policies?
- Are all discounts and performance allowances related to specific (contractual) performance conditions?
- Are there any instances where discounts and allowances are offered as:
    - An incentive to buy without volume or other performance requirements?
    - Custom and practice for a particular account?
- Are your trade terms used fairly and equitably to motivate growth in volume and distribution?
- Recognize the time value of money in all transactions that extend credit at any level of the distribution chain.

Types of motivational discount
Are you using any or all of the following effectively?
- Prompt settlement discounts
    - Designed to improve cash flow
- Performance discounts

	Action points

Checklist 18.2 continued
   – Decreasing price with increasing order volumes
   – Performance rebates at pre-agreed rates geared to annual
     performance
   – Sliding case scale quantity discounts
Minimum orders
● Does the gross margin contribution on a minimum order cover the direct costs of distribution and servicing the call?
● Are call frequencies calculated on the basis that accounts should be able to order at least an economical minimum order each call?
Credit control
● Are all new customers subjected to a credit check?
● Are trade references taken on new customers?
● Are agreed payment terms strictly enforced with all customers?
● Are there instances of credit being extended beyond customers' normal levels of stock cover (i.e. weeks' company product stock cover in relation to sales)?	

Checklist 18.3
Managing wholesalers and trade distributors

	Action points
Five rules for developing and managing wholesalers 1. Build a 'partnership' through active account management policy, building mutual trust. 2. Complement the wholesaler's activities; do not compete in a way that produces conflict. 3. Understand the wholesaler's business – then begin to develop a strategy for partnership and growth. 4. Motivate a wholesaler to push your products by doing something for him that adds value to his business. 5. Focus on what the wholesaler can do with his resources that supports what you do, and focus your resources on what he can do less well. **Using wholesalers to develop business** Would your business development benefit from wholesalers or distributors who: ● Carry stocks of your products to supply trade customers not covered directly by your sales team?	

	Action points

Checklist 18.3 continued
● Extend credit to their customers?
● Generate volume sales through the multiplicity of smaller customers in the various trade channels?
● Cooperate with you, as supplier, in
   – Maintaining and expanding market distribution
   – Generating a regular pattern of orders from the trade customers covered by the wholesalers?
   – Promoting the brands locally?
Do your products better suit exclusive distribution arrangements where your distributor might provide:
● Display and merchandising support for products?
● Cooperation in working towards agreed objectives,
● Competitive market intelligence reports?
● Sales performance and stock data reports?
● Specialist training for their staff?
● Participation in the annual sales and marketing planning process?
● A quality organization structure capable of working to achieving agreed objectives and implementing plans?
● A business using modern technology and systems to develop a high standard of customer service?
 	
Auditing wholesalers
If you need the support of wholesalers/distributors, audit those servicing the market, with a view to identifying:
● How many wholesalers are in the market?
● How many outlets does each cover?
● What are their particular strengths/weaknesses in supplying geographical areas or trade niche sectors?
● How many salespersons does each of the wholesalers have?
● How are their sales teams rewarded?
● How do competitors service and develop customers?
Understand the whole distributor's business:
● The wholesaler's goals and objectives for his business?
● Products each of the wholesalers favours pushing in the market, and why?
● Does he represent on an agency or exclusive distribution basis?
● The financial strengths and weaknesses of each wholesaler?
● The image and reputation of each wholesaler with customers and each other?
● Their terms of trade to their customers?
● The sales service they provide to their customers, etc.?
● The structures of the wholesalers' organizations?
● The pattern of calling followed for each trade channel or category of outlet?	

	Action points
Checklist 18.3 continued	

Checklist 18.3 continued
- How the wholesaler categorizes or prioritizes outlets?
- Special relationships any wholesaler has with any trade channel niche sector or any particular customers?
- What trade customers want from their wholesalers?

Developing wholesalers/distributors
Supplier and wholesaler should each focus on value adding activities.
Focus your team on selling activities that add most long-term value to trade development, e.g.:
- Developing outlet presence
- Selling in new brands
- Increasing share of mind in trade outlets
- Developing customized promotional activity for key outlets

The wholesalers can focus on those activities that have local importance building the market, such as:
- Acting as the order takers and order processors, satisfying volume needs of smaller customers
- Meeting local trade needs for credit
- Maintaining and expanding brand distribution
- Communicating product knowledge to non-direct outlets
- Supporting brands in non-direct outlets by implementing the suppliers' promotions.

Practical ways to add value to wholesaler relations:
- Develop an active transfer order system.
- Pass new outlet leads to wholesalers.
- Let the wholesaler supply some of the better volume accounts, so that he has some of the 'cream'.
- Provide training to wholesaler's sales teams.
- Improve management information systems and order processing systems within wholesaler organizations.
- Improve journey planning for wholesaler salespersons.
- Match the calling cycle of supplier's salespersons to the wholesaler delivery cycle, facilitating transfer orders.
- Support wholesalers with promotional packages that build outlet loyalty to them.
- Develop sales incentive schemes to encourage effort and loyalty amongst wholesaler sales teams.
- Develop preferential support packages for key cooperative wholesalers, additionally motivating them.

19

Sales promotion

Sales managers in smaller companies often have overall responsibility for marketing communications, but in larger enterprises they normally have a much more limited role in that area. Whatever the size of company, sales managers do become very involved in sales promotion activity, in part because the expenditure may be controlled through the sales force, and because its implementation and management are frequently sales force responsibilities. While marketing departments may design sales promotions, their effectiveness is considerably influenced by sales activity at the point of sale.

The need to advertise and promote will depend greatly on the type of product you produce and offer for sale, and the strength of your brand awareness. An industrial product may need a very different approach from a consumer product, and a consumer durable product will need a different programme from non-durable items. Whatever the product or service you are seeking to promote, there are ways and means of active sales promotion, and we will encourage the readers not to discount sales promotion as inapplicable to their products or services, but to think and act creatively. One chapter cannot cover this vast subject, and we will barely touch on marketing communications (the reader can refer to specialist texts on that subject), but it may serve to provide an outline of facets to consider.

The messages that this commentary on basic product promotion should leave you with are the following.

- To maximize the chances of organizing and running successful sales promotions, keep promotions simple and set fundamental objectives that are accepted by all parties (salespersons and customers) as both achievable and measurable.
- Plan each aspect of a promotion in detail with your salespersons and customers to give a measurable sales benefit for each pound spent. Discussions of 'intangible' benefits at a post-promotion review are often just an excuse for having designed a poor promotion or failing to seek tangible, quantifiable results.
- Measure the quantifiable benefits to your customers and your company from participating in promotions, and communicate results to everyone involved so that successful aspects can be incorporated in future promotions, and ineffective elements can be discarded.

Sales promotion

Both advertising and direct sales promotional activities play a role in developing product markets, and may be targeted to one or more of the strategic areas illustrated in Figure 19.1, depending on your assessment of the priorities at the time. In this section I will focus on non-media sales promotion activity.

Sales promotion activity is, in the main, a shorter-term tactical weapon in the sales manager's armoury.

Advertising is normally more costly than

other forms of sales promotional activity and takes far longer to plan and develop. In general, advertising is used to support the main strategic thrust of the marketing programme by creating consumer/user awareness in the target market sectors, developing a brand image, assisting in the creation of market segmentation, and creating, developing or reinforcing consumer perceptions – all of which are aimed to expand sales within the target group, increasing penetration and market share.

Definitions

At this point we should attempt to clarify our definitions of sales promotions and advertising.

- **Sales promotions** can be considered as all supplementary selling and marketing activity that is neither direct media advertising nor direct selling, but which coordinates personal selling and advertising into an effective persuasive force.
- **Below the line promotions** are normally considered as all non-media promotion, historically derived from promotional and advertising expenditures that were not subject to commission compared with above the line activity that was.
- **Advertising** can be seen as all mainstream marketing communications promoting or concerning a product, normally subject to booking commissions, placed with mass media or specialist media, including television, cinema, radio, press, general and technical or specialist journals, posters, etc.

Using promotions in the marketing communications mix

Sales promotional activity is a key, flexible and, if well planned and managed, cost-effective means of communicating product information, benefits and other marketing messages to both the distributive trade chan-

nels and users and consumers. The marketer should adopt an integrated approach, linking above and below the line promotional activities to complement and support each other in the communication mix, ensuring promotional activities geared to any one of the marketer's portfolio of product or brands are:

- not in conflict with the objectives or activity supporting another product or brand at the same time period
- supportive (in terms of objectives, focus and timing) of other mainstream marketing communications (e.g. media advertisements and campaigns) or brand publicity activity and objectives.

Advantages of sales promotions

The main advantages in using sales promotional activity, either alone or to support main stream marketing activity and communications, are:

- very flexible and adaptable in terms of tackling specific problems or supporting mainstream marketing communications at a national or local level
- capable of specific action through a specific focus and structure
- relatively short lead times to design and implement (compared with media communications)
- often more easy to monitor the effect or tangible results
- economical and cost saving, possibly with economies of scale
- can be adapted to large and small markets, major or minor products or brands.

The key to successful use of a sales promotion is to be very clear on its objective, and then design a promotion that is:

- narrow in its focus of objectives
- simple to comprehend and implement (by the salespersons responsible for implementation and participants)
- simple to measure and monitor.

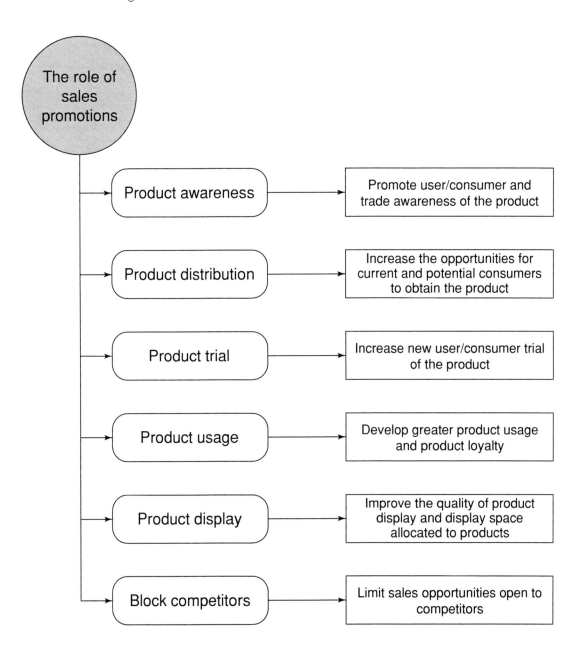

Figure 19.1 *The role of sales promotions*

Figure 19.2 illustrates the typical planned effect of a sales promotion. This assumes that the actual promotion is run for a limited time period, e.g. from time A to time B. If the promotion is successful, then:

- the promotion should increase sales above the level that would occur without a promotion
- sales may remain higher than normal for some period after a successful promotion particularly if new customers have been won to the brand.
- the cost of the promotion can be compared with the additional gross sales revenue during and from the post-promotion period, and with the additional gross profit contribution from incremental sales during and in the post-promotion period.

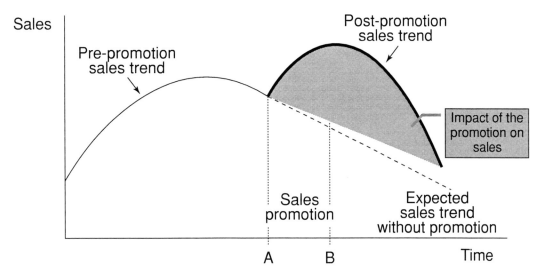

Figure 19.2 *The impact of a sales promotion*

A decision-making framework for evaluating promotion options

In order to ensure that the most suitable promotion is selected to address an issue, problem or objective, a decision-making framework is developed in Figure 19.3. The sales manager might find it useful to adopt this framework when evaluating the options for his or her products, whether industrial or consumer goods.

Types of sales promotions

The type of sales promotional activity the sales manager and his or her marketing colleagues might choose will depend on the type of product being sold, the objectives of the promotion, and who is to be influenced by the promotion (trade buyer, user, consumer). Consider which of the following types of promotion might offer potential for your products in the market sectors and trade channels, and adapt them as appropriate in the annual promotion planning activities. The main types of promotions include those listed on pp. 325–7.

The range of promotional activity illustrated in the foregoing list can be divided into those most suited to promoting sales through the various trade channels distributing the products, and those most suited to promoting sales to users or consumers. Some of the promotion formats are adaptable either to the push of sales through the trade or the pull of sales through consumer demand. Table 19.1 illustrates the typical suitability of the various promotion formats for **trade-push** or **consumer-pull** promotion objectives.

As a rule, an integrated sales promotion programme will run parallel to the main media communications programme, if one is in place, and support its objectives, but also works at a lower level on key tactical objectives, with a mixture of both '**push**' and '**pull**' promotional activities. Appendix 19-A illustrates a range of typical sales objectives tackled through sales promotional activity, and indicates some of the promotion formats that can be used to tackle each objective.

The example form shown in Table 19.2 can help in identifying, listing and evaluating promotion options. Notes can be made under the various criteria relevant to selection of a promotion.

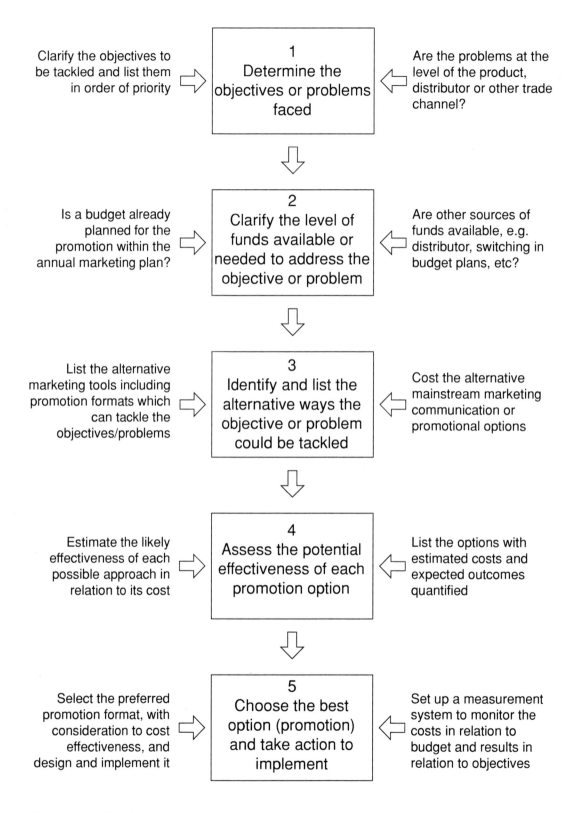

Clarify the objectives to be tackled and list them in order of priority

1
Determine the objectives or problems faced

Are the problems at the level of the product, distributor or other trade channel?

Is a budget already planned for the promotion within the annual marketing plan?

2
Clarify the level of funds available or needed to address the objective or problem

Are other sources of funds available, e.g. distributor, switching in budget plans, etc?

List the alternative marketing tools including promotion formats which can tackle the objectives/problems

3
Identify and list the alternative ways the objective or problem could be tackled

Cost the alternative mainstream marketing communication or promotional options

Estimate the likely effectiveness of each possible approach in relation to its cost

4
Assess the potential effectiveness of each promotion option

List the options with estimated costs and expected outcomes quantified

Select the preferred promotion format, with consideration to cost effectiveness, and design and implement it

5
Choose the best option (promotion) and take action to implement

Set up a measurement system to monitor the costs in relation to budget and results in relation to objectives

Figure 19.3 *The decision-making process for promotions*

Types of sales promotions

Company credit cards	mainly offer scope for retailers of goods and services, some franchised businesses and providers of services such as accommodation (hotel chains), where the company is seeking to build customer loyalty.
Consumer price promotions	(including multi-packs for some lower value retail goods) are aimed to boost trial, entice consumers away from competitors, develop brand loyalty or encourage consumer stocking up with extra product.
Consumer competitions	are normally designed to increase display, trial, usage, loyalty and brand awareness.
Consumer premium offers	usually offer low cost items in exchange for a number of product labels or other evidence of product use and a reduced price for the premium item, and are also aimed at increasing trial, display, usage and product brand awareness.
Couponing	is a promotional format used with either durable or non-durable products, to increase trial and repeat purchase, or to promote linked sales of other products in the supplier's product portfolio.
Dealer competitions	can help to expand distribution or, if aimed at retailers, to increase and improve display, and might possibly be managed by the supplier or a main distributor.
Direct mailshots	have proven benefits, albeit often with low response rates, where the target market of potential users or consumers can be readily identified by job, economic status or other measurable criteria (such as doctors, architects, credit card holders, etc.).
Display bonuses	are usually used where goods are offered for sale through retail distribution channels, and provide a reward to a trade outlet for an agreed display layout or space allocation.
Distributor sales force incentives	are excellent means of directing sales effort to areas needing corrective action or special effort (including new products).
Editorials/advertorials in specialist magazines and journals	are useful to promote specialist products direct to the target user or consumer, and are usually aimed at particular market sectors.
Exhibitions	particularly offer scope to promote industrial or consumer durable products, such as plant and equipment, household durables, ingredients and components, new technology, services, etc.
Free product trial periods	have scope for industrial products and some consumer durable products, the assumption being that trial at the place of use will result in a confirmed sale.
Gifts for buyers	are useful tools to promote product trial, and while gifts for trade buyers are perhaps frowned upon in many of the developed nations, they are a useful promotional activity in many consumer market sectors to gain product trial or approval listing, and also offer scope for products sold through retail channels (e.g. free travel bag with purchase of multiple toiletry items).

Introduction incentives	are much used where specialist services are being marketed (e.g. financial services, home improvements, products or activities requiring an annual membership or subscription).
Lectures, film shows, etc.	are particularly useful where an element of training or education is needed in promoting the product to the potential end users.
On-pack give-aways	are commonly used to promote consumer products, where the free item might either relate to the main product (e.g. a free razor with a pack of blades, or hair conditioner with shampoo) or be a new product aimed at the same target market.
Performance rebates or allowances	encourage buyers to support one manufacturer rather than competitors.
Personality promotions and sponsorships	offer considerable scope with many products to obtain and use the endorsement of famous personalities publicly associated with the products or services (it being essential that personalities involved in sponsoring products are unlikely to do anything to bring the brand name into disrepute).
Point of sale materials	draw attention to products in sales outlets, possibly highlighting the location or product features and benefits.
Promotional aspects of packaging	can enhance presentation through design, presentation of information or illustrations of use and applications, convenience for display, and creating a unique brand identity and impact at the point of sale.
Product merchandising	is often undertaken for products distributed through retail channels by field salespersons or specially trained merchandisers, and can be very effective in creating product awareness at the point of sale, particularly ensuring product is correctly priced, neatly displayed, and highlighted to potential consumers through the use of appropriate point of sale material.
Product sampling programmes	are normally used (mainly with non-durable goods) to increase product trial and entice consumers away from competitive products.
Product training programmes	are normally aimed at increasing the knowledge and expertise of product distributors, enabling them to sell with increased confidence and to offer their customers better support.
Product use demonstrations	create awareness of product features and benefits and encourage product trial by potential users, often highlighting to them the ease of use of the product.
Prompt order bonuses or discounts	encourage the early placement of orders after submission of quotations or demonstrations.
Public relations activities	can be a powerful tool in creating awareness, product trial, and developing a favourable brand image, and have grown in use and importance as a supporting activity in the sales and marketing programme of many companies.

Sales promotional literature	offers a way to gain attention from trade buyers while creating desire and confidence in the supplier as a product source by presenting product features, benefits and applications to buyers.
'Tie-ins' with local special activities	can offer a powerful promotional vehicle in some markets, e.g. carnivals, sports functions and charity activities.
Trade price discounts	to distributors or users encourage stock purchase and increase in stock held in inventories.
Trade channel (dealer) margins	can be adjusted for a specific period or sale to motivate trade buyers to support a product through increased sales activity.
Trade stock bonuses	(sometimes referred to in marketing jargon as 'dealer loaders') can be used to widen distribution or boost stock levels in the distribution chain, e.g. one case free with a 10-case order.
Trading stamps	or similar incentives are aimed at repeat purchase and building loyalty to a product or trade channel issuing the stamps.

Table 19.1 *Suitability of promotional activity to trade or consumer selling*

Type of promotion	Trial e.g. new products	Loyalty e.g. established products
Trade – push		
Dealer competitions	✔	✔
Dealer margins	✔	
Direct mailshots	✔	
Display bonuses	✔	✔
Distributor sales force cash incentives/competitions	✔	✔
Exhibitions/trade shows	✔	
Gifts for trade buyers	✔	
Lectures, slide or film shows, videos, etc.	✔	✔
Performance rebates or allowances	✔	✔
Product demonstrations	✔	
Product training programmes	✔	
Prompt order bonuses	✔	
Public relations activity	✔	✔
Trade credit extensions	✔	✔
Trade magazines or journals	✔	✔
Trade price discounts	✔	✔
Trade sales literature	✔	
Trade stock bonuses (dealer premiums)	✔	✔

Table 19.1 Suitability of promotional activity to trade or consumer selling (continued)

Type of promotion	Trial e.g. new products	Loyalty e.g. established products
Consumer – pull		
Consumer competitions	✓	✓
Consumer exhibitions	✓	
Consumer magazines or journal features/advertorials	✓	✓
Consumer premium offers (self-liquidating promotions)	✓	✓
Couponing	✓	
Customer price specials (e.g. 2 for 1)	✓	✓
Direct mail shots	✓	
Free product trial periods	✓	
Gifts for buyers	✓	
Introductory incentives (e.g. for introducing new customers)	✓	
Lectures, slide or film shows, videos	✓	
Multiple packs (banded packs – same or different products)	✓	✓
On-pack give-aways	✓	✓
Outlet in-store merchandising	✓	✓
Personality promotions/sponsorships	✓	✓
Point of sale material	✓	✓
Price reductions – store price cuts	✓	✓
Product sampling	✓	
Product use demonstrations	✓	
Prompt order bonuses	✓	
Public relations activities	✓	✓
Packaging – e.g. for special promotions	✓	
Product information leaflets at point of sale, etc.	✓	
Recyclable container (re-usable bottles or product containers)		✓
Tie-ins with special events	✓	
Trading stamp and similar incentives	✓	✓
Warranties of satisfaction	✓	

The advertising and promotion plan

The preparation of an annual advertising and promotion programme is an essential process in planned market development. As with most marketing programmes, subsequent developments often cause changes from the outline; such change need not signify a bad plan, just the need to adapt flexibly to any short-term or unforeseen circumstances.

The final version of the **annual promotion programme** should include relevant comment on such topics as:

- the timing of promotions for each product, taking account of seasonal factors such as gift-giving periods and vacations
- the objectives of each promotion or promotional activity, and the ability to control and measure performance against objectives
- special promotional media support or general media support (bear in mind that, if there is a clear seasonal sales trend, a

Table 19.2 *Basic form for evaluating alternative promotion options*

Promotion options evaluation form						
General promotion focus/objective						
Timing:						
Budget:		**Budget source:**				
Alternatives	Specific sales	Budget cost	Lead time	Ease to implement	Ease to control	Measurability of results
Trade sales (push)						
1.						
2.						
3.						
4.						
5.						
6.						
Consumer sales (pull)						
1.						
2.						
3.						
4.						
5.						
6.						

pound spent in the peak sales period generally creates a greater impact on sales than a pound spent in the low period)

- promotional aids (such as sales literature and point of sales materials) and other materials needed to support the promotional activity, including preparation lead times
- special packaging requirements and production lead times
- manufacturing, shipping and other distribution lead times for special promotional goods.

Promotion planning

Each separate promotion programme should have a fully detailed written plan, in addition to the outline annual plan referred to above, incorporating such information as:

- budgeted expenditure in total and by item of expense

- objectives of the promotion
- lead times for preparation of each aspect of copy and artwork connected with design of packaging, display material and media advertisements
- production quantities of each item of advertising and display material, packaging and product
- all rules applicable to any competition, e.g. competitions direct to consumers, retailers and distributor salespersons
- comment on the legality of a promotion in the market and any regulatory approvals needed to run the promotion (e.g. various forms of promotion are restricted in some markets, such as lotteries that may require an approval)
- criteria to measure promotion success and a programme to evaluate success.

The planning stage must ensure adequate lead times for all preparation and production of each special aspect of the promotion, including artwork, schedule advertising, packaging and production of merchandise, even though there may be an element of flexibility in the final promotion dates. If you are working with an advertising agency they should be kept fully apprised of all aspects of planning, and be clearly briefed on their respective responsibilities, although the marketer's job will include monitoring the performance of the sales team and any participating distributors for respective contributions within the plan time span.

Figure 19.4 illustrates some key stages in promotional planning that you might find convenient to elaborate on and adapt to your own planning process.

Preparation of your annual marketing plan in a simple schematic may assist control of the various stages in implementing the marketing programme. In the plan in Table 19.3 promotions for a toiletry range sold into the United Kingdom market give the base for the matrix. There are two main promotions within the budget for the year. First, there is a summer 'travel kit' promotion, which could be a four-item assortment with a free toiletries bag for the consumer. This is supported by magazine advertising in 'lifestyle' image journals. To get the product in displayed distribution, the display period is preceded by a 'dealer loader' promotion (say, one box free with twelve) to fill the pipeline with stock, and a salesperson's bonus competition. Secondly, there is a Christmas promotion as the main event of the year, based on the marketing experience of the marketer that toiletries are popular gift items. This is supported by television advertising, magazine advertising, feature displays, dealer 'loaders', salespeople's incentives, and competitions for best displays. The summer promotion would concentrate on summer skin-care items, such as suntan oils and lotions, and after-sun treatments. The winter programme would concentrate on colognes, perfumes, after-shaves and similar items, and complementary 'luxury' products.

The basic planning principle applies as much to industrial products as to consumer products, but several markets might be linked together for the purpose of promotion planning where they share common activity, such as regional exhibitions. Table 19.4 illustrates an outline promotion programme for navigation equipment, where the size of the markets does not warrant great detail at the level of each market, and the main forms of promotion are through exhibitions and event sponsorships. In this example most activity is concentrated in the spring and summer and particular attention is given by the company, in view of the technical nature of the products, to distributor and agent motivation and training through conferences and factory visits (linked for economy with major exhibitions).

These examples, of course, are not all-encompassing. Every product has promotional techniques to which it best responds, and every company has product attributes and benefits that its own experts and marketing team best know how to exploit. Liaison between the sales manager and the marketing team will promote a cross-flow of ideas and experience to the benefit of the marketing programme.

Setting promotion objectives

As with all marketing activity, any forms of promotional activity should be carefully thought through and have clearly defined and measurable objectives. These must be communicated to, and agreed with, all the parties involved in planning, implementing and managing the promotion, with particular attention to the sales team and distributors.

Most marketing activity is geared to objectives within the general categories of:

- creating or developing brand awareness and building consumer loyalty
- increasing market penetration and share (including by stealing sales from competitors)
- increasing product distribution
- increasing product trial by potential users, or usage by current users

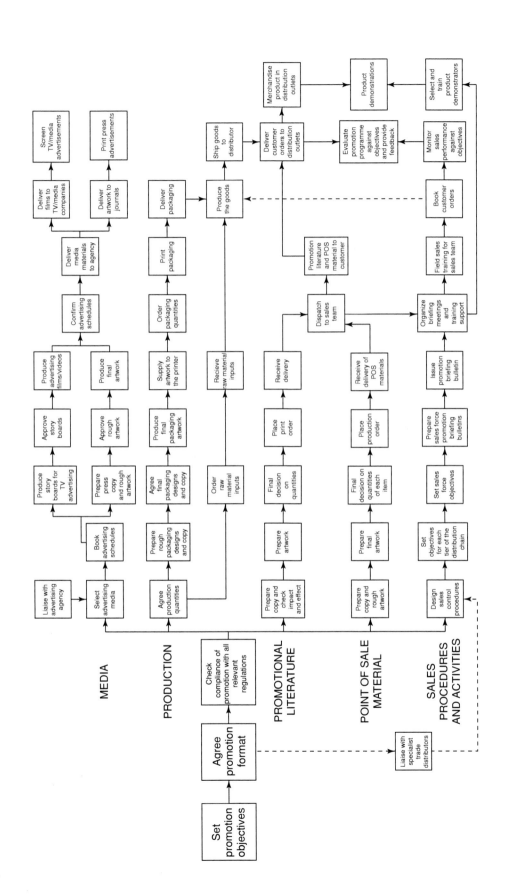

Figure 19.4 Key stages in promotion planning

Table 19.3 Outline of a consumer product sales promotion programme

Sales promotion Programme	Product range: Men's toiletries (winter & summer ranges)											
	Market: United Kingdom								Year: 199			
Promotional activity	Jan.	Feb.	Mar.	Apr.	May	June	July	Aug.	Sept.	Oct.	Nov.	Dec.
Television advertising												
Press advertising												
Key account presentations												
Wholesale/retail trade stock bonuses												
Sales force incentives												
Trade buyers' exhibitions												
Consumer price promotions[1]												
Consumer premium offers[2]												
Special event 'tie-ins'[3]												
In-store product demonstrations												
Point of sale materials												

Winter range activities

Summer range activities

1. Assumes price discounting to clear older stocks before new season sell-in
2. E.g., beach towel with product labels for summer range, or travel bag with winter range
3. These might relate to sporting events, or cultural promotions ('World Games', 'Riviera Week', 'Father's Day')

- generating additional display activity (for consumer goods)
- limiting sales opportunities open to competitors by filling the distribution channels with stock and encouraging users or consumers to 'stock up' in anticipation of future needs.

Within these overlapping categories the sales manager should be able to set specific objectives such as:

- number of additional units targeted to be sold by customer and trade channel, or number of new users expected to result from the promotion
- number of new stockists to be added to

the distribution network
- increase in market share
- measurable increase in brand awareness (in response to market research activity)
- measurable improvement in product displays (for consumer products) within retail stockists, and so on.

Table 19.5 illustrates a draft of an elementary promotion outline with quantified objectives, and this can be refined and expanded as experience permits and circumstances require.

The objectives and the methods to motivate results are obviously interrelated, and from this outline plan the full promotion can be planned in detail to ensure timely produc-

Table 19.4 *Outline of a specialist product sales promotion programme*

Sales Promotion Programme	Product range: ABC Navigation Equipment 'AutoNav' Market: Europe									Year: 199-		
Promotional activity	**Jan.**	**Feb.**	**Mar.**	**Apr.**	**May**	**June**	**July**	**Aug.**	**Sept.**	**Oct.**	**Nov.**	**Dec.**
Specialist trade press and boating magazine advertising		Product related	Product related	Product related		Product related	Product related					
Public relations advertorials and estimates		Product related	Product related	Product related		Event related	Event related					
Trade exhibitions		Geneva	Rome	London								
Direct mailshots to boat builders												
Direct mailshots to mailing list of boat owners												
Distributor/agent conference		Geneva		Factory tour								
Event sponsorships						Cannes ABC Regatta	Round Britain race					
User product exchange plan: part exchange a competitor product for an 'AutoNav' (private boat owners only)					Between 10% and 25% credit on part exchanges							

tion of all display material and sales aids, and the booking of media spots. Remember:

- if the promotion has worthwhile objectives, it is worth thorough planning
- if it is worth the budgeted expenditure, it is worth the management time and effort training the direct sales team and any cooperating distributor sales personnel to ensure effective implementation
- if achievement of the objectives is important to sales development, the results are worth monitoring and quantifying.

Check the implementation of each sales promotion and provide training as necessary. For consumer goods the sales manager should visit the market during the promotion period to conduct extensive random checks on display and distribution and to assess the effective use of point of sale and quality of feature displays.

Appendix 19-A, at the end of this chapter, illustrates a range of typical promotion objectives alongside some of the typical promotion formats that are used by marketers to address the objectives. It can be a useful exercise to prepare a similar type of list specific to your company and products, where you can draw on experience to relate promotion formats to your typical objectives.

Table 19.5 *Draft promotion objectives*

Promotion objectives for a men's personal care range

Distribution objective: increase in distribution from 20% to 30% of all outlets stocking the product category
Method:
- salespersons' new account incentive bonus
- new retailer bonus of 2 free packs for each case of 12 packs ordered (applicable to all size and range variants).

Display objective: 50% of stockists with feature display (say, 15% of all outlets)
Method:
- point of sale display material and product feature boxes
- media support on television and in press
- dealer display bonus or competition
- salespersons' display competition.

Consumer trial: 20% increase in consumer trial
Method:
- consumer premium offer (label redemption programme)
- advertising support on television and in press
- point of sale material and leaflets
- feature displays in retail outlets
- in-store demonstrations and sampling in 50 main outlets.

Promotion objectives for ABC Navigation Equipment 'AutoNav'

Distribution objective: Appoint agents/distributors, with after-sales support facilities, in 4 additional European Union markets, to complete coverage of EU.
Method:
- participation in key European boat exhibitions, actively seeking new agents/distributors
- providing specialist training in products, sales and service to new agents/distributors
- market visits by marketing executives to identify and establish credentials of potential agents/distributors
- advertising and editorial coverage in selected trade journals, focusing on the hi-tech nature of products, encouraging potential distributors to contact the company.

Consumer use objective: Increase European market penetration and share from circa 5% to circa 8%
Method:
- participation and sales promotion at 3 key European boat exhibitions
- sponsorship of two key events, one power boat, one yachting, promoting the product name to the boating fraternity
- product advertising in specialist boating magazines, supported by editorial and advertorial coverage of both the products and the sponsored events
- expansion of distribution network to all European Union markets, with local service centres in main ports in each market, increasing sales opportunities through expanded sales/service network
- direct mailshots to all boat builders and all boat owners listed with national associations and highlighting product features and benefits, distribution and service network and support, and special part exchange arrangements for competitor products.

A promotional brief format

It is customary in the more sophisticated marketing organizations, particularly those marketing fast moving consumer goods, for a **promotional brief** to be prepared, normally the responsibility of a product manager, but some sales managers may be involved in this process. It should communicate specific objectives and criteria for judgement concerned with the development of consumer and trade promotions as a tactical tool. A typical promotion brief framework is illustrated in Figure 19.5.

Evaluating and monitoring promotions

Clearly, as the sales manager in charge of a market you want to be able to see a rise in sales during marketing activity (whether advertising or promotional in nature), and a sustained level of increased sales in the post-promotion period. Where marketing budgets are limited, value for money is essential, and measurement of results from activities will aid future planning of supporting marketing programmes.

Your sales performance figures and graphs may give an indication of improved performance. It is worth pencilling on such charts when and what activity prompted a boost in sales, as a year or two later none of the marketers involved may remember what happened or why, and past lessons are lost.

Other indicators of promotional success may come from: the number of people returning enquiry cards in response to advertisements in trade journals; the numbers of visitors at an exhibition stand requesting a sample or demonstration; the percentage increase in sales during a promotional period compared with some base period; post-promotion performance exceeding the forecast trend line, etc.

Evaluate the outcome of the promotion against the specific quantified objectives agreed and that can be measured from available data, e.g.:

● sales volume through specific (key)

accounts over a set time span compared with a pre-promotion comparable time span (monitor both the trade purchases and stock levels to ensure pipe-line stocks are not accumulating without an increase in throughput)
● increase in product user base
● increase in display facings in monitored outlets (retail goods)
● increase in product distribution over the promotion period, i.e. trade stockists
● increase in product throughput of sub-distributors during the promotion period
● new trade channel accounts being opened (i.e. in response to sales incentives)
● response to consumer audits indicating increased product trial.

It is important to plan all aspects of a sales promotion and to monitor actual costs and incremental sales against budgets. Table 19.6 illustrates a simple control form that will help establish and control promotion budgets and the results of promotions, and promotion achievements can be compared with promotion objectives in both qualitative and quantitative terms.

Your professionalism in developing and presenting promotional plans, and your ability successfully to implement and manage a programme for positive results, will infectiously motivate your sales team and distributors to enthusiastic cooperation in the future.

Key account promotional activity

At the key account level in any market sector very specific (and more easily measurable) promotional objectives can be set and agreed with the account. Key account activity is likely to have spin-off effects on some minor accounts aware of competition and promotion, but if promotions are only offered to key accounts there is the risk of minor account alienation.

A **key account objective planning form** can be used as a control document, and one format is illustrated in Table 19.7. This example might be more relevant to products resold

Figure 19.5 *A framework for developing a promotional brief*

through other distribution channels, such as retail outlets or trade distributors, but a modified version can be designed by the sales manager to suit his or her own products and markets.

This example highlights the current status against key result factors such as product listings, distribution, display, sales volume, and then notes the planned promotional activity focus (e.g. display or price-oriented promotion) and the expected incremental sales the promotion should produce.

An alternative way of planning and monitoring key accounts promotional activity in terms of the sales and cost is illustrated in the form shown as Table 16.9 in Chapter 16 which dealt with typical sales force administrative controls.

Guidelines for developing promotional materials

The trade buyer, consumer or user is normally only exposed to the promotional visual

Table 19.6 Sample form to help promotion budget planning and control

Local promotion design and control form					
Promotion format					
Objectives Qualitative Quantitative			**Achievements** Qualitative Quantitative		
Implementation dates:			Budgets:		
	Lead time	Deadline	Budget	Actual cost	Notes
Check legal compliance					
Literature and POS materials • Design/artwork/copy • Set production quantities • Source/order • Distribute to sales force • Distribute to trade channels					
Media • Agree budget splits • Select appropriate media • Design artwork/copy • Creative execution • Production of materials • Schedule media placements					
Sales implementation • Set sales/other objectives • Design control procedures • Prepare sales instructions • Conduct sales force briefings • Conduct field sales training • Book promotional orders • Monitor performance					

Table 19.7 Key account objective planning form

Account objective planning form	Listing		Distribution		Display		Volume		Promotional activity		Promotional increment (volume/value)	Action by
Account	Current	New	Base	Objective	Base	Objective	Base	Objective	Display	Price		

communication for a very short time, and must absorb the communication content and message and normally move to an action phase within that time. The basic selling principles of getting **attention,** creating **interest,** generating **desire** and provoking **action** should be applied to designing sales literature and point of sale material.

If sales literature is to be used in several trade channels, market sectors or markets, it is wise to keep sales literature straightforward, clear, concise, informative, meaningful and motivational. Good practice guidelines for the design and message communication of promotional visual aids include the following points.

● Keep the message simple: avoid jargon or communicating message content outside the experience of the audience.
● Ensure the choice of print shades and colours makes the message legible and impactful.
● Focus design on impact and suitability of material/visual aid for designated location: ensure it is hangable, fixable or self-supportable if point of sale (POS) material, and of suitable size to make an impact without obstructing venue activity.
● Promote the brand and the brand

proposition at least equally with any supporting promotional activity (e.g. premium product) – avoid making the brand a secondary factor to the promotion except in the case of event sponsorships.
● Focus on the brand benefits and additional promotional benefits that give a reason to buy or try now.
● Relate the promotion to product use venues and use occasions in a way that promotes trial or builds brand loyalty: if premium items are being used (given free or offered at reduced prices) they should be synergistic with the product, e.g. if promoting scotch whisky perhaps use glasses, place mats with Scottish scenes, etc., or if promoting fire extinguishers possible premiums might include fire warning notices, smoke alarms, fire blankets, etc.
● Design your sales literature so that it:
  – presents the product features or attributes clearly;
  – details the benefits to the users/consumers;
  – gives confidence in the supplier as a source of quality merchandise and efficient after-sales service (highlight any sales and service support network);
  – identifies product uses and functions (often pictorially);

- instructs how a product can be used (safely);
- outlines product specifications relevant to the purchase decision;
- illustrates the product, preferably in photographic rather than diagrammatic form;
- presents information in such a fashion as to answer most user/consumer queries;
- generates desire to the point where the potential buyer seeks a sample, demonstration or product trial, or purchases the product at once.

Financing advertising and promotions

Advertising reserves

There are two main ways to generate the funds needed for advertising and promotional (typically abbreviated to A & P) support:

1. making an advertising reserves provision within product costings and including this within the supplier's price, or
2. making a levy on distributors.

As it is not normally practical to make a levy on distributors, unless they have a tied contract such as franchisees, or are exclusive distributors in a foreign market, the normal practice is to build a reserve into costings, depending on the level of advertising and promotion support planned.

The level of the advertising reserve need not be the same for all products, although many companies do just include a standard percentage in the price. There are options, including the following.

- The advertising reserve could be accrued by a variable margin relating to the profitability of products, in which case there could be a cross subsidy from more to less profitable products (such as from established to recently launched products).
- Each product might be costed to provide

the advertising reserves needed for its support and development. This could be problematic in that if higher levels of promotional support were needed for a product, that product might not support a high enough price to generate sufficient promotional funds at certain stages of its life cycle (i.e. in the post-launch investment stages).

Some of the products in your portfolio may develop well with minimal advertising and promotional support, others may need considerable support in the early stages. Highly branded consumer products tend to require greater advertising and promotional support, anything from around three per cent of turnover for mass market products, to 30 per cent of sales revenue for luxury speciality high-margin products (e.g. perfumes historically have large advertising and promotion budgets as a percentage of turnover). Most suppliers of industrial products reserve very limited funds, often under five per cent, for advertising and promotion support. But service providers typically have significant advertising and promotion activity in their competitive markets.

A fundamental concept in marketing is to push your strengths. That may be liberally interpreted as placing emphasis on the market sectors and products with the most potential, where potential may be measured in such terms as:

- consumer incomes and spending power (or user budgets, for industrial and business-to-business products)
- population size and growth
- assessments of market sophistication in matters of distribution or consumption
- cultural acceptance of your products (the market possibly already being developed through competitors' activities)
- freedom from regulatory controls.

Where there are clear risks to your market development programme, such as unstable political environments, arbitrary changes in regulations, or where you can clearly see that developing a consumer franchise is a major long-term project, then, although you perhaps should not abandon the market, you might be wise to allocate very limited promotional funds in the initial stages.

As the timing of promotional expenditures may not be directly related to when the funds are earned from product sales, a system should be agreed with the company accountants whereby accruals for advertising and promotions are noted separately in the accounts as a reserve and not allocated back to profit if not dispersed in the same period as the accrual is earned.

Spend in the marketing mix

In deciding how to spend an advertising and promotion budget consideration must be given to:

- target market and segmentation factors
- product positioning in the portfolio
- weighting of budget supporting the brand
- level of spend.

The marketer with a varied product portfolio needs to:

- clarify the specific target segments (e.g. size and geographical spread)
- identify the range of media and types of promotions likely to reach and appeal to the specific target groups
- cost each alternative likely to achieve the desired level of exposure
- take decisions on the levels of budget allocated to each product variant to enable sales and marketing objectives to be achieved.

Within any product portfolio the available budget for advertising and promotional activity can be weighted in several ways, including:

- by product profit management priority (an attacking marketing strategy might aim to build products with growth potential to build profitable sales while holding a

competitive edge, such as technology, distribution, acceptance, etc.)
- by current sales volumes or assessed sales potential (i.e. sales targets)
- by prioritizing products under particular competitive threat (defensive strategies)
- by weighting budgets taking account of shorter-term strategic or tactical problems (i.e. putting additional budgets behind a product with distribution weaknesses).

The budget level will be a limiting factor in selecting media or promotional formats. Both consumer and industrial products require appropriate promotional support. Specific objectives, as well as budget levels, will have a bearing on the allocation of budgets between alternative forms of advertising and promotion support (see Figure 19.6).

- If your products have a narrow market appeal or target market, but high A & P budgets, then a commonly favoured approach is targeted sponsorships (i.e. events favoured by the target market, such as sports or cultural events – but be wary of the chairman who wants the sponsorship funds to go to his favourite hobby area, if that will not reach your target market) and brands publicity activity.
- If you have limited A & P funds and a narrow target market, lower cost promotional activities can include personal promotion through selling and direct mailshots, advertising in specialist journals reaching the target group, point of sale material, special event promotion or sponsorship, etc.
- If you have mass market products with broad user/consumer appeal and generate large budgets, mass media may be the route for you – media advertising, television, radio, mass circulation newspapers and magazines, and even product placement in major television programmes as a brands publicity exercise.
- And, finally, if your products have a broad appeal, but budgets generated are initially

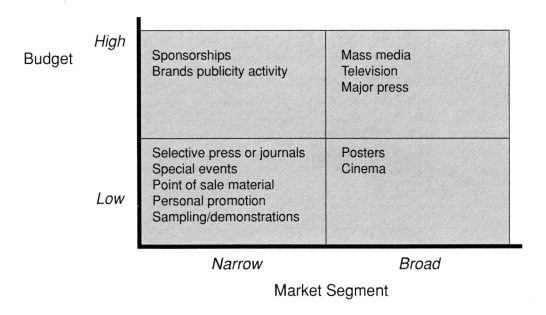

Figure 19.6 *Activity choices in relation to budgets and market segments*

low, then posters in many markets can be very effective, as can limited media communications such as cinema advertising (if your target group includes the profiles of typical cinema goers).

The manager responsible for spending advertising and promotional budgets is going to be concerned with value for money. Some guidelines for selecting media are shown in the following table.

Eight key factors to consider in selecting advertising media

1. **Portfolio aspects of segmentation, e.g.**
   - Price positioning within the company product portfolio and in relation to competition
   - Consumer characteristics of the product/brand
   - Stage in the product life cycle (launch/seed/invest/maintain/harvest).
2. **Budget levels in relation to media threshold levels and costs of medium as a viable choice to reach a target audience, e.g.**
   high budget:
   - TV/press offer wide media possibilities to reach a broad consumer segment
   - Support can come from sponsorships, trade promotions, merchandising and display activity (according to what best suits the products and marketing objectives)
   low budget:
   - Cinema/magazines offer narrow media possibilities to reach more limited (or focused) consumer product segments
   - Support can come from brands publicity activities, trade promotions, direct marketing, sampling/demonstrations.

cost effectiveness: cost per 1000 people or target prospect market reached (this is a simple measure that assumes all the audience for a media are prospects, and does not produce a measure of effectiveness, i.e. cost per sale)

3. **Media availability, e.g.**
   - Range of media available (often limited in less developed markets)
   - Regulatory or legislative restrictions on media use by products
4. **Medium characteristics, e.g.**
   - Geographical coverage
   - Audience mix or special group coverage
   - Frequency of audience coverage
   - Physical limitations such as size, colour, visual limitations for printed media.
5. **Compatibility with brand image, e.g.**
   - Medium quality image
   - Profile of the media audience compared with that of the products (such as orientation towards fun/youth – traditional/conservative)
   - Media popularity within the target group
6. **Medium coverage of target group, e.g.**
   - What proportion of the target group actually see/receive the message placed with each of the alternative media.
7. **Creative suitability of the medium:**
   - Can the chosen medium meet the creative requirements in terms of communicating brand image, perceptions, usage moods, brand message/proposition, etc.?
8. **Media reach versus frequency factors:**
   - The marketer must consider whether to focus on a wide audience (reach) or a narrow audience (frequency) – if all prospects are equally likely to buy reach may be the main criteria, but where only a limited group of consumers seeing the advertisement are likely to respond then frequency may be more important.

Exhibitions

Exhibition planning and management are time-consuming activities, and the marketer will face far more frustrations and problems if the exhibition is actually based in a foreign market. Therefore you will need to concern yourself with:

- selecting only those exhibitions that are anticipated to meet exhibition objectives as part of the overall sales and marketing strategy
- setting exhibition objectives
- planning the details of attendance at the exhibition (of both support personnel and equipment, including samples, literature, etc.)
- organizing post-exhibition follow up with contacts made.

Exhibition objectives

As a starting point it is essential to define your exhibition objectives clearly so that you then participate in only those exhibitions likely to reach the right audience. Some typical objectives might be:

- to expand sales by finding customer for the products or services (for either consumer or industrial products)
- to identify potential agents or distributors (for either home market or foreign markets)
- to solicit immediate sales orders (home market, or export)
- to maintain contact with existing customers/agents/distributors in a forum that enables many contacts to be seen in a short space of time

- to test acceptability of, and obtain feedback on, products or services
- to introduce new products or technology to national or international forums (whether new contacts or existing agents/distributors/customers, who can be briefed on applications and operations of new products through demonstrations and presentations)
- to work with another exhibitor on a cross-endorsement basis, i.e. where the other exhibitor uses the supplier's product as a component, such as a vehicle manufacturer who specifies the supplier's automotive parts as original equipment in its vehicles.

As a supplementary exhibition activity, exhibitors have the opportunity to update themselves on competitive activity and products, learning of their prices, promotions, new developments and marketing activities.

Which exhibition?

The numbers and frequencies of exhibitions seem to be proliferating. The sales manager may have the options of trade-only exhibitions, aimed at domestic and international buyers for the particular product group, or consumer exhibitions (often promoting products with an international 'lifestyle' theme). As the sales and marketing budget is probably quite limited, and human resources even more limited, selection of the exhibitions to include in the marketing programme might take account of such factors as:

- cost of participation (either total or per attendee)
- location (proximity to the exhibitor's centre of operations)
- facilities for the handling of product samples and literature (particularly important if participating in foreign exhibitions, with samples and literature shipped internationally)
- relationship between the company's products and target market and the known parameters of the exhibition's visitor

profiles (job functions, industries, interests, nationalities, etc.)
- international reputation of the exhibition
- quality and quantity of other exhibitors (named exhibitors who will be a draw to visitors)
- competence of exhibition promoters and managers
- timing of exhibitions in relation to company sales cycles or new product launches
- suitability of the exhibition facilities for the display and demonstration of the company's products.

Exhibition planning

Successful exhibitions do not just happen; they are the result of long and careful planning. The sales manager will probably be working with marketing colleagues in planning and participating at exhibitions. With that in mind a few guidelines might be helpful.

- It is preferable to delegate overall exhibition project responsibility to one person, who should be given full access to budgets and the necessary resources of people, time and money, and report to the head of the division (sales director or other top manager) on project matters.
- Book your participation as early as possible to ensure choice of site within the exhibition complex (cancellations may incur penalties).
- Prepare a list of all necessary stand equipment (samples, literature, sales aids) and establish what the exhibition promoter will provide and what you must provide (e.g. if any special equipment is needed such as chilled storage, rotating stands). You will want to know locations of facilities such as electricity and water if needed for demonstrations.
- A critical path plan may help you ensure all deadlines are met, particularly if the exhibition materials must be shipped and cleared through customs. The longest lead time to produce any particular item

needed at the exhibition governs the entire timing schedule for the project.

- Plan the manning of the exhibition stand, using personnel familiar with both products and marketing. Where products are of a low technological nature, and perhaps demonstrations of applications are quite basic (as with some food products and household electrical items), local demonstrators may be available. Interpreters may need to be hired in some instances where you are dealing with foreign contacts.
- You should have enough personnel available to rotate staff every few hours while providing a high standard of company expertise into contact discussions.
- Promote your participation: notify your existing customers, agents, and distributors (domestic and foreign) of your participation in any exhibition through personal letters or advertisements in national and international trade journals.
- Ensure you have adequate supplies of promotional literature and product samples to meet anticipated needs. There is no need to give expensive sales literature to casual browsers, but at the same time many exhibitors run out of promotional aids part way through exhibitions. If interest is aroused with a prospect and you cannot provide all the information, an opening is made for a competitor!
- Have a system for recording who visits the stand and the nature of their enquiry (pre-printed enquiry cards are a help).

Exhibition follow-up

The major post-exhibition problem encountered by most exhibitors is follow-up on leads and contacts generated. Some of the enquiries may have been of a very general nature, needing conversion to a specific product or service. Others will require technical data from other departments. Some may need follow-up visits and meetings; others just need postal (or facsimile or telex) communication. After the exhibition the sales manager or marketer in charge should:

- quantify results in terms of leads generated and orders taken in relation to exhibition participation costs (including the cost of management time)
- analyse enquiries into priority groups according to exhibition objectives, and set a timetable for follow-up visits, demonstrations, sample dispatch, etc. (it is useful to develop a simple follow-up control form to ensure action is happening)
- commit suitably qualified (technical) personnel to pursue leads.

The amount of post-exhibition follow-up will depend on the objectives and nature of the products, and the resources (particularly sales personnel) available to you.

Appendix 19A: *Typical focuses of sales promotions – examples*

Promotion focus/objective	Promotion format
Trade channel pipeline stocks too low	<ul><li>Performance rebates – higher margins with higher sales</li><li>Trade stock bonuses, e.g. 1 free with 10</li><li>Dealer margin increases</li><li>Distributor sales force incentives</li></ul>
Trade channel pipeline stocks too high	<ul><li>Dealer sales competitions</li><li>Product training programmes</li><li>Feature display bonuses</li><li>Price cut specials</li><li>Point of sale material – product information, promotion information</li><li>Local advertising or product/ promotion</li><li>Personality promotions – endorsements, brand ambassadors, etc.</li><li>Couponing</li><li>Tasting/sampling promotions</li><li>Consumer specials: banded packs, etc.</li></ul>
Trade credit/ debt reduction	<ul><li>Early settlement incentives, greater than alternative financial sources</li><li>Increasing scale of performance rebates, etc. linked with prompt settlement, or non-delivery sanctions for non-payment</li><li>Dealer loader premium offers geared to cash with order/ delivery</li><li>Sales force commission claw-backs or distributor penalties for non settlement of accounts</li><li>Positive sales force incentives for debt collections (usually with supply sanctions for slow payers)</li></ul>
Weak trade product knowledge resulting in lost sales opportunities or customer dissatisfaction	<ul><li>Product training seminars, videos, films, etc.</li><li>Field sales team/ brand ambassadors working in outlets</li><li>Trade product literature</li><li>Trade magazine editorials/ advertorials</li><li>Product information leaflets at point of sale</li></ul>
Inadequate product display	<ul><li>Display incentives</li><li>Sales performance rebates, etc. motivating display at key sites</li><li>Dealer display competitions.</li><li>Consumer promotions motivating off-shelf feature displays</li><li>In-store product merchandising teams</li></ul>
Increasing product market share	<ul><li>Performance rebates and allowances, quantity discounts, etc.</li><li>Trade credit extensions</li><li>Trade stock premiums – dealer loaders</li><li>Dealer competitions</li></ul>

Appendix 19A continued

Promotion focus/objective	Promotion format
	• Own sales force or distributor sales force incentives/ competitions geared to volume and display
	• Consumer premium offers
	• Consumer competitions
	• Price promotional price specials.
	• Tie-ins with special local events
	• Sponsorship activities by local opinion formers/ leaders
	• Price reduction offers
	• Couponing
Defending against product sales/share erosion from competitive activity	• Dealer stock incentive promotions – dealer loaders
	• Dealer competitions and gifts
	• Own sales force incentives or distributor sales incentives geared to volume and display
	• Consumer price specials, etc.
	• Couponing
	• Improving in-store display through point of sales material and merchandising
	• Point of sales materials
	• Sampling/ demonstrations/ brand ambassadors
	• Advertorials in trade and consumer magazines
	• Direct mailshots to selected target persons
	• Sponsorships by opinion formers/ leaders
	• Tie-ins with special local events
	• Consumer loyalty promotions – e.g. collectibles, premium offers
Developing brand loyalty	• Trade advertorials
	• Dealer gifts on a build-up/collectable basis
	• Distributor sales force competitions with a build-up/ collectable element, e.g. points against gifts
	• Consumer magazine advertorials
	• Personality promotions/ sponsorships
	• Point of sales material prompting repeat use
	• Consumer premium offers with collectable element (self-liquidating promotions)
	• On-pack give-aways
	• Price incentives – e.g. multiple purchases at reduced prices
	• Couponing
Increasing consumer product trial	• Dealer/outlet sales incentives
	• Inter-dealer/ outlet competitions
	• Special consumer prices for limited period
	• Point of sales material
	• Consumer product information literature
	• Consumer information videos shown at outlets
	• Key site display
	• Sampling

Appendix 19A continued

Promotion focus/objective	Promotion format
	• Visits to outlets by brand ambassadors/ personalities • Demonstrations • Direct mailshots to opinion formers in target market sectors • Couponing • Trial size with established product and variations • Feature displays linked to buying incentive, e.g. special trial price • Cross-product trial offers ('piggy-back' promotions)
Building a customer/ prospect data base	• Coupons on trade magazine advertorials inviting application for vouchers, etc. • Prizes to persons who make productive introductions of new prospects • Free draws for product prizes, etc., possibly connected with a trial promotion such as sampling or product purchase • Data collected from other forms of consumer promotions and competitions with a write in element
New product launch	• Initial order special allowances in price terms or bonus product • Extended trade credit for new products • Trade sales literature • Dealer/ outlet sales competitions • Product introduction seminars • Sponsorships and outlet visits by personalities • Advertorials • Point of sales material • Sampling/demonstrations • Feature displays, possibly with display allowance • On-pack premium offers (give-aways)
Increase sales force effort	• Sales bonuses for new account opening • Performance-related volume sales incentives (commissions) • Bonuses targeted to specific sales force objectives, i.e. particular brand distribution and display objectives • Sales training and product knowledge training • Appropriate product literature • Appropriate point of sales materials • Bonuses for achievement on specific display objectives (on-shelf facings or feature displays) • Trade and consumer promotions that focus attention and activity on achieving extra sales effort and volume

Action points

Agree and set promotion objectives
Consider alternative promotion formats against:
- Promotion objectives
- Budgetary limits
- Sales force resource limits
- Planning and implementation lead times

Check applicable regulations on promotion formats
Fix quantities of special:
- Product
- Packaging
- Sales aids/promotional literature
- Point of sale material

Design copy and artwork for:
- Special packaging
- Promotional literature
- Point of sale material
- Other sale aids

Order production quantities of:
- Special packaging
- Promotional literature
- Point of sale material/other sale aids

Develop supporting media campaigns:
- Prepare copy and artwork and story boards for press and other media campaigns
- Instruct advertising agencies to prepare final media campaign material
- Book media advertising schedules

Sales management of promotional activity:
- Design procedural systems and controls
- Prepare promotional communications to the sales teams, e.g. bulletins and procedural instructions
- Distribute sales team allocations of promotional literature, sale aids, and point of sale material
- Conduct sale team briefings
- Conduct sales team field training
- Set objectives for each customer
- 'Sell in' promotion to customers
- Distribute promotional product to customers
- Conduct in-store promotional merchandising
- Measure performance against promotion objectives
- Prepare a post-promotion evaluation

Action points

The selection of a promotion format will depend on the nature of goods (industrial or consumer) and a clear definition of the objective of the promotion.
Typical promotional formats include:
- Brands publicity and public relations activities
- Company credit cards
- Consumer price promotions
- Consumer premium offers
- Consumer competitions
- Couponing
- Dealer competitions
- Direct mailshots
- Display bonuses
- Distributor sales force incentives
- Editorials/advertorials in special magazines or journals
- Exhibitions/trade shows
- Free product trial periods
- Gifts for buyers
- Introduction incentives
- Lectures, slide/film shows, videos
- On-pack give-aways
- Performance rebates or allowances
- Personality promotions and sponsorships
- Point of sale material
- Promotional packaging
- Product merchandising
- Product sampling programmes
- Product training (e.g. distributors)
- Product demonstrations
- Prompt order bonuses or discounts
- Public relations activities
- Sales and promotional literature
- Tie-ins with special events
- Trade price discounts
- Trade stock bonuses
- Trading stamps and similar incentives

Action points

Select the exhibition
Consider:
- Access to public transport (road/rail/air)
- Proximity to customers/markets
- Reputation of exhibition
- Competence of organizers
- Compatibility of visitor profile with target market profile
- Timing

Objectives
Set objectives:
- Obtaining orders at the stand
- Product launch
- Contact with existing customers/distributors
- Identifying new customers/agents/distributors
- General marketing promotion
- Market evaluation
- Evaluation of competitive activity
- Other (identify)

Planning
Set budgets:
- Participation fees
- Stand design costs
- Delivery/handling/storage of exhibits, etc.
- Hire of furniture, telephones, etc.
- Stand cleaning expenses
- Sales promotion literature and other aids
- Samples
- Foreign language interpreters
- Locally hired demonstrators, etc.
- Staff travel and subsistence expenses
- Advance publicity and public relations
- Insurance of exhibits, etc.
- Customer hospitality
- Others (list)

Facilities check:
- Electricity supply sources
- Lighting
- Stand location
  (proximity to traffic flow, competitive stands, etc.)
- Ease of access for bulky exhibits

Checklist 19.3	Action points

Checklist 19.3

- Catering
- Security
- Communications (telephones, fax, telex)
- Other (list)

Action:

- Develop a critical timetable
- Appoint an exhibition project leader
- Book the exhibition stand
- Decide on exhibition theme
- Design stand and place order
- Design all promotional literature and place orders
- Decide on exhibition manning requirements
- Book hotels and travel for company personnel
- Book hospitality suites
- Plan and book advance publicity
- Notify existing and potential customers
- Prepare and implement public relations campaign
- Prepare exhibits
- Ship exhibits to the exhibition
- Prepare and ship samples to exhibition
- Hire interpreters and local support staff
- Prepare stand manning rota
- Check despatch of all equipment, materials, etc.
- Other (list)

Post-exhibition

- Compare achievements with objectives
- Compare budgets with actual costs
- Prepare and implement a contact enquiry follow-up programme
- Evaluate competitor and market information obtained

20

Merchandising at the point of sale

Merchandising in retail and trade distribution outlets is a key selling activity, impacting on sales volume and account profitability, in many categories of consumer products, and also for some trade products sold through dealer networks. It often attracts less attention than warranted from sales managers and salespersons, perhaps because it seems a less exciting part of the selling process.

The sales manager for products sold through retail or trade dealer outlets has a key role in training his or her team in effective product merchandising, and to promote product merchandising as a key stage in the selling process. Effective product merchandising can make the difference between stock lying in stock rooms or on shelves, or being purchased by customers because of salespersons' skill in displaying the product for maximum impact and drawing attention to it through point of sale material.

A definition of merchandising

Merchandising can be defined as the physical placement of product in a store in a location that is easily identifiable and accessible by the consumers, and enhancement of the display with relevant point of sales material, enabling consumers to make better quality purchasing decisions, thereby maximizing sales through the quality, impact and location of the product display.

The importance of merchandising ■

Product merchandising at the point of sale is growing rather than declining in importance within product marketing strategies and tactics, as part of the marketing communications mix, for several reasons.

- It is becoming increasingly difficult for marketing-led manufacturers to communicate with their consumers away from the point-of-sale. Conversely, retailers and trade distributors are playing an increasingly influential role in the marketing mix.
- The company that invests heavily in advertising its brands to create interest and imagery finds its messages, together with the spend, are lost if they are not endorsed at the point-of-sale where the consumers have the choice to make their selection.
- The supply of product does not end with gaining distribution or even displays; more importantly it is the **quality** of the display versus the competition. This is a sales force function.
- Brand proliferation has caused an over-subscription of space. There is a need to identify new selling tools and improved negotiation methods to gain distribution.

Figure 20.1 indicates why sales managers and their teams should focus on space management and product merchandising for products sold through retail outlets and trade dealers.

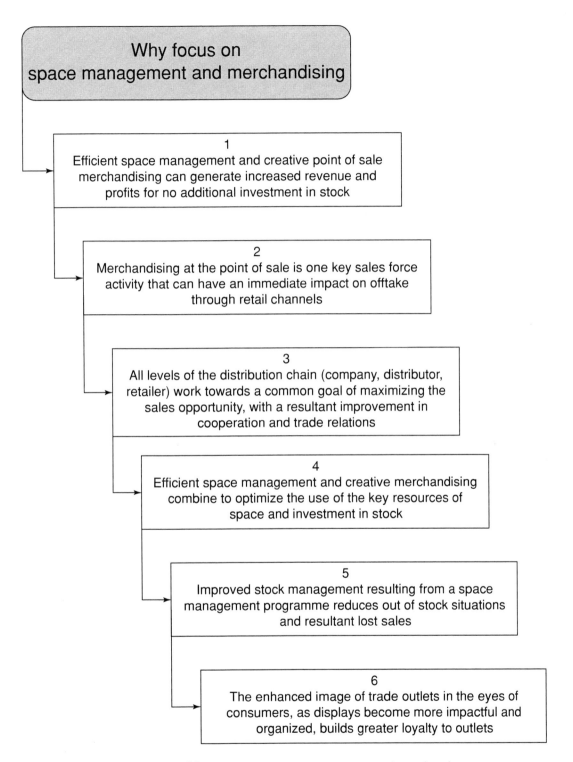

Figure 20.1 *The importance of focusing on space management and merchandising*

There is a tendency for the salesperson calling on trade outlets, such as retailers, trade dealers or wholesalers, to relegate merchandising to a low priority in the field selling activities. We have identified it as a separate stage in the selling process (Figure 10.3) when making selling calls on retailer and other distributive trade channels. It is not as exciting as making the presentation, handling objections and closing the sale. It can often be ranked, along with the post-call administration and follow-up, among those other activities that are really peripheral to the real action, and that are chores that distract from building sales through selling and negotiating. For these reasons merchandising needs to be a key priority training and monitoring focus for sales managers promoting products through retail and trade distributors.

Merchandising in relation to strategy and communications ▬▬

Figure 20.2 highlights the importance of merchandising at the point of sale in the overall marketing strategy for products marketed through retail and trade distribution channels. In this diagram we see that the company's marketing communications focus on positioning a brand in its target market, with messages promoting trial or building loyalty. The sales force must enable the communications messages to convert to sales by enabling consumers to buy and try the products, developing distribution, building volume, and creating attention at the point of sale by focusing display activity on location, layout and impactful use of point of sale material.

All too often salespersons book orders and return on the next sales call to find some of the products are not on display, still in the store room. Figure 20.3 illustrates some of the reasons merchandising can be neglected by the different levels of supplier down the distribution chain – manufacturer, distributor and retailer. The trade channel outlets (retailer, dealer or wholesaler) might rationalize that the product has not been put on prominent display because:

- it is so well known that customers ask for it
- there was no available space on the shelves and display fixtures
- they have been short of staff to price and merchandise the products
- they have other stock they want to clear out before offering this supplier's product
- it has been merchandised and displayed in a secondary site so that they can use the best display locations for other products (perhaps own label brands, or slower products that they want to clear from stock).

Unless the supplying company has some other arrangement for product merchandisers to call on trade channel outlets, such as where a specialist team is hired to fulfil that function, then the salesperson calling on the customer to undertake all the other selling activities must also accept responsibility for product merchandising.

Benefits of merchandising ▬▬▬

All levels of the distribution chain gain from an active space management and merchandising programme – manufacturer, distributor, retailer and the consumer. The benefits are both tangible and intangible, and are illustrated in Table 20.1.

Space management in the selling environment ▬▬▬

Sales managers and salespersons operating in retail market sectors are finding buyers becoming far more professional and discriminatory when evaluating new products. They are concerned with

- fit of the product within the overall product category

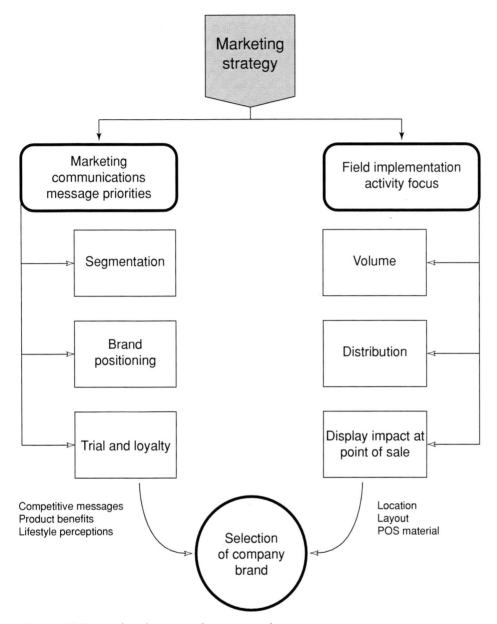

Figure 20.2 *Merchandising in relation to marketing strategy*

- fit of the product within their product mix and in relation to the profile of their own customer base
- innovativeness (bringing something new to expand consumption of the product category)
- merchandising the products within the category
- suitability of the product for sales promotion support

- potential sales volumes and profit from any given space application.

There are positive ways that a focus on space management issues can be developed in sales presentations to retail trade customers, and sales managers will need to highlight these in sales training, as illustrated on page 359. Figure 20.4 illustrates how a sales manager

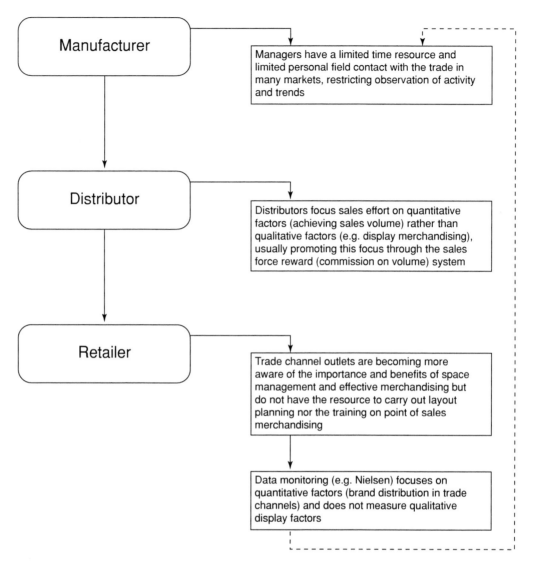

Figure 20.3 *Some factors reducing attention to merchandising*

might develop an action plan to implement space management principles in relation to product merchandising within his or her customer base of retailers or trade dealers. Applications need not just be limited to high street fast moving consumer products retailers, but to a range of durable and non-durable products retailers. In the fast moving consumer goods categories there are well-tried computer programs and models that have broad applications, and are currently used by many major manufacturers and multiple retailers.

Merchandising in the sales call

Although in Figure 10.3 we show merchandising as an activity once the sales presentation is completed and closed, with many fast moving consumer goods there is a strong case for the salesperson to complete the merchandising activity before meeting with the buyer (except where the salesperson needs the buyer's approval to use and locate particular point of sale material). That can give an excuse and opportunity to:

Manufacturers, distributors and retailers in relation to space management and merchandising

Manufacturers and distributors

Typical problems and constraints on progress include:

- limited manufacturer and distributor sales resources, with diverse product portfolios and priorities
- non-recognition of the importance of space management and merchandising in the marketing mix and particularly in field sales activity
- lack of merchandising support or merchandisers untrained in display development and management
- a short-term focus on sales volume, encouraged by sales force reward and incentive systems
- merchandiser rewards not geared to specific display standards, qualitative and quantitative measures ('display dusters rather than display developers')
- an assumption that displayed distribution alone (in stock and out on display somewhere) is sufficient to attract the consumer and influence a purchase decision
- difficulty in quantifying the volume/profit benefit of an effective space management and merchandising programme.

Result

Sales below potential maximum for any given level of sales force resources.

Retailers

Typical problems and constraints on improvement of space management and merchandising at the **retail level** include:

- lack of awareness of **best practice** space management and merchandising principles
- **distrust** of the supplier's motives and integrity in promoting change likely to mainly benefit the supplier
- lack of **technical expertise** and resources to apply space management techniques
- lack of **staff** to focus on qualitative aspects of display
- unfamiliarity with the **key influences** on consumer purchases of the product category
- unfamiliarity with **aspects of brand marketing**, e.g. brand positioning and segmentation communication messages
- display sometimes governed by **current stockholding** levels (of slower brands) rather than product demand factors
- tendency of staff to '**fit product into empty spaces**' rather than merchandise to a consistent layout.

Result

Sales below potential for any given level of space allocation.

- access store rooms to check stock levels
- fill any allocated display space with new stock
- rotate stock if there is any date coding system applied to it
- check shelf prices and promotion prices
- and to place current point of sale material near product display locations.

Product display is a critical factor in influencing customers to purchase retail products, and therefore in achieving your sales targets and potential. Merchandising is concerned with every aspect of 'selling out' of product once it is purchased by the outlet, ensuring that the goods 'sold in' move through to the ultimate consumer. It is a critical factor in achieving sales targets because the trade buyer is always concerned with the rate of stock movement when

Table 20.1 *The tangible and intangible benefits of merchandising in retailing*

Tangible benefits of effective merchandising			
Manufacturer ⇨	**Distributor** ⇨	**Retailer** ⇨	**Consumer**
• More effective use of A & P funds • Develop total product category • Increase turnover • Improve quality of display • Build market share • Monitor impact of promotional activity • Improve product pull through • Assess implication of range extensions prior to launch and monitored after launch • Gain positive control of the marketing mix • Influence retail decisions – buying/ range/ promotion activity	• Sales data from retail outlets • Balance stockholding • Improve turnover on company portfolio • Improve return on investment • Pull product through – improve forecasting • Influence on retail buying/ range decisions • Improve quality and effectiveness of the sales force • Measure performance of promotional activity	• Reduce out-of-stocks • Improve turnover • Balance stock – holding • Improve return on investment • Impactful displays generate greater value • More meaningful data • Quality of display influencing consumer purchasing decisions	• Time saving – finding products easier • Stock available to purchase • Better quality of choice • Improve loyalty • Enhanced displays allow more opportunities to make purchases

Intangible benefits of effective merchandising			
Manufacturer ⇨	**Distributor** ⇨	**Retailer** ⇨	**Consumer**
• Established as the product category manager and as a concerned supplier • Competitive edge • Improve quality of display at the point of sale • Greater impact of the total product category on consumers • Elevate the profile of the product category to consumers • Improve distributor relationships: demonstrate the benefits to them • Gain retailers' respect from expertise and genuine contribution to their growth • Endorse brand messages at the point of sale	• Establish reputation as the local product category manager and expert • Better relationships with retailer • Greater influence at retail level • Retail respect from expertise and genuine contribution to their growth. • Improve quality of display at point of sale	• Enhance image with the consumer	• Gain information on retailer • Increased satisfaction • Easier to shop from a logical layout • Receive correct brand messages and knowledge

Sharing information	● A greater sharing of **information** on sales and access to valuable retail data will increase recognition that both manufacturers and distributors can, and want to, develop total sales.
Space management	● Space management as a selling issue is **non-confrontational**; it helps to move the negotiations away from the **price** platform.
New listings	● In seeking **new listings** recommend where the product should be located, what the projected sales are and thus required number of facings. (Suggest where space can be freed up on shelf to house the product correctly.)
	● Logical layouts will enable the manufacturer to build a consumer profile of the store (check this against other product groups) possibly creating additional **listing opportunities** where there are products in the marketer's' company portfolio that match the consumer profile.
	● Do competitor brands have listings for additional sizes?
Promotional slots	● The retailer will be more receptive to your **promotion initiatives** where these take account of space management issues, and therefore place value on your suggestions.
Better use of promotion budgets	● **Promotion budgets** should be used for off-shelf displays but not shelf space, using space management rationale and logic to obtain shelf space.
Promotion effectiveness	● Measuring the results of sales promotions that have been merchandised according to a logical space management programme will highlight which **promotions** have greatest impact on sales, and facilitate better and more effective promotion planning.

placing orders, and both merchandising activity and promotional activity have a significant effect on the rate of stock movement.

There are a number of areas where you can focus your merchandising activity, as indicated in Table 20.2.

On-shelf display

The importance of shelf display will vary between different product categories, but in general shelf display offers the best opportunity for ongoing sales volume, reserving off-shelf daily features for promotional activity supporting short-term sales objectives.

Regular shelf display area should not be neglected for merchandising as an important sales location because it:

● is the regular area of display, generating the normal volume of sales as consumer traffic circulates the store

● is a reactive area and responds to consumer demand (people shopping off the shelves usually know what to look for and where to find it in their regular stores)

● can be used as a market 'barometer' since this is where consumers have the choice in what to buy and with a range of prices in any product category, where all similar products are displayed alongside each other.

In Figure 20.5 we can see how people shop from shelf fixtures, in that the primary purchases are planned, and selection is made in a very short time, with the impact of the shelf display having a significant opportunity to influence choice, particularly where the allocation of the shelf space reflects the normal pattern of sales volumes of the respective products within any product category.

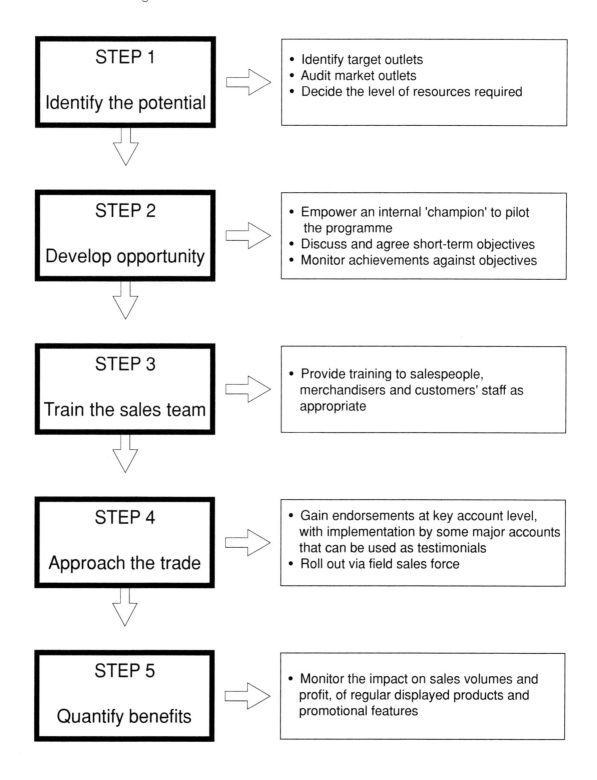

Figure 20.4 *Implementing space management in the market: an action plan*

Table 20.2 *The focus of merchandising activity*

Merchandising to increase the rate of sale	
In the retail trade	**In the wholesale trade**
Product facings on shelf fixtures: • Increase number of brand facings on shelf fixtures • Ensure facings agreed for a key account are maintained • Manage shelf space allocated to company brands (and whole section) according to turnover/ profitability principles (space management) • Keep shelf fixtures full **Improve display siting:** • Locate displays in main traffic flow areas • Merchandise products in best position within a section (normally waist to eye level) **Key sites for promotional features:** • Note the high traffic locations for off-shelf floor displays on customer record card, and negotiate for these during promotions **Implementing correct prices:** • Check shelf pricing is correct (and as per any key account agreement on price) • Check brand price positioning is correct versus competition • Price any unpriced stock on display **Point of sale material:** • Locate in clearly visible locations close to product (do not obstruct traffic flow) **Rotate stock:** • Check that display stock is correctly rotated where appropriate **Tidy stock:** • Dust product • Dust or tidy shelves and shelf stock	**Increase product facings on stock shelf fixtures:** • Ensure storage space allocation reflects rate of sale to avoid out-of-stock situations • Ensure stocks are maintained at levels reflecting offtake • (Ensure packaging clearly identifies product) **Improve display siting:** • Ensure product is clearly visible and accessible to staff picking orders • If possible, locate product displays within view of trade customers **Develop key sites for promotional features:** • Negotiate to place promotional products where customers to the trade outlet can see them (at key traffic flow points and where customers are waiting to place orders) **Increase number of product display or stock positions:** • If a product presents opportunities for impulse sales, seek to locate a display near customer service points, or near other products relating to its use **Place product literature:** • Locate product literature where customers can see and reach it while they are browsing or placing orders • Place other promotional point of sale material in key locations visible to customers **Ensure competitive pricing:** • Advise trade customers of typical trade prices in their neighbourhoods, and alert them if their prices reduce their competitiveness

Off-shelf feature displays

The off-shelf display features, seen so prominently in many mass merchandising retail and trade outlets, are a major generator of additional product sales volume. Just as with on-shelf displays, location is critical, as are the sheer size and impact of the promotional display if it is to have maximum effect on sales demand and profitability from the allocated space. The sales manager, in training salespersons to build effective feature displays, should emphasize (as illus-

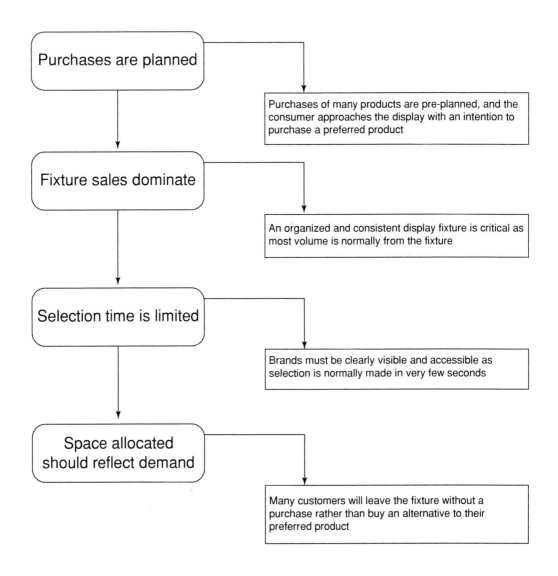

Figure 20.5 *Shopping from the regular shelf display fixtures*

trated in Figure 20.6) for **off-shelf display** that:

- it is a proactive area that should create demand and develop incremental sales
- **impact** is crucial to generating volume

sales (through size of display, creative use of display material, prominent featuring of the promotion offer and benefits, etc.)
- **location** should be in the highest traffic flow areas possible.

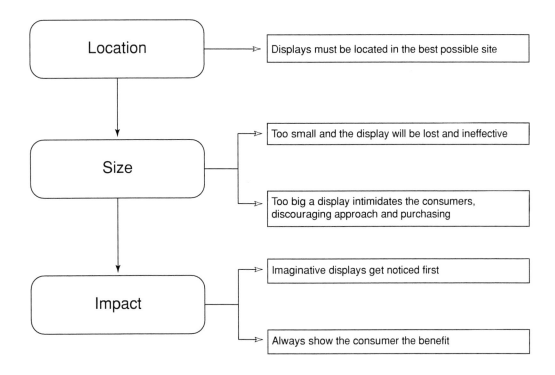

Figure 20.6 *The keys to effective off-shelf feature displays*

Point of sale material

Many companies produce **point of sale material** for products, brands and promotions. Examples are seen in retail stores, banks and other financial institutions, hotels, chains of fast food restaurants, car dealerships, and so on. It is an effective selling tool in influencing the buyer and consumers in both retail and other trade outlets. It is also a significant item within the marketing budget for most companies, and therefore best use must be made of available point of sale material in all outlets.

Use of point of sale material by the salesperson

Point of sale material can often be quite a powerful tool in influencing buyers during sales presentations. It demonstrates that a supplier is concerned not just with selling product into distributive outlets, but also in working with the distribution channels to increase product trial and usage. Buyers usually recognize that producing effective point of sale material can be costly. In order that current point of sale material is used by the salesperson during sales presentations it should be taken into all customer calls, and can either be included within the **sales presenter**, or, if it is bulky, kept separate from it, but in either case it should be used as a sales tool in sales presentations to influence the buyer and progress the sales proposition. It can be used by the salesperson with particular effect:

- when focusing on a single brand, perhaps during a brand talk, to highlight support for the buyer in promoting the brand to his or her customers
- when looking to sell in a special promotional programme, featuring a product, with accompanying display activity and promotional material
- when looking for an excuse to get hands on stock to re-position a display.

Guidelines for maximizing sales from off-shelf feature displays

Finding the best sites

- Tour the store, stand at certain locations within it and watch the customer flow, look for the most worn-out floor area.
- Choose a high traffic area, such as:
  - entrance
  - by the till
  - on the 'main' route of customer flow (i.e. the area connecting the tills, freezer section and entrance)
  - avoid dead ends or 'separate' areas.
- Salespeople should be responsible for 'booking' the site when promotional activity is agreed.

Impact – how it should look

- Positioning at an angle attracts attention from more than one direction.
- IIf possible, obtain free-standing displays.
- Show the features and benefits. Ensure that the consumer understands the message.
- Ensure that product is priced.
- Ensure that product is clean and display is kept free of debris.
- Create a 'finger gap' – if the display is too symmetrical it will intimidate consumers and deter them from drawing from the display.
- Never mix product in a display, if at all possible, to keep a consumer focus on the promoted product.
- Always ensure the display is full up with stock.
- Maximize the impact of branding.
- Look for cross-merchandising opportunities but ensure that these are in addition to the normal product display; i.e. do not affect the amount of stock in the product category area by allowing another product group to take its place.
- Ensure the display is accessible to the consumer.
- Be creative! The only constraint to building displays is the imagination.

- Effective use of **point of sale material** can increase sales significantly.
- Its use can be short-term or permanent, but ensure that the material is relevant for how you want to use it.
- The incremental sales gain normally far outweighs the initial costs.
- POS should always be used to support above the line (media) campaigns, as well as for supporting in-outlet promotions.
- Always replace point of sale material when it is damaged.
- Always remove promotional material when a promotional feature ends.

Table 20.3 *Examples of point of sale material and possible use locations*

Where to use point of sale material	
Location	**Typical POS material to use**
● **Shelves (and tables, etc.)**	● Shelf edge strips ● Wobblers ● Purpose-built displays ● Price cards ● Show cards
● **Small displays**	● Display stands/floor dispensers ● Cut cases ● Header/case cards ● Print cards ● Product dispensers ● Leaflets ● Show cards
● **Pallet displays and larger features**	● Pallet wraps ● Talker boards ● Price cards ● Posters ● Eye-catching items (e.g. umbrellas) ● Balloons ● Pennants/bunting ● Product leaflets and dispenser ● Product shapes ● Moving displays ● Stickers
● **Ceilings**	● Pennants ● Stickers ● Suspended product shapes ● Mobiles
● **Walls**	● Friezes ● Pennants ● Posters ● Stickers ● Clocks (featuring brand)
● **Glass entrance/ exit doors**	● Adhesive stickers ● Mobiles ● Branded open/closed signs
● **Roof tops/ exterior walls (prominent large expanses)**	● Permanent POS – neon signs, billboards/ posters, product shapes
● **Check-out/tills counter**	● Carrier bags ● Stickers ● Display areas for small sizes ● Counter displays with product and literature

Point of sale material should normally be taken into the sales call in the sample case or salesperson's attaché case, unless it is a particularly bulky piece.

From the perspective of the marketer and the salesperson, every visible or accessible space (on walls, shelves, certain floor areas, ceilings, windows, doors, exterior walls and roof tops) offers scope for product or service promotion, and appropriate point of sale material can be designed that makes an impact while suiting the trading or display environment.

Table 20.3 illustrates a few point of sale material formats, and where they are typically used. In designing and placing POS material, ensure that it:

- suits the location where it is designed to be located (size, stability, visibility, impact)
- is durable enough to last at least the life of the promotion that it is supporting
- is easy to fix or attach in place, without major effort or time, or the need for a multiplicity of tools.

Checklist 20.1
Merchandising in retail and trade outlets

Action points

Focus of merchandising activity
Retail trade
● Increase product facings on retail shelf fixtures
● Improve product display siting
● Develop key sites for promotional features
● Implement correct prices for brands
● Place point of sale material
● Rotate stock
● Tidy stock
Wholesale trade and trade dealers
● Increase product facings on stock shelf fixtures
● Improve display siting
● Develop key sites for promotional features
● Increase number of product display or stock positions
● Place product literature
● Ensure competitive pricing
Typical merchandising activity in the retail trade
Improve product facings on shelf fixtures:
● Increase number of brand facings on shelf fixtures
● Ensure facings agreed for an account are maintained
● Manage shelf space according to best space management
  principles
● Keep shelf fixtures full
Improve display siting:
● Locate displays in main traffic flow areas
● Merchandise products in best position within a section
Negotiate for key sites for promotional features:
● Note the high traffic locations for off-shelf floor displays,
  and negotiate for these during promotions
Implement correct prices:
● Check shelf pricing is correct
● Check brand price positioning is correct versus competition
● Price any unpriced stock on display
Place point of sale material:
● Locate in clearly visible locations close to product
Rotate stock:
● Check that display stock is correctly rotated as.
Tidy stock:
● Dust product
● Dust or tidy shelves and shelf stock

Checklist 20.1 continued	**Action points**

Typical merchandising activity in wholesale outlets

Increase product facings on stock shelf fixtures:
- Ensure storage space allocation reflects rate of sale
- Ensure reserve stock levels reflect offtake
- (Ensure packaging clearly identifies product)

Improve display siting:
- Ensure product is clearly visible and accessible to staff
- If possible, locate product displays within view of trade customers

Develop key sites for promotional features:
- Negotiate to place promotional products where customers to the trade outlet can see them

Increase number of product display or stock positions:
- For products presenting impulse sales opportunities, locate a display near customer service points, or near other products relating to its use

Place product literature:
- Locate product literature where customers can see and reach it while they are browsing or ordering
- Place other promotional point of sale material in key locations visible to customers.

Ensure competitive pricing:
- Advise trade customers of typical trade prices in their neighbourhoods, and alert them if their prices reduce their competitiveness

Have you developed point of sale material to suit your products with regard to:
- Location of POS material & product displays, e.g.:
Shelves, tables, etc.?; Small displays, pallet displays and large feature displays?; Ceilings?; Walls?; Windows & doors?; Exterior walls & roof tops?; Check-out points and till locations?
- Practicality and impact of the alternatives, e.g.:
  - Shelves/table displays and POS material (price cards, show cards, edging strips, wobblers, etc.)?
  - Feature displays (bunting, posters, price cards, leaflets, moving displays, price cards, talker boards)?
  - Ceiling material (pennants, mobiles, hanging shapes)?
  - Wall POS materials (posters, stickers, pennants)?
  - Doors and windows (adhesive stickers, mobiles, etc.)?
  - Exterior signs on walls/roofs (neon signs, billboards, posters, product shapes, etc.)?
  - Check-outs/tills (branded carrier bags, stickers, counter displays, product literature)?
  - Product literature (dispensers at accessible locations)?

**Checklist 20.2
Creating impact at the point of sale**

Action points

The market
Have any limiting factors that inhibit progress with 'best practice' space management and merchandising been identified in the market, i.e. in respect of: the company?; distributors or key retailer?

Action plan

1. Identify the potential

Identify targets
● Audit market
  – Identify space allocated to your product category
  – Identify space allocated to each sub-category and manufacturer's range
  – Identify number of facings by brand and shelf location
● Decide on resource needs
  – Ascertain potential workloads
  – Define jobs of merchandisers

2. Develop the opportunity
● Make a commitment
● Empower a 'champion'
● Set short-term objectives
● Monitor progress

3. Train the sales team
● Has a 'champion' for merchandising been appointed?
● Has a separate merchandising team been developed?
● Is the merchandising job defined?
● Do rewards reflect the skills and opportunities to influence the quantity and quality of display?
● Intensive training of the 'champion'
● Training of sales team and merchandisers
● Has training been undertaken in respect of:
  – product knowledge
  – merchandising skills
  – on-shelf display management
  – off-shelf displays
  – use of point of sale materials
  – criteria for effective merchandising
  – location
  – size of display
  – impact

4. Approach the trade
● Gain endorsement within the retail trade
● Approach key accounts (conduct 'tests')
● Roll out through field sales force

5. Quantify local benefits
● Monitor impact on sales volumes and profitability

21

Key account management _____

Key account management is becoming a more important focus of sales management activity, with sales managers either managing a range of major customers themselves, or developing a key accounts team within the sales organization. In part this need arises from the consolidation of buying points, in industrial and retail organizations. In many developed countries a handful of retailers dominate most product categories, able to exercise 'buyer power' in negotiating and selecting products. Similarly, within industrial and commercial organizations buying is becoming more professional and concentrated, with concern for greater efficiency in supply chain management, improved margins, reducing costs, and so on.

The stages in key account management ▬▬▬▬▬▬▬

The main stages in key account management are summarized in Figure 21.1. This highlights that managing major customers is a lot more than just calling to make presentations. In fact the frequency of presentations to major accounts is low, but the allocation of time in developing an understanding of their business, building relationships with a network of decision makers and influencers, and monitoring their performance against agreed objectives is large. A key account manager will typically have a small portfolio of accounts to manage, but often have a complex web of relationships to develop and manage in each of the accounts (see Figure

21.2). While the key account manager's main contact may be with the titular buyer, he or she will have to network within the buying organization, collecting information and feedback, and developing support and interest in his or her products, amongst a range of decision influencers, carefully building contacts and relationships and communicating effectively, but not gossiping, politicking or usurping anyone's authority.

Trade channel mapping ▬▬▬

This topic has been covered in Chapter 18, and at this point I would want to refer readers back to that section.

In summary of action points in pulling together trade channel mapping as a tool in key account management:

- **Collect data** on the product category volume purchases or usage by all customers/users as low down the volume purchase/usage tree as possible.
- **Identify (ranking as best possible) the major accounts** in terms of volume purchases or usage (depending on whether the products are for onwards sales and distribution, or for internal consumption as an industrial or commercial input).
- **Clarify which accounts you will treat as key accounts** (do not limit yourself only to your current customer base within category purchasers/users – at this point you must recognize also those major

Identify the trade channels for company products
Identify the key accounts in each channel

Trade channel mapping

Categorize key accounts according to relevant profile parameters
Match key account parameters to company brand target outlet profiles

Developing key account profiles

Develop an in-depth understanding of the buyer and his or her role in the account
Use knowledge in developing presentation strategies

Getting to know the buyer

Build a network of contacts with persons involved in any aspect of the account's business relating to the sales of company products
Establish a relationship of trust with key contacts that can be built on in negotiating and influencing the account

Building relationships within key accounts

Develop company sales and marketing programmes with an account consistent with the account's own objectives and strategies, and that increase the sales and market shares of company brands with that account

Account penetration and development

Give a clear focus to key account meetings and to developing strategies with the accounts
Provide a basis for measuring the effectiveness of key account managers in developing company business through the key accounts

Setting key account sales objectives

Use strategic selling and negotiating skills to match company objectives with a key account's needs, strategies and opportunities, to increase the overall level of company business with the account

Key account negotiating

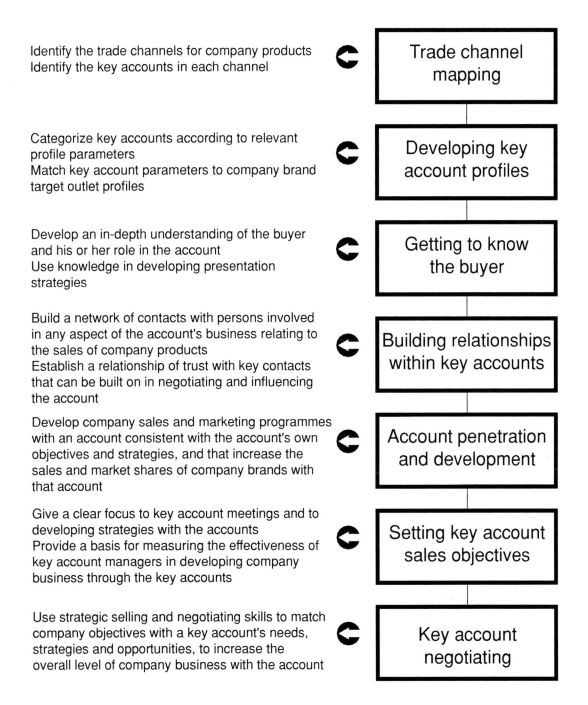

Figure 21.1 *Stages in key account development*

accounts who are not currently your customers, but who should be classified as key accounts in order to receive the development attention needed to penetrate and gain trial or distribution). As a guideline only, in many categories we would identify as key accounts any purchaser/user who absorbed over 1 per

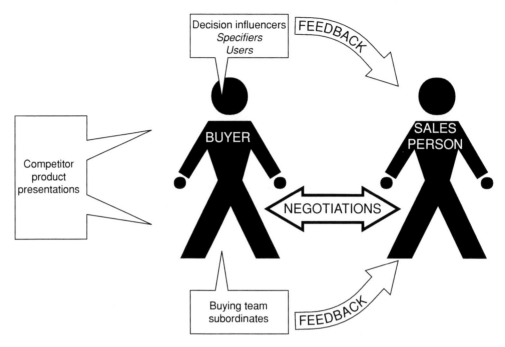

Figure 21.2 *Some communication interactions in key account management*

cent of the total category purchases or usage.
● Set account objectives, develop specific account development strategies and tactics.

Developing key account profiles ■

The objectives in developing key account profiles are to:

● categorize each key account according to its rating on relevant profile parameters
● match key account parameters to your company brand target outlet profiles.

The next stage in formalizing an approach to key account management is to develop a profile of each key account. Typically a form such as that in Table 16.1 (the customer/prospect record card) might help in this exercise, or, alternatively, a format of a customer record card such as either of those illustrated in Tables 21.1 and 21.4 might suffice.

A key aspect in developing an account pro-

file is to know the buying patterns and practices of each customer, with a focus on the points illustrated in the table on the following page.

A form of the type illustrated in Table 21.3 can be used to build a profile of national or territory accounts. In that example we are looking at the various trade channels selling alcoholic beverages either for consumption on the premises (*on trade*) or for take home consumption (*off trade*). The various outlets will have very different customer profiles for parameters that relate to the purchase and consumption of individual alcoholic drink brands, such as in terms of location, income, social class, ages, sex. With this kind of customer analysis the supplying company can decide exactly which individual outlets it wishes to target as locations where it would like particular brands distributed and displayed.

Getting to know the buyer ■

It is important to develop an in-depth understanding of the buyer (see Figure 21.3), both

Understanding the buying practices of key accounts	
1. **Establish the company's share of the customers' business in the product category**	• Ask questions to establish purchase/sales data • Observe visible information (display units in use) • Collect any published information (accounts data) • Is the company share growing or declining? • Is the company gaining or losing penetration?
2. **Clarify future company potential with the account**	• Establish their plans (markets, products, people) • Will they need more or fewer of your products to meet their plans?
3. **Identify trends in the customer's business and your business with it**	• How are they reacting to positive trends or countering negative trends? • Allocate more effort to growth accounts and less to declining accounts • Policies regarding multiple suppliers or any favoured supply sources
4. **Understand procurement policies and procedures**	• Policies concerning particular product groups • Alternative points of sale on the premises • The system of gaining approval for products or other proposals • Paperwork systems for new products and repeat purchases • Structure of any buying committees
5. **Establish buying criteria (in theory and in practice)**	• Product pricing or positioning • Trade buying terms • Product source or type • Advertising and promotional support • Merchandising support • Delivery options
6. **Know the competition and competitive products**	• Why were they chosen? • What volumes are purchased? • What share does each have of the account's sector purchases? • What is competition doing to retain or expand business? • Does any market research exist to provide an insight to competitors?

from the perspective of his or her role in the key account and as a person.

Establishing relationships

When working with major accounts the selling relationship is not normally a quick, hard sell, but protracted negotiations over a period of time, often supported with substantial figure work and analysis of products. The key account manager must work over time to build an appropriate business rapport and relationship of mutual respect and equality (see Figure 21.4 and the table on page 377).

Building relationships within key accounts

The objectives of developing relationships with key accounts are to:

• build a network of contacts throughout the account with persons involved in any aspect of the account's business which impacts on the actual or potential sales of your products
• establish a relationship of trust with key contacts that can be built on in negotiating and influencing the account to take favourable decisions.

Table 21.1 *Example customer record card for an industrial client*

Customer record card					
Company name **Address**	**Tel:** **Fax:** **Telex:**				
Ownership/affiliations	**Nature of business**				
Best visit times	**Budget period** **Credit rating**				
Office & Facility locations					

Trading History
(a) Account turnover
(b) Account expenditure on
    input categories
(c) Company turnover with Account
    (c) as % share of (a)
    (c) as % share of (b)
	19—	**19—**	**19—**	**19—**	**19—**

CONTACTS Buyers/Users/Specifiers **Name Position Function**	**Organization structure notes**				
Account strategies **Policies/philosophies** **Target markets for products** **Consumer profiles**	**Trade terms** **Payment terms** **Discounts/allowances** **Other**				
Product testing and approval procedures	**Product usage points in client operations** **Special production or delivery requirements**				

Table 21.2 Example customer record card – retail customers

Customer record card					
Company name Address	Tel: Fax: Telex:				
Ownership/affiliations	Nature of business				
Best visit times	Budget period Credit rating				
Office & Facility locations					

Trading History
(a) Account turnover
(b) Sector % share account
    turnover
(c) Company turnover with Account
    (c) as % share of (a)
    (c) as % share of (b)
	19—	19—	19—	19—	19—

CONTACTS Name Position Function	Organization structure

ACCOUNT STRATEGIES	TRADE TERMS
Policies/philosophies	Margins
Target markets	Payment terms
Consumer profiles	Discount allowances
	Other

MERCHANDISING/DISPLAY
Policy
Format:
    Planogram
    Discretionary
 	
Branch calls:
    Sales
    Merchandising
 	
Point of sale material:
    H.O.   Branches
	MARKETING
	Promotional policies
	
	Promotions permissible:
	    National
	    Regional
	    Branch
	Cooperative advertising
		DISTRIBUTION
		Central warehouse
		Regional warehouses
		
		Branches
		
		Authorized products:

Table 21.3 Example key account profile form for a drinks company

Account profile form / Account name	Type of drinks licence	No. of outlets	On trade channels Hotel/restaurant	Bar	Other	Off trade channels Super-market	Liquor	Other	Customer base Socio-economic ABC1	C2D	E	Age profile < 25	25-40	>49	Sex M/F	Latest year account turnover Total £m	Category sector £m	Latest year company turnover Value £m	% share of category sector	Company brands stocked	Company opportunities
Central Leisure	On	14			Club				X			X	X		M/F	12.6	8.3	2.2	26.5%	6	Highlander Palace Gin
Acme Markets	Off	96					X		X	X			X	X	M/F	42.0	34.0	4.9	14.4	All	Promotions
LowCost Hypers	Off	22				X				X	X		X	X	F	28.8	3.2	0.5	15.6	4	Premium brands

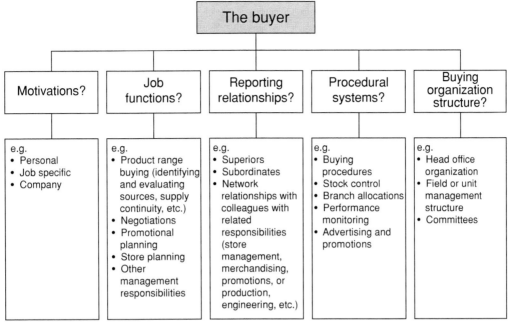

Figure 21.3 *Getting to know the buyer*

Relationships with key accounts

What do we mean by a business rapport?

- A process of two-way communications between the account manager and key account, not a monologue situation in meetings nor a demand-and-respond situation in non face-to-face contacts.
- An ability to raise contentious issues without rancour, and to discuss them without animosity or conflict, but from a position of mutual respect and a willingness to identify and address issues impacting on the performance and objectives of either party.
- Personal relations at a satisfactory level where social contact passes smoothly but are not the dominant aspect of relationships to the point that active and effective account management is inhibited.
- A level of mutual trust demonstrated by the key account through a willingness to discuss his or her business, its performance and issues with the account manager

What do we mean by a relationship of equality?

- Mutual respect between the account manager and key account, i.e. for:
  - their roles and responsibilities
  - their particular expertise and inputs to developing a mutual business
  - their respective goals and objectives
  - their needs (for the businesses and personally).
- Neither assuming or projecting a dominant or submissive role or attitude towards the other.
- Either party being willing to seek or heed the advice of the other.

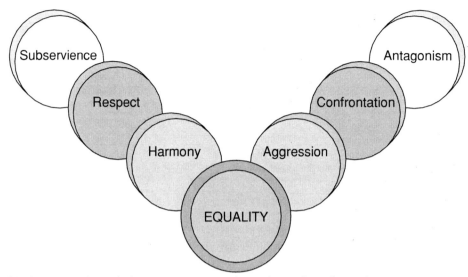

Figure 21.4 *Moving through the spectrum towards a relationship of equality*

Within a key account organization there is normally a network of managers who take decisions or influence decisions that impact on the opportunities for your products to develop through the account. Even within an entrepreneurially owned key account the owner will normally be supported by a management structure.

Therefore it becomes critical in effective key account management that the key account manager develops:

- detailed knowledge of the internal management structure of each key account organization, including any power or political factors
- relationships with all the managers who have any input to the buying, testing, specification, use, merchandising and marketing of the product category in general and your products or brands in particular.

For any particular account the key account manager must make a list of the network of contacts to be developed (who can normally be categorized as illustrated in Figure 21.5), and allocate time to developing his or her relations with this network, as all will have various inputs to, and influence on, the buying process.

Once the network of contacts is identified then the key account manager can build his or her knowledge, getting to know the buyer and the buying organization in depth. We can build on Figure 21.3, and, as illustrated in Figure 21.6, focus now on collecting, collating and building on information about the buying organization, covering:

- the buyer and the buying company's motivations
- the buying organization's business
- the market environment the buying organization operates in (getting to understand the buyer's industry, markets, competition, etc.)
- your role, function and importance as a supplier to the buying organization.

Contacts to develop and follow up with

Key account management is all about team work, both linking to the buying team and within your own organization. Align your organization with the account.

- For retail customers ensure merchandising experts such as those with space planning skills are in contact with key account merchandising departments, and that your field sales management is working with

Typical contacts to make and cultivate

Industrial and commercial products

Build and cultivate relations with managers involved in:

- buying
- product specification
- product trial and testing
- product use
- product maintenance and servicing
- other approvers or authorizers who make inputs to the buying process.

Retail products

Build and cultivate relations with managers involved in:

- buying (include any members of buying committees)
- product range distribution policies (decisions on which outlets will stock which brands)
- marketing (e.g. store advertising and promotion programmes)
- merchandising (specifying store section product display layouts)
- store operations (management at the regional, area or branch levels)
- physical distribution of goods (central warehouse management, if the account handles its own distribution from a central warehouse)
- accounts (on processing payments).

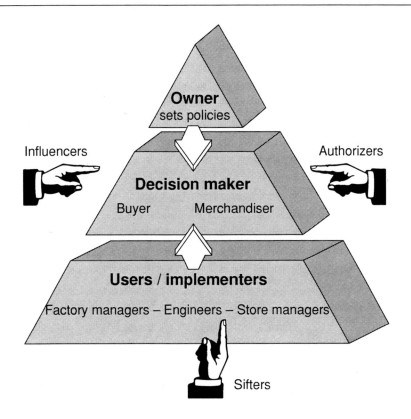

Figure 21.5 *The buying network*

key account field management (store controllers or branch managers, etc.) as locally appropriate.

- For industrial customers put your technical experts (engineers and researchers) in touch with those in the client company concerned with technical issues (specifications, performance, maintenance).

Contacts must be maintained and developed, and Table 21.4 indicates some typical job functions where liaison may be advantageous. An account manager is responsible for driving this process, but must also delegate appropriately to allow time to work on prior-

ities and key result areas. The degree or level of interaction will depend on the sophistication of the account and the depth of your backup services available.

Supporting relationships with a value-adding approach to account management

The starting point in looking for ways to add value is to recognize the different objectives of the supplier and the customer account within the market place, and look for ways to add value to the account's business through help in achieving its objectives for its business rather than relying solely on relation-

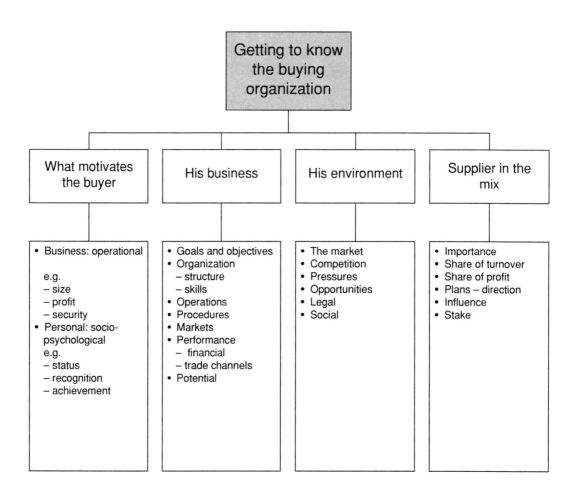

Figure 21.6 *Getting to know the buying organization*

Table 21.4 *Linking the buying and selling organization*

The buying organization	Link to	The supplier organization
Buyers	⟷	Account managers
Buying committees		Field sales managers
Area field controllers	⟷	Field salespersons
Branch managers		Brand ambassadors
	⟷	Demonstrators
	⟷	Product trainers
Stock controllers	⟷	Distribution departments
Distribution managers		Order processors
Industrial product end users	⟷	Product trainers
Retail or distributor sales teams		
Merchandising and marketing staff	⟷	Merchandising specialists
		Marketing experts
Technical specialist staff	⟷	Technical support teams
		Production/design teams
Accounts departments	⟷	Accounts departments

ships. Table 21.5 highlights typical focuses of objectives for a supplier and industrial or retail key accounts.

This table helps us develop a model that recognizes the importance of relationships in a very competitive trading environment and also the need to find ways that add value to an account's business, and Figure 21.7 illustrates the two-pronged approach to motivating and managing key accounts.

The professional account manager will work to excel in his or her development of relationships, but will also ensure that every call has a **value-adding theme**, aiming to sell more of his or her product while enhancing the customer's progress towards achieving its own goals and objectives.

Table 21.5 *The focus of objectives in key account management*

Supplier's focus of objectives	Industrial buyer's focus of objectives	Retail buyer's focus of objectives
● Volume	● Profit from trading activities	● After-sales service and support
● Profit	● Input cost control	● Profit
● Brands' market share of product category	● Input reliability and availability	● Cost control
● Distribution (by brand)	● Performance in use	● Growth without direct investment in brand development
● Brand awareness		● Market share within its trade channel and product categories
		● Risk spreading through range development

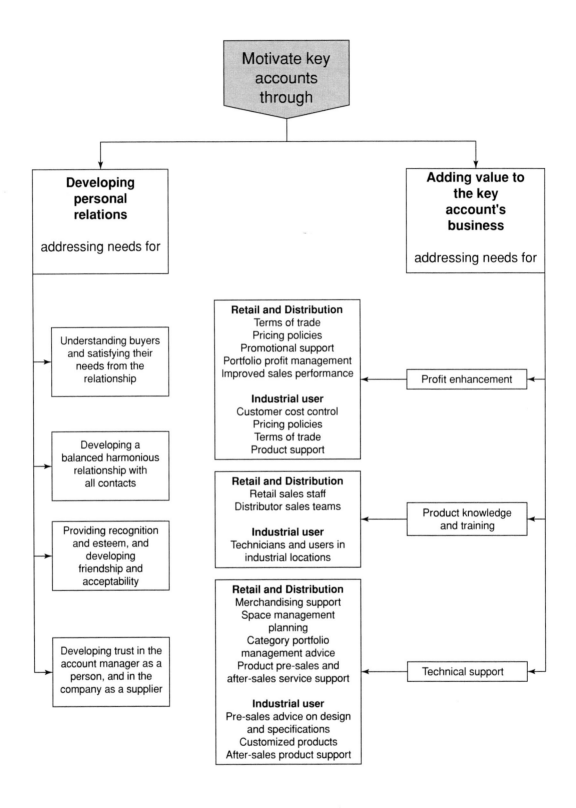

Figure 21.7 *Motivating key accounts*

Typical account penetration and development objectives

Retail products

- Developing your company sales and marketing programmes with an account that are consistent with the account's own goals, objectives and strategies, and that increase the profitable sales and market shares of your brands with that account

Industrial products

- Maximizing the sales and usage of your product within the account's business by developing relationships, sales and usage at all locations that can make use of the product within the account organization

---

Account penetration and development

The supplier's objectives with an account will depend on whether he or she is selling products for re-distribution (retail) or for use in industrial establishments.

Effective key account penetration is essential if the account is to be managed to maximize your sales and profits from each key account. Account penetration revolves around two aspects of knowledge:

- in-depth knowledge about the buyer and the buying team
- in-depth knowledge about the account in

terms of its goals and objectives, how it operates, and how your products fit into its operations.

It takes time to build up knowledge in both these areas. Knowledge is added to rather as building blocks in Figure 21.8. The key account manager should develop the edge over competition by ensuring he or she works to develop knowledge at the level of fine detail on each key account, and then to use that in planning his or her sales and marketing strategies and proposals. Checklists at the end of this chapter expand on the range of key account information useful for developing account penetration strategies.

Factors to consider in developing a strategy

The interaction between the key decision makers, e.g.:

- Know who has an input to the buying decisions
- Know the relative level of influence of each decision maker
- Know the internal power plays and relationships
- Know the individual needs and product interests of each decision maker and influencer
- Make contact with each decision maker personally to address their needs and interests

The physical flow of goods through the account, e.g.:

- Are deliveries timely?
- How will your goods be delivered?
- Does the account run out of stock because of production/delivery problems?
- What are the handling and processing procedures at 'goods in'?
- Convenience of storage of your products at the accounts premises?

	• How will your goods be distributed internally to users or to branches?
	• What are the weaknesses of your products versus your competitors' products in the physical flow cycle?
Hidden costs to change	• Tangible or intangible costs to a prospect changing supply sources exist, e.g.: – adapting handling or storage facilities or procedures; – changing computer stock/range listings; – changing working procedures; – training in product knowledge or use (including maintenance); – changing production processes to incorporate new products ; – changing merchandising layouts; – losing customers through dissatisfaction at range change, or with a finished product incorporating different inputs.
Competitive strategies	• Competitors will not stand by while you steal their markets – keep abreast of their marketing programmes, advertising and promotions, product developments, trading terms.
Reciprocal trading opportunities	• Ils the company, or could it be, a customer for your customers' products? • Is a customer buying from a competitor because of reciprocal trading relations, and can you undermine this by stressing competitive advantages or encouraging value analysis?
Multiple sourcing policies	• Many companies develop informal policies to buy supplies from multiple sources where practical, particularly for consumable inputs or where products are for resale – encouraging such a policy may help you make inroads where you are not currently supplying product.
The influence of key individuals or companies respected in the trade The mileage of windfall publicity	• Cultivate relationships to supply products to key players in the market, or obtain endorsements from them that will help you promote sales to other prospects. • If your products or your company receive positive publicity for any reason use that to your benefit by drawing it to the attention of clients and prospects.

Agreeing a modus operandi for account management

It is important when managing a key account to have a framework of standard systems and procedures – a *modus operandi*. This provides a meaning and focus to meetings. Issues to be agreed by discussion with the account will include:

- the frequency of calling on the account head office buyer (and other related functions, such as the merchandising department)
- the annual account development planning process
  - annual sales performance targets
  - terms of trade
  - promotion plans

Peripheral account knowledge

Retail distribution
e.g. turnover; number of branches and locations; buyer
Industrial product users
e.g. turnover; number of use locations; buyer

More detailed insights to the account

Retail distribution
e.g. organization and reporting structures; decision-making processes; overall company performance; network of personnel; budget periods
Industrial product users
e.g. organization and reporting structures; decision-making processes; product approval processes; overall company performance; network of personnel; budget periods; service needs

Fine detail

Retail distribution
e.g. account's plans, goals, objectives; operational procedures; sales and profit performance by branch; product category performance; strategies; timings of all strategic and development activities; promotional plans; competitive performance and activity; personal contacts with all head office and field management
Industrial product users
e.g. account's plans, goals, objectives for its own products; operational procedures that impact on use of the supplier's products; sales and profit performance by location; account's performance in its product category; account strategies for its markets; timings of all strategic and development activities; account product innovation; usage levels of the products or substitute products; personal contacts with all product end users, product specifiers, and key influencers; competitive performance and activity

Figure 21.8 Building account knowledge to improve account penetration

- branch outlet calling frequencies and activities
- meeting agendas, agreed and prepared in advance
- exchanging information
  - account and product performance
  - market intelligence
- recording details of meetings
- meeting contact reports, or other written confirmation of meeting discussion and content.

A formalized structure to account management meetings reduces the risk of time wasting meetings. **Every meeting should have a selling purpose**: the account manager should avoid falling into the trap of 'courtesy meetings', just calling on the account to pass the time of day with casual conversation – the common excuse for this is maintaining relationships, but it quickly slides into a negative form of relationship where the buyer learns that he or she can have a meeting and avoid discussing business issues or making commitments.

It is useful with most accounts to schedule ahead **quarterly** review meetings, specifically to:

- monitor detailed performance within the account against annual sales objectives by brand and account development plans, and compare with overall market performance
- consider any corrective action promotion activity to counter shortfalls against sales targets
- update on the key account's strategy in its markets and with its outlets
- update on the key account's overall performance in the market place against its objectives and competitors
- update plans for the balance of the planning year, and fine-tune plans in detail for the coming quarter
- discuss product developments (new products, pack changes, advertising campaigns, etc.)
- exchange relevant market intelligence.

Preparation for meaningful key account

meetings is time consuming, but essential if the role is to be conducted in a serious business development fashion, and not just be treated as any routine call on a smaller customer.

Key account negotiating

The objective of negotiating with key accounts is to use strategic selling and negotiating skills to match your company objectives with a key account's needs, strategies and opportunities, and to increase the overall level of your business with the account (in terms of volume, turnover and share of product sector).

Within the scope of this text we can only give limited coverage to the topic of negotiating, in a fashion that will mainly assist sales managers in some negotiation training sessions.

Negotiating takes place where either or both the key account manager and the key account have needs for changes to progress their businesses (e.g. product ranges or mix, marketing programmes), and where a programme or proposition offers ways for each party to progress towards his or her objectives, but where each party has areas of difference that need to be resolved (e.g. cost, resources, timing, monitoring, etc.).

As illustrated in Figure 21.9, the gap closes through a series of concessions. Each party concedes on a point where he or she feels the value of the concession is less to him or her than it is worth to the other, so trades it for something he or she values more.

Typical pattern to the annual round of negotiations

At the annual round of negotiations the key account buyer may bring up a variety of issues, but in the main they will normally revolve around issues of:

- price, terms, discounts, rebates, allowances, etc.
- profitability

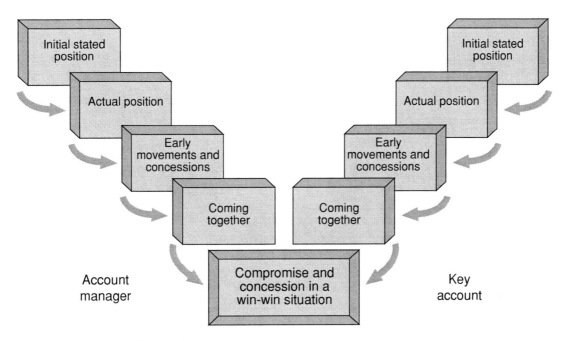

Figure 21.9 *Moving through the negotiations to points of agreement*

- turnover (for retail products) or volume needs (for industrial products)
- cannibalization of sales for other brands (for retail products)
- continuity of supply contracts (for industrial inputs).

The key account manager must develop a presentation that addresses all these issues, in whatever form they are raised. When negotiating with retail trade distributors the key account manager must particularly focus on demonstrating to the satisfaction of the key account that his or her proposals will produce a net increase in account turnover and profit for the product category, after allowing for any cannibalization or steal from other category products. That will require good knowledge of the account's overall sales performance within the product category, and the preparation of detailed calculations to support proposals. Negotiations are likely to be drawn out over several meetings, as illustrated in Figure 21.10.

The actual process of negotiating can be broken down to show the stages the negotiator typically passes though en route to a contract,

the processes he or she will be going through to achieve a satisfactory conclusion, and the outcomes he or she will be aiming for at each of the stages. This is illustrated in Figure 21.11.

Follow-up to negotiations

Negotiations may finish when the deal is signed, but the key account manager's job does not. When all the negotiating is concluded the key account manager must work to ensure all the commitments are met, and that the customer is completely satisfied with the product and the service. There are invariably significant amounts of follow-up activity within the supplier company, and also within the customer organization.

Follow-up with retail accounts

- With retail accounts ensure follow-up to motivate local branch ordering/display in the buying organization with other departments or with individual branch managers and their field controllers. Persons likely to be the focus of post-order follow-up contacts include:

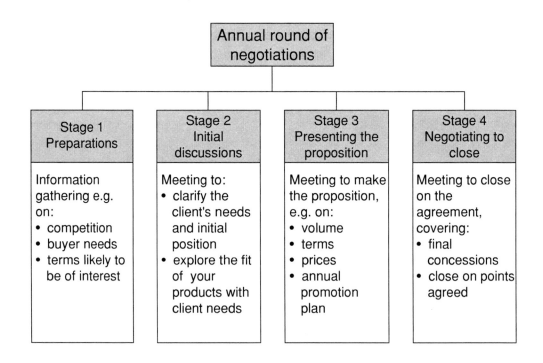

Figure 21.10 *Stages in the annual round of negotiations*

- buyers
- area field controllers
- branch managers
- stock controllers
- product end users
- merchandising and marketing staff.
● Ensure follow-up through your own sales office departments to ensure efficient order processing, and also within your field sales force if there is a network of other salespersons involved in contacting branches or customer field managers. Internal follow-up is likely to be with:
  - order processors
  - distribution departments
  - field sales managers
  - field salespersons
  - brand ambassadors
  - sales promoters
  - marketing specialist (on promotional activity).

Follow-up with industrial and commercial key accounts

● Ensure follow up to motivate use in the client company, and satisfaction with performance. Persons likely to be the focus of post-order follow up include:
  - end users (production managers, engineers, technical staff, etc.)
  - product specifiers (research specialists, engineers, technical experts, quality control personnel, etc.)
  - other section managers in the account likely to be able to benefit from use of the product in their immediate environment.
● Ensure that your organization provides full training and technical support.

The sales manager will normally have responsibility for recruiting and training a key account management team, and for establishing the systems and controls to support their activity.

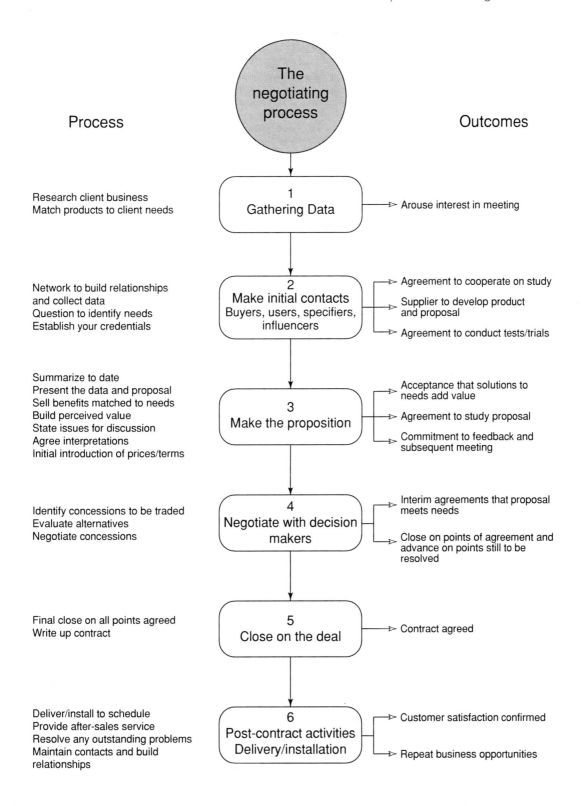

Figure 21.11 *The negotiating process*

Category management ▬▬▬▬

Category management is an aspect of management that combines a range of marketing and sales management issues in working with major customers to maximize sales and profits from a product category, and in the case of each supplier, from his or her products within a particular product category, and that are supplied to customers (direct or through distribution outlets).

What is category management? ▬▬▬

Category management is about the **active** and **responsible** development of the overall market for a group of products seen together as a category (e.g. frozen food products, wines and spirits, tobacco products, household cleaning products, home entertainment products, personal communication products, and so on). A supplier typically is actively involved in category management in terms of promoting the growth in volume and range of goods on offer and the places where these can be purchased.

Where a company markets products that attract any form of regulatory control, that supplier will want to demonstrate it is **responsibly involved in category management** in that it will only promote the purchase and use (or consumption, perhaps) in a manner that complies with all local legislation and regulatory control, and that encourages a responsible attitude to product marketing and use amongst its customers and consumers.

Category management operates at two levels, that of:

- your company as a supplier
- your salespersons acting as key account managers, developing sales through the trade distribution channels.

The supplying company's role

The supplier should start by developing a view of what its role should be in relation to the product categories it markets. The larger share of any category a supplier has, the more it will be pressured to demonstrate category leadership, which typically includes:

- taking a responsible position in the profitable development of the product category through its marketing and sales policies
- meeting consumer needs through a range of high quality brands that are attractively packaged and sold at prices that offer value to the consumer at the various price points within each market segment
- meeting trade needs by offering the highest standards of customer service, cooperative support for building its brands and the markets, competitive trade terms, and providing a source of objective industry comment on trends and future developments.

The key account manager's role

The key account manager should:

- be able to articulate company policy as expressed above and in terms beneficial to the key account at all levels within each account
- have an insight into the key account's buying and decision-making processes, and how the buyer and his or her colleagues measure performance and judge success, e.g. by the modelling of the product category on computer programs including brands, pack sizes, distribution, display space allocations, selling prices, margins, etc., so that the effect of any decisions can be predicted before the presentation of a proposition to the key account
- be able to understand a buyer's circumstances, positions and needs, and to think like a buyer in order that he or she can advise the account on general market trends in such a way that it can benefit from these and develop sales propositions that have a positive effect on

the product category within each key account
- have a high level of company, industry, market and competitive product knowledge, and be able to use this knowledge effectively in his or her relations with the key account and in developing the category within the account's product mix.

Developing the product category ____

If the product category can be stimulated to grow overall, a proactive supplier will gain its share of this growth. The account manager must be alert to opportunities to work with accounts, and possibly even with competitors occasionally, to develop the overall category market through promotion, either geared to immediate sales and consumption, or aimed to improve offtake through improved display.

The buyer and category management —

The buyer is not concerned with a supplier's profitability, nor probably with the depth and breadth of the supplier's range he or she carries. A retail buyer is concerned with maximizing his or her profit from the category section with whatever product and brand mix will give that maximum profit. The buyer is well aware that a higher percentage margin on one product category, or even a particular brand, does not mean he or she should allocate more space to that particular product category or brands within that product category. The buyer recognizes the need to offer his or her customers a choice of products and brands, since too narrow a range is a disincentive to an outlet's customers. But too wide a range is a problem to buyers in failing to optimize the utilization of the available space as low turnover items (even if they have a higher percentage margin!) block space that can be allocated to brands that will yield a higher gross margin per linear or per square metre.

The key account manager will only progress his or her proposals with key accounts if he or she looks at category management from the perspective of the buyer, and recognizes that each proposal must add value to the key account through increased profit.

The key account buyer will be making assessments of the volume sales potential for each new brand or pack offered, and will quite possibly use a computer model to program in:

- the percentage profit on retail
- the cash profit per unit sold
- estimated consumer demand for the item
- the cannibalization effect of the new item on sales and profits from other product categories, brands or pack sizes (including through the allocation of the scarce resource of shelf display space to a new item).

The buyer can calculate the expected effect on overall profit of changes in any of the parameters. A lower margin on a higher volume item may add more to profit than a higher (percentage or cash margin per unit) profit on a slower selling item.

While very many salespersons will only make presentations from the perspective of their own brands and company position, the key account manager seeking to develop a relationship of greater trust as a consultant to the customer is wiser to operate as a category manager. He or she should have an in-depth understanding of how an account will evaluate a proposal and measure a product's performance, and develop proposals that will show an account added value and increased profit potential based on its own criteria of measurement and evaluation.

Managing key accounts is a specialist function within the broader sales management field. It requires a high standard of planning, as well as advanced selling, negotiating and interpersonal skills. This chapter has given some insight to aspects of selling and sales management that can be applied in key account management.

Checklist 21.1
Key account profiles

Action points

The objectives in developing key account profiles are to:
- Categorize each key account according to its rating on relevant profile parameters
- Match key account parameters to company brand target outlet profiles

Collect account information covering:
- Account name and address
- Phone/fax/telex details
- Contact names
  - Buyers
  - Product specifiers
  - Other influencers
- Ownership structure
- Trade channel type
- Trading history
  - Turnover last 3 years
  - Product category turnover or share of account turnover
  - Company turnover or share of product category
- Organization structure and reporting relationships
- Details of other suppliers to the account
  - Turnover
  - Share of account's category expenditure
  - Products used
- Information on account's markets
  - Target market segment
  - Marketing philosophies & policies
  - Needs of account's customers
  - Technology-related needs
  - Customer service needs
- Consumer or customer profiles of account's target market
- Product promotion policies (retail consumer outlets)
  - Centrally organized
  - Branch promotions permitted
- Merchandising policies (retail consumer outlets)
  - Display layouts
  - Point of sale material
- Annual budget period
- Attitude to associate company or branch calling
- Distribution requirements
  - Central
  - Direct to associate companies or branches

Checklist 21.2
Key account knowledge

Action points

Know the customers' buying patterns and practices, e.g.
- **The company share of the customers' product category business:**
  - Ask questions to establish purchase/sales data
  - Note visible information (display units in use)
  - Collect any published information (e.g. accounts)
  - Is the company share growing or declining?
  - Is the company gaining or losing penetration?
- **Future company potential with the account:**
  - Establish their plans (markets, products, people)
  - Will they need more or fewer company products to meet their plans?
- **Trends in the customer's business and company business with it:**
  - How are they reacting to positive trends or countering negative trends?
  - Allocate more effort to growth accounts and less to declining accounts
- **Procurement policies and procedures:**
  - Policies regarding any favoured supply sources
  - Policies concerning particular product groups
  - Alternative points of sale on the premises
  - The system of gaining proposal approvals
  - Paperwork systems for new products and repeat purchases
  - Structure of any buying committees
- **Buying criteria:**
  - Product pricing or positioning
  - Trade buying terms
  - Product source or type
  - Advertising and promotional support
  - Merchandising support
  - Delivery options
- **Competitive products:**
  - Why were they chosen?
  - What volumes are purchased?
  - What share do they have of the sector purchases?
  - What is competition doing to retain or gain business?
  - Does any market research exist to provide an insight to competitors?

Action points

Identify and list the buying functions for the buyer.
What do you know about the buyer?
- **His motivations:**
  operational needs?
  socio-psychological needs?
- **His personality** (type/characteristics)
- **Job functions:**
  His job responsibilities, e.g.
  – buying?
  – promotional planning?
  – store planning?
  His breadth of buying portfolio?
  His purchasing budget?
- **Reporting relationships:**
  Who he reports to?
  Who reports to him?
  How he interrelates with other departments?
- **Procedural systems?**
  How are products selected or approved?
  Is there a buying committee – if so, who is on it?
  What paperwork is involved with new products or repeat orders?
  What other procedures apply to collecting orders (e.g. checking damaged products)?
  Are new products allocated to branches?
  How are product sales monitored?
  What promotional support procedures apply?

Who else in the buying organization is influential in buying or related decisions:
- Superiors?
- Subordinates?
- Other decision influencers?

Develop an organogram of the key account organization:
- How do buying and merchandising inter-relate?
- What is the structure of branch management?

Checklist 21.4
Building relations with key accounts

Action points

Note all the key account contacts involved in the decision-making processes for your products, and identify their roles (selection, promotion, merchandising, specifying, testing, maintenance, etc.), e.g.:
● Buyers
● Authorizers
● Influencers
● Users
● Sifters

The range of key contacts will vary in multiple retail or distribution accounts from single location key industrial accounts. Typical contacts to identify and develop include:
● Buyers
● Area field controllers (retail or distribution)
● Branch managers (retail or distribution)
● User department managers
● Stock controllers
● Distribution managers
● Warehouse managers
● Merchandising managers (retail or distribution)
● Advertising and promotion managers (retail or distribution)
● Accounts departments (payments)
● Sales personnel (retail or distribution)
● Engineers and technicians (industrial users)
● Research departments (specifiers in industrial users)
● Factory and production managers (industrial users)

Liaising with buying committees
● Identify the members of a buying committee
● Provide sets of information for each buying committee member
● Develop contacts with members of the buying committee
● Assist the buyer progress a proposal through the committee

Get to know the account
Motivations
● Operational motives, e.g.:
  – size/ growth
  – profit
  – technological leadership
  – security in supply sources
  – other (identify & list)
● Buyer personal motives, e.g.:

	Action points

Checklist 21.4 continued
status/ recognition/ achievement, etc.
other (identify and list)
Business
● Account goals and objectives
● Organization structure and skills
● Operations
● Procedures (e.g. buying and distribution)
● Markets served
● Performance
  – financial
  – trade channel shares for its sectors or products
  – potential
Environment
● The markets (trends and opportunities)
● Competition to the account
● Pressures on the account
● Legal environment (e.g. regulations governing sale or use of its products)
● Social environment (e.g. attitudes to your products or the products made/distributed by the account)
Your company in relation to the account
● Importance of your company as a supplier to the account
● Your company share of account turnover or expenditure
● Your company share of account profit (retail products)
● Your company's influence, e.g. share of your product sector, technological leadership, product range, display layouts (retail)
Motivate key accounts through:
Developing personal relations
● Understanding buyers and satisfying their personal needs
● Developing harmonious relationships
● Providing recognition and esteem
● Developing friendship and acceptance
● Developing trust in yourself and your company
Adding value to the account's business
● Helping the account build profits through:
  – competitive terms of trade
  – pricing policies
  – better cost control
  – promotional support (retail products)
  – portfolio profit management (retail products)
  – improved sales performance (retail products)
  – product support (pre-sales & after-sales)
● Providing product knowledge training:
  – retail sales staff
  – distributors' sales teams
  – technicians & users in industrial locations
● Technical support:	

Checklist 21.4 continued	**Action points**

– merchandising support (retail products)
  – space management planning (retail products)
  – category portfolio management advice (retail products)
  – pre-sales and after-sales technical support
  – customized products (industrial)
  – advice on design, specifications, optimum product use,
     performance, maintenance, etc.	

**Checklist 21.5
Detailed key account knowledge**

	Action points

Use as relevant for retail or industrial customers

Basic data
- Number of outlets, branches or product usage points
- Location of retail outlets or product usage points
- Size of retail outlets (sq. metres, checkouts, capacity)
- For industrial users – production capacity, production usage rate, or other data relating to potential market for your product
- Number of employees (head office and by outlet) or location
- Locations of distribution warehouses or product storage facilities (and any capacity limitations that can affect)

Organization structure
- Organogram of organization and reporting relationships
- List of names and contact details for all head office and field management personnel
- List of key persons in decision-making process
- Composition of any buying committees
- Movement of any key personnel within the organization
- Criteria by which managers are measured and rewarded
- Internal formal and informal communication networks

Suppliers/products
- Policies on 'own label' for retail outlets
- Policies and attitudes towards your product category in its product mix (for retail products)
- Attitudes towards your company and other main suppliers
- Note any favoured supplier situations
- Data on competitive supply contracts: duration, pricing, trade terms, allowances, volumes, etc.
- Note any special relationships with suppliers
- Standard terms for dealing with suppliers

Distribution
- Warehouse facilities and locations
- Supplier order processing procedures (including paperwork)
- Goods in/out handling procedures (including paperwork)
- Branch ordering systems and procedures
- Branch distribution procedures (including paperwork)

Communications
- Communications systems with retail field management and branches (frequency and format)
- Style of product and retail promotion data communicated
- Standing instructions, e.g. on range, display, pricing, promotions, supplier contacts and relations, etc.

Checklist 21.5 continued

Use as relevant for retail or industrial customers

Action points

- Internal communications notifying of product approvals, usage, stock levels, product knowledge training (if relevant), care and maintenance, etc.

Buying

- Procedures for reviewing proposals and products (including paperwork)
- Timing for sales visits
- Lead times for new products and other proposals
- Budget periods
- Budget levels by product category
- Criteria for product or proposal selection or acceptance

Financial

- Organization structure of finance department
- Scope of responsibilities
- List of key personnel
- Annual accounts history
- Budgetary periods
- Budgetary levels by relevant product category
- Trade credit ratings
- Investment strategies and plans
- Supplier invoicing processing systems (re payments)
- Standard margins by product category (for retail products)
- Turnover trends by product category (this year/ last year comparisons)
- Profit trends (overall and by product category)

Store/ outlet matters (retail products)

- Outlet location list
- Branch management list
- Store/outlet layout diagrams
- Display space utilization guidelines
- Display space allocations by product category
- Display space agreements by product with any suppliers
- Product category section display layouts
- Details of local discretionary areas of decision making on display matters
- List of product approvals for stocking in each branch

Merchandising (retail products)

- Organization structure of merchandising department
- Scope of responsibilities
- List of key personnel
- Product merchandising policies and procedures
- Authorized display layouts
- Information of display agreements with competitors
- Application of space management technology and principles
- Flexibility for local negotiation on display
- Policy towards brand (supplier) merchandising support and brand promotion

<table>
<tr><td>

Checklist 21.5 continued
Use as relevant for retail or industrial customers
- Policy towards use of supplier point of sale material (centrally delivered or merchandised at branches)
- Specific branch merchandising opportunities for your company

Marketing
- Organization structure of marketing department
- Scope of responsibilities
- List of key personnel
- Annual plan timings and procedures
- Policies, goals and objectives
- Current strategic focus and priorities
- Target markets: customer base and profile
- Product range focus
- Planned promotional programmes and activity
- Forecasts and budgets by product category
- Fit of your products with account's markets

And specifically for retail products
- Your company's annual promotion programme agreed with the account (for retail products)
- Competitive annual promotion programmes agreed with account – obtain details (for retail products)
- Account category pricing policies – your products versus competition
- Assessment of your product's sales potential with account (account's view)

Performance data and information technology
- Criteria by which the account measures its performance
- Use of information technology in the account's head office, warehouses
- Use of information technology in retail branches (e.g. EPOS, stock control, product sales monitoring, turnover by brand, etc.)
- Available feedback data on supplier and competitive brand performance
- Your company's share of product category (either of sales for retail products, or inputs for industrial products)
- Historical performance comparisons of your products versus competition, by volume and share of sales/purchase values

</td><td>

Action points

</td></tr>
</table>

Checklist 21.6
Key account development

Action points

Agree a modus operandi with the account, covering:
- frequency of calling on the account head office
- the annual account development programme
- retail branch calling frequencies and activities: order taking; merchandising; sales promotion.
- meeting agendas
- exchanging information
- reporting on meetings (contact reports) and field visits to branches, subsidiaries, etc.
- periodic (quarterly) reviews to address
  - performance against agreed plans or targets
  - corrective action to counter negative deviations
  - update on the key account's strategy in its markets
  - update on the key account's performance against objectives and competitors
  - update plans for the balance of the planning year
  - supplier/customer marketing plans and product developments
  - exchange market intelligence

In developing key account strategies:
- Plan your time allocation to accounts according to their sales and profit potential
- Build on customer service
- Cultivate the entire buying team
- Promote points of competitive advantage
- Provide supporting independent research data
- Offer practical assistance where appropriate
- and recognize
  - the hidden costs of change faced by an account
  - competitive strategies and counter strategies
  - the influence of key individuals and customers on other trade customers and product users
  - the mileage of windfall publicity and advertorials to the supplier.
- Take account of the key account's:
  - own marketing strategies and policies
  - organization
  - financial and other resources
  - use of information technology
  - technological position in relation to competitors and current state of the art in the product sector

22

Alternative sales or distribution operations _____

Telephone selling ▬▬▬▬▬▬

Earlier in the text we looked at the typical costs of a field salesperson. Quite apart from cost factors there are situations where tele-marketing or tele-selling can fulfil a very useful temporary or permanent role in linking the company to its customers. Companies have preferences as to the label attached to this activity, and there are variations in the functions a department might fulfil in the overall sales/marketing mix.

Some of the typical sales support situations where a tele-sales department can provide useful contact include:

- cold call canvassing to identify and qualify prospects
- emergency contact where a regular salesperson is unavailable to call
- coverage of small accounts or geographically remote customers
- tele-ordering where customers phone in to place regular repeat product orders
- promotional thrusts focusing on special activity
- customer satisfaction research
- other customer-oriented marketing research.

Cold call canvassing _____

Suppliers of all types of products (industrial, consumer and business-to-business) have opportunities to develop telephone selling to make initial contact with potential customers, frequently for later follow-up for a direct selling call in person by a salesperson.

For the sales manager supervising cold call canvassing tele-sales operations there are several points that typically need attention (see page 403).

To avoid wasting time and money on telephone calls, it is important to structure contact according to simple framework:

- State who is calling and provide a credible reason for the contact
- Mention a referral source if there is one (i.e. enquiry card, friend, neighbour, colleague, associate, etc.)
- Ask relevant questions that help to clarify if the contact could be a prospective customer:
  - Focus on establishing a product need, and financial resources (if possible)
  - Clarify whether the contact matches any key customer profile parameters relevant to the product target market
- Establish who is the main decision maker for contact
- If interest is aroused agree the process and timings (appointments if appropriate) for follow-up contact
  - literature
  - further telephone contact
  - direct selling visit by salesperson or other needs surveyor
- Seek other referrals (either within a

Cold call canvassing: supervising, training and motivating

Identifying leads	● Possible contact sources include:
	  – reader enquiry cards returned in response to advertisements;
	  – trade directories;
	  – professional directories;
	  – membership lists for societies whose members match consumer profiles.

Establishing scope and objectives of contact	● Tele-sales staff must be clear on their objectives and scope of contact, and know how to action positive response.
Scripting opening dialogue	● While scripted speeches can be transparent and annoying to the prospect, they do provide a useful approach to starting a conversation for tele-sales contact. Staff should be trained to work to a series of prompts that can guide them through the various expected scenarios, so that they sound as if they are following a conversation naturally, rather than delivering a 'canned' speech.

Training	● Staff need to be trained in
	  – basic tele-sales and related communication skills;
	  – recognizing levels of interest (positive/negative signals over the telephone);
	  – handling objections and rejection.

Motivation and supervision	● The contact rejection rate is high in tele-sales environments, and team members need supervision, constant feedback and motivation to maintain enthusiasm and motivation. ● Some companies keep staff working in teams in open plan areas, where there is a lot of activity and cross-flow of ideas and exchange of results that can prove motivational.
Follow-up	● Many companies devote considerable resources to identifying prospects through tele-sales operations, and then fail to have adequate systems and resources to follow up quickly. It is important that these are in place at the start of a tele-sales campaign.

---

company, for industrial and commercial products or services, or within peer groups for consumer and other direct sales products).

Emergency contact with customers

Where a field sales force is in place, there are occasions when it is impossible to visit customers as scheduled. For major non-repeat products this may be less of a problem if a visit is delayed a few days, but where the products are for repeat consumption (consumer products or many commercial input supplies), it can be important not to lose the immediate sales volume. Also, failing to call to collect an order leaves an opening for competitors.

In this situation, either the territory salesperson could make telephone contact with customers personally, or a tele-sales department could fill the gap in coverage by placing a call. A second call might be needed if a customer needs time to check stock levels prior to ordering.

Coverage of small accounts or geographically remote customers

Where business volume is too small to justify a direct sales call or there is no other effective means of gaining and maintaining distribution (i.e. no satisfactory local wholesale distributive outlets), it might still be cost-effective to maintain direct distribution at the lower sales costs levels of the telephone sales department.

Tele-ordering for regular repeat product orders

If tele-sales contact is to be a regular feature of customer management, it is usually best to develop an approach to training and motivating the customer in a way that the customer sees as beneficial. For example, the telephone call can be placed at a regular time each week, so that the customer can expect it and prepare a stock count in advance.

Tele-sales can provide an excellent support to the occasional salesperson's call, especially where the customer's ordering frequency (possibly because of storage limitations or credit restrictions) is greater than a physical call could justify. When physical calls are made it then becomes important to:

- check stock levels and rotation (if age is a factor in the product design or formulation)
- present promotions and new products
- check for damaged stock (if the supplier accepts some responsibility for that)
- present current marketing support (advertising and promotions)
- note competitive activity and any new marketing intelligence
- network amongst the buying team and other decision influencers
- check for any technical issues that need to be addressed.

Promotional thrusts focusing on special activity

Tele-selling can have an important role in some product categories to alert customers to special offers. This may be as an alternative to a salesperson calling, or as a preliminary to establish if customers or prospects would accept a visit from a salesperson to promote the special offer.

Customer satisfaction research

Companies are now becoming increasingly sensitive to customer attitudes and reactions to their service and support. Tele-marketing departments provide an excellent means of organizing post-sales surveys of customers to establish levels of satisfaction.

Other customer-oriented marketing research

Quite apart from customer satisfaction surveys, tele-sales or tele-marketing (the one department may double in the functions it fulfils) can be developed as a source of market research, either in surveying existing customers or for contacting prospective customers for responses to structured surveys.

Training

The tele-sales team need training to meet their special functional responsibilities and activities. Training needs are likely to be identified in the areas of:

- making 'cold calls' to unknown contacts who are identified as prospects
- identifying and accessing decision makers
- techniques for penetrating beyond persons who act as sifters to reach direct to decision makers (whether that be family members for direct to consumer sales, or staff in a buyer's team who are a blockage to accessing the buyer)
- quickly and effectively relaxing the contact to create a receptive atmosphere, rather than an immediate rejection and disconnection
- gaining the contact's attention, and creating interest to enable the conversation to progress to a brief telephone presentation

- use of questioning techniques to elicit interest or clarify or create potential needs or use opportunities
- making effective telephone sales presentations
- dealing with objections by telephone
- closing the sale, or arousing interest to the point where contact can be followed up with literature or, preferably, a direct sales call by a representative
- recording results in a systematic manner (using any appropriate database preferred).

Telephone salespersons are more likely to be received positively if they:

- have voices that project warmth, maturity, friendliness, sincerity, and authority
- are clear, concise and logical communicators
- are good listeners, patient and able to lead the direction of the conversation
- establish at the outset of each call if the contact is free to talk and, if he or she is not free, seek to arrange an alternative convenient time to place the call. A contact will be more receptive to a call if the tele-salesperson mentions a referral from another person at the beginning of a call.

Wholesalers, distributors, brokers and agents

Wholesalers and distributors

Where a product user does not warrant a direct call from a manufacturer's representative, perhaps because of low volume orders, remoteness of location, or simply a limitation on sales resources such that all potential customers cannot be covered by the supplier's team, another alternative is to introduce the customer to a **wholesale stockist** or other **distributors** who can provide the products and any supporting service. These other distributors are not agents, in that they take title to the goods and resell on their own behalf.

They may have a formal territorial franchise or distribution agreement with the supplier, or simply take goods on a non-exclusive wholesale basis. Exclusive distributors may be more aggressive in pushing a supplier's products, but often have the limitation of not covering all of the potential customers within any assigned geographical area or trade channels.

Brokers and agents

An extension of wholesale distributors could be the appointment of **sales brokers** (see Figure 22.1), who effectively act as sales agents on a fee or commission basis without taking title to the goods. Some brokers will go beyond a pure agency role, and actually hold stocks where they have the facilities to provide logistical support such as physical distribution, invoicing and credit control. The role of sales brokers is well established in the USA where few companies can afford a national sales organization. In other markets the term broker may not be in use, but the role is often filled by independent sales agents.

Customer contact

At some point in the selection process it will be essential to visit potential customers and end users (for industrial products) to satisfy yourself that the potential agent or distributor has market acceptance and credibility, and to get a feel for how aggressive the potential agent may be in pushing your products.

Should you be marketing consumer products, there is no substitute for your own random store check to establish:

- strength of competitive products (e.g. user attitudes, usage, distribution, display, etc.)
- which distributors, brokers or manufacturers are most effective in obtaining displayed distribution (retail products)
- which agents and distributors are known and respected by store managers or

(a) All sales through appointed distributors

(b) Sales through brokers/agents, with manufacturer handling distribution logistics

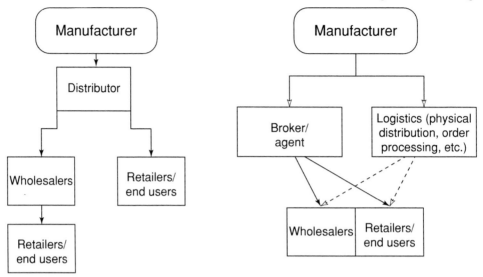

(c) Sales through broker/agent who organizes physical distribution and logistics

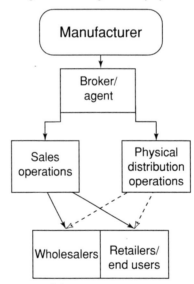

Figure 22.1 *Alternative distribution models*

product end users: strength of agent/distributor relationships (e.g. reputation and goodwill) with customers
- a distributor's practices in respect of display, merchandising, pricing and promoting products
- market pricing practices for the product category through the various trade channels (e.g. product price levels, key price points, trade margins and terms)
- sales achievements of your potential agent or distributor with products already represented
- your potential representative's ability to implement your marketing plans and programmes
- your potential agent's/distributor's selling skills.

Agreements with agents and distributors

Before entering into any exclusive agency representation or distribution agreement, check the local laws that may be applicable to such agreements in the market. Some countries have agency laws that will give protection to agents, after termination of a contract, in respect of future commissions on business from customers introduced by them (this is the position within the European Union).

There are probably as many different forms of agreement as there are lawyers, or so it seems to the lay person, but the key points essentially cover:

- product exclusivity and product range or extensions
- territorial exclusivity
- rights to supply other parties
- limitations to export to other territories
- method of quoting prices
- duties of the principal
- duties of agent/distributor
  - performance clauses
  - special storage, handling and packaging
- principal's right to accept or refuse orders
- market pricing and costing guidelines
- marketing programmes and planning
- promotional responsibilities and materials
- payment terms
- commission arrangements
- reporting/marketing information reports
- training of agent or distributor's personnel
- warranties
- indemnities
- limits of authority
- confidentiality clauses
- trademark/patent protection
- dispute handling
- duration of the agreement
- assignability
- termination
- non-waiver clauses
- entire agreement clause
- force majeure clause
- applicable country for legal enforcement and interpretation.

The reader with responsibility for drafting or negotiating agreements should refer to Chapter 8 in my companion volume, *The CIM Handbook of Export Marketing* for comprehensive topic coverage.

Other ordering or distribution methods

Exclusive retail stockists

Manufacturers of some specialist products (such as perfumes, cosmetics, home computers, fashion products, etc.) may not require a large sales force, but may work through a network of appointed retail outlets that have an exclusivity for distribution in an area. This is more commonly the distribution format where the product is not aimed at a mass market, but at a clearly defined niche consumer profile.

Postal orders

A system of postal orders is used to solicit business through mail order catalogues, mentioned shortly, and can also have applications in some other situations, such as where:

- trade is basically seasonal in nature, and direct sales calls are not always justified, with the customer having the option to replenish stock with mail orders
- customers are required to submit payment with an order
- products are customized to a degree, and requirement details are solicited on an order form.

Postal order systems are a lot less personal than tele-sales contact, but they are often a preferred route, or optionally combined with telephone selling, where customers need product literature in order to make informed product choices. A new order form and current catalogue can be despatched with each order.

Direct mail campaigns

Direct mail campaigns are commonly used to promote sales direct to end users or consumers, or buyers with special interests in a product category. Their effectiveness hinges upon tightly identifying the target market group, and named individuals who should have an interest in the products. The user profile should be carefully defined, and contact researched to whatever degree is practical for a match with the target profile (possibly a mix of age, income, education, social class, residence location, employment type, etc. for consumer and household products). Target groups may be identified from directories, society membership lists, and a host of sources including mailing lists that can be purchased or leased for defined target groups.

Mail order catalogues

Mail order catalogues seem to rise and fall in popularity. They can be useful both in increasing sales of general products (such as jewellery, clothes, some household goods), and in promoting specialist products to narrow target markets (such as collectibles, stamps, seeds, hobby-related items, and so on). Their effectiveness, just as with other direct mail campaigns, is a function of the accuracy in targeting the market and the specific individuals to receive the catalogue.

Ideally purchase through a catalogue should offer the purchaser some tangible benefit over purchases at other distributive outlets to gain interest and encourage action. The benefit may be in terms of: price advantages, a broader product range, scarcity value (collectible products), convenience of ordering, beneficial payment terms, additional guarantees or warranties, product trial before payment.

Computer ordering

While the comments of the previous section might apply largely to computer ordering, this is an area that sales managers and marketers will want to be exploring for its future potential in most product categories. It lends itself to the promotion and communication of information in all product categories, industrial, commercial and consumer. As more companies promote their products and services on the computer networks, so consumers will also become more familiar with computer marketing and more comfortable with making choices and placing orders via computers.

Direct home distributors – network marketing

Over recent years a number of companies, particularly in the United States and some Asian markets, have built enormous sales volumes by achieving effective distribution, high product loyalty, and promotion by personal referral through various forms of network marketing. In some instances the distributors are self-selected, in that they apply to a company to become a distributor. In general these distributors do not receive any local franchise, but are all in competition with each other to promote through their group of contacts. Each distributor is typically a product consumer also.

Network marketers promote cost-saving benefits through the shorter distribution channel, from manufacturer to final consumer without a multiplicity of middlemen. Cost savings can arise through lower sales and marketing costs, lower absorbed physical distribution costs (in that a retail product normally has physical distribution costs included in pricing structures, but a networked product frequently has the distributor paying separately for delivery), and fewer levels in the distribution chain taking profit margins.

Action points

Is there a need or role for a telephone sales department for:
- making initial cold contacts?
- replenishing stocks?
- emergency call cover?
- small accounts?
- remote geographical customers?

Has a telephone sales sequence been developed?

Are telephone sales staff trained in:
- cold call telephone canvassing?
- identifying decision makers?
- gaining access to decision makers?
- relaxing contacts?
- identifying and clarifying customer needs?
- presenting the goods or services?
- handling objections?
- closing sales?
- arranging direct sales visits by salespersons?
- questioning and listening techniques?
- recording notes on results of contacts made, and complying with administrative and database system requirements?

Have support internal administrative systems been developed for:
- identifying potential customers?
- customer ordering and order processing?
- arranging payments (i.e. credit cards, etc.)?
- invoicing?
- arranging direct sales visits by salespersons?
- recording customer information (such as stock details) obtained over the telephone?

Other alternatives

Do any of the following offer viable alternatives or complement a direct sales organisation:
- wholesalers?
- distributors (exclusive or non-exclusive)?
- agents or brokers?
- distribution direct to branches of multiple account customers?
- exclusive retail stockists?
- postal ordering systems?
- direct mail campaigns?
- advertising producing direct orders and enquiries?
- mail order catalogues?

Checklist 22.1 continued	Action points
● direct home distribution and network marketing?	
● computer-linked ordering systems?	
● exhibitions?	
● franchising?	

Checklist 22.2
Selecting agents/distributors

Action points

Essential topics to be addressed with your potential agent or distributor will include:

The distributor's organization
- Size of the organization
- Office, branch, warehouse and other locations
- Access to necessary levels of capital resources for investment expansion (taking new distributorships)
- Corporate history (how long established, etc.)
- Ownership and corporate structure
- Correct legal titles and address
- Compatibility of existing distribution facilities

Financial resources and performance
- Financial performance history
- Paid up capital and reserves
- Three years' accounts and financial data
- Trade and bank references
- Profit margin expectations

Marketing and sales performance
- Marketing performance history and capabilities
- Products currently represented
- Current product range compatibility
- Sales performance with other agency lines
- Commitment to your marketing plans
- Willingness to provide performance data
- Market sector shares and trends
- Market outlet coverage (of users/consumers)

Management resources
- Shareholder management involvement
- Details of key officers and managers
- Company organization and staffing
- Marketing organization
- Management skills and experience
- Management training and succession
- Distributor management style

Physical distribution capabilities
- After-sales service capabilities.
- Distribution capabilities
- Availability of special distribution facilities
- Administrative systems and controls

23

Developing international markets _____

Within many companies the responsibility for export sales falls within the control of the sales director. This could be either because the company is too small to warrant a separate division with board-level representation, or because the nature of the goods or services being offered makes it more practical for the same team to manage sales activity. The reader with export responsibility will find that my companion volume, *The CIM Handbook of Export Marketing* (Butterworth-Heinemann), provides extensive coverage of aspects of practical export market management that we can only touch on here.

How the company benefits from exporting

An individual company benefits from exports through:

- increased plant utilization
- spreading operating costs over a larger output
- reduced input costs through volume purchases
- additional profit contribution
- new markets for domestic product range
- diversification opportunities into new market sectors using domestic technology
- increased volume opportunities through modifications to existing products
- developing international brands and/or company image
- improved rate of technological progress through exposure to world markets

- opportunities to sell support services, consultancy, training, technology licensing.

The broader international opportunities

While most companies start their international business activities by direct exports of goods or services to foreign markets, as the volume of business develops often other opportunities develop. Depending on the nature of your products and markets some of the typical range of opportunities might include the following.

- Exporting existing products and services. This is where you can export products designed for the domestic market without any further modification.
- Exporting modified products to suit end market requirements (customer preferences or regulatory requirements) or opportunities.
- Developing new products or services specifically for export markets, using existing skills and technology, and research and development expertise.
- Providing consultancy expertise (solo or in consortia), for example where you are an industry leader in technology or distribution relating to certain markets.
- Licensing products, patents, trademarks or brand names, technology, and other know-how into markets where it is not practical to develop the market profitably through direct exports.

- Franchising trademarks, know-how, business formats, etc. into markets where the franchisee acquires local distribution and marketing rights in exchange for fees and royalties. Franchising primarily, but not exclusively, operates in consumer markets.
- Opening foreign branches or subsidiaries to control local marketing or distribution.
- Forming joint ventures with local market partners who have local strength to increase market penetration (either just for distribution, or to include local manufacture).
- Inward import to the home market of goods synergistic with domestic range or distribution, and which will increase your sales turnover, market share or penetration, or help in other strategic ways to achieve goals.
- Inward licensing of products, technology, brand names, and/or inward joint ventures that open new market opportunities to you in your home market, such as taking you into new market sectors, enabling you to incorporate new technology, saving you time and development costs, etc.
- Foreign sourcing of inputs, where you can cost-effectively have inputs required in your production or marketing operations produced in foreign markets to your quality standards.

There are many ways to build international markets, sales and profits, including but not limited to direct exports.

The export sales manager

Role of the export sales manager

The export sales manager's responsibilities are not dissimilar to the home market sales manager, but are rather broader in scope and need a slightly different mix of skills and qualities. The typical key job functions include:

- accepting responsibility for achieving objectives and export targets (volume, value, profits) by direct selling efforts and/or with the sales support of agents or distributors
- finding foreign markets for existing company products or services, or suitable products for foreign markets
- establishing an international network of agents, distributors or customers capable of importing the goods, obtaining acceptable levels of distribution, and providing after-sales service (if necessary)
- maximizing the sales effort by providing management support and advice, training and feedback in the foreign markets
- coordinating the planning of international marketing efforts
- maintaining morale and motivation amongst the network of foreign agents or distributors
- interpreting and filtering company philosophies, policies and objectives to the foreign representatives
- communicating effectively with agents and/or distributors through regular market visits, sales and planning meetings, informative bulletins and performance feedback data
- becoming the company expert on business development and business practices in foreign markets, with the objective of increasing the company's global sales and market shares in foreign markets.
- identifying and prioritizing export markets
- forecasting potential sales volumes by market
- establishing company export prices that ensure competitive destination market prices
- identifying, setting and achieving market sales objectives, targets, budgets, and profit plans
- developing field programmes to implement the company's sales and marketing plans in each destination foreign market
- assisting agents and distributors develop sales organizations and management structures to achieve plans and objectives

- converting overall export plans and objectives, in liaison with the foreign importers, into specific standards of performance, sales targets, and programmes for each individual market
- developing an export office sales support function, customer service function and shipping department to handle:
  - credit control
  - invoicing and general export documentation
  - order processing
  - enquiries, invitations to quote, complaints
  - dispatch of sales promotional materials
  - market performance monitoring and feedback reporting
  - export costings
  - export distribution
- selecting and training all subordinate export marketers and shipping executives
- selecting and training all the foreign agents and distributors, and any appointed sub-distributors, dealers, service agents, etc.
- liaising with departments concerned with forecasting, domestic marketing, product development, budgeting and product costing, production planning, production, distribution, etc.
- setting export terms of trade, prices, scale discounts, promotional allowances, etc.
- communicating with subordinates, direct export customers and distributors on plans, programmes, policies, objectives, products and performance feedback
- assisting in developing and test marketing new products and seeking out new product opportunities in the foreign markets
- developing expertise in foreign market rules and regulations (including those relating to labelling, health, safety, import licensing requirements, foreign exchange regulations, product liability, agency laws) and ensuring product compliance, and limiting the exposure of the company to risk.

Skills in the international marketer

The range of job functions facing international marketers is more diversified than for the equivalent level of sales or marketing managers operating in the domestic market. Export marketers need a broader range of skills, developed to a good level of competence. While they may not need or have the depth of expertise of their domestic marketing colleagues, in providing support to their agents and distributors they will cover competencies ranging through:

- finance and accounting and general commercial skills
- marketing and marketing research
- sales management
- personal selling and negotiating
- management and sales training
- strategy development, forecasting and planning
- foreign legislation applicable to agency and distributor relationships and sale of goods in foreign markets
- shipping practice and regulation
- business systems, performance measurement and management controls
- human resource management.

The export manager will normally be taking decisions away from the base office, without the immediate support of colleagues with functional expertise. In order to function successfully in an international environment, the export marketer will need to have **linguistic** skills in addition to being highly **numerate**. He or she will also need to demonstrate a mix of personal skills and qualities that includes: organization, administrative and communications skills, decisiveness, good judgement, initiative, personal stature and authority, adaptability to various cultures and business practices, intelligence, integrity, independence and maturity to work alone abroad, and reliability to honour commitments to customers and contacts. Often managers who are experienced in domestic selling and marketing, or who are technical specialists, are transferred into export management positions without any special training, the assumptions being that the skills and balance of personal qualities needed are the same.

Measuring the export marketers' performance

The effectiveness of an organization can be monitored or measured by its achievement against goals and objectives. Once the broad export goals and objectives are established, a range of quantitative and qualitative objectives that relate to current plans can be established for each market. These are highlighted in the following list.

Individual companies may choose to focus on some of these more than others, according to what is relevant to their markets, distribution system and products.

Desk research

Desk research is an important export market management activity, as the cost of foreign travel is invariably higher than in the domestic market, and time available when on a market visit is very limited.

In most countries it is customary that,

Measuring the exporter's performance

Quantitative performance measures
- Changes in market share:
  - in total
  - by brand/product
  - by trade sector
- Gross profit by market
- Profit by brand or product
- Increase in profit over base/target
- Distributor's profit derived from company products and activities
- Budgets as a percentage of turnover/profits by market/brand
- Achievement of sales value/volume export despatch targets
- Achievement of market sales targets (depletions from a local distributor's stocks, where a distributor holds stocks)
- Growth/decline in market sales volumes: by export despatches or depletions from distributor stocks
- Changes in recorded brand distribution or usage
- Managing debtors within agreed credit limits and time spans.
- Effectiveness of promotional activity: measurable impact on sales/market shares
- Measures of parallel trade shipments (where parallel trade – imports into the market by routes not part of the formal distribution system – is a factor in the product category or market distribution)

Qualitative performance measures
- Preparation of strategic marketing plans:
  - macro level/ micro level
  - by country
  - by distributor/agent
- Preparation of detailed sales, tactical plans by market/distributor/agent
- Preparation of detailed advertising and promotion plans and budgets
- Accuracy/quality of information files for each market
- Distributor or agent relationships
- Control of expenditure within budgets
- Distributor's effective implementation of, or adherence to, marketing and sales plans
- Distributor management skills, systems and controls
- Distributor sales force skills, systems and controls
- Distributor sales force effectiveness
- Distributor compliance with company reporting requirements

when an export takes place, the exporter must report to some authority (such as customs and excise) the nature of the product under appropriate **customs tariff** headings, the volume of exports, and the value. As a starting point, the export marketer should make a study of home market **export statistics**, which will normally show:

- whether exports are taking place already
- where they are going
- the volume and value of exports
- any seasonal pattern to exports in your product categories
- who is exporting.

Home market export statistics will normally be available from government sources (e.g. customs authorities) or through trade associations, chambers of commerce, business libraries or government export promotion agencies. You will be surprised at the data uncovered by a meaningful analysis.

If it is known that other countries are producing similar products and are exporting them, then access to their export statistics will yield the same information on potential markets as I have noted above, and will additionally provide a basis for analysis value/volume comparisons of:

- comparative export prices
- competitive export quantities
- magnitude of import trade to key markets
- any seasonal trends (in the case of raw materials or commodities).

In addition to the desk research into exports and imports, and patterns of movement of goods, some further desk research, such as through the government resources of the Department of Trade and Industry for the United Kingdom, will normally yield data on:

- health and ingredient laws
- labelling and packaging
- import licences and procedures
- import quotas
- export licences and quotas

- exchange control restrictions
- product registration/approval
- import/duties/tariffs/taxes
- import/export documentation
- agency and distribution agreement, and other relevant regulations in foreign markets.

When the desk research is at a suitably advanced stage potential markets will have been identified, and an exercise to **prioritize markets** can begin by looking at criteria such as:

- existing or potential consumer or user demand in the foreign market
- suitability or adaptability of the products to meet specific needs in the foreign market
- sales volume and value potential for your company in the face of competition from other sources (e.g. competition in terms of price, availability, quality, traditional supply sources, etc.)
- existence of foreign market manufacturers with compatible production facilities or products, either to utilize your products as inputs or to compete with local product on advantageous terms
- a local distribution infrastructure suited to the product needs (i.e. refrigerated trucking for delivering frozen goods, or dealers capable of supporting product with after-sales service)
- existence of local distributors capable of marketing the products
- current or potential protection (from imports) for locally produced products
- availability of foreign exchange for imports
- availability of import licences (if required).

Distribution channels

At an early stage in the evaluatory research processes the exporter needs to be considering channels of distribution and their cost, because each link in the distribution chain clearly increases the final price to the end user. The distribution chain may be very short, as in direct export to the end user (common with industrial products), or long, as in the case of a consumer product requiring handling, storage and redistribution at several wholesale and retail levels before sale to an end user or consumer. Your objective should normally be to maximize sales consistent with using the shortest possible distribution chain, minimizing the inflationary effect each link has on the final user price. Figure 23.1 illustrates that there are several ways of developing foreign markets.

Factors in studying distribution needs ___

Some of the factors that should be considered when studying the product's distribution needs in relation to the market's available tiers and channels of distribution include the following.

- The need to achieve and maintain **price competitiveness** in the foreign market if the product is not sufficiently differentiated such that price is a lesser factor in the marketing mix.
- The **physical distribution capabilities** of those distributors able and willing to

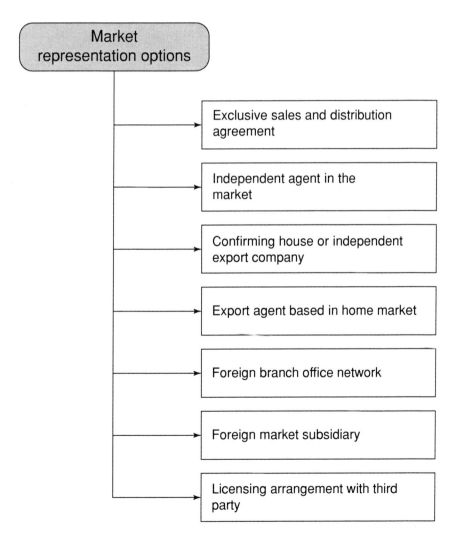

Figure 23.1 *Some alternative ways of developing markets*

handle the products, and the effective modes of distribution within the market infrastructure. Some potential end users may be in remote rural areas, not easily accessed, while major distributors may be concentrated in major cities. Also the provision of after-sales service in remote areas may be a problem for distributors.

- The number and geographical spread of effective and **available distribution points**, e.g. depots, industrial end users, wholesalers, retailers.
- Possible product **after-sales service** needs (without necessary product support buyers will become dissatisfied).
- Traditional **locally established distribution mechanisms** and infrastructures, e.g. trading houses, importers, primary, secondary and tertiary wholesaling.
- **Demographic characteristics of target market sectors**. You will need to study the demographic characteristics of each market or conduct a locational analysis of end user industries, and decide the best means to ensure distribution to potential worthwhile outlets.
- **Available media for marketing communications**. Certain media may be mainly effective in cities, whereas the product may have strictly rural demand. Consumer products particularly benefit from advertising and promotional support. Urban populations in some developing nations may have access to television, cinema, magazines, etc., and have a higher literacy rate than some rural populations. In rural areas promotional support might be limited to basic point-of-sale material, posters and word of mouth communication aimed at a less literate community.

There is, of course, quite a range of distribution options, even when working through agents and distributors. Figure 23.2 shows some alternative distribution networks, and your chain might include a mix of these in the different markets you choose to target.

The market requirements or best approach will possibly vary. If the product has very few potential users, as may be the case with industrial plant or ingredients, the chain may consist only of exporter and end user. However, depending on the degree of service needed by the exporter, product or importer, even that chain may benefit by being lengthened. For example, it is unlikely that it would be cost effective for an exporter of heavy plant and machinery to maintain an inventory in a region where demand might be minimal, such as dairy plant in the Middle East; but the same exporter might well feel that a market such as North America warranted local branch operations and inventories of some or all of the product range and spare parts.

In the case of branded consumer goods, the exporters are likely to find that they need a lengthier distribution chain, probably similar to that in the home market. Main and sub-distributors may be necessary to hold stock or provide spare parts and service, and to provide sales operations to distribute to the wholesale and retail trade. Direct sales by the exporter to a number of competitive wholesalers frequently results in certain of the wholesalers trying to claim sole rights on the grounds that they represent the bulk of imports and sales. However, giving sole rights to a company seen locally as only another wholesaler (as opposed to main distributor) may result in other wholesalers ceasing their sales effort. A main distributor can be involved in managing marketing plans, including media, and can offer goods on comparable terms to all local wholesalers, who will often be competing to supply the same retail outlets. A new branded consumer product frequently requires much effort and investment of time and resources to create the initial demand and distribution at consumer and retail levels in order to develop active wholesale support. A mass market consumer item therefore needs a much greater margin between landed cost and retail price to support the frequently longer distribution chain, margins and promotional activity. Early market investigations should ascertain the expected profit margin required by each tier in the distribution chain, in order that product pricing is consistent with desired positioning.

(a) Direct exports to end users

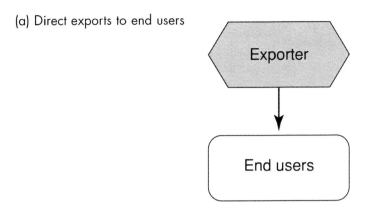

(b) Industrial product exports through agents or distributors

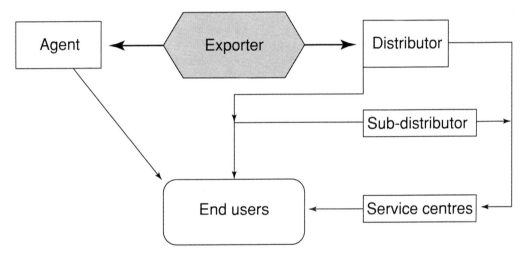

(c) Consumer product exports through agents or distributors

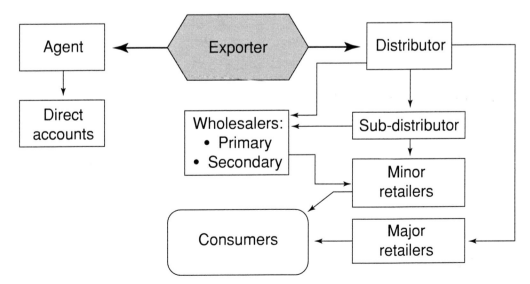

Figure 23.2 *Some alternative distribution networks*

Identifying and selecting agents and distributors

Many companies enter exporting as an opportunistic exercise, where some enquiries come from foreign markets, and once a shipment is made the company is an exporter! Frequently, before long one of the foreign customers asks for sole market agency or distribution rights, and a company that has limited resources and expertise to investigate opportunities and markets might well be tempted to make a formal appointment, on the basis that there is nothing to lose at that point in time. The problems usually come some time later, when the exporter becomes aware of greater sales opportunities than the agent or distributor seems able to develop into orders. To change an agent or distributor can be both very disruptive in the market and very costly, particularly where they can claim any compensation.

A more formal approach to selecting and appointing agents and distributors will reduce the risks of later dissatisfaction or under-performance in the market.

When interviewing a potential representative for the role of agent, distributor or importer, you will need to establish certain basic information to assist your evaluation. Essential topics to be addressed will include the following points.

- Correct legal title and company address
- Locations of all offices, branches, subsidiaries, warehouses, and their proximity to markets and customers
- Ownership of the company and date of establishment
- Paid-up capital and reserves
- Three years' accounts and financial data
- Products represented and length of representation, and performance history with other lines represented
- Trade and bank references
- Distribution capabilities
- Special facilities required for the distribution of your products
- Staffing levels and company organization charts

- Sales and marketing organization
- Market outlet coverage (how much of the total potential customer base they cover and at what frequency)
- Sales performance history with current agency lines, and market share data
- Distributor company policies and strategies
- Administrative systems and controls
- Training policies and programmes (are their staff trained and competent?)
- Ability and commitment to implement your marketing plans
- Willingness to provide market performance data
- After-sales service facilities for customers/end users
- Commission or gross profit margin expectations, and normal margins in other levels of trade distribution channels

Some of the questions likely to be on your mind include the following.

- Is the distributor able physically to distribute goods (and provide any requisite after sales service) either nationally or regionally, or have they only limited geographical abilities?
- Do they grow by building on the base of existing agency lines or simply by taking on new lines to sell to a limited range of customers?
- Have they an effective management, sales and marketing organization, and management succession and training programmes?

The export manager should personally visit all the relevant facilities of the potential importer to verify their existence and suitability. Every effort should be made to establish that staffing levels are as claimed, particularly if you are dealing with smaller, less established companies. It is also essential to visit some potential customers to satisfy yourself that your prospective agent or distributor has credibility and market acceptance.

If you also visit some potential customers

with a salesperson from your potential representative, you can then form initial views on his or her acceptance, trade relationships and professionalism in the market.

Should you be marketing consumer products, there is no substitute for your own random store check to establish:

- strength of competitive products (e.g. distribution, display, use)
- which distributors are most effective in obtaining displayed distribution (retail products)
- which distributors are known and respected by store managers or product end users: strength of agent/distributor relationships (e.g. reputation and goodwill) with customers
- local methods of merchandising and packaging products
- market pricing practices (e.g. product price levels, key local price points, trade margins)
- sales achievements of your potential agent with products already represented
- your potential representative's ability to implement your marketing plans and programmes
- your potential agent/distributor selling skills.

Managing agents and distributors

There is no simple magic way to maximize sales through agents and distributors. The principles of managing wholesale distributors (Chapter 18), and also those for developing key accounts (Chapter 21), all have very practical application when managing a network of agents and distributors.

Your agents and distributors will look to you mainly as a provider of support and assistance, particularly in respect of:

- resolving all problems that arise in connection with orders (often concerning: product availability, packaging, labelling, quality, dispatch, shipping documents)
- providing a two-way link between your

company and the distributor, exchanging information relevant to the distributor–principal relationship (such as knowledge of developments outside the distributor's market that might benefit the distributor)
- imparting product knowledge to the distributor and their sales team, who will look to you for a level of expertise they cannot expect to acquire as a multi-product marketing organization
- training in selling skills to enhance the performance of the distributor's sales team (particularly for your products, but with spin-off benefits for other products represented)
- assisting in developing management systems that can be adapted for use by the distributor in their own company, with benefits for all parties through improved control
- planning marketing and sales activities designed to increase sales and profits, in conjunction with the distributor, using your more specialized knowledge and multi-market experience
- providing direct sales support by presenting products to key accounts in the foreign market alongside the distributor's sales team.

Market activities

While visiting markets and working with your agents or distributors it is likely that your main discussions and activities will fall into the categories of:

- communicating
- planning
- motivating
- performance monitoring
- training.

Within the earlier chapters of this text we have covered all these topics, and your experience and expertise in these areas will fit well for export market management. Our export markets invariably operate to different cultural norms than ourselves, and we must be the chameleons, adapting to their local culture while propagating 'best practice'.

While in the foreign market, on what is usually a rather short visit, you will be under a great deal of pressure (much of it self-generated) to accomplish a variety of tasks and objectives. During your extended working day time will normally be spent in meetings with your representative, customers or end users, and perhaps monitoring performance in the market place (field checking distribution). While with the distributor or agent some of your key activities will usually include:

- reviewing sales performance
- providing feedback on company and general distributor performance (such as your export performance compared with that of other home market exporters, your share of imports to destination market, and other available data supporting estimates of performance)
- presenting new products, advertising plans and promotions
- providing appropriate sales and management training
- planning annual (or other periodic) sales and marketing programmes (or rolling forward current plans)
- reviewing achievement against current plans and programmes
- developing action programmes to counter deviations from current plans
- assisting in distributor sales team and sales management recruitment
- assisting in major sales presentations with local key accounts
- developing goodwill for the company and products.

Field work

Of course there is more to do on a foreign market visit than just hold meetings in an office. Field work with the agent or distributor's sales team, or sometimes alone conducting distribution audits, is another important market activity function. There are several aspects to field work, including:

- making sales presentations with agents and distributors (particularly with key accounts or where the prestige of a direct visit from the manufacturer may clinch a deal)
- conducting field sales training with members of the agent's or distributor's sales team
- conducting field distribution checks (for products distributed through retail outlets) on known customers and on a random selection of outlets (to measure actual distribution versus potential distribution)
- assessing market reaction to your products, prices and promotional activities, and collecting and collating information useful in the planning (or corrective action) and performance monitoring process
- seeking and identifying new opportunities for your company to expand its range of sale activities
- problem solving (trouble shooting) where identified problems have not been handled by the agent or distributor, or where he or she needs your specialist assistance
- visiting distribution outlets (sub-distributors, wholesalers, specialist stockists, etc.), distribution depots, after-sales service centres
- monitoring competitive activity (pricing, distribution, product range, distributor effectiveness, promotional activity, sales performance, acceptance, etc.).

The experienced international marketer may be involved in all these activities without thinking; new representatives may want to develop personal checklists to remind themselves of the factors relevant to their particular products and markets. Those sales managers who transfer from domestic market operations into the export function will find that they are well prepared if they have a broad competence in the subject matters covered in this text and the companion volume, *The CIM Handbook of Export Marketing* (Butterworth-Heinemann).

Checklist 23.1
Exporting – the benefits and opportunities

	Action points
How would you benefit by exporting?	

How would you benefit by exporting?
- Increased plant utilization
- Spreading operating costs over a larger output
- Reduced input costs through volume purchases
- Additional profit contribution
- New markets for domestic product range
- Diversification opportunities into new market sectors using domestic technology
- Increased volume opportunities through modifications to existing products
- Developing international brands and/or company image
- Improved rate of technological progress through exposure to world markets
- Opportunities to sell support services, consultancy, training, technology licensing

What are your international opportunities?
- Existing products and services
- Modify products to suit end market requirements
- New products or services using existing skills and technology
- Consultancy expertise (solo or in consortia)
- Licensing products, brand names, technology
- Develop new products for new markets using Research and Development expertise
- Foreign branches, subsidiaries or joint ventures
- Inward import of goods synergistic with domestic range or distribution
- Inward licensing of products, technology, brand names, and/or inward joint ventures
- Foreign sourcing of inputs (value added opportunities to foreign sourced inputs)

Index _____